# Zhou Enlai
## A Political Life

*Barbara Barnouin & Yu Changgen*

**The Chinese University Press**

*Zhou Enlai: A Political Life*
By Barbara Barnouin and Yu Changgen

© **The Chinese University of Hong Kong**, 2006

ISBN 962–996–244–6

**THE CHINESE UNIVERSITY PRESS**
The Chinese University of Hong Kong
SHA TIN, N.T., HONG KONG
Fax: +852 2603 6692
      +852 2603 7355
E-mail: cup@cuhk.edu.hk
Web-site: www.chineseupress.com

Printed in Hong Kong

revolutionary, an experienced administrator, a successful negotiator, an efficient organizer, and a capable troubleshooter. Under a cloak of suavity, he could be ruthless or conciliatory. He had an indomitable will but could be flexible and adjust to changing circumstances. He was shrewd, worldly wise, and sophisticated, capable of resigning himself to adversity and of enduring humiliation and of acting against his own better judgment. His talent for public and human relations was remarkable. With seductive charm he invited affection and confidence. His wittiness and urbane manners, resourcefulness and subtlety won public admiration.

Kissinger was particularly fascinated by Zhou's intellectual gifts, describing him as "equally at home in philosophy, reminiscence, historical analysis, tactical probes, humorous repartee" and as "one of the two or three most impressive statesmen I have ever met."[3] Another biographer, Han Suyin, went so far as to state in public that she could not find any fault with him, however much she had tried. Many Chinese to this day venerate him as one of the most humane leaders in twentieth-century China. The official view similarly puts him on a pedestal and extols his virtues as a dedicated and self-sacrificing leader, who remains a symbol of the continued worth of the Communist Party, in contrast to Mao, who has been officially recognized as having committed political mistakes.

But Zhou also has his critics. A popular saying characterized him as a weighted doll that always bounces back after having been pushed over (*budaoweng*), implying that he was a political opportunist. In complex political situations, he often avoided a clear stand, and became instead elusive, ambiguous, and sometimes enigmatic.

Clearly, Zhou had a genius for political survival. Several times, he narrowly escaped death. But considering that the history of the Chinese Communist Party was full of internecine power struggles, his capacity for surviving politically and retaining his position at the center of power throughout his life was even more remarkable. During the last ten years of his life, overshadowed by the Cultural Revolution, survival became even more problematic. By then Mao had established himself as a demigod accountable to no one. His paranoiac megalomania led him to demand the subservience of his fellows, purging all those suspected of disloyalty and manipulating the entire country into a frenzy. Zhou's Confucian upbringing and cautious, well-organized, disciplined, and hierarchy-oriented character had not prepared him for such a scenario. But his loyalty to Mao and interest in his own self-preservation led him to accept it. When his acceptance seemed less than enthusiastic, he accused

Europe. This inaugurated his lifelong career as a major leader of the communist movement.

During the Long March, when Mao Zedong began his ascendancy as China's supreme leader and ideologue, the relationship between the two leaders would become the major determinant in Zhou's political life. Disagreements that had flared up between two leaders before the Long March subsided as Mao gradually settled into the role of supreme leader. At the same time, Zhou, the very picture of modesty and humility, appeared to be immune to higher ambitions. A good deal of evidence shows that he was content with the number two position and that he attached greater importance to the revolutionary cause than to its leadership. Not only was he prepared to stand back in the interest of his cause, but he was able to swallow his pride. "For the sake of our revolution we can play the role of a concubine," Zhou once declared, "even of a prostitute if necessary."[2]

Even at this early stage in his political career, Zhou showed a remarkable capacity for reconciling divergent opinions and mediating among contending comrades—a capacity that expanded over the years and often used to brilliant effect.

Yet he was also capable of Machiavellian shrewdness in the name of the communist cause. While he was the urbane communist representative to the Nationalist government in the 1930s, his office was largely funded by the GMD. However, this did not prevent him from opposing it with every means at his disposal and of seeking other channels to raise funds. For this purpose, he organized and personally directed underground and secret service operations. To accumulate additional funds, he established capitalist enterprises and did not hesitate to promote opium production and sales to finance his operations.

When the leading organs of the Party were reorganized in the 1940s, Zhou was one of the central figures within the Communist Party and later within the communist government structures. He occupied the third rank in the communist hierarchy, a position he retained throughout his life. From the time of the founding of the People's Republic in 1949 to his death in 1976, he was premier of the government while remaining involved in the country's foreign affairs. Although his contribution to the revolution, especially to the administration of the country, was considered second only to Mao's, he was never regarded as a potential successor to Mao. Nonetheless, he gained the admiration of many people inside and outside China who saw in him a bright and gifted politician, a charismatic

Zhou Enlai was born into this society. As a young child, he received the traditional Chinese education based on Confucian values that molded his character and personality helping him to develop a strong sense of responsibility, of self-discipline, of moderation and of readiness to compromise. All of this heavily influenced his approach to problems, and later made him a 'trouble-shooter' par excellence. As a high school student at Tianjin—the coastal town which was the maritime access to Beijing—he was exposed to China's most modern educational system and to one of its great educators, Zhang Bolin. Zhang instilled in him the spirit of public and civic duty (*gong*) and of cultivating the ability to fulfil one's patriotic obligations (*neng*). He gave Zhou the confidence that he was competent to contribute to the strengthening of China and to the re-establishment of its international respectability. As the biographer of his early years, Chae-jin Lee observed that growing up and maturing in the midst of political decay and social uncertainty enabled Zhou to develop an ability of "adjusting to the dynamics of China's shifting environment."[1] His exposure—in his early twenties—to Japan and Europe nourished the alertness and flexibility of his mind. This in turn allowed him to espouse Marxism as a theory of social change contributing to the improvement of people's social and economic conditions and, above all, to national salvation. As a young adult, when he could have chosen scholarship over action, he was drawn into militant action and became a major actor in the Chinese revolution.

Zhou's contribution to the Chinese revolution in all its different phases was indeed remarkable. As was the case with many socially alert young Chinese, the May Fourth era left a deep impact on his mental outlook. It was really a landmark in Chinese history that inspired future reformers and revolutionaries.

Zhou's life as a revolutionary began in Paris, where in 1921 he organized Chinese youth into a communist party before such a party had been founded in China. Paris was also where he established relationships with an important network of politically like-minded Chinese, relationships that would endure for the rest of his life. Returning to China in 1924, he was immediately drawn to the center of action challenging the existing political regime. Three years later, when the Guomindang (GMD; Nationalist Party) government under Chiang Kai-shek openly broke with the communists, Zhou became a member of the Politburo of the Chinese Communist Party, which had been founded in China during his sojourn in

# Introduction

Zhou Enlai was born during an era of profound transformation unparalleled in China's long history. It coincided with the end of a dynastic cycle and an external challenge of unprecedented magnitude. Although China had been a target of several invasions in the course of its history, its invaders were nomadic in origin and they had always been sinicized in the end. This time history did not repeat itself. For the first time, Japan and the Western powers had deeply encroached upon Chinese territory in their attempt to dominate the empire. In so doing they reduced the country to what was later called a "semicolony." The emergence of the Western powers, compounded by economic decline, aggravated the plight of the Chinese peasantry, resulted in the degeneration of the local gentry, and accentuated the inability of the ruling elite to deal with these problems generating the emergence of new social and political thinking. Its prominent features were something totally alien to what China had always lived with—a Confucian loyalty to the "son of heaven" and the social order emanating from him. Much of what China had represented since time immemorial was downgraded, broken and devastated.

But it was really at the turn of the twentieth century that this movement of discontent became shapelier and more cohesive. A relatively small number of intellectuals—among them many who had been exposed to western thinking and education—began to develop ideas for change, which later proved to be of great significance to the evolution of Chinese political and social reforms. The ramifications of all this were horrendous: massive revolts snowballed all over the country, and calls for the establishment of a powerful China became more and more tenacious and more and more pronounced. Inevitably all this resulted in the spawning of a "self-strengthening" movement in the second half of the nineteenth century.

## II. YEARS IN POWER

# Contents

ZHOU ENLAI

himself of "poor understanding" of Mao's thinking, giving the appearance of compromising with forces that he secretly loathed and that, in private, he called his "inferno."

Zhou's political position was seriously threatened on several occasions during this period, but, with Mao's help, he was able to prevail, virtually alone of all other members of the upper echelon of leadership during the Cultural Revolution. He adjusted to all the twists and turns of Mao's most irrational and absurd policies, notwithstanding how harmful they seemed and how many victims they targeted. He supported, at least verbally, the purges of veteran revolutionaries, many of whom had been his long-time comrades, and flattered Mao's coterie, especially his wife, Jiang Qing, who often inspired senseless and cruel political measures. But there were also instances of his persecution of others, seemingly motivated by the desire for revenge.

It has been argued that he had no choice—that no statesman can achieve his objectives unless he stays in power. Had Zhou resisted Mao's radical policies, he undoubtedly would have suffered the same fate as many of his colleagues. As one of his biographers remarked, "He preferred to risk being seen as scared of such martyrdom than to allow the whole structure of government, which he had personally so painstakingly built up . . . to be completely destroyed."[4] Yet it has also been argued that, in fact, Zhou sustained Mao's regime and, without him, the state might have crumbled. Clearly, Zhou's efforts to keep the country afloat in the face of adversity also served Mao's purpose. Despite his apprehension that the chaos of the Cultural Revolution hampered the functioning of the state, he was Mao's willing helper in the implementation of his policies, a fact of which Mao was aware and thus never failed to rescue his premier whenever he was politically threatened.

A major objective of the Chinese Communist Party since Deng Xiaoping's rise to power in the late 1970s was to maintain its prestige, which had been seriously weakened by the Cultural Revolution. Until this point, Mao had been the focal point of twentieth-century Chinese historiography. The erosion of Maoism in the wake of the Cultural Revolution, however, forced the leadership to locate another, more sedate symbol of the Party's greatness and its infallibility, if it was to set forth a new model for the otherwise discredited Party. Mao's numerous disastrous policies, ranging from the Great Leap Forward to the Cultural Revolution, could no longer represent the finest hour of the Party, but Zhou Enlai could. He was built up and projected as the irreproachable hero of "New China."

The researcher seeking to fill out a true picture of Zhou at this point in time finds much literature praising his contributions to the communist cause, his humanitarian approach to politics, and the goodness of his heart. Many hitherto enigmatic aspects of his life have become better known. Some archival material became available, allowing Chinese scholars to seriously research and document certain aspects of Zhou's life that were previously hidden. An official biography and a chronology of his life— the final volumes of which were published in time for the centenary of Zhou's birth in 1998—also helped clarify many hitherto obscure events in his life. Memoirs written by his former colleagues and assistants describe different periods and activities. Some light has been shed, for example, on his intelligence and underground activities from the late 1920s to the 1940s that were almost entirely ignored by his earlier biographers.

Zhou's placement on a political pedestal has naturally led to his glorification. It sometimes reaches a crescendo with authors depicting him as having functioned in a political environment lacking the presence of Mao Zedong. This, of course, was never the case. Mao was always there, omnipresent in Zhou's (and other leaders') political life, to the point that it is difficult to write about Zhou without constantly referring to Mao. But to discuss him in such a vacuum would ignore historical facts. Zhou began his political career in the service of a cause, but ended it in the service of a tyrant.

# I

# YEARS OF STRUGGLE

# 1

# Formative Years (1898–1924)

## *Childhood*

Zhou Enlai was born on 5 March 1898, during a period of dramatic change in China's history—a change characterized by the decline of the Qing dynasty (1616–1911) and an unprecedented encroachment of foreign powers on Chinese soil. These historical events, with their adverse social, economic, and political ramifications, had a direct impact on Zhou's large family of scholar officials, whose economic fortunes were decimated by the economic decline in the empire.

Zhou's grandfather, Zhou Panlong, a county magistrate during the Qing dynasty, had settled in Huai'an, Jiangsu province, in southeastern China around 1870.[1] This pleasant old city is located on the banks of the Grand Canal linking China's two great rivers, the Yangtze and the Yellow rivers, which, for centuries, had been China's main channels of communications between the north and the south. Yet Zhou did not regard Huai'an as his ancestral home, something given great importance in Chinese tradition. In Zhou's case, it was not the place of his own birth but, rather, that of his grandfather, who was born in Shaoxing county in Zhejiang province, that he considered the home of his ancestors. Zhou Enlai saw himself as hailing from Zhejiang and viewed Shaoxing county as the locus of his clan's long lineage.[2] By the end of the nineteenth century the turmoil caused by the declining Qing dynasty had ensnared his family, now struggling to maintain the standards established by the grandfather.

Zhou's father, Zhou Yineng, was born in 1877, the second of four sons. He did not succeed in occupying a position worthy of his family background and traditional education. Despite his reputation for honesty, gentleness, intelligence, and concern for others, he was generally considered "weak" and "lacking in discipline and determination." Unsuccessful in his professional life, he drifted from one occupation to another, living variously in Beijing, Shandong, Anhui, Shenyang, Inner Mongolia, and Sichuan.[3] Zhou remembered his father as always away from home and unable to support his family.[4]

"Enlai," which means "advent of grace," was the first of four brothers born to his family. As is common in Chinese families, all male members of the same generation had the same character—in this case "*en*"—in their given name. Zhou Enlai also had a nickname—Daluan (big, fabulous bird)—and a courtesy name—Xiangyu (soaring over). Later he used the motif of flying birds for his pen name, Feifei (fly and fly) or simply Fei.

At the time of Zhou's birth, his father's youngest brother, Zhou Yigan, was critically ill with tuberculosis, and it was clear that he would never be well enough to have children. This inability to produce an heir, specifically a male heir, was considered a great tragedy, for according to Chinese tradition, maintaining the continuity of the family line was of vital importance, as was a son to comfort, look after, and act as companion for a widow after her husband's death. In a remarkable demonstration of brotherly love and family solidarity, Zhou's father gave the four-month-old Enlai to his brother, even though, at that time, he was his only son. After Zhou Yigan's death in 1899, Chen (given name unknown), his widow, kept Enlai as her son, lavishing on him all her tenderness and affection.

Madame Chen was born in 1878 to Chen Yuan, a distinguished scholar and medical specialist. Her father, who had no sons, insisted that his daughters receive a classical Chinese education. Excelling in literature, poetry, calligraphy, and painting, she passed on her skills to her adopted son. Enlai, an able student, was able to read and to recite Tang and Song poetry at the age of four.

Chen left perhaps the most lasting impression on Zhou, for in addition to giving him affection she was also able to devote herself to Zhou's education. "My aunt," Zhou told the American writer and journalist Edgar Snow in 1936, "became my real mother when I was a baby. I did not leave her for even one day until I was ten years old—when she and my mother both died."[5] In 1946 he told another journalist: "Even now I very much appreciate my mother's instructions. Without her love and protection, I would not have had such educational advantages."[6]

Since, as part of a traditional multi-generational Chinese family, she and Zhou's real mother lived in the same household, Enlai was considered to have two mothers, a situation that even as a young boy he came to regard as normal. He addressed Chen as "mother" and called his birth mother "adopted mother" (*ganma*).

Zhou's birth mother, Wan Dong'er, was born in the prefecture of Huai'an the same year as her husband. She was well educated in Chinese classical arts such as literature, calligraphy, and painting.[7] Zhou spoke of her as a "very beautiful, virtuous, and cheerful" lady.[8] Her father, a scholar official, served as a magistrate in Jiangsu province for over thirty years. Her mother, a farmer's daughter with little education, gave justification to Zhou's later claim that he was from peasant stock—a claim made at a time when family background was a cardinal element in his career as a revolutionary.[9]

The third woman in Zhou's early life was Jiang, his wet-nurse. She often took Enlai to her home in a poor but bustling neighborhood of Shanyang, so her children became his playmates.[10] From a very early age he was exposed to the living conditions of people living in poverty and acquired sensitivity about their predicaments.

After Zhou Enlai's adoption by his aunt and uncle, his birth parents had two more sons, named Enbo and Enshou, who were one year and six years younger than Enlai respectively. In 1904, when he was six years old, the two families moved from Huai'an to Qingjiangpu, Huaiyin county, where his father had found work. They all moved into the home of Zhou's maternal grandfather. His grandfather's library housed a rich collection, including all the Chinese classics. The first book that Zhou read, when he was age six, was *Xiyou ji* (Journey to the West), the story of a Buddhist monk who went to India to collect holy scriptures and who, on his way there, met with numerous fantastic adventures. Beginning at age eight, he read other classical Chinese novels, such as *Shuihu zhuan* (Water Margin), *Sanguo yanyi* (Romance of the Three Kingdoms), *Shuo Yue quan zhuan* (The Story of the General Yue Fei), and *Honglou meng* (Dream of the Red Mansion). To be able to comprehend such literature was a remarkable achievement for a boy of his age. Because of the complexity of the traditional Chinese written language, most Chinese children are unable to read even much simpler texts before the age of ten.

The Wan clan had many members, among them many boys of Zhou Enlai's age, who became his playmates and his classmates in the Wan family school. There he studied such Chinese classics as the Confucian *Lunyu* (Analects), the *Daxue* (Great Learning), the *Zhongyong* (Doctrine of the Mean), and the *Shijing* (Book of Poetry).[11] These works locate the value of man in the concept of self-cultivation, an essential virtue in Confucian ethics. According to its teachings, the first task of a learned person is to establish order and harmony and to serve his country and its people. The path to achieving this (*ren*) is to learn kindness and love for others, beginning with one's family.[12] Self-cultivation, the raising of a decent family, the administration of the country, and the search for peace in the world (*xiushen, qijia, zhiguo, ping tianxia*) were basic principles that Zhou aimed to put into practice during his entire life. Closely linked to these principles was the promotion of the doctrine of the mean: the avoidance of excess and the tendency toward moderation as crystallized in the Confucian maxim "to go beyond is as wrong as to fall short." Zhou, like many traditional intellectuals, was strongly influenced by these concepts. Even as a fervent revolutionary Zhou never allowed himself to go beyond what he considered appropriate. Loyalty to the king was another essential element of Confucian teaching, one that Zhou employed in his relations with the modern Chinese emperor, Mao Zedong, to whom he was the very picture of devotion.

Self-restraint—distilled in the maxim "he who cannot take small insults or setbacks is liable to spoil big plans"—was another postulate of Confucian teaching in which Zhou excelled. He demonstrated his ability to swallow "small insults" on numerous occasions, even at a time while he was already part of the "power center." During the internal conflicts that divided the Chinese Communist Party (CCP) throughout its history, he showed extraordinary self-restraint, especially when he was forced to be on the defensive. Zhou attributed his skill at self-restraint—a virtue that contributed greatly to his political survival—largely to his adoptive mother as she supplemented his lessons at school with episodes in Chinese history that were imbued with Confucian principles. Though not prone to talk about personal matters, he admitted that her example of self-restraint had left a deep impression on him.

His birth mother also had a significant influence on him. As a capable woman competently managing a household in declining circumstances, she demonstrated her talent for administration as well as mediation. Big families like the Wan clan tended to have frequent disputes. Wan Dong'er was usually the one called on to mediate and to resolve problems. As the eldest son, Enlai often witnessed his mother's efforts and may well have called on the lessons from these experiences when required to play a similar role in his political life.

Those early years were probably the happiest in Zhou's childhood. But in 1907, when he was nine years old, his birth mother died, followed a year later by his adoptive mother, who suffered from tuberculosis. The loss of both women within such a short time undoubtedly was a severe emotional blow. Steeping in his traditional training, he never bemoaned his fate but, rather, emphasized the responsibilities that now fell to him, as the eldest son of his generation, even though he was still a young boy.

Afterward Zhou's father left his three sons behind as he settled in Hubei province, where he had found a better position. In 1908, Enlai returned to Huai'an with his two brothers. The little money that his uncles and father irregularly sent back supported him. Part of the family home was mortgaged to pay debts. To feed the family, Zhou pawned his mothers' belongings. "I learned to know the hardships of life at a very young age," he later recalled. "I took up household duties, taking care of food supply and family relations when I was ten or eleven."[13]

The following year, 1910, was a turning point in Zhou's life. He left home for Mukden (the present-day Shenyang), the capital of Manchuria, to live in the home of his eldest uncle and to start formal schooling. He never returned to Huai'an though he retained fond memories of his childhood there.[14]

This uncle, Zhou Yigeng, and his wife, who had no children of their own, followed Chinese family tradition by taking in their young nephew, providing his living and schooling expenses in Mukden and later in Tianjin. In his new environment, where he was free from the burden of family responsibilities, Zhou was able to expand his mental horizons. He received a modern education at a public school, including a Western education. He was convinced that this important change in his life influenced not only his way of thinking but also his future. "I certainly would not have achieved anything in my life if I had not left home," he later recalled. "I would have come to a sorrowful end, like my brothers who stayed at home."[15]

The politically oriented intellectual debates of the day that followed the collapse of the Qing dynasty in 1911 also left their imprint on Zhou. Under the influence of some of his teachers, he began to read political literature that exposed him to contending schools of thought represented by the radical democrat Zhang Binglin (1868–1936) and the reformer Kang Youwei (1858–1927). His history teacher, Gao Gewu, who was a member of Sun Yat-sen's revolutionary party, the Revolutionary Alliance (Tongmenghui), introduced him to the works of Zhang Binglin, whose writings deeply influenced his ideas about patriotism and democracy at that time. He also read the essays of Zou Rong (1885–1905), who, in his pamphlet *Revolutionary Army* (gemingjun), denounced the Manchu regime, called on patriots to join the army of revolution, and advocated reforms, such as the introduction of a republican form of government modeled after that of the United States. Another influential text was Chen Tianhua's (1875–1905) *Alarm to Arouse the Age,* which urged people to take up arms and fight against foreign aggressors in order to achieve national independence.[16]

Zhou's geography teacher, a Manchu named Mao, who was a member of the Protect the Emperor Society (Baohuanghui), introduced him to the works of the more moderate reformers Kang Youwei and Liang Qichao, both of whom advocated constitutional monarchy for China. Liang Qichao, who wrote in the vernacular language (*baihua*), was particularly accessible to young people and acquainted them with the problems of China's relations with the outside world.

Strengthening China and pushing it to progress became deeply held goals for Zhou, like many other young people at the time. Once, when his teacher asked him what the purpose was of studying, Zhou replied that he wanted to learn "for the sake of China's rise in the world." The same sense of purpose was apparent in a composition that he wrote at the age of fourteen, in which he declared that the reason for receiving an education was to "become a great man who will take up the heavy responsibilities of the country in the future."[17]

In 1913 Zhou Yigeng with Enlai and the rest of his family was transferred to Tianjin to take up a position at the Office of Salt Transportation. The move to Tianjin was important for Zhou's intellectual growth. Life and cultural activity were very different in this metropolis compared with the cities in China's interior where he had previously lived. Its important sea port and the concessions occupied by the British, French, Russians, Germans, Japanese, Belgians, Austrians, Italians, and Americans gave it an international atmosphere much like that in Shanghai. Tianjin's industry, commerce, and educational system were well-advanced, benefiting from new ideas and ideologies flooding in from all directions.

The political situation in the city, as in the whole country, was one of unrest and uncertainty. The 1911 Revolution, spearheaded by Sun Yat-sen and his Tongmenghui, overthrew the Qing dynasty and proclaimed the Republic. Thereupon followed the ascension to power of Yuan Shikai, the commander of the Northern Army. In 1912, Yuan declared himself the president, but ultimately nursed an ambition to restore imperial government with himself as the emperor. For this he needed the backing of foreign powers, especially Japan. In 1915, Japan pledged its support but as compensation insisted on the fulfillment of "Twenty-one Demands," claiming control over vast parts of northern Chinese territories. The demands sparked nationwide opposition to Yuan, who was overthrown in 1916.

Whereas daily life remained relatively untouched by political events in large parts of China, they had a great impact on Tianjin, located only 100 km from the capital. Zhou experienced them at a particularly impressionable age and with an awakened political consciousness.[18]

## *Modern Education*

The relocation of Zhou's family to Tianjin gave him the opportunity to attend one of the most progressive institutions available at that time to students of his age, the Nankai Middle School. This school had been established by Yan Xiu, an intellectual well-versed in traditional Chinese culture, who had held high positions at the prestigious Hanlin Academy as well as in posts in the provincial and central government. The setbacks that China suffered at the turn of the century drew him toward Western learning and the Japanese system of reform, which stimulated his intellectual curiosity.

Yan Xiu belonged to the group of reform-minded intellectuals who, in 1905, composed a memorandum (called a memorial) proposing the replacement of the ancient imperial examination system by one more in line with modern requirements. In the ensuing educational reform, he played a central role in establishing modern educational institutions throughout China. After the 1911 Revolution, he was offered several high-level positions, but declined them all, preferring to devote his time and energy to the establishment of the Nankai school.

Yan Xiu nominated Zhang Bolin president of the school. The association between the two men proved extremely fruitful. While Yan Xiu represented the best intellectual and moral tradition of old China and was able to combine it with a progressive educational orientation, Zhang Bolin, a modernist emphasizing Western science and physical exercise, was an advocate of reform and moral renewal for the sake of national salvation.

Zhang Bolin is considered one of the pioneer educators of his generation. His educational program, implemented at Nankai, was a synthesis of Japanese and American methods based on the traditional Chinese concept of self-cultivation. Zhang was convinced that China suffered from five illnesses: ignorance, weakness, poverty, disunity, and selfishness. The cure that he proposed consisted of physical education, scientific education, group activities, and moral training with a special emphasis on encouraging the ability to contribute to national salvation. The slogan that Zhang adopted for the school was embodied in the two Chinese characters *gong* (public spirit) and *neng* (ability). They expressed Zhang's aspiration to mold his students into future public leaders endowed with a spirit of integrity, dedication, and civic responsibility, and possessed of practical abilities to efficiently confront China's predicament.

Nankai was a boarding school with strict schedules, discipline, and moral codes. Each room housed four students. Everyone was awakened at 6:30 A.M. for physical exercise under the supervision of the teachers. The rest of the morning was spent in the classroom. The time after lunch until 4:00 P.M. was devoted to independent study or labs. The rest of the afternoon was for extracurricular activities—sports, drama, music, speech, and group activities. Study time resumed after dinner between 7 and 9 P.M. Lights out was at 10 P.M. This schedule was strictly adhered to, just as it was in any British school.

Physical exercise played an important role in the educational program at Nankai. Zhang was convinced that students needed to develop their physical as well as their mental abilities, and he went to some effort to break down the traditional Confucian contempt for physical exercise and manual labor. He considered himself not only a teacher but also a model for his students, using their common washroom to instill basic principles of hygiene, eating with them, and participating in their exercises. Such close association with students was uncommon in China (and elsewhere, too, for that matter), and it distinguished Zhang as a pioneer of modern educational methods. It certainly contributed to the depth of his influence on his students and to the admiration that most of them felt for him throughout their lives.[19]

Zhou was an excellent student and soon received a scholarship. His skill in literature and composition won him several awards and in time caught the attention of Yan Xiu, who proposed that Zhou marry his daughter. Fearing that his financial prospects were not promising and that, as his father-in-law, Yan would dominate his future, Zhou declined, explaining his reasons to his schoolmate, Zhang Honghao.[20]

Zhou's interest in political history prompted him to read the works of progressive writers of the Qing dynasty such as Gu Yanwu (1613–1682) and Wang Fuzhi (1619–1692). Among the Chinese classics his favorite was *Shiji* (Records of the Grand Historian), by Sima Qian (145–87 B.C.). Because Western cultural influence was particularly pronounced in Tianjin, many works of Western literature were available to the students in translation. Zhou familiarized himself with works that already had inspired a whole generation of young Chinese since the turn of the century: Thomas Huxley's *Evolution and Ethics*, Jean-Jacques Rousseau's *Social Contract*, Montesquieu's *The Spirit of Law*, Adam Smith's *The Wealth of Nations*, and Charles Darwin's *On the Origin of Species*.

At the same time, Zhou became increasingly engaged in extracurricular activities. In 1915, he founded an association called Jingye lequnhui (Society for Respecting Work and Enjoying Community Life), which provided a forum for discussion with the principal goal of advancing intellectual development, in part by promoting book exchanges.[21]

Several times a year the association published articles by its members in a journal called *Jingye* (Respect Work). Having contributed numerous articles and poems, Zhou developed a strong interest in publishing and editing the journal. Its first issue was published in October 1914, the last one in June 1917, during Zhou's last year at school. But after he graduated, the journal ceased because no one else had the inclination to follow in his stead. Already by that time the thoroughness and conscientiousness of his future work-style had become apparent. Meanwhile, Zhou also was active at the school's weekly newspaper *Xiaofeng* (School Wind), where he worked his way up from reporter to editor in chief and, in his senior year, to general manager.[22]

Some of Zhou's writings of that period have been preserved. Among them is an essay about Daoism and Aldous Huxley's theory of evolution, which he wrote in 1916 at the age of eighteen. In the essay, called "Laozi Emphasizes Concession and Huxley Competition," he stated that "the civilized world was formed by cycles substituting the new for the old.... Both Laozi and Huxley are aware of this eternal law of survival." He argued that, although the two men lived under different historical conditions, they both attempted to comprehend the essence of life and death. While Laozi emphasized "concession," Huxley stressed "competition," but both had the same understanding of the law of the world, albeit observing it from different vantage points.

Even more representative of Zhou's thinking at the time was his preoccupation with such subjects as the determination to accomplish a certain objective, by which he meant the strengthening of China. He was absorbed by the political situation in the 1910s, following the 1911 Revolution, and wrote several articles expressing what he viewed as the critical issues of the day.[23]

One popular activity at Nankai was drama performance. Both Yan Xiu and Zhang Bolin consider it of high educational value as a group activity to advance social and political awareness. Zhou was an enthusiastic actor, recalled for one performance in particular. Fair of complexion and handsome, he was particularly suited to the role of the leading heroine in the play *One Dollar*. The play had a moralistic message of upholding virtue, loyalty, and true love that was resonated so strongly with the Tianjin public that it remained on the school's repertoire for several years.[24]

The high esteem in which Zhou was held, not just for his excellent academic achievements, but also his personal qualities led to his selection as the graduation speaker in June 1917. In addition to his academic accomplishments, however, his schooling at Nankai had also given him the basis for emotional resilience and intellectual growth. He was also appreciated for his personality: "gentle and honest, affectionate to his fellow students and true in friendship." He was praised for "doing his best for the sake of common interests and friends" and described as "versatile ... good at public speech and writing."[25] These comments are some of the earliest on record about Zhou.

By the time Zhou left Nankai, Zhang Bolin's teachings of *gong* and *neng* had been so deeply ingrained in him that he was ready to commit himself to public service and wanted to acquire the necessary skills to do so. Zhang's pragmatism and flexibility and Yan Xiu's posture as a Confucian gentleman and scholar official also had left a deep impression on Zhou, and he mirrored these traits of his mentors throughout his life. His participation in debating and stage performance certainly contributed to his eloquence and powers of persuasion, which were useful in his later political career. Even as a middle school student, Zhou demonstrated the ability to use modesty to disarm potential rivals.

## *Japan*

Zhou, like many other Chinese students, decided to continue his education in Japan. En route, he returned to Mukden in July 1917 to visit his uncle, who had returned there a year earlier, and took the opportunity to visit his classmates from primary school, in particular Guo Sining. Before leaving Mukden, he wrote a note to Guo saying: "We shall meet again when China has risen high in the world."[26] Thirty-two years later, when the two friends met again, Zhou was premier of the newly established People's Republic and Guo a low-ranking functionary in Shenyang who had come to Beijing carrying a slip of paper with these words. Thus reminded of their long friendship, Zhou invited him to dinner at his home in the leadership's compound at Zhongnanhai.

Continuing his education in Japan seemed an obvious choice for Zhou. Although he was critical of Japan's policies toward China—a resentment he had expressed in some of his political essays[27]—he also believed that China had much to learn from Japan. The country was admired for its reforms and industrial modernization and for its teaching of modern sciences. It was widely believed that Japanese methods of developing national prosperity would offer models and concepts for the development and modernization of China. Zhou clearly wished to find in Japan a path for China's salvation.

However, Zhou was, in many ways, disheartened by his stay in Japan (July 1917–September 1919). It was in Tokyo, where the news of a death in the family reached him. His uncle, Zhou Yikui, had died in Huai'an after a long illness. In his diary he described his feelings of loss: "The bad news struck me. I almost fainted." His sorrow over the death was compounded by his anxiety about the family fortunes. "There is no suitable man at home," he wrote, "there is no money, only debt. There is nowhere to borrow from. There is no place to ask for food even if one does not care about losing face."[28]

His inability to master the Japanese language was another cause of anxiety. His diary entries of January 1918 record that he had made little progress in the Japanese language and therefore could not attend classes at a university. Unless he registered at a university, he would lose his eligibility for a Chinese educational stipend. To reduce expenses he moved several times within a few months in search of the cheapest possible accommodations.

He became discouraged by his difficulty in making progress with language studies. After having failed his entrance examinations twice, he wrote: "What is the use of talking about national salvation? What is the use of my loving my family? The humiliation will never be washed away if I fail to enter a school with a government stipend."[29]

In his biography of Zhou, Chae-jin Lee suggests that foreign languages had never been Zhou's strong point. Achieving the Japanese language proficiency required to pass entrance examinations to any of the Japanese colleges, which would have entitled him to receive a Chinese government grant, would have taken at least a year and a half—almost a year more than Zhou had allotted for preparation of the exam.[30] In addition, his growing political activities began to take up an increasing amount of his time.

Zhou had arrived in Tokyo at a time when Japanese chauvinism was at its peak and its behavior toward China had become insolent and disdainful.

Even more important was that Zhou did not find the Japanese model relevant to China. After nineteen months in the country, he concluded that it was far from an ideal society and that Japanese policies were characterized by external expansion and internal suppression. He became particularly critical of militarism and elitism, which he had previously believed might serve as a model for the salvation of China. As Japanese expansionary ambitions with regard to China and its collusion with northern warlords became increasingly evident, Zhou's disappointment with Japan became even stronger. "Territorial expansion is essential to militarism," he said, and "the primary principle of militarism is power, yes, justice, no!" He considered militarism unacceptable in the twentieth century. "I realized that I was totally wrong to believe that 'militarism' and 'elitism' could save China," he wrote in his diary in February 1918.[31]

In the summer of 1918, Japan was rocked by nationwide riots provoked by the soaring price of rice. In Zhou's view, the inability of the Japanese authorities to find a solution to the problem and the recourse to martial law and to control by the armed forces to restore order exposed the government's weakness.

Thus, Zhou decided, Japanese government policies should not be followed in China. But Japan was interesting from another perspective: Socialist thinking was emerging there, and elsewhere, in the aftermath of the Russian Revolution of October 1917. Information and literature on Marxism, Leninism, and the Russian Revolution were readily available, more so than in China. This provided Zhou with the opportunity to study the basics of these subjects. He followed the events closely, commenting on them in his diary: the revolutionaries, who had overthrown the tsar, were deeply divided between moderates (*wenhepai*) and extremists (*guojipai*), by which he meant the Bolsheviks under Lenin's leadership. Since he was convinced that "the principles (of the extremists) are most suitable to the minds of the workers and peasants," he predicted that Lenin's group would ultimately prevail.[32]

During that period, Zhou also became increasingly absorbed in writing on social affairs. He read John Reed's *Ten Days that Shook the World* and became an avid reader of *Social Problems Research,* a magazine published under the direction of the pioneer Marxist Kawakami Hajime. Hajime (1879–1946), a professor of economics at Kyoto Imperial University, enjoyed great intellectual influence on a large number of his contemporaries. Many of his books—among them *The Tale of Poverty* and *Social Organization and Social Revenue*—were translated into Chinese and inspired numerous future Chinese leaders, including Mao Zedong.

Zhou Enlai's attention also turned to new Chinese thinking on social problems. He was increasingly taken with *Xin qingnian* (New Youth), a leftist literary and political journal published by Chen Duxiu (1880–1942).[33] This publication recommended the complete break with old traditions, arguing that independence should replace servility; progress should replace conservatism; and a scientific approach to life should prevail over indulgence in fantasy. Chen Duxiu was particularly critical of Confucianism, which he held responsible for most of China's ills. He recommended the "smashing of the Confucian shop" and the seeking of advice from two Western gentlemen, Mr. Science and Mr. Democracy.[34]

Although *Xin qingnian* had been available at Nankai, Zhou—as he later explained—did not read it carefully at that time. In Tokyo, he rediscovered it anew, reading incessantly the issues at his disposal and absorbing concepts and ideas, which undoubtedly helped him clarify his thinking. Zhou suddenly realized that all he had "previously thought, done and learned is totally useless." He was full of joy about his "great new awakening," which he considered a rebirth that convinced him to "give up everything" he had learned in the past "to pursue 'new thinking' to seek 'new knowledge' and to 'do new things.'"[35] Although for a time his thinking on all these issues remained vague, it nonetheless catalyzed him to find new purpose. In the spring of 1919, he returned to China, where the first momentous revolutionary event was about to unfold.

## The May Fourth Movement

Zhou's destination in China was Tianjin. There, he enrolled at Nankai University. But his interests were mainly social and political and so he never became a serious student. Although Marxist ideas were still relatively unknown in the politically interested circles in the city, indignation against imperialism and feudalism was widespread, finding dramatic expression in the May Fourth movement. This movement had germinated in May 1919 as demonstrations against the Chinese government and its acceptance of the Versailles treaty that allowed the Japanese to annex parts of Shandong province, but it grew to include opposition to Confucianism. It ushered in a new phase in the Chinese revolution in which radical intellectuals began to play an important role.

The police ordered to suppress the demonstrations and arrested thirty-two of the three thousand students marching in Beijing's Tiananmen Square.

This apparently trivial incident had immediate and far-reaching consequences. Hearing of the events in Beijing, students in Tianjin and Shanghai as well as other cities began to stage their own protests. In Tokyo, too, several thousand Chinese students demonstrated against the Japanese claims on Chinese territory. They were dispersed only after repeated charges by police and cavalry that left twenty-nine students injured. Under heavy pressure, the Chinese government was forced to release the students that it had arrested. Their fellow students escorted them triumphantly back to their universities.[36]

According to the official Chinese bibliography, Zhou had returned to Tianjin in April 1919, just in time to play an active part in the early stages of the May Fourth movement. But Chae-jin Lee gives another version of events. Zhou Enlai, he wrote, was "conspicuously absent" and "his name does not appear in the extensive written records" of the activities during May and June. Moreover, he throws doubt on Zhou's participation in the establishment of the Tianjin Student Union, a coalition of student organizations from various schools and universities throughout the city. This organization was to play a significant role in the continuation of the May Fourth movement by staging mass rallies, organizing boycotts of Japanese goods, and advocating political reforms and democracy. It is, however, certain that Zhou took charge of the Union's daily newspaper, the *Tianjin xuesheng lianhe huibao* (Tianjin Student Union Bulletin), a task compatible with Zhou's inclinations and talent. Setting the tone of the student demands in the inaugural edition of the bulletin, Zhou called for the promotion of reform policies and appealed for a change of mind and a change of society. Demonstrating his characteristic devotion to editorial work, Zhou arrived at his office early in the morning and left only at midnight. The *Bulletin* soon exceeded a circulation of over 20,000, which included student leaders all over China. Zhou closely observed the student movement and its reception by official policy. On 6 August 1919, he wrote one of his most moving pieces, "The Forces of Darkness," denouncing the suppression of an anti-Japanese demonstration in Shandong ordered by the provincial military commander Ma Liang. Such official policy, he contended, not only was oppressive but was directed against fundamental Chinese interests. Soon Zhou became increasingly involved in student activism, accompanying his friends to the continuing demonstrations in Beijing and publishing reports about student activities in the *Bulletin*. It was on one of the train journeys to Tianjin from Beijing, where they had participated in demonstrations against Ma Liang, that he and others decided to improve their own organizational structure by establishing the *Juewushe* (Awakening Society). The society was founded on 16 September by twenty student leaders, including members of the Tianjin Association of Patriotic Women, the youngest of whom, at the age of sixteen, was Deng Yingchao, Zhou's future wife. Instead of going by their names, the founding members used numbers to identify themselves, thus ensuring confidentiality. Zhou Enlai was number five (*wu hao*), a pseudonym that he later used for several essays.

The Awakening Society was to become an important forum for discussion on student activism and on political and social issues. Because Zhou was instrumental in forming the organization, he was offered the chairmanship, a position that he declined according to Lee "out of modesty."[37] In a precursor of later events, he showed that he was satisfied with a secondary role, leaving the top position to someone else.

According to Zhou, the major purpose of the society was to imbue the Chinese people with a new awareness. He solemnly declared, "Anything that is incompatible with progress in current times, such as militarism, the bourgeoisie, partylords, bureaucrats, inequality between men and women, obstinate ideas, obsolete morals, old ethics … should be abolished or reformed."[38] One of the society's activities was to invite guest speakers to discuss subjects of common interest. Most of them came from Beijing University where a remarkable center of progressive thinking had been established by its president, Cai Yuanpei. One of the first speakers to address the Awakening Society was Li Dazhao, who, on 21 September 1919, presented his views on Marxism and the Bolshevik revolution. Unlike Li Dazhao's class at Beijing University, the Awakening Society was not devoted purely to the study of Marxism; its members were interested in a wide range of political thought. Socialist and Marxist influence nonetheless was clearly prominent among members of the Awakening Society, for, over the next few years about three-fourths of its members joined the Chinese Communist Party or the Socialist Youth League either in Europe or in China. Li appears to have had great influence on many young students, and he certainly supplemented Zhou Enlai's studies of Marxism, which had been based largely on Kawakami Hajime's writings.

The end of 1919 and the beginning of 1920 witnessed a continuous upsurge in student demonstrations against Japanese encroachment in China. The situation reached a climax in November 1919, when Japanese consular guards and residents in Fuzhou killed and injured Chinese students involved in various anti-Japanese activities. Chinese citizens reacted by accelerating their boycott of Japanese goods and demanded protection from the Chinese government. In Tianjin, as well, students, together with the Alliance of All

Circles for National Salvation, devised schemes to expose Chinese merchants who imported Japanese goods and to confiscate these goods. These activities, however, were not universally applauded. The governor of Zhili province soon came under heavy pressure from segments of the Chinese population that disapproved and from the Japanese. The governor banned the boycotts and tried to crack down on the Students' Union and the Alliance, a decision that only inflamed anti-Japanese sentiments in the city all the more.

Zhou Enlai became an energetic student organizer, using the *Bulletin* to urge his fellow students to participate in anti-Japanese activities. Twenty thousand students and citizens in Tianjin demonstrated on 20 December to protest the Fuzhou incident. The demonstrators listened to patriotic and anti-Japanese speeches, in addition to burning Japanese goods that they had previously confiscated. Student leaders including Ma Qianli, Shi Zizhou, Guo Longzhen, and Li Yitao, played a prominent role in the organization of the rallies. Zhou's name, however, was not mentioned in the relevant press reports;[39] no doubt, as usual, he remained in the background.

The boycott of Japanese goods gained new momentum, on 23 January 1920, after students discovered a large cache of Japanese lampshades at a store selling foreign goods. When the students proceeded to confiscate them, the Chinese storeowners called for protection from some Japanese hired bullies, who attacked the students and then escaped into the Japanese concession in the city. During the protests that ensued against this incident, several student leaders were arrested, and the police closed down the Student Union and the Tianjin Alliance.

Zhou Enlai and other members of the Awakening Society immediately protested these measures, pressed for the release of the arrested students, and urged the government to punish the Japanese thugs and their Chinese collaborators. On 29 January several thousand students marched to the governor's office, this time under the command of Zhou Enlai, who no longer hesitated to come to the forefront in their defense. But he also sought to fend off violent confrontation, calling for discipline and the avoidance of unnecessary disturbance. He and others had prepared a petition to be presented to the governor as a basis for negotiation. As the small student delegation headed by Zhou penetrated the premises of the provincial government's offices, they were immediately arrested. At the same time, sixty students demonstrating outside the gates were severely wounded and more than eight hundred others were injured to some degree.[40]

Zhou and most of his fellow students remained in prison for six months.

Their treatment was lenient, and they used this opportunity to discuss Marxism. For Zhou, it was a period in which he tried to sort out his own thinking. As he later recalled, during the time he spent in prison, the embryo of revolutionary ideology began to take shape in his mind.

While Zhou and other members of the Awakening Society were incarcerated, the organization had been busy with preparations for the establishment of a nationwide coalition of reformist organizations. After his release, Zhou immediately espoused this goal. In August he, together with other members of the Society, went to Beijing to discuss this idea with representatives of other progressive groups there. At one of the meetings, he and Deng Yingchao exposed views on coordinating activities between organizations in Beijing and Tianjin. They were so convincing that the participants agreed to establish a reform federation. Li Dazhao became instrumental in the formation of the federation and its spread in Beijing and elsewhere. The federation developed a populist movement advocating liberty and equality and "going to the people" with the goal of educating the "common people" and advancing women's independence. For Zhou, the federation also offered an opportunity to strengthen his cooperation with Li Dazhao and to become acquainted with other student leaders. At the same time, Zhou was preparing to leave for Europe a plan that had taken shape while he was in prison, when he and other detainees from Nankai learned that they had been expelled from their university.[41]

Yan Xiu—in cooperation with the Sino-French Educational Commission—provided the necessary organizational help and scholarships for Chinese students to attend university in Europe. Zhou and one of his closest friends, Li Fujing, were selected to receive such stipends. They and 196 other students embarked for France on 7 November 1920 on the French postal ship *Porthos*, which docked at Marseilles on 13 December.

## Europe

Unlike most other Chinese students in Europe, who lived in France on a Sino-French work-study program, Zhou had regular income from his scholarship. In addition, he had accepted an assignment from the Tianjin newspaper *Yishibao* to work as a special correspondent in Europe. Compared to most of his fellow students, Zhou was thus well provided for and did not need to do any work during his stay in England, Germany, and France, so he was able to devote his time to revolutionary activities.

In a letter to a cousin, dated 30 January 1921, Zhou described what he wanted to achieve during his stay in Europe: to discover the social conditions in foreign countries and their methods of solving social problems, in the hope of applying these methods to China on his return. However, he had yet to adopt a specific ideology. "As for the belief in a specific ... ism," he wrote in the same letter, "I still have to make up my mind."[42]

His first destination was England. From Marseilles via Paris, he arrived in London in January 1920, just in time to witness a large-scale miners' strike. He found this confrontation between workers and employers fascinating and immediately wanted to study the incident closely. So deep an impression was left by these events that he wrote a series of articles for *Yishibao* that were sympathetic toward the striking minors.

After five weeks in London, he moved to Paris, where living expenses were lower than in England. The impact of the October Revolution in Russia could be felt in France, where a Communist Party was founded that was admitted to the Communist International (Comintern) in 1920. Works by Marx, Engels, Lenin, and other socialist writers were readily available to Zhou, who was taken with the wide variety of socialist thinking. In addition to studying Marxist theories, he also read about anarchism and Fabian socialism. As he wrote in a letter to his cousin, there seemed to be two possible paths for China. Either "China's ills had to be cured by violent means," like the October Revolution in Russia, or "by gradual reform," as practiced in England. "I do not have a preference for either the Russian or the British way," Zhou continued, "I would prefer something in-between, rather than either one of these two extremes."[43]

Seeking lessons that might be applicable to China, Zhou closely followed developments in Russia. His sympathy for that country began to grow, leading him to conclude that communism would provide the best cure for China. He declared in a letter of March 1922 to his friends in the Awakening Society that the "ideology of the Awakening Society is not satisfying and not clear.... We should believe in the theories of communism and in the two principles of class revolution and proletarian dictatorship. But we will have to adjust them to practical requirements."[44] In an interview in Chongqing in 1946, Zhou recalled his transformation into a communist revolutionary. At first, he was attracted by anarchism, but then decided that assassination would not solve Chinese problems. Thereupon he began to appreciate the Fabian Society. It was only after reading the *Communist Manifesto* and Karl Kautsky's *Class Struggle* that he became convinced that communism was the right way for China. The death of a friend—Huang

Zhengpin, who had been arrested and executed by a warlord during a cotton mill workers strike in Changsha—as Zhou put it, "strengthened my commitment to communism. I believe I shall prove worthy of my dead friend…. I will never change my ideology, and I will continue to work for it and propagate it."[45]

The precise date of Zhou's adherence to the Communist Party is not known.[46] By 1920, even before the Party was officially founded in July 1921 in Shanghai, several communist groups began operating in cities such as Beijing, Wuhan, and Changsha. Member of these groups included Chen Duxiu, Li Dazhao, Mao Zedong, and Dong Biwu. Chen Duxiu and Li Dazhao had played a leading role during the May Fourth movement and had been discussing the founding of a communist party since the summer of 1920. In the beginning of 1921, Zhang Shenfu, a young lecturer at Beijing University and a member of the Beijing communist group, came to Lyon with Liu Qingyang, the first chairwoman of the Tianjin Association of Patriotic Women and a member of the Awakening Society, to teach at the Sino-French University established in that city with the help of the Chinese government. They arrived there with clear instructions from Chen Duxiu to organize communist groups among the Chinese students. Together they established a small communist cell in Paris, which Zhou joined in March 1921.[47]

The Chinese government had become increasingly concerned about the radicalization of Chinese students sojourning in France under the work-study program. In early 1921 it suspended the meager financial support hitherto provided to the students through the Chinese legation in France. The Sino-French University in Lyon was instructed to exclude the Chinese students already in France and to invite only new students coming from China. Protesting these policies in front of the Chinese legation, the Chinese students clashed with the French police. A group of Chinese communists, organized by Zhou and others, was dispatched to Lyon on 20 September to occupy the Sino-French University. Most of them were promptly taken into custody by the French police, escorted to Marseilles, and deported to China in October 1921.[48]

Zhou, who escaped this fate, continued to play an active role in the Chinese student movement in France. Together with twenty-two other Chinese communists he established the Chinese Youth Communist Party in Europe as a branch of the CCP. The Party in Europe had a three-member executive committee consisting of Zhao Shiyan (general secretary), Zhou Enlai (director of propaganda), and Li Weihan (director of organization). In

February 1923, the name of the organization was changed to Chinese Communist Youth League in Europe, which operated as a branch of the Chinese Socialist Youth League established in China in May 1922. Zhou was elected general secretary of this organization.

In June 1923, the third national congress of the CCP decided that the Party should cooperate with Sun Yat-sen's Guomindang (GMD) in its efforts to eliminate the northern warlords. At the same time, Sun sent Wang Jingqi, a left-wing member of his party, to France to establish a branch of the GMD there, and did so in November 1923 in Lyon. Zhou Enlai had received instructions to work with him and, along with other communists, joined the GMD in their personal capacity. At the branch's inaugural meeting, Wang Jingqi was elected chairman of its executive committee while Zhou Enlai was nominated as director of the general office and Li Fuchun director of propaganda. Nie Rongzhen, who had returned to France from a work-study program in Belgium, was appointed director of the Paris liaison office of the Guomindang.[49]

Zhou had put aside his academic ambitions in order to devote himself to organizational and publication work. Because of his publishing experience, he was put in charge of the party journal *Shaonian* (Youth) later renamed *Chiguang* (Red Light), where he published extensively on social and ideological issues. He opened an office in Paris at the Godefroy Hotel at 17 rue Godefroy, near the Place d'Italie. Thus began his association with a nineteen-year-old work-study student named Deng Xiaoping, whom he had asked to operate the mimeograph machine to make copies of the journal.[50]

In 1924, the revolutionary movement, led by Sun Yat-sen in cooperation with the CCP, began to develop and to attract more and more recruits, which it needed badly. The Communist Youth League in France decided that the best course of action was for the activists to return to China. Most of them traveled via Moscow, where they received brief training before proceeding to China. Zhou Enlai and others, such as Deng Xiaoping, Li Fuchun, and Nie Rongzhen, were the exceptions in that they returned directly to China. Before Zhou left Paris in July 1924, the Chinese Communist Youth League remarked of him: "Zhou Enlai, age 26, born in Zhejiang, has a cordial and gentle temperament. He is very active, energetic, eloquent, witty and quick in writing. He has profound knowledge about 'ism' [a Chinese way of summarizing ideological concepts such as communism, socialism, capitalism, dogmatism, etc.] and, as a result, is totally proletarianized. Good in English. Can read French and German."[51]

Unlike other Chinese students, who divided their time between work and study, Zhou devoted all his energies to writing and to revolutionary activities during his three years and eight months in Europe. For over a year, he wrote weekly dispatches on diplomatic events and international relations. He actively participated in the establishment of Communist Party organizations all over Europe and became himself an important leader of the communist youth. During his stay in Europe, Zhou began to work with many Chinese activists who later became important leaders of the party and the state. When he left Europe in the summer of 1924, Zhou thus had established an important network of relationships, upon which he would draw for the rest of his life.

# 2

# Revolutionary Years (1924–1949)

## *The First "United Front"*

When Zhou Enlai returned to China in September 1924, the country was in turmoil. The Republican government established after the overthrow of the Qing dynasty was never able to assert itself. Warlords had run rampant, and foreign pressure had become ever stronger. Under the circumstances, nationalism was the only viable road for China to take and its only option for self-assertion. A call for a greater and stronger China, capable of liberating itself from internal and external oppression, rallied the public to protest under a single banner.

Seeking to spread communism in Asia and recognizing the importance of nationalism as a motivating force, Stalin's instrument, the Communist International (Comintern), was to play a major role in the Chinese revolutionary movement. Stalin had shaped a strategy that he thought, would fit into Chinese circumstances. Its core was the creation of a united front between the Nationalists and the Communists. Through agents who began to arrive in China in June 1920, the Soviet Union offered organizational, military, and financial support to the Nationalist Party (Guomindang, GMD), founded by Sun Yat-sen. Beset with financial difficulties and isolated, Sun was all too ready to accept Soviet support. The tiny Chinese Communist Party (CCP) was pressured to accept an alliance with the GMD, which they would join as "individuals" while maintaining their affiliation with the CCP.[1] By joining GMD, the Communists expected to transform it from within into a driving force of revolution. Their ultimate goal of the strategy was to use the GMD as a vehicle for communist goals, to control it from within, and ultimately to lead it. This very objective was to become the seed of serious discord between the two groups.[2]

Although he had just returned from abroad, Zhou Enlai was perceived as the right person to implement such a strategy effectively. His reputation as a revolutionary and as an organizer had preceded him; moreover, he was seen as having a personality that would facilitate getting along with partners who were not Communists. Thereupon he was made the secretary of the Communist Party of the Guangdong-Guangxi region and, at the same time, was appointed the political director of the Whampoa (Huangpu) Military Academy in Guangzhou, founded by the GMD in cooperation with the Comintern. The Whampoa Military Academy and the soldiers that it was training were modeled after the Soviet Red Army, in which Party representatives controlled all organizational, cultural, and political work. Soviet advisers, including Mikhail Borodin and General Galen (Vassili K. Blykker), ensured that the Soviet model was faithfully copied. Party representatives formed a separate and parallel chain of command in military activities. They were responsible for the loyalty of officers and troops and for discipline in the field. They were expected to show bravery during military campaigns and to protect the civilian population from excesses by the troops. Zhou's official mandate was political indoctrination of the cadets, who were expected above all to embrace a political cause that would motivate them on the battlefield. But, informally, he was also assigned the discreet task of counteracting and containing GMD influence at the academy. As director of the political department of the academy's First Army, and as the CCP representative with the rank of major-general, Zhou was in an excellent position to promote the communist cause within the academy. Through a special branch established under his overall control for this specific purpose, he established a series of front organizations—the Spark Society, the Red Flower Theater, and the Young Soldiers League—all of which assisted in the recruiting of new members.[3]

The elimination of regional warlords, who continued to threaten the Nationalist government established in Guangzhou, gave Zhou a chance to test the effects of his political teachings on the battlefield. During a campaign against a war lord of the area in February and March 1925, the political indoctrination of the Whampoa troops bore fruit. Soldiers and officers alike demonstrated discipline and high morale while propaganda teams escorting the troops worked to rally the population to support the military campaign. By the end of the year, the Nationalist army, now battletested and hardened, had brought all of Guangdong province under its control. Zhou's participation in these campaigns thoroughly acquainted him with military operations. His contributions to operational planning as well as his experience on the battlefront gave him ample training to become a military commander.

At the political front, too, Zhou's efforts to expand the Party were fruitful. The policy of cooperation with the Nationalists allowed the CCP to infiltrate the GMD and, at the same time, contributed to the speedy growth of the CCP. At the beginning of 1925, the Party membership totaled only 994, but by little more than two years later, its membership had increased to 57,900.[4] An increase in membership also followed demonstrations in Shanghai on 30 May 1925 that erupted after a Japanese manager of a cotton mill killed a communist worker. This incident exacerbated anti-Japanese feelings that were already running high in the wake of the May Fourth movement. Two weeks later, the continuing outrage reached a crescendo with a large rally of students and workers, broken up by British police with a firmness that resulted in the death of some of the demonstrators. The unrest that followed became known as the May Thirtieth movement. Public outrage spread to other areas, including Guangdong and Hong Kong, where a hundred thousand people marched in protest against the killings. The Whampoa Military Academy was also swept up in events. On 23 June, Zhou led a protest march of two thousand instructors, cadets, and soldiers. Once more, British troops retaliated, killing 52 people and wounding about 170 others. A series of strikes involving several hundred thousand people followed over many months, blocking Hong Kong harbor and seriously disrupting economic life in both Hong Kong and Guangzhou.

Amid this swirl of upheaval, Deng Yingchao arrived in Guangdong. While in Europe, Zhou had maintained correspondence with her and had become convinced that her dedication to the revolutionary cause would match and support his own. Attending the fourth Party congress in Shanghai in January 1925, Zhou had broached the subject of his marriage with Party officials. According to communist ethics that were valid at the time and that basically did not change during Zhou's life time, a person of Zhou's position could not take a decision about his private life without the approval of the Party leadership. In this context, Zhou went to see Peng Shuzhi, a member of the Central Committee to discuss his marriage plans with him. Peng expressed his approval and, in July 1925, Deng set out on her journey by boat from Tianjin to Guangzhou. When she arrived in August, no one was at the dock to greet her. Zhou was occupied with organizing a strike. The young man he had sent to the dock with Deng's picture failed to recognize her, and thus she had to make her way to Zhou's small lodgings with only an address on a piece of paper. This event was symbolic of their future life together: the work of the revolution took priority over everything else; private life was secondary, even nonexistent. They married on 8 August 1925, but as Deng later recalled, they had no ceremony, no registration, and no witnesses. They simply started living together.[5] Despite its unheralded beginning, their marriage—unlike that of many other communist leaders—lasted a lifetime.

Zhou's contribution to the remarkable expansion of the communist movement among peasants and soldiers began to alarm the GMD. With increasing concern, right-wing GMD leaders demanded the expulsion of Communists from their ranks and the termination of all relations with Comintern agents. Chiang Kai-shek, now in charge of the Whampoa Military Academy, was also worried about the widening influence of the Communists within the army. In October 1925 he asked Zhou to provide him with a list of all Communists serving in the First Army and enrolled at the Whampoa Military Academy. In March 1926 without Chiang's knowledge a gunboat with a largely Communist crew had moved along the river from Whampoa to Guangzhou. Chiang used the transfer, later called the Zhongshan gunboat incident, as a pretext for cracking down on left-wing forces in the city. Nie Rongzhen—although he does not contribute much to the clarification of the incident— suggests in his memoirs that the gunboat had moved in protest because Zhou Enlai had been arrested.[6] In order to reinforce his grip over Guangzhou, Chiang ordered the seizure of the boat, declared martial law, and surrounded communist strongholds in the city. Continuing his pressure, Chiang dismissed procommunist members of his Party, demanded the departure of some 250 communists working at the Whampoa Military Academy and sent his rival, Wang Jingwei, the leader of the GMD left wing who was sympathetic to the communists, on vacation in Europe.

Although he wished to curtail communist influence in the GMD and the army, Chiang still needed Soviet military and financial support as well as the left-wing troops in the army in order to pursue his Northern Expedition to subdue the warlord governments in northern China. The communist crackdown after the Zhongshan gunboat incident had given rise to disagreement about further communist support for the Northern

Expedition. For Zhou, whose priority was the defeat of warlords and of foreign imperialists, the success of the Northern Expedition was critical. The left-wing armed forces did not have the strength to reach these goals without the Nationalist army. Zhou aimed to ensure a strong and disciplined communist presence in the armed forces and their propaganda squads. Since communists could no longer operate within the Whampoa Military Academy, he worked with the Guangzhou Military Commission of the Provincial Committee of the CCP to increase the Party's influence in the various units of the Nationalist army. The first army unit directly under communist command, the Independent Regiment of the Fourth Army, which had an armored unit as its core, was established at that time.[7] On 1 May, Zhou and Ye Ting, a devoted communist who commanded the Independent Regiment, instructed all the officers of the regiment from the company level upward about the CCP's target in the Northern Expedition: it expected them to make every effort to storm the warlord bases up to the Yangtze River. To keep control over his forces, Zhou appointed Nie Rongzhen as liaison between himself and the communist officers of the armed forces.[8]

The Northern Expedition, which started in the summer of 1926, had as its first target—before pushing farther north—the valley of the Yangtze River. In a two-pronged thrust, one army consisting largely of communist and left-wing forces headed northwest starting from Guangdong Province toward Wuhan, while Chiang Kai-shek was leading his units northeast toward Nanjing and Shanghai. In a forceful campaign, the communists and leftists led by Ye Ting and the Soviet adviser General Galen quickly pushed toward the Yangtze River. By the end of August they occupied all of Hunan province. Two months later, they took Wuhan, a city with an important industrial center where they established a Left-GMD government. Chiang Kai-shek in the meantime showed no hurry to proceed along the eastern part of the country toward Shanghai. From the very start of the expedition, he had intended to let the left-wing troops do most of the fighting while allowing his personally groomed troops avoid military engagement. He established his military headquarters in Nanchang, a conservative medieval town lacking any significant industry. From there, Chiang planned the demise of his leftist rivals by using his long-standing association with the Shanghai mafia. This association was instrumental in helping Chiang reach his goal of removing the communists and left-wing activists from the GMD.[9]

## *Defeat*

Shanghai, a lively port city with a large foreign presence, a sizable commercial and financial community, and a rudimentary industrial base, had become an important center of communist activities. Harboring a major portion of China's impoverished proletariat—which, according to Marxist theories should form the basis of revolution—it appeared to be the ideal location for the CCP's Central Committee, but turned out to be a difficult environment in which to work openly. Although the Communists had been able to organize a General Labor Union, they were opposed by a well-established right wing of the GMD, which maintained close links with the financial, commercial, and industrial community. The Green Gang, one of the major organizations of the Shanghai mafia controlled large numbers of the city's workers, thus presenting a direct challenge to the General Labor Union. Moreover, the union had to cope with Sun Zhuangfang, a local warlord hostile to the Communists, who controlled much of the city and its surrounding areas.

Despite those obstacles, the CCP expected to lead workers into revolts against the Shanghai establishment that would bolster the prestige of the CCP and of the left wing of the GMD. Soon, however, it became clear that the Party leadership had underestimated its opposition. The first major uprising organized by the communists in October 1926, was forcefully put down by warlord troops. The CCP, following instructions from the Comintern, maintained their insurrectional policies nevertheless. When Zhou arrived in Shanghai in December 1926 he immediately began to plan further agitation. At a meeting of the CCP Central Committee, he was appointed secretary of the Organization Department and member of the Military Commission. Both positions gave him large authority in the organization of workers' revolts.

Working out of his apartment at 29 rue Lafayette in the French Concession, Zhou organized an uprising, planned to take place at the approach of the National Revolutionary Army. A general strike staged on 19 February in expectation of the Army's arrival had been suppressed, with students handing out leaflets arrested and, in some cases, executed without trial. Some reports in the foreign press in Shanghai described displays of severed heads carried around the city on poles.[10]

The atmosphere in the city became extremely tense. Rumors circulated about a communist coup against Chiang Kai-shek or a coup by Chiang against the communists. Zhou, nonetheless, continued to prepare the next uprising on 21 March. Eight hundred thousand workers took to the streets of Shanghai. Fierce fighting broke out between the protesters and the police. Within a few days, Zhou was able to establish control over the city, with the exception of the foreign concessions. He ordered all fighting to stop and formed a provisional government to welcome the approaching National Revolutionary Army.

The merchant community and foreign residents in Shanghai feared becoming victims of a massacre. Meanwhile Chiang's alliance with the Green Gang leader had become more active. They acted in concert to launch an armed attack against workers and communists on the night of 11 April, for which Chiang diverted troops of his Twenty-sixth Army, originally destined to take part in the Northern Expedition to pacify warlords.

Despite signals that should have aroused the suspicions of the communist leaders, the attack took them by surprise. On the eve of the attack, Wang Shouhua, the head of the CCP Labor Committee and the chairman of the General Labor Union, had accepted a dinner invitation from Big-eared Du, but after he arrived, he was strangled. Zhou Enlai was nearly a victim of a similar ruse. He was invited to meet with Si Lie, one of the commanders of Chiang Kai-shek's Twenty-sixth Army, at his headquarters, but this invitation, too, was a trap, and Zhou was arrested upon his arrival. Despite rumors that Chiang had put a high price on Zhou's head, he was, surprisingly, released the next day. After all, Zhou was the most senior communist in the city at that time, and the cooperation agreement between the CCP and the GMD was still officially in effect. Chiang Kai-shek's plans to exterminate the communists had been shrouded in secrecy, and many GMD officials had not been informed about the attempt on Zhou until the last possible moment. Zhou was released after the intervention of Zhao Shu, a representative of the Twenty-sixth Army who believed that Zhou's arrest had been a mistake. This was one of many attempts on Zhou's life.

The following day Zhou organized a rally of about a thousand people to protest the suppression and arrest of workers. They marched to the headquarters of the Twenty-sixth Army to demand the release of those who had been arrested. The soldiers guarding the headquarters opened fire on the unarmed crowd, killing an estimated hundred demonstrators and wounding more than a hundred others.[11]

Over several months, a pattern of violence against leftist forces had developed in GMD-controlled areas. Labor militancy caused economic setbacks and instilled a climate of panic over the "Bolshevik threat." The

Shanghai business community—Chinese as well as foreign—began to perceive Chiang Kai-shek as the only man capable of protecting it from that threat. Chinese businessmen were ready to finance the suppression of communists with generous loans. In Beijing, controlled by Zhang Zuolin, a fiercely anti-communist Manchu warlord, allowed Chinese police to search the Soviet embassy, where local communists had taken refuge. In the process Li Dazhao was captured and killed.

It is difficult to understand why Zhou, depicted in today's Party history as a brilliant Party organizer, did not realize the threat Chiang Kai-shek posed to the left-wing forces at that time. He had witnessed Chiang's actions against communists in Guangzhou, yet did not recognize the threat to the Party in Shanghai and elsewhere.

After the events in Shanghai, the massacre of communists and their supporters spread to other parts of the country. In May, Nationalist troops stationed in Hunan and Hubei began to suppress communists and their sympathizers. In the area around Changsha, more than ten thousand people were killed within twenty days. It was estimated that, in the year after April 1927, more than three hundred thousand people were killed.[12]

Six days after the massacre of communists in Shanghai, Chiang Kai-shek established a Nationalist government in Nanjing. Within the next few weeks the Left-GMD in Wuhan began to disintegrate. Its leader, Wang Jingwei, transferred his allegiance to Chiang Kai-shek, which officially terminated the policy of alliance with the CCP. By the end of the year, the Left-GMD also collapsed, and Wang Jingwei, fearing persecution as a communist sympathizer, fled to Europe. Borodin and other Russian advisers to the GMD were forced to leave China. This officially terminated Soviet cooperation with the Nationalists. Borodin was quickly replaced by Lomidnadze, Stalin's arrogant and inexperienced envoy who demanded strict adherence to Comintern directives regardless of whether they were adapted to Chinese conditions. The Communists though forced underground, remained under Comintern influence.

At an emergency conference of CCP Central Committee held on 7 August, Chen Duxiu, the secretary general of the CCP, was blamed for the disaster, forced to resign, and replaced by Qu Qiubai, who had the support of the Comintern. Policies did not fundamentally change under his leadership. The Central Committee had been planning a series of peasant uprisings in several provinces to be staged during the Autumn Harvest Festival in September, a period when tensions between peasants and landowners were usually high because rents (which the peasants would have difficulty paying) were due. But, before that, a military uprising was to take place in Nanchang. Zhou was appointed secretary of the front committee in charge of the operation—an appointment that gave him overall responsibility and direct command over the uprising. About twenty thousand troops of the National Revolutionary Army commanded by communist generals (Zhu De, Ye Ting, He Long, and Lin Biao) were involved in the uprising. According to a plan developed by General Galen, the troops were expected to move southward in the direction of Guangdong province immediately after their operations at Nanchang were completed. Their objective was to seize an area with an outlet to the sea and eventually to occupy the entire province. It was expected that the uprising would receive support from the Soviet Union via the sea. Zhou Enlai considered Galen's plan workable. While Chiang Kai-shek controlled only the provinces along the middle and lower reaches of the Yangtze River, the provinces in the north and the southwest of the river were ruled by warlords. Zhou believed that, by using the south as a base and by relying on the support of worker and peasant organizations in the area, it would be possible to launch a second Northern Expedition under the leadership of the CCP. It turned out, however, that he greatly underestimated the difficulties of the undertaking.[13]

In early August, after initial success in Nanchang, the communist troops moved toward Guangdong. Little was done to consolidate their position in Nanchang itself. The rapidity with which the main forces proceeded southward left the remaining troops either in disarray or in the mood to desert, and the main unit that was marching nonstop under a scorching sun began to disintegrate. Battle fatigue and lack of food and water undermined morale and left them prey to illness. The tired and sick soldiers were unable to carry artillery, weapons, or ammunition, much of which had to be abandoned. A battle at Huichang at the end of August and another at Changting (both in Jiangxi province) in early September caused heavy casualties and numerous defections. Later, during the same month, Zhou and his regiments seized Chaozhou and Shantou, an important outlet to the sea. But another two thousand and more people were lost in a battle at Jieyang at the end of the month. Zhou retreated to the area of Haifeng and Lufeng, where he hoped to receive support from a relatively well-developed peasant movement. But the entire insurrection collapsed after another defeat, inflicted this time by the Eleventh Division of the Nationalist army. This new setback led Zhu De and Chen Yi to abandon their drive southward. With remaining troops numbering no more than eight hundred, they marched toward the Jinggang mountains, where they joined Mao Zedong and established a Red base area.

As Nie Rongzhen later recalled, many strategic and tactical errors contributed to the disaster that followed the Nanchang Uprising. Many of the troops who were only temporary allies were unreliable. The military leadership tended to be impetuous and reckless. And none of the leaders, not even the usually cautious Zhou, had considered the option of avoiding a confrontational situation. Clearly, he was unable to coordinate the troops and to establish an efficient vertical command structure, much of which was apparently due to the tremendous difficulty of establishing lines of communication. But obsession about rigid internal Party discipline also played a role. Submission to orders from the top had become so ingrained among the commanders that they lost all flexibility to adapt to changed circumstances, to the point that earlier instructions would be carried out even if they no longer made any sense. Another factor contributing to the disaster was the lack of local support on which the communist forces had counted. The workers had been so suppressed with such force since the Shanghai massacre that they were either unable or unwilling to support the insurgents. Toward the end of the campaign, Zhou Enlai fell seriously ill with malaria. In a state of recurrent unconsciousness, he dreamed of battles in which he shouted at his troops to charge. Nie Rongzhen and Ye Ting decided to secretly transport him by sea to Hong Kong, where he would be able to receive medical treatment. But, as Nie recalls, he and Ye Ting had only one pistol to defend themselves and could not communicate with the local people since they did not speak their dialect. Finally they managed to find a leader of a local Party organization, Yang Shihun, who was willing to help them. In his memoirs, Nie recounts the difficulties of the voyage to Hong Kong in a small boat. "The craft was too small for the four of us—Zhou, Ye, Yang and me—plus the boatman. We put Comrade Zhou Enlai in the cabin, which could accommodate only one person, and all the others stayed outside. The boat tossed so violently in the choppy waves that we had to tie ourselves to the mast with ropes. We reached Hong Kong after two days and one night of rough voyage." Yang entrusted Zhou, who was disguised as a businessman named Li, to the care of the local Communists, who arranged medical treatment for him.[14]

Though a military failure, the Nanchang Uprising was considered politically correct and was seen as an important event in Party history and in Zhou's political life. It marked the start of the Party's independent military action as well as the beginning of Zhou's career as a leader of the Chinese Revolution.

The Nanchang Uprising was only one of many failures. Plans to stage other revolts came to nought. In Hunan, where Mao was in charge, a planned revolt, called the Autumn Harvest Uprising, did not succeed. But despite all these setbacks, the Central Committee, chaired by Lominadze, continued to emphasize that the Chinese Revolution was experiencing a "high tide."[15] He argued that "objective factors"—weakness of the enemy and desolate conditions of peasants and workers—favored insurrections. In his view, all the debacles that had occurred between July and November 1927 could be attributed to "subjective" inadequacies that meant that in effect—despite the "favorable" conditions—leadership had been incompetent. Mao was blamed for the failure of the Autumn Harvest Uprising, while Zhou and others were made to take responsibility for the failure of the Nanchang Uprising. Zhou even was demoted—albeit temporarily—to alternate member of the Politburo. While admitting some mistakes, the Central Committee continued to harp on the correctness of communist tactics in the uprisings and reiterated its determination to continue with the uprisings—a determination that was again made visible in December 1927 with the staging of another uprising in Guangdong and the establishment of the Guangzhou Commune. But this too failed. After only three days the commune was suppressed by the Guomindang authorities.[16]

Maintaining its unrealistic appraisals of the revolutionary situation in China and hostile surroundings, the Comintern forced Zhou to operate on two planes. On the one hand, he was caught at the center of endless debates about the course and direction of the revolution. On the other hand, Chiang Kai-shek's persecution of communists and their sympathizers—the "white terror"—had forced him and the CCP to operate underground. According to a decision by the emergency conference on 7 August, the Party had to transform itself into a "strong, secret and combative organization."[17] Zhou was appointed the head of the powerful Organization Bureau of the Standing Committee of the Politburo, which was to handle organization, propaganda, military affairs, investigation, the secret service, communications and publications. This bureau was, in fact, the leading organ of the CCP involved in day-to-day affairs of the Party.[18]

The debacles resulting from the series of miscalculated revolts catalyzed the Party leaders to re-evaluate their policies. The sixth congress of the CCP, which took place 18 June to 11 July 1928, was the occasion for such a reassessment. At Stalin's invitation, the congress met in Moscow. Meeting in the Soviet capital shielded the Chinese communists from the ever-expanding "white terror," but Stalin had another reason for hosting the meeting on his territory: he was eager to tighten control over foreign communist parties. Bringing the Chinese communists to Moscow was meant to keep them in line.

For the Chinese delegates, it was indeed an adventure to travel through China to Moscow. In many areas, GMD control was so tight that many, including Zhou, had to leave the country in disguise in order to avoid being arrested. Dressed as an antiquarian, Zhou left Shanghai with Deng Yingchao in early May 1928.

The revolutionary situation in China was the main theme on the agenda of the congress. The eighty-four delegates and thirty-four alternates discussed the nature, the targets, and the tasks of the revolution. Was the revolution at a "high tide" or a "low tide"? Acting as the general secretary of the congress, Zhou delivered a long and sober speech, insisting that the revolutionary tide was ebbing. Zhou criticized those who were impatiently insisting on revolutionary insurrections. In Zhou's view, the major task at present was to win over the masses to help develop the revolutionary momentum.

These statements were vague enough to cover a wide range of possibilities. The most important passage in Zhou's speech, however, related to the possibility of establishing a separate regime in southern China, by which he meant soviet base areas of the type that Mao Zedong and Zhu De had already began to establish. The masses, Zhou said, should be prepared to rise up to establish a soviet regime. With these statements, Zhou, for the first time, stressed the importance of the countryside for the Chinese Revolution.[19]

Zhou's views carried the congress. Although Xiang Zhongfa, a colorless figure with a working-class background, was made secretary general, he soon proved to be incapable of fulfilling his role, so Zhou emerged as the de facto leader of the Party. He was then thirty years old.

After his return to China from Moscow, Zhou began to implement the policies agreed on at the congress. He repeatedly emphasized that "armed insurrection is not yet a call for action but a slogan of propaganda," and he focused his efforts on the revival of Party organizations in GMD-held areas, on the expansion of Red bases in the countryside, and on the growth of the Red Army.[20]

Clearly, at that stage, it was Chiang Kai-shek's political stature—not the communist revolution—that was on the upsurge. After the defeat of the communists in Shanghai, he started the third phase of his Northern Expedition to conquer Zhang Zuolin's stronghold in northern China. Zhang, with half a million troops under his command, represented a considerable challenge. But Chiang was able to consolidate various military forces and to amass the financial resources needed to carry out the operation. His alliance with the Shanghai mafia and his astute brother-in-law, the finance minister T.V. Soong, had been instrumental in the success of his actions. Surrounded by armies on three sides, Zhang was forced to abandon Zhili province and to retreat to Manchuria. En route to Manchuria in June 1928, he was killed by Japanese troops who blew up his train. In July 1928, having established a Nationalist government in Nanjing, GMD troops marched into Beijing, whose name at this point was changed from Beijing (Northern Capital) to Beiping (Northern Peace).

The Great Depression in 1929 inspired the Comintern again to overestimate the Chinese revolutionary potential. Stalin arrived at the conclusion that the deeply critical economic situation in capitalist countries had created new prospects for revolution—an opportunity that the Chinese party had to seize. In the view of the Comintern, it should "prepare the masses to overthrow the regime of landlords and of the bourgeois coalition by revolutionary means, and to establish a workers' and peasants' dictatorship according to the Soviet model."[21]

Zhou reacted ambiguously to these new calls for revolt. He did not consider the time ripe for immediate revolutionary action. Officially, he accepted the Comintern's views and drafted resolutions in support of its instructions. But he also warned against "'left adventurism" and repeatedly emphasized discretion and prudence in the implementation of revolutionary activities.[22]

Although Zhou apparently endorsed Comintern policies, differences persisted between him and the Far Eastern Bureau of the Comintern, which was established in Shanghai in the late spring of 1929. While he was in Moscow for talks with Stalin and the Comintern in early 1930 some problems surfaced within the central leadership of the CCP. Zhou's absence opened the door for Li Lisan, also a member of the Central Committee, to strengthen his own leadership position. Li Lisan firmly believed that conflicts within the GMD and the international economic crisis in the wake of the depression had made the situation in China ripe for upheaval, he began to design a more aggressive revolutionary strategy. In his estimation, Wuhan should be the center of activities organized by the communists. The various Party organizations—leading organs of the CCP, the Communist Youth League, the labor unions—there should merge into action committees that should strive at bringing to a standstill all day-to-day work. Communist military forces formed the core of his strategy. While workers were to strike and revolt, the Red Army was to march into the cities to support the workers.[23]

Li Lisan's policies, though unrealistic, were, in fact, based on policies the Comintern itself had made explicit in four letters of instructions sent to the CCP in the course of 1929. But a few months later, in a reversal of positions, the Comintern regarded these policies as examples of "left adventurism." After his return to China in August, Zhou had to grapple with the situation created by Li. At a meeting of the Central Committee in late September, Zhou attempted to reconcile the positions of the Comintern and Li by concluding that, although Li had made some tactical mistakes, there were no fundamental differences between them. Pavel Mif, who had arrived in December 1930 to take over the Comintern office in Shanghai, pressed for another meeting of the Central Committee that would thoroughly criticize the Li Lisan line and Zhou's "conciliatory line." In January 1931 Zhou's position was reversed. He "acknowledged" his mistakes in compromising with Li and even offered to resign from the Politburo and its Standing Committee. In the ensuing reshuffle of the Politburo—in which Mif made all the decisions—Zhou was retained, while such top leaders as Li Lisan and Qu Qiubai were removed. Mif condescendingly commented, "Comrade Zhou Enlai should, of course, be beaten on the buttocks, but he is not to be thrown out. He should mend himself through his work."[24] Evidently he was convinced, as Mao later was, that Zhou's services as Party leader were indispensable and that Zhou was willing to cooperate with whoever was holding the reign of power.

## *Underground Work*

While the Comintern was disputing the degree of revolutionary potential in China, Zhou, operating underground, tried to rebuild the decimated Party in Shanghai. The greatest danger was the GMD secret service, which had been founded in 1928 and given the specific task of rooting out communists. To avoid being snared in its net, Zhou had to be careful not to attract their attention. He and his wife led a transient life, changing residence frequently, sometimes staying in one place for only two weeks or a month. With each move they changed their names, and Zhou was often disguised as a businessman, sometimes sporting a beard. Only two or three people knew of their whereabouts. Both the Party center in Shanghai and the Jiangsu Provincial Party Committee disguised their offices, scattering them throughout the area. About two hundred people worked at the underground nerve center of the Party. Party organizations were located in different buildings: the Politburo met at 447 Yunnan Road, the liaison office of the Military Commission at 112 Central Zhejiang Road, and the Organization Department of the Central Committee on Chengdu Road. Passwords were needed to enter any of these locations. Zhou attended meetings either from five to seven o'clock in the morning or after seven o'clock in the evening. He never used public transportation, nor did he appear in any public place.[25]

In November 1928, the CCP established its own intelligence agency, the Special Service section of the Central Committee (Zhongyang Teke, abbreviated as Teke), of which Zhou took charge. He was assisted by Xiang Zhongfa and Gu Shunzhang, a man with strong ties to secret societies who had become an alternate member of the Politburo. Teke had four operational sections responsible for the protection and safety of Party headquarters, for intelligence gathering, and for internal communications respectively. The fourth, known as the "Red Squad," was an assassination team.[26]

Zhou's main concern was to establish an efficient anti-espionage network within the GMD secret service. Within a relatively short time, Chen Geng, who, as head of the intelligence section, directed these operations, succeeded in planting an impressive network of moles in the very center of the GMD secret service, in the Investigation Section of the Central Operations Department in Nanjing. Among them were three particularly outstanding men: Qian Zhuangfei, Li Kenong, and Hu Di.[27] Zhou later referred to them as "the three most distinguished intelligence workers of the Party" in the 1930s.[28] Qian Zhuangfci was the first to infiltrate GMD intelligence. He had joined the CCP in 1925 as student of medicine in Beijing. In 1929 Zhou Enlai asked him to join a wireless communication training class in Shanghai run by Xu Enzeng, head of the Nationalist Investigation Department. The purpose of the training class was to recruit special agents for Xu Enzeng's Investigation Department. This department had an urgent need for personnel to gather intelligence about political parties hostile to the GMD. The CCP was only one of them. Qian, talented and hard working, won Xu Enzeng's trust, advanced to the position of Xu's personal secretary and was put in charge of the recruitment of additional special agents. This created many opportunities to plant CCP men into Nationalist organizations. Two of them, Li Kenong and Hu Di, took up their posts in the GMD secret service by the end of 1929, providing carefully selected information and disinformation about the activities of hostile parties—which Zhou personally controlled—and reported directly to Zhou about Chiang's designs. Thanks to their intelligence reports, the plans for the first two "encirclement campaigns" that Chiang had devised against the Red Army in Jiangxi province were no secret to Zhou, who was able to use this information in designing his operational response to the enemy's plans.[29]

During the two years after the sixth congress, when the CCP remained relatively evasive, Zhou's efforts to reorganize the Party began to show signs of success. The CCP slowly recovered and even gathered strength. So did the Red Army, now numbering about seventy thousand troops, mostly in base areas (more than ten of which had been established). The underground network in GMD-ruled areas became increasingly active, while the Great Depression affected the Shanghai merchants and the GMD's financial supporters. For the first time since the setbacks of 1927, the CCP's outlook became more positive.

But not for long. Zhou's intelligence operations on which much of the CCP's success was dependent confronted some major obstacles. In late April 1931, Gu Shunzhang, Zhou's chief aid in security affairs, was arrested in Wuhan. Party members who were arrested by the GMD had few options for release and were subjected to heavy torture and round-the-clock interrogation. Having used similar methods in his own interrogations, Gu was fully aware of this. Moreover, as a former labor leader with strong connections with the Shanghai mafia, his communist convictions were shallow. To save himself, he informed the authorities about the CCP organizations in Wuhan. The police immediately carried out raids, apprehending and executing more than ten leading communists in the area. Insisting that he would talk only to Chiang Kai-shek in person about such matters, however, Gu refused to disclose information about the Party center in Shanghai. A telegram that the Wuhan police sent to Nanjing to request instructions was intercepted by Qian Zhuangfei, who—deeply disturbed by the terrifying prospect of Gu's betrayal—sent his son-in-law to Shanghai to report to Zhou Enlai about the matter. In the meantime, the Wuhan secret police transported Gu by boat to Nanjing, where he was to meet with Chiang Kai-shek. This gave Zhou two days before Gu's arrival in Nanjing to evacuate the Party offices and the residences of its leaders and to change the communication codes and procedures, all of which were known to Gu.[30]

After his meeting with Chiang Kai-shek, the GMD secret police escorted Gu to Shanghai, where, with his help, they attempted to root out Communist agents. But they arrived too late. The offices of the CCP and the residences of its leaders were empty. Nonetheless the CCP suffered heavy losses. Gu knew too much about their Shanghai operations and their links to the Jiangsu organizations not to cause major damage. Many Party members who could not be warned in time were caught and executed. Another wave of persecution of left-wing sympathizers also began. The result was perhaps the largest number of casualties since the massacre of 1927.

Zhou's reaction to the episode was extreme. In a style reminiscent of the Soviet Cheka as well as Chinese traditions, which demanded the punishment of the family for the misdeeds of one of its members, he turned on Gu's relatives. Gu's wife, Zhang Xinghua, and some of his relatives also worked for Teke and thus had become a security risk. On Zhou's orders, more than fifteen members of Gu's family were executed in one night by the Red Squad, their bodies hurriedly buried in several quiet residential areas in Shanghai.[31]

Zhou's retaliation did not stop there. Wang Bing, a leading member of the GMD secret service, became his next target. Wang Bing, who was accustomed to moving around the city in rickshaws and without protection, was an easy target. The Red Squad ambushed and shot him in a busy downtown area. This operation was meant to make visible in Shanghai the continuous presence of the Party despite the wreckage caused by the Gu incident. Zhou's reaction to Gu's betrayal was not the exception but the rule: morality had no place in the face of the cruelty of the GMD agents against left-wingers. But Gu's arrest was a major blow for Zhou's intelligence operation and for the security of Party leaders. The four members of the Politburo's Standing Committee dispersed. Zhang Guotao had already joined He Long at the Jiangxi Base Area. Wang Ming had left for Moscow, where he was to represent the CCP at the Comintern. Xiang Zhongfa and Zhou would leave for the Jiangxi Base Area in the coming year. Before his departure, Zhou reorganized the Teke, whose most efficient staff members had become exposed through

Gu's disclosures. The chief of the intelligence section, Chen Geng, and the undercover agents Li Kenong, Qian Zhuangfei, and Hu Di were transferred to safe havens at the Red base areas. Pan Hannian, one of Zhou's chief aides not yet under suspicion, took over as the head of the section.[32]

But Zhou's ordeals with his intelligence operations were not yet over. In June 1931, before Xiang Zhongfa was scheduled to leave for the base area, Zhou suffered another blow. Xiang was one of the most wanted men in Shanghai. Before leaving Shanghai, he spent his last night with his mistress at a hotel, ignoring Zhou's warnings about the danger. In the morning, an informer who had been following his movements for some time located Xiang as he was leaving the hotel. Xiang was arrested on the spot and taken to a prison in the French Concession. This gave Zhou some hope that extradition to the GMD authorities might be avoided. To stop the extradition, his agents tried to bribe the Chinese chief of police in the French settlement with a large sum of money. But the chief of police did not have much to say in the matter, since the GMD authorities were in direct contact with the French, who agreed to surrender Xiang to General Xiong Shihui, the head of the Shanghai Garrison Headquarters. Once in their hands, he was subjected to relentless interrogation. Zhou's hope that Xiang might be transported to Nanjing, which would provide a chance to kidnap him during the journey, also came to nought. General Xiong's interrogation had yielded all the results that the GMD could expect from a person of his status. Chiang Kai-shek considered further questioning futile and ordered his execution. However, Teke succeeded in buying copies of Xiang's interrogation records. Clearly, Xiang, like so many others before him, had folded under the interrogation methods used by the GMD secret services. Zhou read with apprehension and shock to what extent Xiang had betrayed the Party and how much information he had spilled. Among other things, he had informed the authorities of the location of Zhou's residence. Another wave of arrests and executions followed Xiang's revelations.[33]

Having abandoned their apartment on the morning of Xiang's disappearance, Zhou and his wife were able to escape in time. The Standing Committee of the Politburo established in 1928 was scattered. In September 1931, a Provisional Center of the CCP was established in Shanghai, with Bo Gu as secretary general and Zhang Wentian, Li Zhusheng, Kang Sheng, Chen Yun, and Lu Futan as members.[34]

## The Red Base Areas

After the failure of the Nanchang and Autumn Harvest Uprisings in 1927, Mao had retired to the Jinggang mountains, where he was joined by Zhu De and others. Seeing that the Bolshevik strategy of staging revolution in the cities had failed, Mao and his comrades turned to the countryside, where they established and gradually expanded their bases. The Central Soviet Area was the first of three major base areas which was functioning at the time. Founded in the spring of 1928, it occupied vast territories in southwest Jiangxi and in the border regions of Hunan and Hubei. In November 1931, a "Provisional Government of the Chinese Soviet Republic," with Mao as its chairman, was established in Ruijin. The First Front Army, with Zhu De as its commander and Mao as its political commissar, was stationed at this base. At its peak it comprised more than eighty thousand troops. This was paralleled by the founding of other base areas at the border of Hubei, Henan, and Anhui provinces. A number of smaller ones were scattered throughout Fujian, Guangdong, Jiangsu, Zhejiang, and Sichuan. The Red Army in those areas reached its greatest strength in 1933, when it totaled a force of three hundred thousand.[35]

Even in the relatively secluded base areas, communist leaders felt threatened by enemies they could not see and by internal dissension. This perception of looming danger grew stronger as the soviet areas expanded and as different factions of the Party drew different conclusions about the causes of past failures. There was a great deal of suspicion about the possibility of defectors returning as spies and GMD agents infiltrating the base areas. In the early 1930s Mao, eager to eliminate hostile agents and to consolidate his leadership, began a major purge among the communists in his base area. Zhou, who then headed the Party center in Shanghai, also had reason to suspect that a large number of GMD spies had infiltrated communist organizations and the Red Army. According to recent Chinese studies, he supported the purge and perhaps set it in motion.[36]

Claiming the need to eliminate counterrevolutionaries operating as the Anti-Bolshevik (AB) group, the purge was directed against not only alleged spies but also people whose ideological outlook was different from Mao's.

Without a doubt, the communist leadership was faced with a real danger of persecution but it had also become suffused with paranoia and a craving for power. The ruthlessness that Mao employed against those that he believed were fomenting opposition to him became quickly apparent. Using cross-examination and torture to extract confessions, the purge developed into an exercise in psychological and physical depredation. On explicit orders from Mao, "ancient methods of torture" were used, "thrashing suspects with bamboo sticks after hanging them up by their hands. If that has no effect, next came the flame of a kerosene lamp.... Torture ceased only after confession.... Wives who came to the *yamen* to seek news of their husbands ... were tortured even more brutally than the men; the soldiers cut open their breasts, and burned their genitals."[37] Suspects were forced not only to confess their own affiliation with the AB Group but also to denounce others as members. The "evidence" obtained from such confessions led to more arrests, which, in turn, yielded more confessions resulting in still more arrests. The snowball effect of these tactics led to the exposure of thousands of "counterrevolutionaries." Even those in charge of carrying out the purge were not safe from persecution. The purge of the AB Group soon spread from Party organizations to the Red Army; a large number of commanders at different levels were executed as enemy agents. Even Chen Yi, who was then the commander and political commissar of the Jiangxi Military Region, was accused of being a member of the AB Group. These events finally provoked violent reactions against the persecutions, culminating in what became known as the Futian Incident in January 1931.[38]

While all this was happening, the CCP leadership in Shanghai was deeply engulfed in internal disputes. It was only after a complete reshuffle of the central leadership that Zhou and the Politburo were able to focus again on the problems in the base areas. In a letter of February 1931 to the Front Committee in the Central Soviet Area, also named Central Base Area, both Zhou and the Politburo stressed that organizations like the AB Group were the "most powerful organizational instruments" of the Chiang Kai-shek government and that the Red Army "would not be able to defeat the enemy unless it purified its own ranks." The letter called for the intensification of the struggle against all counterrevolutionaries.[39]

The Politburo appointed Zhou Enlai, with Ren Bishi and Wang Jiaxiang as his deputies, to investigate the Futian Incident. They condemned the revolt at Futian as a counterrevolutionary action of the AB Group and its allies. Based on these findings, the Politburo, on 28 March, adopted a resolution affirming that Mao had followed the correct line in waging a persistent struggle against the enemies of the Party. It dispatched Ren, Wang, and Gu Zuolin to the Central Soviet Area to assist its leadership in the elimination of the AB Group. Throughout 1931, the purge intensified in all major base areas. Mass arrests and killings reduced the army from a force of more than forty thousand to one of a few thousand in a short period. Chinese historians estimate the total number of victims in all the base areas at about hundred thousand.[40] The purge can clearly be regarded as a test run for later campaigns. Similar purges were carried out, on a smaller scale, during the Yan'an rectification campaign in the 1940s and, on a larger scale, during the campaign to purify class ranks in the late 1960s and early 1970s.

If Zhou supported the elimination of counterrevolutionaries, he was sensitive to the excesses of the purge. His apprehension became even stronger after he met with Ouyang Qin, who, in August 1931, had come in person to Shanghai from the Central Base Area to report about the purge. In a letter written at the end of August to the leadership in the Central Soviet Area, Zhou criticized the "excesses, the panic, and the oversimplification" practiced by the local leaders, which had led to the "widening of the scope" of the AB Group during the purge. When he arrived at the base area in western Fujian on his way to Ruijin in December of that year, his investigation of the problem revealed that much had gone wrong during the interrogations. He questioned many people who had carried out the purge. After a year of investigation, he concluded that all sorts of people—including landlords, rich peasants, and Party members who had committed political mistakes—had been accused of affiliation with the AB Group. The scope of the threat had thus been grossly exaggerated, Zhou said. He also pointed out that "a very dangerous way of thinking" had developed that "focused on ferreting out counterrevolutionaries as the key to all work." He continued by denouncing the practice of using torture to obtain confessions. A resolution was passed on 7 January 1932, incorporating all of Zhou's conclusions on the purge of the AB Group; thereafter, the campaign gradually subsided.[41]

The events leading to the Futian Incident were a manifestation of a more general problem generated by the expansion of the Red base areas in the Chinese hinterland, namely, the inefficiency of the command structure and flow of information between the Party center and the base areas. The same applied to communications among the base areas themselves. The center was unable to exercise control over the activities of Party and military leaders at the base areas. For their part, they found it difficult to accept instructions from the Party center, which they believed did not take into consideration the conditions under which they were operating. When Zhou, in August 1930, proposed the establishment of a Soviet Area Bureau of the Central Committee (abbreviated as Central Bureau), he had all these factors in mind. The lack of control and coordination between the Central Committee in Shanghai and the soviet areas and the latter's relative success might have been decisive elements. But, perhaps most important, the persecutions in urban centers had made underground work increasingly difficult. Workers' support for the cause of the revolution was rarely forthcoming. The Politburo on 26 August 1930 accepted Zhou's proposal and nominated him as the bureau's secretary general. The bureau was set up in January 1931 in Xiaobu (Ningdu county, Jiangxi province) while a curtailed provisional center continued to operate in Shanghai. Pending Zhou's arrival in the area, Xiang Ying and later Mao were acting secretaries of the bureau.[42]

After four years as an underground Party leader in Shanghai, Zhou, one of the men most wanted by the Nationalist authorities, left the city in early December 1931 to start his hazardous journey to Ruijin. Teke had been planning the itinerary for months and had finally established a special route for Zhou. Accompanied by a guide, Zhou left Shanghai for Hong Kong on a British steamer. From there, a local Party liaison man escorted him to Shantou. All along the route, the CCP had established underground communication lines with local Party organizations in Guangdong, Fujian, and Jiangxi who made careful arrangements for Zhou to move from county to county and from town to town through GMD-dominated areas. It took several weeks before he reached Ruijin by the end of December.[43]

## *Zhou Enlai and Mao Zedong*

At the base area in Jiangxi, Zhou began his lifelong relationship with Mao, who would become the most influential person in his life. Although they had met briefly in Guangzhou in 1927, they were separated for many years because of the various needs of the Party following the failure of the Nanchang and the Autumn Harvest Uprisings. Mao moved to the Jinggang mountains, while Zhou was relocated to Shanghai, where he attained greater prominence in the Party hierarchy. In fact, in late 1931, his position as the secretary general of the Central Bureau made Zhou the leader of all base areas, making Mao his subordinate.

The two men were fundamentally different. Mao was a rebel by nature, much less given to Party discipline and much less ready to compromise than Zhou. He was frequently at odds with the Comintern and much of the CCP leadership. In his famous report on the agrarian movement in Hunan published on 20 March 1927, he presented the unorthodox thesis regarding the vital importance of the peasantry—more vital than the proletariat—for the revolution in China. Because he was thoroughly acquainted with the countryside, he was capable of appreciating the vast revolutionary potential of the peasants. "All China is littered with dry faggots which will soon be "aflame," he wrote in 1930.[44] The countryside was remote from the national government, yet, in his view, it was the ideal location for maintaining and developing "separate armed soviet bases," with the potential to be self-sufficient and defensible by a strong and disciplined Red Army.[45] Mao disagreed more or less openly with most of the central leadership's revolutionary strategies— largely inspired by the Comintern. In February 1929, the Comintern invited Mao and Zhu De to travel to Moscow to familiarize themselves with Soviet military strategy and tactics. Neither Mao nor Zhu considered the invitation anything but a trap devised to draw them out of their own country and into the influence of Soviet interests. Both were convinced that their presence in China was more important than listening to Stalin's lectures; they therefore refused his invitation.[46]

While Mao was a rebel, Zhou Enlai was a highly disciplined Party member who readily adopted official policies. If he had any reservations, he expressed them in a nuanced manner—he was rarely openly defiant. But Mao's military strategy finally drew Zhou to him. The repeated failures of revolutionary strategies promoted by the Party center and his close contacts with Mao at the base areas convinced Zhou that Mao's arguments were sound. Mao continued to reason that, as long as the communist forces were inferior to the Nationalist troops, direct attacks on key cities could only lead to defeat. He recommended focusing on the enemy's weak spots. For the same reason, Mao was in favor of mobile guerilla strategy rather than regular warfare.[47]

Zhou evolved toward Mao's position only gradually and in several stages. He overruled Mao's reservations and ordered an attack on Ganzhou in February 1930. In an article in *Shihua* (Speak Frankly), the official newsletter of the Central Bureau in Ruijin, he made an optimistic appraisal of the general revolutionary situation in China and called on the Party and the Red Army to carry out the revolutionary war and to "seize key cities." As Mao had predicted, the attack on Ganzhou proved a failure.

After thirty-three days of fighting, which resulted in heavy casualties, it had to be abandoned.

After the debacle at Ganzhou, Mao suggested setting up a new base area in northeastern Jiangxi where the enemy was weak. This suggestion was rejected as a manifestation of "right opportunism," while attacks on key cities along the Gan river valley continued to be proposed. Zhou, who also had rejected Mao's proposal to move toward the northeast, did, however, approve another of his suggestions: leading an army to western Fujian to attack the cities of Longyan and Zhangzhou because Nationalist troops in that area posed a threat to the Central Base Area. Mao's tactics proved correct. He wiped out four Nationalist regiments, seized two [77] counties, and took fifteen hundred prisoners of war.[48]

Despite Mao's success, the leadership remained divided. As in the past, there were those who continued to propagate an urban-oriented strategy called the "forward and offensive line." Zhou, though formally a supporter of that official policy, was increasingly confronted with the harsh realities of the base areas, which convinced him that the Red Army was still too weak to accomplish the tasks assigned to it by the proponents of offensive strategy.

As arguments over the correct strategy continued to place the Central Bureau and the Provisional Center in Shanghai in opposition, Zhou drew increasingly closer to Mao's views. He and Mao, as well as Zhu De and Wang Jiaxiang, were in favor of moving the Red Army to areas where the enemy was weak and could thus be eliminated. They continued to argue against attacking key cities, which were heavily guarded by government troops. But they remained a minority, with the rest of the leadership insisting that the army should move farther north to attack such cities as Fuzhou and ultimately to threaten Nanchang, the provincial capital.

On 24 August 1932, Zhou led his troops to Nanchang, where he discovered that the government had sent heavy reinforcements to the city, which appeared to him as a strongly guarded fortress. Zhou suggested abandoning all plans to attack Nanchang and retreating to the area of Nanfeng, where the enemy was weak and might be more easily confronted. His suggestions were rejected. Between 23 September and 1 October, eleven cables were sent between Ruijin and the headquarters of the First Field Army to settle the issue, but no agreement was reached. Finally, it was decided to attempt a reconciliation of the conflicting views at a meeting of the Central Bureau in Ningdu in the first half of October 1932.

At the Ningdu conference, several leaders, acting on behalf of the Comintern and the Provisional Center at Shanghai, dominated the proceedings. They used the meeting as a platform for opposing Mao's strategy. The attack at Ganzhou had failed, in their view, because Mao had been deliberately passive and "sluggish in his work." He was accused of having preferred "to wait for the attacks of the enemy" and of failing to demonstrate respect for the central leadership.[49]

Zhou also came under fire. There was, it was said, not much difference between him and Mao in their attitude toward the revolution, which, generally speaking, was considered too passive. Both "laid stress on preparation" and adopted a "wait-and-see attitude." Zhou was accused of failing to criticize Mao's errors explicitly and of trying to explain and even to defend him at times. In the past, it was recalled, Zhou had already displayed the same (erroneous) conciliatory attitude toward Li Lisan.

During the conference, Zhou demonstrated his remarkable ability of agreeing with everyone. To the Provisional Center, he admitted that the some leaders "surely entertained the idea of waiting. Zedong exhibits this trend more than others." The members of the Central Bureau were correct, he pointed out, when they criticized the caution displayed by some leaders. But, in his view, they underestimated the seriousness of the enemy's attacks and their criticism of Mao was excessive. Having become "more moderate" in his criticism of Mao, he suggested that Mao remain at the forefront of revolutionary operations, where his talent was more evident than elsewhere. Mao had great experience in warfare, he said, and therefore he should stay at the front. But Zhou's suggestions were rejected, and the conference appointed him to take over Mao's post as general political commissar of the First Field Army. Thus deprived of his post, Mao returned to the rear areas to serve as a figurehead in the soviet government.[50]

The Ningdu conference was an important episode in the relationship between Mao and Zhou. Mao never forgot the humiliation that he had suffered, but he also remembered Zhou's defense of his policies. More than thirty years later, he recalled that "during the Ningdu conference, Lo Fu (Zhang Wentian) wanted to expel me, but Zhou and Zhu De did not agree."[51] In due course, all those who had opposed Mao during the conference were either purged or demoted.

Chiang Kai-shek's continuing harassment made it increasingly difficult for the Provisional Center, then headed by Bo Gu, to function in Shanghai. In January 1933, it was transferred to the Jiangxi Base Area.

The Comintern representative, Otto Braun, also left Shanghai and settled in Jiangxi province in October 1933. Bo Gu, who had little experience in military matters, appointed him chief military advisor, thus making Braun the de facto commander of the Red Army. With their arrival, the Central Bureau merged with the Provisional Center. This decision made Zhou's post as secretary of the bureau redundant. The new Party center proceeded to reshuffle the army's command structure. In May, it moved the Military Commission from the front to Ruijin and appointed Xiang Ying as its acting chairman. Zhou retained his post as general political commissar of the Red Army, while Zhu De was commander in chief. This allowed the Party center in Ruijin to control front operations directly.[52]

## The Long March

Having achieved his goal of placating the warlord armies by 1930, Chiang Kai-shek turned to attack communist strongholds in the base areas. During the next four years, he launched five military campaigns against the Jiangxi-Fujian base that became known as encirclement campaigns.

The Red Army had been able to avoid significant damage during the first four campaigns, but the fifth campaign, which got under way in September 1933 with a new strategy, proved much more difficult to contain. Chiang deployed a larger number of troops than before and used "blockhouse tactics," whose objective was to seal off conquered territories with a line of blockhouses resembling small medieval castles. They were close enough to permit overlapping fields of fire. Although the advance was slow, it permitted the entrenchment of the army at every step, which thus avoided being drawn into communist ambushes. The strategy proved successful; within a few months, the GMD armies advanced steadily into the border region, where they captured major communist strongholds.[53]

Bo Gu and Braun organized the defense by adopting tactics of regular positional warfare. Their plan was to attack two Nationalist strongholds north of Lichuan with the aim of later recovering the town itself. Zhou, although opposed to this strategy, directed the military operations, which ended in failure. He and other military leaders were blamed for the debacle. Despite the defeat, the fifth plenum of the sixth congress of the CCP, which met at Ruijin in mid-January 1934, adopted a resolution declaring that "an immediate revolutionary situation" existed in China, that the latest encirclement campaign provided the chance to prove "who will conquer whom" and to demonstrate whether "the soviet road or the colonialist road" would dominate.[54]

At the meeting Zhou was elected to the Politburo. Moreover, along with Bo Gu, Zhang Wentian, and Xiang Ying, he was chosen as one of the four members of the Standing Committee and appointed vice chairman of the Military Commission.[55] Although Zhou's cautious approach to the revolution gave rise to considerable reservations among the hard-liners, he had proved his ability to compromise on most issues where differences were mainly tactical. His organizational talent and his devotion to work had made him indispensable. Moreover, he had never shown any ambition to reach for supreme power in the Party and was accepted as a leader by different political factions.

Between January and March, the enemy was advancing steadily. Bo Gu and Braun continued to employ tactics of regular warfare, with the result that the Red Army lost a series of campaigns and battles. In April, the Nationalist army began to attack Guangchang, a city that was considered the gateway to Ruijin. In an attempt to fight a "decisive battle" against the enemy Bo and Braun divided the Red Army into "six routes" (six armies). These tactics did not work. In October, GMD troops defeated the Red Army and drove deep into the heart of the Central Soviet Area. When Ruijin became exposed to GMD attacks, the CCP leaders were faced with the choice of either remaining and perishing or breaking through the enemy encirclement and deserting the base area.[56]

Since the Central Base Area could no longer be held, the Standing Committee appointed Bo, Braun, and Zhou to organize its evacuation. They were in charge of politics, military matters, and the implementation of military planning, respectively. In other words, it was Zhou's responsibility to organize and supervise the logistics of the withdrawal. Since the enemy was relatively close, Zhou made his preparations in utter secret. It was not disclosed who was to leave and when. Even senior leaders were informed only at the last moment of the planned movements. The route that the troops were to take was equally uncertain. Although the bulk of the forces was able to break through before Nationalist troops succeeded in occupying the bases, many were left behind. Among them were many wounded, who presumably were sheltered by peasants in the area, and some of the most capable leaders, including Xiang Ying, Chen Yi, Tan Zhenlin, and Qu Qiubai. It is not known what criteria were used to determine who was to go and who was to stay. Those staying behind clearly were risking their lives. But the force of sixteen thousand that was left behind was able to act as a rear guard and to divert the Nationalist troops, thus permitting the main force to depart well before Chiang Kai-shek's troops became aware of their movements.

The exodus of about eighty-four thousand people began in early October 1934. The general goal was toward the west to join He Long and his Red Army units in Hunan and Hubei and to set up a base area there. To do so, they had to break through four blockade lines, of which only the fourth was occupied by Chiang Kai-shek's troops. Others, as Zhou's intelligence agents had been able to ascertain, had been set up by troops under the command of General Chen Jitang, a warlord in Guangdong. Zhou believed that he preferred to preserve the strength of these troops, rather than fight. He sent Pan Hannian to negotiate with General Chen, who agreed to permit the Red Army to pass through the territory under his control.[57]

Zhou left on the evening of 10 October 1934, marching with the first column of the Field Army. He embarked on the voyage with two blankets, one sheet, one sweatshirt, and some wrapped up cloth to serve as a pillow. His wife, who was suffering from tuberculosis, walked with the company of the old and the sick. She had asked to be allowed to stay behind, but her request was denied. Zhou told her that the Party center had made the decision that she leave.[58]

The Red Army broke through the first three blockades without much fighting. But in early December, when it attempted to cross the Xiang river in Hunan, Chiang Kai-shek's troops intercepted the communist forces and inflicted serious casualties. Their numbers were reduced from eighty-six thousand to thirty thousand. How many were lost and how many dropped out, no one is prepared to calculate.[59]

The defeat completely demoralized some of the leaders. Bu Gu, for example, played with his pistol, sometimes pointing it at his head. Nie Rongzhen, then commissioner of the First Army Corps, had to tell him to be careful with his weapon. Braun lost a considerable amount of his self-confidence and became much less arrogant. Zhou kept his calm and retook command.[60]

As it became increasingly evident that Chiang Kai-shek intended to intercept the remnants of the Red Army in western Hunan, the direction of the Red Army's movements had to be reconsidered. The plan to march toward Hunan to join He Long's troops had become too risky. Mao proposed changing direction, to move toward Guizhou. In Guizhou, Mao told Zhou, the local army could be expected to be relatively weak. A meeting at Tongdao, a small town in western Hunan near the Guizhou border, was convened to discuss the question on 12 December. On that occasion, Zhou endorsed Mao's proposal. His unequivocal support permitted the leaders to overrule Bo Gu's and Braun's objections. But the controversy flared up again after the troops reached Liping, in the mountainous southeast of Guizhou, where Braun and Mao clashed about the direction of the march. Zhou later recalled the "sharp disputes [which] erupted at Liping. Li De held that we should go to eastern Guizhou. But [according to Mao] there was a great danger that we would march into the arms of Chiang's troops. Chairman Mao suggested going to the western part of the province, which borders on Sichuan, to establish a base area there." Zhou sided with Mao, which made Braun "fly into a rage because he was overruled in the debate." At the meeting it was decided that the Red Army should follow Mao's suggestion and move toward Zunyi in western Guizhou.[61]

On 1 January 1935 the Red Army reached the Wu river, which had to be crossed on the way to Zunyi. Bo Gu and Braun insisted again that the army should move toward western Hunan to join the other communist troops in that area. But their stature in the Politburo had considerably declined by this point; it rejected their request. In the face of Bo Gu's and Braun's stubbornness, even Zhou began to lose patience. He proposed a new rule, to take effect immediately, that all military plans had to be submitted to the Politburo for approval. The motion was passed, clearly depriving Braun of the right to direct military affairs.[62]

A few days later, on 7 January, the Red Army seized Zunyi, the second-largest city in Guizhou. As Mao had predicted, the defenses of the Guizhou army were weak and the Nationalist forces were too far away to constitute an immediate threat. Zhou used the respite to call an enlarged Politburo meeting to examine the causes of the communists' repeated defeats. The meeting, held between 15 and 17 January, was expected to draw lessons from the failures of the past and to develop new strategies for the future. The discussion revolved around the question of whether the defeats suffered by the Red Army were due to circumstances or inadequacies of the leadership. Bo Gu, the first speaker, attributed the Red Army's misfortunes to objective causes, such as the overwhelming numerical superiority of the enemy forces and the poor coordination between the communist forces. As Wu Xiuquan, Braun's interpreter, later recalled, Bo Gu's arguments did not impress his audience and he came across as someone who wanted to avoid responsibility. Zhou Enlai was the second speaker. The mistakes, he said, owed to wrong decisions at leadership level. As one of the three persons responsible, he felt he was accountable for the debacles. His willingness to accept responsibility was well received by the other participants in the meeting. Zhang Wentian, whose report to the conference was based largely on conclusions drawn from lengthy discussions he had recently had with Mao, attacked Bo Gu and Braun directly and criticized their strategic and operational errors. Mao followed suit, analyzing the erroneous tactics and strategies developed by the two leaders. With Zhou's explicit backing, Mao succeeded in winning over the meeting, whose twenty participants—with the exception of Bo Gu, Braun, and He Kequan—argued in his favor. The withdrawal of support to Bo Gu and Braun put an end to their domination of the Politburo.[63]

The Zunyi conference and its outcome has been a subject of dispute among historians, the main question being whether Zhou had relinquished his leadership position in favor of Mao. Chinese historians see Zunyi as a turning point in Party history because it ended the dominance of the "left adventurist line" and became the starting point of Mao's ascension to supreme leadership. According to a recent Chinese version of the events at the conference, Zhou was held partly responsible for the Red Army's defeat during the fifth encirclement campaign. Explicitly, it was stated that "three comrades, A (code name for Braun), Bo, and Zhou made mistakes in military command, but comrade A and Bo should bear the main responsibility."[64] But it was also recognized that Zhou's attitude toward military tactics had changed considerably. His differences with Bo Gu at the Ningdu meeting, his successful tactics during the fourth encirclement campaign, and his resolute support of Mao during the Zunyi conference were cited as examples of this shift. This explains why Zhou, unlike Bo Gu and Braun, was not eliminated from the upper strata of power. But it was, in fact, in March, two months after the Zunyi conference, that a major change in the command structure was inaugurated in the form of a three-man group. Within that group, Zhou was empowered to make final decisions on military matters while Mao was his assistant (*bangzhuzhi*). Wang Jiaxiang, the third member of the group, was in charge of Party affairs.[65] Mao was promoted to the Standing Committee of the Politburo. This marked the beginning of his political and military authority at the summit of CCP leadership, but it does not mean that, at that point, he acquired an unchallenged position.

When the Red Army had reached Zunyi, it was already depleted, counting little more than ten thousand members. Many had deserted in the first few months of the march; those who remained had encountered severe harassment from warlords in front and heavy pressure by Chiang Kai-shek's troops in the rear. To avoid fatal confrontation with the enemy, Zhou and Mao maneuvered their troops in tortuous patterns across Guizhou, Sichuan, and Yunnan, feigning attacks on Guiyang and Kunming, remaining forever elusive and untraceable. On 9 May, the Red Army crossed the Yangtze River, finally extricating itself from enemy pursuit. But that was not the end of its problems. From then the army confronted physical obstacles of dangerous peaks, rough climatic conditions, wild rivers, hostile tribes, in addition to shortages of food, clothing, and equipment for the exhausted troops. In June, the Red Army crossed the snowy mountains at Maogong in northwestern Sichuan, climbing up to a peak of 4,000 meters. Many men were lost during the ascent. Freezing temperatures and snowstorms took their toll. Those carrying cooking and other equipment succumbed to the thin air and lack of oxygen.[66]

## *Encounter with Zhang Guotao*

In June, the much reduced Red Army met the Fourth Front Army under the command of Zhang Guotao at Lianghekou. Zhang had taken a different route and arrived at the meeting point with eighty-four thousand men in relatively good condition. The fact that his unit was in such good condition allowed him to challenge both Zhou's and Mao's leadership, whose major strength at that time stemmed from the Party center's support. Zhang demanded that one of his generals, Chen Changhao, take over Zhou's post of political commissar of the entire Red Army. Then Chen Changhao suggested that Zhang Guotao replace Zhu De at the Military Commission. He argued that such a reorganization would create a more equal army leadership. On 18 July 1935, Zhou relinquished his post as political commissar, and several leading positions were taken over by generals from the Fourth Front Army. However, these changes had no practical significance because Zhang and Mao disagreed over the direction of the army. While Zhang insisted on going toward the southwest, Mao decided that it would be better to move northward. No agreement was reached, and the armies finally split, each going its own way.[67]

In August, the remaining marchers advanced northward, passing through the vast grasslands of Xinghai. Stretching on a plateau from six thousand to nine thousand feet high, with a vast, mosquito-filled swamp, the grasslands presented an even greater challenge to the exhausted men than the mountains. During the daytime, Zhou walked with his troops. In the evening, he worked until well past midnight. He had a horse, but he did not dare to ride it, for fear that, in his exhausted condition, he might go to sleep while riding and fall off. While the army was crossing the marshland in the August heat, he fell seriously ill, with a high fever that often made him unconscious. When he was unable to walk, Peng Dehuai, then commander of the Third Army Corps, organized a team of soldiers to carry him on a stretcher through the difficult terrain. Yang Lisan, the director of the army service station, volunteered to join the soldiers in carrying the stretcher. For six days, the men walked through the marsh with the stretcher on their shoulders. As a token of gratitude, when Yang Lisan died nineteen years later, Zhou Enlai (by then prime minister) insisted on helping to carry Yang's coffin at his funeral.

In October, about eight thousand survivors of the Long March in Mao's Red Army arrived at the border region of Gansu and Shaanxi, meeting forces under Liu Zhidan, Gao Gang, and Hu Haidong, who had established a soviet base in northern Shaanxi. They were joined there by He Long's Second Front Army and by a much smaller Fourth Front Army under Zhang Guotao, who—having suffered considerable losses en route—was no longer in a position to challenge Mao. The Long March had lasted an entire year and covered a distance of more than three thousand miles. It was glorified as a great achievement of endurance, which it undoubtedly was for the few who survived. For Mao and Zhou, it represented a critical period of their lives. At the time, no one foresaw that the dramatic events were going to create links between them which were to last during their lifetime.

In November 1935, shortly after settling in northern Shaanxi, Mao officially took over Zhou's leading position in the Red Army. He became the chairman of the new Military Commission, with Zhou and Peng Dehuai as vice-chairmen. After the arrival of the Red Army forces who were under the command of Zhang Guotao, Zhu De, and others, the Military Commission was reshuffled again. Mao remained chairman, with Zhou and Zhang Guotao as vice-chairmen.[68] This marked the beginning of Zhou's role as second to Mao, a position he was to maintain for the rest of his life.

## The Second "United Front"

Uneasy about the concentration of the Red Army forces in northern Shaanxi, Chiang Kai-shek established a "northwest headquarters for the suppression of bandits," as he called the communists, located at Xian, the ancient imperial capital in Shaanxi province. This post was of such importance that he took over command. His deputy was General Zhang Xueliang, the son of the Manchu warlord Zhang Zuolin whose Northeast Army, driven out of Manchuria by the Japanese, constituted the bulk of the armed forces in the area. Doubtful of General Zhang's loyalty, Chiang also deployed his own army in Shaanxi. The purpose of this mobilization was to destroy the Red Army before it could consolidate its base in northern Shaanxi.

While Chiang continued to pursue communist armies, Japanese troops occupied three provinces in northeastern China and began to move toward northern territories in inland China. Hostility toward the occupation grew into an anti-Japanese movement throughout the country. Shanghai became the center of Chinese boycotts against Japan, some of which turned violent and left some Japanese dead. The Japanese navy retaliated with heavy and protracted shelling of the city. Anti-Japanese sentiment spread to large segments of the Chinese military and became particularly pronounced within the Northeast Army, whose territory of origin, Manchuria, was under direct occupation. Demands grew for the establishment of a national united front to fight against the Japanese, rather than against the Chinese communists.

The Comintern, too, had its reasons for calling for a united front in China. Since Hitler's rise to power in 1933, Stalin had felt threatened by the anti-communist and anti-Soviet stance of fascism in Europe. Beginning in the spring of 1935 talks between Berlin and Tokyo on cooperation against communism added to his apprehension. To counter these anti-communist tendencies, the seventh congress of the Comintern, which met in July–August 1935, established a new political line propagating the establishment of a united front of cooperation between communist parties and socialist and bourgeois forces to combat the rise of fascism. Stalin could do little to prevent an alliance between Japan and Germany, but he could attempt to persuade the Western countries to join him in a fight against fascism, which threatened them all. In China, a united front under Chiang Kai-shek, still the only leader capable of managing such an internal alliance, was seen as the only option for restraining the aggressive Kuantung Army, which, Stalin feared, might strike in Siberia.

The Soviet Union had some difficulty in conveying the Comintern's new united front policy to the CCP leadership. Contact between the CCP and the Comintern, essentially radio contact, had been interrupted since November 1934, during the early stages of the Long March. It had been reestablished for a few weeks in the fall of 1935, only to cease again until new radio equipment arrived from the Soviet Union in May or June 1936.[69] During the seventh congress of the Comintern, which met that August in Moscow, Wang Ming issued a CCP manifesto advocating an anti-fascist united front. Since there was no contact with the CCP Central Committee, its leadership could not have been aware of this initiative.[70] In November 1935, communications were briefly reestablished through Lin Yuying, a member of the CCP delegation to the Comintern and the Comintern's emissary to the CCP headquarters in China. After a long search for the Red Army's whereabouts, Lin located it at Wayaobao in Shaanxi Province. There, he told the Red Army leaders about the united front policy of the Comintern congress to the CCP. Because he had not dared to carry any official communist documents, he had to relay the policy verbally. The main thrust of the message was summarized as follows: the previous policy of "opposing Chiang Kai-shek and resisting Japan" was to be replaced by "uniting with Chiang Kai-shek to resist Japan."

In view of the intensifying anti-Japanese feelings in many circles of Chinese society, the CCP, independently from the Comintern, had begun to consider a new kind of united front policy. On 23 December 1934, the Politburo adopted a resolution on "Problems of Military Strategy." It stipulated that the Red Army should "unite the civil war with the national war." In practical terms, this meant that the Red Army should combine the consolidation and active defense of the soviet area with "fighting to clear the way for resistance againstJapan."[71] Anti-Japanese sentiment throughout Chinese society was expanded to an anti-imperialist struggle, which the communists believed would unite all political, military, and intellectual forces in a common effort to combat Japanese occupation. On 23 December, another resolution adopted by the Politburo, later known as the Wayaobao Resolution, widened the concept of anti-Japanese forces to include elements of the national bourgeoisie, rich peasants, and landlords with small holdings. But the then prevailing Chinese communist view held that not only the Japanese imperialists but also the "traitor Chiang Kai-shek" were the primary targets of the united front.[72] The Comintern's demand to "unite with Chiang Kai-shek" must have stunned the CCP leadership. Though long accustomed to practicing internal discipline in the face of directives from the top, CCP leaders found this difficult to accept and showed strong resistance. Nevertheless, they put their propaganda apparatus to work in underscoring the anti-imperialist struggle and winning over army units and commanders to the cause of cooperation. Zhou was instrumental in the implementation of this policy. By December 1935, the CCP had established contact with Yang Hucheng, the commander of the Nationalist Northwest Army. Zhou Enlai made special efforts to win over Zhang Xueliang, who was well known for having anti-Japanese sentiments. Zhang's deep-rooted anti-Japanese sentiments, his doubts about Chiang Kai-shek's willingness to oppose the Japanese, and the CCP's indication that it was ready to advance against the invaders made him well disposed toward joint action with the communists. Zhou established a northeast working committee with the sole purpose of promoting cooperation with Zhang. New slogans insisting that "Chinese must not fight Chinese," urged Zhang's Northeast Army to unite with the Red Army in its struggle against Japan and to retake Manchuria.[73]

Using secret contacts, Zhou established communication with Zhang and finally met with him in Yan'an, then under Zhang's control. During their first encounter, which took place in a church on 7 April 1937, Zhang showed great determination to stop the civil war, to unite the country, and to fight the Japanese. However, he emphasized that Chiang Kai-shek was firmly in control of the national government, and it would be difficult to achieve national unification against Japan without his cooperation. The CCP, he said, had to give serious consideration to finding a modus vivendi with its archenemy.[74]

While Zhou was developing secret contacts with Zhang, Chiang Kai-shek began to feel increasingly dissatisfied and suspicious about Zhang's inaction against the communists. Chiang ordered his own generals and troops to advance to Shanxi and issued instructions to his deputy to attack the Red Army in northern Shaanxi without further delay. But the conspiracy between Zhou and Zhang against Chiang Kai-shek had reached such proportions that, in order to foster a deception, they deployed mock military units, creating the impression that the Northeast Army and the Red Army were engaged in battle. While Zhou was moving armed forces around the east bank of the Yellow River to transfer the headquarters of the CCP to Bao'an, he stopped at a hamlet called

Beijiaping to meet the American journalist Edgar Snow. Snow, en route
to the headquarters of the communist base areas, vividly describes his
meeting with the "notorious Zhou Enlai." It was Snow's impression that
Zhou appeared just at the right time to save him from being captured by a
young Red Guard leader who took him for a "white," thus an enemy.[75]

Zhang Xueliang, convinced that a national united front against Japan
could not be achieved without Chiang's cooperation, was also certain that
some coercion was necessary to force Chiang into an alliance with anti-
Japanese forces, including the communists. When Chiang arrived in Xian
in December to take charge of another campaign against the CCP, Zhang,
in cooperation with General Yang Hucheng, arrested him.[76]

Chiang Kai-shek was held in captive at the Huaqing gong (Palace of
Glorious Purity), where the Tang emperor Xuanzong used to take his
beloved Yang Guifei to bathe in hot springs. His captors, the two generals,
issued an eight-point statement demanding, among other things, the
reorganization of the Nanjing government into a "National Salvation
Government" that should end the civil war and give priority to the
struggle against the Japanese invasion, in which all anti-Japanese forces
act in concert. They invited Zhou to Xian for consultations about the
future destiny of Chiang Kai-shek, whose execution was demanded by
numerous officers of Zhang's and Hu's armies, as well as some CCP
leaders. Mao Zedong and Zhu De, for example, demanded a public trial
of Chiang Kai-shek, while Zhou and Zhang Wentian were concerned that
Chiang's execution might release strong anti-communist forces and
increase the danger of a civil war. Moreover, Moscow had sent
instructions ruling out anything but a compromise. Stalin wanted a united
front that Zhou was to negotiate. Soon after Chiang's arrest, the Nanjing
government split into two factions. A pro-Japanese group, represented by
General He Yingqin, the defense minister, and Wang Jingwei, who
favored a "punitive expedition" against Chiang Kai-shek's captors, was
ready to march against Xian. Fearing that such a military action might
result in Chiang's death and his replacement by Wang Jingwei, Chiang
Kai-shek's wife, Soong Meiling, and her brother T.V. Soong, strongly
opposed such an initiative.

Zhou Enlai arrived in Xian in the evening of 17 December with an
entourage of about twenty men, to find that Zhang Xueliang and Yang
Hucheng disagreed about the future course of action concerning Chiang
Kai-shek. Whereas Zhang was ready to negotiate Chiang's release, Yang
was in favor of executing him. Acting as moderator, Zhou employed

extreme caution and courtesy in long hours of intensive negotiations and succeeded in reconciling their positions. While he was keen on ensuring Chiang's safety, Zhou was also convinced that pressure had to be brought to bear to persuade Chiang of the need to abandon his policy of pursuing a civil war and to organize all patriotic forces willing to oppose the Japanese. As an immediate priority, however, Zhou proposed the formation of a military alliance between the Red Army, Zhang Xueliang's, and Yang Hucheng's forces against the "punitive expedition" planned by General He and any future retaliation that Chiang might plan against his captors.[77]

On 20 December, T.V. Soong arrived in Xian to investigate the situation. Two days later, Soong Meiling joined her brother in the discussions concerning Chiang's fate with Zhang, Yang, and Zhou. After ten years of civil war, during which the communists had been referred to as "bandits," it must have been gratifying for Zhou to sit at the negotiating table with government representatives and to discuss the future orientation of the country's policies. Chiang Kai-shek never participated in the negotiations, having delegated matters to T.V. Soong and Soong Meiling. At first, Chiang strongly opposed the participation of CCP representatives in the discussions, but under pressure from his family and supporters, he realized that his life and freedom depended to a large extent on communist goodwill toward him. He felt compelled to accept, however reluctantly, communist demands to end the civil war and to cooperate with the Red Army in the anti-Japanese war. Moreover, having been persuaded by T.V. Soong and Madame Chiang, Chiang received Zhou for a meeting on the evening of 24 December. This was the first time that Chiang and Zhou met since Zhou's departure from the Whampoa Military Academy more than ten years earlier. Zhou started the conversation by saying: "In the ten years since we have met, you seem to have aged very little." Chiang nodded and said, "Enlai, you were my subordinate. You should do what I say." Zhou replied that, if Chiang would stop the civil war and begin to resist the Japanese, then not only he but the entire Red Army would be willing to accept Chiang's command. After listening carefully to Zhou's statement concerning CCP policies toward the GMD government and the Japanese invasion, Chiang promised to end his policy of communist suppression, to cooperate with the Red Army against Japan, and to invite Zhou to Nanjing for further talks.[78]

Chiang was released and departed for Nanjing on 25 December, accompanied by General Zhang Xueliang, who, as a gesture of goodwill, agreed to leave with Chiang—only to be placed under house arrest as soon as they reached Nanjing. After Zhang's arrest, the officers of the Northeast Army rose in protest against Chiang's double-dealing, demanding the release of their general. There was disagreement about how to obtain his freedom. Whereas General Wang Yizhe, representing some high-ranking officers, advocated peaceful persuasion, some middle- and lower-ranking officers insisted upon carrying out a punitive military action against Chiang Kai-shek. The differences between the two groups became so heated that, on 2 February 1937, several angry young officers who held General Wang responsible for the lack of response to Zhang's arrest broke into Wang's residence and killed him.

Immediately after Wang's death, rumors began to circulate that the CCP was behind his assassination. This was followed by insinuations that, in order to force the army to adhere to the CCP, more generals from the Northeast Army were going to be killed. As soon as Zhou heard about Wang's violent death, he went to his house and found the general's family in a state of grief and confusion. Taking matters into his own hands, he took care of the traditional funeral arrangements. His thoughtfulness touched Wang's family deeply, and they were convinced that Zhou and the CCP were not involved in Wang's assassination.

But this was not the end of the story. A few days later, a group of angry young officers rushed to Zhou's office, surrounded him, and accused the CCP of having instigated the Xian Incident and of having betrayed General Zhang, who had acted as a friend. At gunpoint, they threatened to kill Zhou. With complete self-control Zhou maintained his composure and, eloquently defending his case in this perilous situation, he succeeded in calming down the young officers, who finally departed, leaving him unharmed.[79]

In several meetings with government representatives or with Chiang Kai-shek in Xian, Hangzhou, Lushan, and Nanjing between February and June 1937, Zhou tried to obtain General Zhang's release. But Zhang remained under house arrest, first on the mainland, then in Taiwan. He was released only in 1990, when he was more than ninety years old.

*     *     *     *

The outbreak of the hostilities between China and Japan at the Marco Polo bridge (Lugouqiao) on 7 July 1937 and the occupation of Shanghai by Japanese troops on 13 August 1937 once more changed the relationship between the CCP and the Nationalist government. As Japanese hostilities spread throughout northern and eastern China, the Soviet Union signed a nonaggression pact with Chiang Kai-shek on 21 August. The next day, three divisions of the Red Army, numbering forty-five thousand, were officially reorganized into the Eighth Route Army under the Nationalist army, but retained de facto independence under the command of the communist generals Zhu De and Peng Dehuai. In central China communist guerrilla troops were regrouped into the New Fourth Army. On 12 October, its troops were placed under the command of the communist generals Ye Ting and Xiang Ying. The GMD recognized the communist base area as a regional government on 6 September. On 22 September, the CCP and the GMD formally established their alliance but issued separate statements. The GMD declared its intention to enlist the support of all nationals against the Japanese invader and the CCP promised to honor its commitments to the Nationalist government.[80]

These understandings, however, only papered over the problems that existed between the parties. Zhou was realistic enough to recognize that many issues under negotiation between the Nationalist government and the CCP would remain unsettled. The area of jurisdiction of the border region government was one of them. The expansion of the Eighth Route Army from three to six divisions that Zhou demanded was also rejected. In his discussions with the GMD, Zhou put aside other issues such as the supply lines for the Eighth Route Army and the New Fourth Army and their location. But neither side was ready to compromise, and the negotiations ended in stalemate.

In fact, from the very beginning, the cooperation agreement was doomed to failure. Within the CCP, stormy debates raged about its meaning and implementation. Between 22 and 25 August, an enlarged conference at Luochuan became the forum of a heated discussion on the organization of the Eighth Route Army. Zhu De, supported by Zhou, argued that, for the sake of efficient military resistance against Japan, the Eighth Route Army should be integrated into the military structure of the Nationalist army. But this implied that military representatives from the GMD General Staff would be able to intervene in its command structure, something that Mao was not willing to accept. His primary concern was the Red Army's independence, so he refused to accept any form of effective control by the Nationalists.

Disagreements also surfaced on military strategy. The question was whether the Red Army, in cooperation with the Nationalist army, should predominantly use guerrilla tactics in which it was widely experienced or should employ mobile warfare as well. Mao argued that the Red Army was not sufficiently strong or well equipped to have any effect in a conventional war. It should therefore disperse behind enemy lines and engage in guerrilla warfare. Most important, it should expand communist bases and, in the process, its own military strength. Zhou was opposed to this strategy. If the Red Army refused to confront the enemy face to face, he said, it would discredit itself and throw doubts on its anti-Japanese stance. No agreement was reached on these issues.[81]

An enlarged Politburo meeting in December further discussed the issue of military organization and strategy. Wang Ming, a member of the Comintern presidium and its chief CCP representative, had returned from Moscow in November 1937. At the meeting he explained the Comintern's new united front policies, established at its seventh congress. According to Wang Ming, the basic principle for cooperation with the GMD was that "everything should go through the united front," and "everything should be submitted to the united front."[82] Mao, however, reasserted "independence and initiative" as the guiding principle for Party and army strategy. This implied that he was determined to retain his own initiative in military operations. He had serious doubts about Chiang Kai-shek's willingness to combat the Japanese, believing that Chiang was ready to wage, at most, "a war of partial resistance," as Mao called it. He thought that the CCP should guide the resistance movement.[83] Wang Ming's approach was different. He accused Mao of being too independent and of taking too many initiatives without consulting the GMD, instead of increasing his efforts to strengthen unity between the two parties. Wang also showed little interest in guerrilla warfare, emphasizing that mobile warfare, for which the Nationalist army was trained, would be instrumental in winning the war against Japan.[84]

Zhou Enlai echoed some of Wang Ming's views at the December meeting. He was not as pessimistic as Mao about the Chiang's disposition to compromise with the Japanese and suggested that, for the sake of combating the common enemy, the CCP should be more sincere about its cooperation with the GMD. Zhou believed that the Eighth Route Army should not engage in guerrilla warfare alone, but should also be ready for mobile warfare, if the conditions were right. He cautioned against the application of the principle, favored by Mao, of "independence and initiative," which implied that Mao did not want to wait for the decisions of the GMD before taking his own initiatives in the war as he saw fit. All this might harm the united front and thus the effectiveness of the resistance against Japan. He criticized the Politburo for failing to give priority to the "war of resistance above all."[85]

On 13 December 1937, Nanjing fell to the Japanese without much resistance. The Nationalist government retreated to Wuhan, where it established its temporary war capital on the eighteenth, while Wang Jingwei, who remained in Nanjing, installed a pro-Japanese government. Within the framework of the new cooperative arrangement between the GMD and the CCP, the CCP established representation in the Nationalist government. Zhou was appointed to head the liaison office in Wuhan. Parallel to the official representation, Zhou set up a Yangtze Bureau of the Central Committee, a clandestine operation under the cover of the office of the Eighth Route Army. It focused on the recruitment of new Party members and the formation of new Party structures in southern China.

In February 1938 the Nationalist government appointed Zhou to the post of deputy director of the Political Department of its Military Committee under General Chen Cheng. Zhou's rank of lieutenant general made him the only communist to hold a high-level government position. This position allowed him to make a contribution, in March 1938, to the strategic planning of Tai'erzhuang campaign, one of the early victories of the Nationalist army against the Japanese. Several armies were involved in the campaign. Generals Bai Chongxi and Li Zongren, leaders of the Guangxi warlord faction, led their troops into battle. Other army units, including Chiang Kai-shek's own forces, also converged toward the war zone. However, a central command structure was absent. Zhou, aware of the problem and convinced of General Li's military abilities, recommended his appointment as commander over all the troops involved in the battle, which totaled four hundred and fifty thousand. To persuade Chiang to grant Li overall command of the troops in the war theater could not have been an easy undertaking. After all, in 1936, Li and Bai had revolted against Chiang's hesitant policies toward Japan. Zhou's promise of support from the Red Army apparently tilted the balance. He offered assurances that the Eighth Route Army would intervene from the north and the New Fourth Army would cut off the Tianjin-Pukou railroad, critical for Japanese supply lines. This consolidation of the command structure proved a major element in the Chinese attack that killed twenty thousand Japanese soldiers and resulted in the seizure of a large amount of booty.[86]

## Mass Mobilization

On 12 August 1937, the CCP issued instructions on united front work and national resistance to all Party units. The directive stressed the importance of open propaganda and mass mobilization and, at the same time, of underground activities aiming at the establishment, promotion, and penetration of mass organizations as well as communist infiltration of government and army units at different levels. Zhou was a master organizer, and these tasks clearly appealed to him. Shortly after his arrival in Wuhan, the communist newspaper *Xinhua ribao* (New China Daily), which had just began publication, became a major tool for the spreading of communist propaganda in GMD areas. Paradoxically, it was formally authorized and even financially subsidized by the Nationalist government. The communists thought of it as "a dagger pointing at the heart of the GMD." The Nationalists later regretted it as one of their "biggest mistakes" to have allowed and even financed such a propaganda instrument.[87]

Zhou enlisted the talented Guo Moruo, a recognized intellectual, scholar, writer, historian, dramatist, and poet, to help him to mobilize the masses. Though officially heading the Third Bureau of the Political Department of the National Military Commission, which was in charge of propaganda, he was a clandestine member of the CCP. Zhou counted on his devotion to the communist cause and on his personnel reputation to engage a large number of left-wing and middle-of-the-road intellectuals to organize scores of artistic and cultural events propagating resistance to the Japanese invasion. Lecturing teams, expected to persuade people that they should participate in the anti-Japanese movement, were dispatched throughout the city. The highlight of these activities was a propaganda week in celebration of the victory over Japanese troops at Tai'erzhuang organized from 7 to 12 April in Wuhan. The propaganda week was a big success. Between four hundred thousand and five hundred thousand people took part in parades; and more that ten thousand formed a chorus singing songs of resistance. Fund raising in support of the war effort yielded more than a million yuan in only five days. Chen Cheng donated 10,000 yuan on behalf of the Political Department of the Military Commission, while Zhou Enlai donated 240 yuan, his monthly salary as the deputy director of the Political Department.[88]

Building up the Party, which Zhou regarded as one of his main tasks in Wuhan, extended to the many foreign residents and visitors there. This made Zhou the CCP's main contact person with the outside world. He routinely received foreign visitors and eventually arranged their visits to the Red base area in Yan'an. A Canadian medical team headed by Norman Bethune, for example, was able to visit Yan'an in early 1938. Zhou extended his help to a Dutch film director Rodney Evans for the production of a documentary on China, entitled *400 Million People*. Zhou met with the Indian medical team headed by Dr. Dwarkanath Kotnis. He developed good relations with such foreign journalists and writers as Edgar Snow, Agnes Smedley, Anna Louise Strong, and Rewi Alley, all of whom became sympathetic to the communist cause and extensively wrote about it in the foreign publications. Through Wang Bingnan, his secretary for foreign affairs at the Yangtze Bureau, he maintained contact with more than forty reporters in Wuhan. All these activities contributed to a change in the image of the CCP, which the GMD, during the previous ten years of civil strife, had described as a group of bandits.

Zhou's efforts in image building were in some way deflected by Zhang Guotao's defection to the GMD, which dealt a serious blow to the prestige of the Party. Zhang, a founder of the CCP and, at the time of his disillusionment with the Party, a member of the Politburo and acting chairman of the government of the Shaanxi-Gansu-Ningxia (abbreviated as Shaan-Gan-Ning) Border Region, continued to disapprove of Mao's authoritarian leadership methods. His latest disagreement was over how the united front was being implemented.

On 4 April 1938, Zhang left Yan'an on a ceremonial visit to Xian. A few days later, he arrived in Wuhan, accompanied by two GMD special agents. The defection of such a high-ranking official was embarrassing to the CCP and its policy of enhancing its image in China and abroad. Zhou attempted to detain Zhang at the railway station, where he dispatched Li Kenong, his chief of intelligence, and two uniformed and armed men. Zhang firmly refused their invitation to accompany them to the office of the CCP. Both Zhou and Zhang wished to avoid a public showdown, so Zhang offered to take up lodging at a hotel where not only Zhou's men but also GMD agents would be able to supervise his movements. Using all his diplomatic talent, Zhou attempted to bring about a reconciliation. In several talks with Zhang—in which Wang Ming, Bo Gu, and Li Kenong also took part—Zhou proposed that Zhang either resume working for the CCP or take leave from it for a period of rest and reflection. If these alternatives were unacceptable to him, he would be expelled from the Party. The proposals were rejected: Zhang clearly had made up his mind to turn his back on the CCP. Refusing any compromise, he left the meeting under the protection of the GMD secret police. The next day, 18 April, the CCP Central Committee announced its decision to expel Zhang; two days later, he issued a statement accusing the CCP of sabotaging efforts to resist the Japanese and expressing his full support to the Nationalist government.[89]

## Underground and Intelligence Operations

As Japanese troops approached Wuhan in the autumn of 1938, the Nationalist government abandoned the city without a fight and removed its offices to Chongqing in Sichuan province. On his way to Chongqing, Zhou witnessed the "fire of Changsha," in which more than twenty thousand lost their lives and hundreds of thousands became homeless. This event was caused not by the Japanese army but by the Nationalist government's lack of concern for the local people. After Wuhan fell to the Japanese, Chiang Kai-shek believed that Changsha, the capital of Hunan province, would be next. Rather than leaving the city to the advancing Japanese troops, he decided to set it on fire. The plan was to warn citizens through air raid alarm before the city was set ablaze. But because of an organizational error, so it was later claimed, the fires started before people could be warned.

Zhou was almost caught in the fire. He arrived in Changsha on 27 October. During the early hours of 12 November, he and Ye Jianying were awakened by Zhou's bodyguard, who was urging them to leave their lodgings then threatened by the blaze. Zhou, Ye, and their guards joined a large crowd of refugees who converged on the banks of the Yangtze River to escape the fire. Taking refuge in a Buddhist temple in a neighboring village, Zhou organized the evacuation and retreat of the Changsha office of the Eighth Route Army toward Guilin.

The fire lasted for three days, destroying two-thirds of the city. Newspapers in the whole country were in an uproar against the authorities, which had declared that the fire had been the work of unruly masses. Zhou approached the Nationalist government, demanding a thorough investigation of the causes of the fire and the punishment of those responsible. He also insisted that reparations be paid to the victims, that the city be thoroughly cleaned up, and that accommodations be provided for the homeless. The government blamed the commander of the Changsha garrison, the commander of the third regiment of the garrison and the director of the Changsha secret services bureau for the fire. All three were summarily executed.[90]

## Chongqing

Theodore White, a correspondent for *Time* magazine who arrived in Chongqing in April 1939, drew a vivid picture of the city at that time. A footbridge from the Yangtze River led from the docks "to the foot of a gray cliff, and there, high above the cliff, ran the city wall of old Chongqing.... Sedan chair bearers carried the visitor and his belongings up the hundreds of steps carved into the cliff."[91] The city wall was replaced by a road, but visitors still walk up the steps, and their suitcases may still be carried up the cliffs on bamboo poles. The city still sits on top of the cliffs, squeezed together by the Jialing and Yangtze rivers, which join at the tip of the wedge.

Chongqing was then home to three hundred thousand people. Their houses, in narrow and hilly alleys, and their way of living had not changed for hundreds of years. The city was the gateway to Sichuan—one of China's most fertile areas, where, according to an old Chinese saying, rice and fish were abundant. The government's move to the city brought with it some two hundred and fifty thousand people, causing culture shock among the local population. The newcomers dressed differently, talked differently, smoked cigarettes, and drank foreign brandy; worst of all, most of them did not eat the spicy food typical to the region.

Zhou and his staff arrived in Chongqing at the end of December 1938. They settled down at 50 Zengjia'an lu, which was also the seat of the liaison office and of the South China Bureau, as the Yangtze Bureau was now named. The house that they occupied was an old and ramshackle building located in a small alley. White describes its reception room, which contained several armchairs and a sofa, spring-broken, lumpy, uncomfortable; all covered with the same coarse, blue cloth worn by Chinese peasants and workers. As in Wuhan, Zhou's mission was multifaceted. His official function was to maintain relations with the GMD and to negotiate with the government on various issues. But he attached as much importance to the development of contacts with different circles with the aim of winning sympathy and support for the CCP's efforts in the struggle against the Japanese. He thus served as a bridge between the remote Party headquarters and the outside world. But the expansion of CCP underground network in GMD-controlled areas was again the major task of the clandestine work of the South China Bureau.

The South China Bureau started operations on 16 January 1939. Zhou headed its Standing Committee, which functioned officially as the Chongqing office of the Eighth Route Army. Zhou, with Dong Biwu as his deputy, headed the United Front Department and the department in charge of Party work in enemy-occupied zones. The bureau also included a Propaganda Department headed by He Kequan; an Organization Department directed by Bo Gu; an Overseas Chinese Department headed by Ye Jianying; a Department of Women's Affairs led by Deng Yingchao; a Youth Department, where Jiang Nanxiang was in charge; a Research Office on International Affairs directed by Zhang Hanfu; and a Secretariat headed by Tong Xiaopeng. Two official communist publications were published: *Xinhua ribao,* directed by Wu Kejian, and *Qunzhong* (The Masses), a periodical edited by Qiao Guanhua. During its peak, the full staff of the office totaled several hundred people.

With the beginning of the second united front, the CCP began to reconstruct its organizations in the southern provinces, which had earlier been seriously reduced by the GMD. Under the united front agreement, Zhou negotiated the release of political prisoners who were still in the hands of the GMD. They were often experienced organizers, whom Zhou reassigned to the reconstruction of the Party. Before sending any leading cadres to the southern provinces, Zhou discussed the specific details and conditions of their assignment with them.[92]

The revival of Party organizations became a focal point of Zhou's activities in December 1937, after the Politburo stated that the upsurge of anti-Japanese sentiments and the general outcry of patriotism created favorable conditions for the establishment of new Party structures at the level of municipalities, counties, and various localities. A resolution of March 1938 called for the recruitment of new Party members in large numbers. This effort was helped by the Japanese occupation, which inspired large numbers of people, especially those who were already left-wing, to join the Party and other progressive movements. In Sichuan, for example, only 340 had already joined the Party by March 1938. Within a few months, membership expanded tenfold. In Hunan, the situation was similar. From a few hundred at the beginning of the year, CCP membership increased to more than seven thousand by the end of the year. By September 1938, CCP membership in all thirteen southern provinces had increased from an insignificant number to 67,780.[93]

The vigorous growth of the CCP threatened the GMD. As in the 1920s, Chiang hoped to reinforce his control over the communists by integrating them into the GMD. He proposed a merger between the two parties, which implied that the communists would have to give up their membership in the CCP. Zhou, whose memories of the 1927 massacre were still fresh, turned down the proposal. In January 1939, Chiang made further overtures for a merger. The official response from Yan'an, which Zhou had requested, was similarly negative. Because Chiang's offers were falling on deaf ears, the GMD, in April 1939, issued an internal directive ordering the introduction of "measures to restrict the activities of alien parties," which were aimed at containing and opposing the CCP.[94] Relations between the two parties began to deteriorate.

In July 1939, while in Yan'an to attend a series of Politburo meetings, Zhou reported at length about the war situation, the problems of the united front, and the general work of the South China Bureau. During his stay, Zhou had an accident while horseback riding, falling and fracturing his right elbow. There was very little medical care available in Yan'an, so, accompanied by Deng Yingchao and their adopted daughter, Sun Weishi, Zhou went to Moscow for treatment. He arrived in September and received surgical and medical treatment until December, but too late to mend the fracture. His arm remained bent for the rest of his life.

The Comintern in Moscow was concerned about developments in China. In particular, it deplored the evolution of the united front. Zhou admitted that there were "serious frictions in the united front." Stalin was so displeased with the CCP's independent policy toward the Nationalists that he refused to talk to Zhou while he was in Moscow for medical treatment. Without seeing Stalin, Zhou returned to Yan'an in March 1940 and then traveled to Chongqing at the end of May.

During his absence, relations between the CCP and the GMD had further deteriorated. In addition to a series of clashes between military units, Nationalist blockages of Party organizations in the south also had become increasingly frequent. Party members were harassed, arrested, and often executed. When, in April 1940, two leading members of the CCP Special Committee of Sichuan and Tibet were arrested, Zhou was convinced that the time had come for the CCP to change its modus operandi in GMD areas.[95] At a meeting of the Central Committee Secretariat in Yan'an on 29 April, he argued convincingly that Party members and organizations should go underground and no longer operate openly. In the white (GMD) areas, it would be preferable for communists to operate in disguise, no longer participating in activities such as strikes and demonstrations. On 4 May, the Politburo accepted Zhou's proposals. It issued a guideline, reversing instructions promulgated in the first half of the 1930s, stating that "in GMD areas, our policy is to have well-selected cadres working underground for long periods, to accumulate strength and bid time and to avoid rashness and exposure." The major preoccupation was "to build up strength by using GMD laws and decrees that can serve our purpose."[96] The directive allowed communists to join the GMD if they were forced to do so. The purpose was to infiltrate the GMD administrative system and, wherever possible, the educational, economic, and military establishment.

In the months that followed Zhou adopted a series of measures to put the May 4 guidelines into practice. Under the cover of the Office of the Eighth Route Army, which had moved to a stately building on the outskirts of town, the South China Bureau was involved in both open and underground activities. Zhou's strategy was, as much as possible, to separate the two types of operations, for which he used different people. To enhance the efficiency of underground work, Zhou introduced a high degree of centralization and a strict command structure for Party organizations. He established two area working committees: the Southwest China Working Committee, covering Sichuan, Yunnan, Guizhou, western Hubei, and Hunan; and the South China Working Committee was in charge of Guangdong, Guangxi, Jiangxi, Fujian, Zhejiang, Hong Kong, and Macao. The committees answered directly to Zhou. While the leading organs of the underground Party were being restructured, Zhou transferred Party members who had been exposed to the GMD, to the Shaan-Gan-Ning Border Region, or to base areas in Japanese-occupied zones. He encouraged Party members who remained in the GMD areas to find work, preferably as schoolteachers, a profession that would allow them to influence the younger generation. Although Zhou considered the infiltration of GMD agencies a priority for the CCP, he was also conscious of the fact that GMD agents would penetrate the CCP. This might have been particularly easy for them during the period when a large number of new members—motivated by anti-Japanese sentiments—had been pouring into the Party. In a drive to expose such agents, he instructed Party organizations at various levels to examine its members closely.

Aside from the restructuring of Party organizations, Zhou concentrated his efforts on the establishment of a complex underground communication network in GMD areas. As the nerve center of Party activities in the GMD areas, the South China Bureau established two lines of communication with clandestine CCP organizations. A semi-open line allowed communications between the liaison offices of the Eighth Route Army and the New Fourth Army in various cities; and a secret line linked underground Party organizations in various GMD-controlled areas. Sun Youyu, Zhou's assistant in the South China Bureau, supervised operations along the two lines of communication.[97] The financing of Party activities presented another major problem. No financial contribution could be expected from the border regions. Whereas the expenses of the Office of the Eighth Route Army were covered by the government, additional funds were needed to finance the undercover operations of the South China Bureau. Financing was needed for communist publications and bookstores, work demanded by Yan'an, local underground organizations in the southern provinces, support activities for left-wing mass organizations, and basic needs of useful "friends of the Party" faced with economic difficulties. The bureau received donations from the China Defense League supported by Song Qingling (the widow of Sun Yat-sen and sister of Soong Meiling), from sympathetic foreigners, and overseas Chinese. But this was not sufficient to cover its growing financial needs. Demonstrating a great capacity for leaving aside ideological considerations when it came to solving practical problems, Zhou was convinced that the bureau should find solutions to its financial needs by running its own businesses. In mid-1940, he cabled Liu Xiao, the underground Party chief in Shanghai, to locate experienced businessmen among the city's Party members. Liu recommended Lu Xuzhang and others with experience in business related to Western medicine, medical instruments, and postal services. When they arrived in Chongqing, Zhou suggested that a company be established to engage in various businesses. Under Lu's direction, the Guangdahua Company was founded and developed into a thriving enterprise, with branches in several other cities. The same year, Zhou oversaw the establishment of the Xinhua Trading Company in Hong Kong. The success of Lu Xuzhang's business in Chongqing encouraged Zhou to establish a silk and satin store in the same city. The different businesses run clandestinely by the Party were so successful that it encouraged Zhou to set up more companies, among them one supplying raw material for industries and an oil refinery. The Dasheng Company set up in Chongqing by Liu Xiao, with branches in other cities, made large profits from the production and trade of cotton yarn and cloth, Western medicine, and other products. In addition to commercial activities, some of the Party's businessmen began to master currency trade and speculation, especially in U.S. dollars and gold, which became a profitable business during the war. The most lucrative business, however, was based on opium plantations that Zhou had authorized in the border regions. The CCP, as soon as it came to power, was deeply engaged in the eradication of opium smoking habits, but this venture allowed the generation of huge profits from opium trade in GMD areas, not to mention the debilitating effects on combat ability from opium addiction.[98]

During his time in Chongqing, Zhou developed an intelligence network centered at the South China Bureau. His deputy, Pan Hannian, ran a large espionage organization in the south, assuring communication lines with the intelligence apparatus of the communist armies in northeastern China and with Yan'an, where a Social Affairs Department—as the intelligence unit headed by Kang Sheng was discreetly called—had been established. Pan operated from his headquarters at the South China Intelligence Office in Hong Kong, which was established in the late summer of 1939 with the help of Liao Chengzhi. Hong Kong was the center of activities for many Chinese and foreign secret services, which sometimes cooperated but most of the time competed with one another. The major GMD intelligence agencies, the Bureau of Investigation and Statistics under General Dai Li and the Central Bureau of Investigation and Statistics headed by Chen Lifu, were both active in Hong Kong. Often they were chief targets of communist intelligence. Pan succeeded in planting his agents in Dai Li's Hong Kong organization thus gaining access to information about the relations between the Nationalist government and the United States and Great Britain and about their secret contacts with the Japanese. He also was able to gain the sympathy of Hu Egong, an adviser to the powerful and manipulative H.H. Kung (Kong Xiangxi, Soong Meiling's brother-in-law and Chiang's finance minister), who maintained his own secret service. In Hong Kong Hu introduced him to high society circles that largely facilitated Pan's activities and allowed him to develop a working relationship with the Soviet Far Eastern Information Bureau in Hong Kong.[99]

Shanghai was another focal point of communist intelligence. Here, too, secret agents from Chongqing mingled with their Japanese, American, British, French, and Soviet counterparts and with those of the pro-

Japanese Wang Jingwei puppet government in Nanjing. Liu Shaowen, head of the South China Bureau's Information Department, and Liu Xiao, leader of its underground Party organizations, represented Zhou Enlai's intelligence apparatus. They were joined by Pan Hannian's agents, who established a branch of the South China Intelligence Bureau in the city and greatly reinforced the Party's intelligence work there. Under Zhou's direction, telecommunication facilities linking Shanghai, Hong Kong, Chongqing, and Yan'an were established.

The CCP's intelligence operations were flourishing. Two of its agents were particularly ingenious. One was Yuan Shu, whose career in the secret service dated back to the early days of Teke. He became a quadruple agent, infiltrating, first, a special service section at the Central Committee of the Guomindang; then, the Japanese consul in Shanghai, which recruited him for his own intelligence operations because he spoke fluent Japanese. He also became an operator in Dai Li's branch office in Shanghai and, lastly, was a member of the secret service of the Nanjing puppet regime. Yuan's complex activities were coordinated by Pan Hannian, who worked out all the information about the CCP to be transferred to his different employers. Yuan managed to operate throughout the war years without being discovered until he left Shanghai for the communist-controlled areas in 1946.

Guan Lu, a well-known female writer and a secret member of the CCP since the 1930s, was another example of Zhou's success in planning and executing intelligence operations. Through her friendship with his wife, she infiltrated the household of Li Shiqun, a former communist who had thrown his fate in with Wang Jingwei and was in charge of the secret service and of the Ministry of Police in Nanjing. Li Shiqun was himself a triple agent, working not only for the Nanjing puppet government but also for the Japanese and the GMD secret service. In 1942, the CCP ordered Guan Lu to work publicly for the Japanese as an official representative of Shanghai cultural circles. In this function she became a notorious "traitor" to the communists while gathering information of great utility to them.[100]

In the early 1940s, Zhou was confronted with steadily worsening relations with the GMD government. While the CCP clearly was not ready to abandon its political and military independence or any of its territorial gains, Chiang Kai-shek became increasingly intolerant of communist demands. Instead of complying with Zhou's requests to recognize the border regions and to increase the potential of the Eighth Route and the New Fourth armies, he demanded that they should be abandoned and that the communist-led armies north of the Yellow River, should be reduced and redeployed. Wherever possible, Chiang intensified the persecution of CCP members and encouraged military clashes that culminated in the Southern Anhui Incident of January 1941 where nine thousand soldiers in the Communist-led New Fourth Army were ambushed, and their commanders killed or imprisoned by government troops.[101]

From Yan'an, Mao lodged a strong protest with the Nationalist government over the Southern Anhui Incident. In Chongqing, Zhou used the network he had established to promote the CCP's view of the incident. He openly condemned General He Yingqin—the commander of the government troops involved in the incident—for his role in the incident, calling him "a criminal against the Chinese nation for a thousand years." He called upon the GMD General Zhang Chong to protest the government's actions. He visited the British and the Soviet ambassadors to advise them about the incident, as well as meeting with the U.S. envoy to China. All his subordinates who were able to communicate in a foreign language were instructed to contact foreign reporters, and to openly express the CCP's indignation at the massacre of the communist armies.

Because of the strict censorship by the Nationalist authorities of the communist press and the continuous attempts to shield foreign journalists from the CCP, it was difficult to publicize the communist version of the event. But Zhou succeeded in contacting Anna Louise Strong, who agreed to publish an article about the affair in the foreign press. *Xinhua ribao* also was able to circumvent official censorship and cover the event.[102]

The GMD secret service continued its operations against communist organizations. It raided and closed down liaison offices of the Eighth Route Army in Guilin, Guiyang, and Xian. In one of its most effective strikes against a CCP underground organization GMD agents captured a messenger of the western Hubei special committee. This led to the arrest of He Gongwei, the head of the special committee. After he refused to cooperate, he was summarily executed, and about a thousand Party members were arrested.

A series of arrests of leaders and members of the CCP in Jiangxi province prompted Zhou Enlai to streamline further the leading organs of the underground organizations. Party members representing the CCP and the Office of the Eighth Route Army in Chongqing, working publicly, were ordered to cut contacts with underground Party members. Thereafter, members did not hold meetings but maintained contact with the Party individually through a contact person. Membership in Party branches was limited. Rather than having a large number of members in one branch, parallel branches were set up. There was no horizontal linkage between underground Party members and branches. So, if a branch organization was exposed, the others could continue to operate. Secrecy and safety were the primary goals of this structure. Residences of leading Party members were known only to Zhou Enlai, Dong Biwu, and Kong Yuan, the three major leaders of the South China Bureau.[103]

In Zhou's view, the essence of underground activities was to work among the masses and to influence them. "The first thing to be done," he said at a meeting of the South China Bureau at the end of 1941, "is to gain access to the GMD, the Nationalist Youth League, to workers' organizations, associations at schools, cooperatives in villages and to all important administrative departments." The target was to set up a Party branch, or indeed several parallel branches, in all major units—factories, schools, villages, and government offices. To operate successfully, underground Party members were encouraged to acquaint themselves with both the normal activities and the emergency measures of the central and local GMD authorities, and of those of its secret agents in particular.[104]

Despite all these precautions, CCP underground organizations shrank during the course of 1941. The Jiangxi Provincial Party Committee was eradicated, which interrupted communications with Chongqing. An envoy sent to Jiangxi by the South China Working Committee to investigate the situation was intercepted and forced to guide the GMD secret police to the office of the Northern Guangdong Party Committee. Its leaders were arrested on the spot. Two days later, on 29 May, Liao Chengzhi, a leading member of the South China Working Committee, was also arrested. Fang Fang, the secretary of the committee, narrowly escaped arrest. The situation had become so serious that Zhou transferred all leading cadres to safer places and, in December of that year, dissolved the South China Working Committee.[105]

The year 1941 was critical for Zhou's work in Chongqing. In China, the Southern Anhui Incident marked the formal collapse of the second united front. Internationally, the Soviet Union had concluded a neutrality pact with Japan in which Stalin pledged to respect the territorial integrity of the Japanese-occupied area of Manchukuo while the Japanese reciprocated with regard to Mongolia. Both regions were widely regarded as Chinese territory. In the first half of the year, the international situation was in so much flux that Zhou felt compelled to redouble CCP intelligence efforts in this area.

Zhou was persuaded by his secret service that U.S. President Franklin Roosevelt was intent on appeasing Japan at China's expense and that the United States and Japan were in the process of negotiating an agreement to settle the Chinese problem. He feared that such a settlement would be attractive to the GMD, whose opposition to Japan had always been shallow. Mao Zedong took Zhou's warning seriously. On 25 May, he published a directive to "expose the plot for a Far Eastern Munich" and launched a large-scale propaganda offensive against the plot designed to exert pressure on Chiang Kai-shek.[106]

But it was speculation about a possible German war against the Soviet Union that was the talk of Chongqing. Yuan Baohang, a secret Party member active in diplomatic circles there, informed Zhou that Hitler was planning to attack the Soviet Union on 22 June. Under Zhou's signature, this information went to Yan'an and from there to Moscow on 20 June.

The German attack on the Soviet Union, which took place as expected on the twenty-second, led to much speculation at CCP headquarters as to what would happen with respect to Japan. Would Japanese forces attack the Soviet Union in the north in support of Germany, or would they be directed south to engage the United States, Great Britain, Southeast Asia, and areas in the South Pacific? Between July and October 1941, the CCP Intelligence Bureau in Hong Kong sent several cables to Yan'an relaying information obtained from various Japanese sources concerning Japanese military plans. Zhou's agents at the office of the Japanese chief of staff in central China reported that the emperor of Japan had warned of an attack on Siberia. Other agents at the Japanese consulate in Shanghai learned that the Japanese might launch a preemptive war against the United States in the Pacific. This intelligence was supported by information from other sources leading into the same direction. By October, it seemed clear that Japan had all but completed war preparations against the United States. All this information was transmitted to Yan'an and, from there, passed on to the Soviet leaders.[107]

Zhou expanded his intelligence network into the Nationalist army. Since the 1930s, when nationalistic, anti-Japanese sentiment had become widespread in China's cities, many students had joined the CCP. Some of them were chosen by the Party to enlist in Chiang Kai-shek's army. This was such a delicate and dangerous assignment that Zhou had specified the qualifications such an agent had to possess in order to survive. He had to come from a well-to-do family, be young, and be well educated, especially with respect to Sun Yat-sen's political ideas; politically, he needed to have the profile of a centrist; he had to be circumspect, have a good memory, and feel at ease in a changing environment. One of those whom Zhou himself recruited to join the First Army Corps was Xiong Xianghui, then a recent graduate of Qinghua University in Beijing. Xiong, then nineteen years old, satisfied Zhou's requirements and served successfully as a CCP agent in a high position in the Nationalist army until 1949.[108]

Another recruit was Qian Junrui, a well-known intellectual and a secret Party member, who became the chief of the Cultural Work Committee in the fifth war zone, in Guangxi. Two other clandestine Party members whom Zhou enlisted were able to infiltrate the headquarters of the Guangxi troops, under the command of Bai Chongxi and Li Zongren. One of the agents, Liu Zhongrong, served as a senior adviser to General Li. The other, Xie Hegeng, rose to the position of private and confidential secretary of General Bai with the rank of colonel. His role was further enhanced when Bai was appointed deputy general chief of staff of the Nationalist army during the anti-Japanese war. From that position he relied on secret channels of communication and became a reliable and continuous source of information to Zhou. Moreover, he was active in distributing disinformation to the Nationalist general chief of staff, which had been carefully checked and revised by Zhou.[109]

By the early 1940s, Xiong Xianghui had worked his way up to the position of secretary to General Hu Zongnan, commander in chief of the important eighth war zone, headquartered in Xian. Hu was responsible for the defense against the Japanese of a long stretch of the Yellow River and for the blockage of the Shaan-Gan-Ning Border Region controlled by the CCP. In 1943, Chiang Kai-shek planned to launch an attack on the border region. Xiong was one of the few people with access to Chiang's orders to General Hu and to the operational plans developed for his army. Through his clandestine channels of communications, he sent the information to Yan'an. Mao decided that the best countermeasure to Chiang's plans was to make them known to the entire nation. He launched a large propaganda offensive before Chiang's armies went into action. It started with a cable that Zhu De, commander-in-chief of the communist armies, sent to Hu Zongnan on 4 July 1943, protesting the planned attack and pointing out that such an internecine struggle would only serve the purposes of the Japanese invaders. Thirty thousand people rallied in Yan'an to protest and to declare their determination to defend the border region. *Jiefang ribao* (Liberation Daily), the communist newspaper, carried an editorial entitled "Some Pointed Questions to the Guomindang," in which Mao launched a sharp attack on the Nationalist government. The allies, who supported Chinese efforts to repulse the Japanese invaders and opposed civil war, denounced Chiang's plans. The attack was abandoned.

After civil war broke out in mid-1946, Xiong participated in preparations for General Hu's attack on Yan'an and thus was able to transmit the full operational plan to the CCP headquarters.[110] This enabled communist leaders to evacuate the area without a fight. Mao and Zhou, chairman and vice chairman of the military commission, respectively, directed operations against Hu's army. Employing mobile warfare tactics, they fought many successful campaigns, which defeated large number of Nationalist troops and permitted the recovery of Yan'an in April 1948.

## The Fate of Zhou's Agents

After the establishment of the People's Republic of China in 1949, many of Zhou's agents, including those who had taken exceptionally high risks and had been remarkably efficient, found themselves on the wrong side of the prevailing political stream and thus were ostracized. Zhou had personally recruited many of them and undoubtedly had detailed knowledge about their performance, yet failed to come to their defense. When Guan Lu joined the communist base in Yan'an after the Japanese surrender in 1945, her reputation as an ostensible traitor had been so firmly established that she never gained the full trust of the Party. Wang Bingnan, later a famous diplomat with whom she fell in love, was not allowed to marry her. After 1949, she disappeared from public life. During the Cultural Revolution she was brutally interrogated because of her association with the Japanese. Zhou Enlai, who had been well aware of her role as a double agent in Shanghai, which enabled her to provide valuable information about the Japanese occupation forces there, did not come to her rescue. She lived alone and died in 1983 in deep depression.[111]

In the 1940s Li Zongren sent Xie Hegeng to the United States, where the Jiangxi army was operating a propaganda office directed against Japan. With Zhou's approval, Xie and his wife, the film actress Wang Ying, settled in Washington DC, where they continued to work for the communist cause. They returned to China in the early 1950s, when the McCarthy period made their stay in the United States increasingly difficult. Shortly after their return Xie was arrested during the anti-rightist campaign in 1957. In the 1960s, he was arrested again, this time together with his wife. Both were charged with having acted as American spies. Xie died in prison.[112]

The fate of Pan Hannian, Zhou's master spy, shows to an even greater extent Zhou's indifference toward his former agents. After the establishment of the People's Republic, Pan was appointed vice mayor of Shanghai, with the special assignment of eradicating secret societies and special agents, then flourishing in the city, and "counterrevolutionaries," as people who sympathized with the old regime were called. In March 1955, while participating in a conference in Beijing, he was suddenly arrested. Still under arrest eight years later, he was accused of being a "clandestine traitor" and sentenced to fifteen years in prison. The reason for his fall from grace was that, in 1943 he had an unscheduled meeting with Wang Jingwei, then head of the Nanjing puppet government. He had failed to report the meeting, which he considered insignificant, to the communist authorities at that time, but he talked about it in 1955. Mao then ordered an investigation of his earlier activities, which revealed that while working in Shanghai he had used former agents of Wang's secret service. That was enough to send him and his wife to a labor camp in Hunan, where he died in 1977. Five years later, the Central Committee rehabilitated him, declaring that he had been falsely accused.[113] Once again, Zhou did nothing to ameliorate the fate of these agents, who, in the course of many years, had proved their loyalty to the CCP and to Zhou personally, and had risked torture and death at the hands of the GMD.

## Social Life in Chongqing

Despite worsening relations with Chiang Kai-shck, Zhou was a political star in Chongqing social circles. His charming personality, intelligence, and eloquence enabled him to make friends with different kinds of people regardless of their political affiliation, though his preference naturally was for those who were at odds with Chiang Kai-shek. He became friendly with General Feng Yuxiang, the commander of the Northwest

Army, who was known as the Christian general because he had converted to Christianity early in the century and baptized his soldiers. Feng developed deep respect for Zhou and greatly admired his intellectual brilliance. The growing friendship between the two men made it possible for Zhou to cultivate a number of GMD generals who had been Feng's former subordinates. Zhou also respected General He Jifeng, the deputy commander of the GMD Seventy-seventh Army, who had fought the Japanese at Marco Polo bridge. Zhou's public declaration that He was a national hero made a deep impression on the general. In early 1939 Zhou arranged for him to visit Yan'an, where he became a secret member of the CCP. Later, in early 1949, he played an important role in the famous Huaihai campaign of the civil war in which 800,000 GMD troops lost their lives.

Zhou's intelligence agents penetrated the Sichuan armed forces under the command of General Deng Xihou, a former warlord who had joined the GMD. His agents paved the way for negotiations between General Feng and Zhou in Chongqing, which resulted in Deng's agreement to supply ammunition to the communist New Fourth Army. Another Sichuanese general, Liu Wenhui, also agreed to cooperate with Zhou against the Nationalist government by allowing the installation of a radio transmitter which—far removed from the interference of the GMD secret service—ensured the communication between Chongqing and Yan'an.

While he was in Wuhan in 1938, Zhou befriended Zhang Chong, the commander of the 184th Division of the Yunnan Army, and Nong Yun, the governor and commander of the Yunnan armed forces. Both cooperated with the CCP against Chiang Kai-shek and eventually became secret members of the Communist Party. As a result, a clandestine radio station broadcasting pro-communist propaganda began operating from the building of the provincial government in Kunming, which became an important center of student opposition to Chiang.[114]

Unlike in Wuhan, popular demonstrations against the Japanese invasion could not be staged in Chongqing because it was under frequent heavy fire by the Japanese air force. Zhou therefore focused his attention on cultural activities, particularly the theater. His friend, the historian Guo Moruo, with the help of noted left-wing playwrights and actors, was able to stage plays critical of the Nationalist government. Zhou enjoyed mingling with them to discuss problems and their art. The 1940s became a highly productive period for Chinese modern drama, much of which originated in Chongqing. Zhou also established personal ties with scholars such as the progressive educator Tao Xingzhi, the sociologist Ma Yinchu, the historian Jian Bozan, and the philosopher Hou Wailu.[115]

Zhou became the CCP representative to the outside world. His charming and urbane ways, simple life, and dedicated work-style were in stark contrast to the corruption and the ostentatious life-style of Chiang Kai-shek and his coterie and made a favorable impression on many foreign envoys. Despite Chiang's attempts to isolate him from the international community, Zhou was able to establish regular contacts with American, British, Canadian, Russian, and other foreign diplomats in the city. He was always ready to receive foreign visitors, regardless of their status, taking into account their potential usefulness to the cause of the CCP. In 1941, Ernest Hemingway and his wife, Martha, visited Chongqing. Marsha later published her impressions of their meetings with H.H. Kung, Chiang Kai-shek, and Zhou Enlai. The meetings with Kung and his wife, Song Ailing (sister of Song Qingling and Soong Meiling), and with Chiang Kai-shek and his wife, Soong Meiling, were a disappointment to the Hemingways. They noted Song Ailing's extravagance in wearing a Chinese dress with diamond bottoms, a sharp contrast to the poverty of the Chinese people. Kung acted as if he were Martha's uncle, offering her a Chinese dress that, in her view, would have been suitable for a prostitute. Chiang talked about the Southern Anhui Incident, asking about the reactions to it in the Western press, and commented at length about the necessity of eliminating the Red Army. But the Hemingways could not comment since they had never heard anything about the Southern Anhui Incident. Their impression of Chiang Kai-shek, according to Martha, was that of pouring water onto the sand.

During their stay, they were approached by a woman—reportedly Wang Bingnan's German wife—who asked them whether they would like to meet Zhou Enlai. Martha had never heard of Zhou, but Hemingway recalled that he was a friend of Rodney Evans, the famous Dutch film producer and director, and thus agreed to meet with Zhou. According to Martha, this was the first time they had met with a Chinese with whom they were completely at ease. They knew very little about Zhou and the CCP and were unable to ask any significant questions on the subject. Later, they could not even remember what they had talked about. But they were enchanted by Zhou's personality, his sense of humor, and his easy laughter. And, as they later told State Department officials, they had become convinced that the communists would take over China after the war.[116]

Zhou also spent hours with *Time* reporter Theodore White. Years later, recalling his stay in Chongqing, he wrote that Zhou "had a way of entrancing people, of offering affection, of inviting and seeming to share confidences," and he added, "I cannot deny that he won my affection completely."[117]

Zhou motivated many literati and artists to play an active role in popularizing the communist cause in left-wing journals and books published under control of the South China Bureau. He established personal and long-lasting ties with many intellectuals and artists. But, as it was the case with his collaborators in the secret service who had risked their lives working under his instructions, his relationship with his artistic friends was often outweighed by political considerations. He was of little help to many of them when they came into trouble politically.[118]

In Chongqing, Zhou's cooperation with other political parties and their leaders paved the way for an anti-Chiang front to be established a few years later. He extended his tentacles to the upper echelon of GMD officials and succeeded, on the eve of Chiang's collapse, in winning over many of them to the communist side. He also used his stay in Chongqing to establish secret contacts with local warlords in southwestern China, thus leading them to turn to the CCP in the final phase of the civil war.[119]

## *Conversion to Maoism*

The year 1943 was a turning point in Zhou's life. His three-year stay in Chongqing came to an end when he was called back to Yan'an. In May 1941, during his absence, Mao had initiated a rectification campaign to rid the Party of Soviet influence and internal dissension. Mao was no longer willing to tolerate arguments on politics and ideology. His timing of such a campaign was well chosen for several reasons. First, Hitler's invasion of the Soviet Union in June 1941 demanded all of the Soviet leaders' attention and considerably reduced their willingness to intervene in the internal affairs of other communist parties. In 1943, Stalin dissolved the Comintern, through which he had attempted to control the entire international communist movement. All this allowed Mao to purge Stalin's representatives, particularly the Moscow-trained Bolsheviks grouped around Wang Ming, who occupied high-ranking positions within the CCP. Second, the "mopping-up operations" of the Japanese army led many communist cadres from war areas to retreat to the safety of Yan'an, thus allowing Mao's rectification campaign to reach a large number of people. Third, the campaign created an opportunity for ideological training of an increasing number of young people and intellectuals who had flocked to Yan'an in protest of the Nationalist government's inaction in the face of the Japanese invasion. Their motivation to join the CCP stemmed perhaps more from anti-Japanese sentiments than from genuine conviction about the communist cause, so they needed to become acquainted with Mao's brand of communism.

The campaign quickly turned into a brain-washing operation with heavy ideological overtones. It began with the study of Marxism-Leninism and the criticism of "dogmatism," "subjectivism," and "sectarianism"—concepts Mao used to criticize intellectuals, whom he viewed as a dangerous group of independent thinkers.[120]

But Wang Ming and other followers of the Comintern who had promoted the policies of the Communist Party of Soviet Union (CPSU) at the CCP Central Committee—this was dubbed the "Wang Ming Line" — became the focal point of criticism. The fact that most of them had supported Mao on many occasions did not weigh in their favor. They were labelled "Bolsheviks," "internationalists," or "dogmatists." Others were condemned as "empiricists" because they had followed, at some time or another, the Comintern and the Wang Ming line. Zhou Enlai and Peng Dehuai, for example, were accused of the latter.

The method used in the campaign demonstrated Mao's unique ability to enhance his own power status and to organize control at all levels of the CCP, repeated later during the Cultural Revolution. According to a document produced by the CCP Propaganda Department, the Party center established a General Study Committee headed by Comrade Mao Zedong, with Kang Sheng as his deputy. The document stipulated that "all organizations under the direct jurisdiction of the Party center must establish a first-level study committee, led by Kang Sheng and Li Fuchun, with branches in individual organizations." The same applied to the military, where "all organizations under the direct jurisdiction of the Military Affairs Commission must establish a first-level study committee led by Wang Jiaxiang and Chen Yun." Under this committee study groups were established "covering all its departments, branches, and troop units." The same system applied to the entire Party structure, to all schools, and all other organizations in Yan'an and the base area. A centralized network was thus created to permit the examination of every cadre at every level. It was indeed a massive operation.[121]

The first major result of the rectification campaign was the reshuffling of the leadership officially sanctioned in March 1943 by the Politburo. Mao was elected chairman of the Politburo and of the Central Committee Secretariat. In addition, he became chairman of the Central Committee's Military Commission and was given "the power to make final decisions on questions discussed by the Secretariat."[122] Final veto power ensured Mao's dominance of CCP policies. His superior position was further enhanced by the introduction of the term "Mao Zedong Thought" as the sacred tenet of the CCP. Wang Jiaxiang, writing on the occasion of the twenty-second anniversary of the CCP in 1943, used the term for the first time: "Mao Zedong Thought is Marxism-Leninism, Chinese Bolshevism, and Chinese communism" all at once.[123] Liu Shaoqi (later, in the Cultural Revolution, Mao's first and most prominent victim) declared that "our Party, the proletariat, and the revolutionary people of our country have finally found their own leader in comrade Mao Zedong after the twenty-two-year-long, hard, and complicated revolutionary struggle." Mao, he stated, was a great revolutionary who had long been tested, was well versed in Marxism and Leninism, and was infinitely devoted to the cause of the Chinese people.[124] This was the official initiation of Mao's personality cult and the inauguration of the alliance between Mao and Liu that dominated Chinese politics until the Cultural Revolution.

Such was the political atmosphere Zhou encountered upon his arrival in Yan'an in July 1943. Although he had not been unreserved in his support of either Wang Ming or Mao, he now jumped into the fray. Speaking at a meeting organized to welcome his return to Yan'an, he now committed himself to Mao:

> At many critical junctures and on many key issues during the past three years, Comrade Mao Zedong's leadership and instructions have ensured that our Party did not in any way lose its bearing or take the wrong course. Nothing offers clearer proof than the march of events of the last three years. Those who opposed, or were skeptical about, Comrade Mao Zedong's leadership or his views, have now been proven to be utterly wrong. The twenty-two-year history of our Party has shown that Comrade Mao Zedong's views have developed throughout this period into Chinese-style Marxism-Leninism, a Chinese-style of communism. Comrade Mao Zedong's orientation is the orientation of the Chinese Communist Party. Comrade Mao Zedong's political line is the Chinese Bolshevik line.[125]

On 30 August and 1 September, Zhou delivered his report on the work of the South China Bureau that he had directed over the previous three years. Subsequently he was drawn immediately into the rectification campaign. As a member of the Politburo he was expected to clarify his own political and ideological stance. Zhou read large amounts of documents and archival material, wrote four reviews about the subject, and presented them in several speeches to the Politburo. Before his peers, he criticized the dogmatism represented by Peng Shuzhi, Chen Duxiu, and Wang Ming, who had long been able to dominate Party policies. He attributed Wang's success as a communist leader to the "empiricist trend" that existed in the CCP and had permitted dogmatism to prevail. In an effort at self-defense, he divided empiricists into two categories: those who collaborated with the dogmatists "with ulterior motives" and those who did it for lack of ideological understanding. The former needed serious self-examination while the latter—among whom he counted himself—needed to improve their understanding of Marxism.

Despite Zhou's efforts to conform to Mao's ideological and political line, Mao criticized him severely. Of all the members of the Central Committee elected at the sixth Party congress fifteen years earlier, he said, only five (Mao Zedong, Zhou Enlai, Xiang Ying, Ren Bishi, and Liu Shaoqi) had survived. But only two of them (Mao himself and Liu Shaoqi) had been clearly opposed to the Wang Ming line, while the other three had supported it.[126]

In the face of this offensive, Zhou began another series of confessions and self-criticisms. He realized that his ability to convince Mao of his unconditional support would be the key to his political future. Zhou's statements were the longest and the most elaborate of those delivered by the leaders, lasting five days. This was expected, since he was the only leader who had been involved in all major Party events since 1927. Analyzing all the important issues that had been disputed since that time, he examined his own involvement in each of them. He accused himself of having been too moderate in the repudiation of the Li Lisan line and too conciliatory toward Wang Ming after Wang—with the help of Pavel Mif and the Comintern—had seized power at the fourth plenum of the sixth Central Committee in 1931. He apologized for failing to "learn conscientiously from those comrades who had worked in the soviet areas for a long time" and for implementing erroneous strategies formulated by the Provisional Center in Shanghai with respect to attacks on key cities. He stressed his own responsibility in following Braun's strategy during the fifth anti-encirclement campaign, which had forced the Red Army to embark on the Long March. He further recognized his mistakes during the early period of the anti-Japanese war on such issues as relations with the GMD, the united front, and military strategy against the Japanese. But the major themes running through his speeches were praise for Mao, Mao Zedong Thought, and his own unconditional acceptance of Mao's leadership.[127]

Although Zhou had accepted Comintern policies until the Zunyi conference in 1931 and had cooperated with Wang Ming in the beginning of the anti-Japanese war, Mao did not view him as belonging to the Wang Ming group. He regarded Zhou, like some army generals (Peng Dehuai, Liu Bocheng, Ye Jianying, and Nie Rongzhen), as an "empiricist." Zhou, who was "versed in practical work ... but who belittled the study of Marxism-Leninism," Mao said, became "a collaborator and assistant of dogmatism during the period when this tendency dominated political thinking."[128]

It was not only Mao that Zhou had to convince but also Mao's fierce loyalists who launched sharp and, according to Hu Qiaomu, excessive attacks on Zhou. Hu did not disclose their names, but this group could have comprised Liu Shaoqi, Peng Zhen, Bo Yibo, and others who had never followed the Wang Ming line. In their view, the mistakes made by Wang Ming, Bo Gu, Zhang Wentian, and Wang Jiaxiang had been so thoroughly exposed and criticized that they could no longer be regarded as a threat. But the danger posed by empiricism had not yet been neutralized.[129]

Zhou Enlai's predicament during the rectification campaign was compounded by the problem of the so-called Red flag parties, or Party organizations that pretended to be communist but were effectively controlled by GMD special agents. Kang Sheng, a member of the Politburo and Mao's major assistant during the campaign, was convinced that hundreds of communist cadres in Yan'an were in fact special agents of the GMD who had infiltrated the Party. His mania for political persecution led him to believe that most of the underground Party organizations that had grown under Zhou's jurisdiction in Gansu, Sichuan, Henan, Hubei, Yunnan, Guizhou, Zhejiang, and Shaanxi were "Red flag parties." Li Weihan, also a member of the leading group in the rectification campaign, confronted Zhou Enlai with this problem, but Zhou firmly denied that any of the Party groups established under the South China Bureau had been dominated by Nationalist agents. The accusation was finally withdrawn, but only at the very end of the campaign.[130]

The news about the rectification campaign created considerable apprehension in Moscow. Although the Comintern had been dissolved, its former head, Georgi Dimitrov, wrote a personal letter to Mao expressing concern about the campaign and about the treatment of Wang Ming and Zhou Enlai. The letter, dated 22 December 1943, states: "I consider politically incorrect the campaign being waged against Zhou Enlai and Wang Ming, who are being incriminated with the Comintern and endorsed national front policy, as a result of which they have allegedly led the Party to schism. Persons like Zhou Enlai and Wang Ming must not be severed from the Party."[131]

Zhou's untiring self-accusations and repeated acknowledgments of his faults and of his misjudgments of the true political line, and his persistent reassurances that he had recognized Mao's leadership genius, finally made his conversion to Maoism credible even to the distrustful and paranoid Mao. To have convinced Mao was, under the prevailing circumstances, a precondition to his own political survival.

When the seventh congress was finally convened at Yan'an from 23 April to 11 June 1945, it was a major landmark in the Party's history. First, it confirmed Mao's dominance over the Party, thus terminating the perennial conflict between the Maoists and the internationalists supported by Moscow. Second, it heralded the postwar era in which the leadership made concerted efforts to build up Mao not only as a Party leader but also as a figure of national status capable of challenging Chiang Kai-shek. Mao's personality cult reached a new height at the congress, where Liu Shaoqi, on behalf of the Central Committee, presented a report on the revision of the Party constitution that mentioned Mao's name no fewer than 105 times. The report devoted a special section to the interpretation and the celebration of Mao Zedong Thought, which was enshrined as the sacred creed and guiding principle for the entire Party.[132]

## Negotiations on Postwar Settlement

After the Japanese attack on Pearl Harbor on 7 December 1941, the Sino-Japanese conflict became a part of World War II. The U.S. presence in the China-Burma-India (CBI) war theater and its alliance with Chiang Kai-shek gradually increased American involvement with China. But the inability of the Nationalist government to contain Japan and its unwillingness to do so—despite U.S. military aid—disillusioned the U.S. military and diplomatic personnel in China. The Communist Party, in the meantime, continued to increase its ranks. Despite its anti-Japanese rhetoric, it also wished to conserve its troops for a final showdown with Chiang Kai-shek. With the exception of one major battle fought by Peng Dehuai and Zhu De in northern China in the fall of 1940, communist troops remained behind enemy lines engaging in guerrilla warfare and striving to expand. The resurgence of communist forces, which, according to Zhou, comprised more than half a million men, supported by 2.3 million militia, and the ever-expanding base areas, with more than ninety million people, attracted the interest of an increasing number of Americans in China—among them were many military men whose mission it was to support China's was efforts, as well as journalists and other observers of the political scene—who had become increasingly disillusioned with the Nationalist government's indifference and inefficiency. Their success in communicating their frustrations with Chiang and their interest in the communists to top levels of the U.S. administration led Vice President Henry A. Wallace to impress upon the Generalissimo the American desire to send an observer team to Yan'an.[133]

In June 1944, Chiang Kai-shek, at the time blockading access to the communist areas, reluctantly agreed to authorize the visit to Yan'an of a "military observer group" known as the Dixie mission.[134] Mao and Zhou welcomed the American team, seeing in it a certain measure of international recognition and a chance to persuade Americans to end the Nationalists' exclusive right to U.S. military aid. They intended to present the observer group with a positive image about the social and military conditions in the base areas. Zhou established two teams to tend to the mission's well-being and need for information. The first—consisting of Ye Jianying, Huang Hua, Chen Jiakang, and George Hatem (called Ma Haide in Chinese), an American doctor working in Yan'an—was instructed to make its life in the harsh conditions of Yan'an as comfortable as possible. The second team—composed of such leading communist generals as Peng Dehuai, Chen Yi, Lin Biao, Nie Rongzhen, and He Long—was to brief the Americans about the military situation behind enemy lines and about the conditions in Japanese-occupied areas. Mao and Zhou, either together or separately, held numerous talks with the members of the mission concerning relations between the GMD and the CCP and the communist need for U.S. aid. On 23 August, Mao and Zhou emphasized that the only way to avoid a civil war in China was for American support to be granted to both the GMD and the CCP. On two other occasions, Zhou talked with John Stuart Service and John Paton Davies, both members of the Dixie mission, about the need to put an end to the GMD's one-party dictatorship and to reform the Nationalist government. U.S. military strategy in the Pacific war and military cooperation between communist and U.S. forces against Japan was another topic. The communist leaders pledged the support of the Red Army for U.S. military operations if the United States entered the war on Chinese soil, for example, landing its troops on the eastern or southern coast of China, on the Shandong peninsula or the Bay of Hangzhou. Until the end of the year there were numerous discussions about this issue as well as about possible joint military operations between the United States and the CCP in northern China. As a gesture of goodwill, CCP guerrilla units were ordered to rescue allied soldiers, mostly members of the U.S. air force who had been stranded in the rear of the Japanese-occupied zones in the latter period of the Pacific war. The Communist charm offensive proved successful. Members of the Dixie mission were convinced that the CCP "a party seeking orderly democratic growth towards socialism" and suggested the establishment of formal cooperation between it and the U.S. authorities.[135]

## Hurley's Good Offices

In September 1944, Zhou summarized the CCP position in a note to General Joseph Stilwell, commander of the CBI war theater, who had become increasingly disillusioned with Nationalist government policies toward Japan and whose personal relations with Chiang Kai-shek had reached the point of mutual mistrust and even contempt. Zhou, taking advantage of the tensions between the two, stressed the dramatic situation on the battlefields and in the areas controlled by the GMD. He argued that, under those circumstances, one-party rule was no longer sustainable, suggesting the establishment of a coalition government as the only viable solution for China. This implied full recognition by the Nationalists of the military and civil resistance to the Japanese that the CCP had successfully organized. Zhou demanded that communist jurisdiction of the areas under CCP control be fully acknowledged and that the CCP, in view of its military efficiency, receive a share of American weaponry equal to that provided to the Nationalists through the lend-lease program.

These demands were in complete contrast to Chiang Kai-shek's position. Providing Chinese communist troops with weapons and ammunition was an anathema to him. Chiang concentrated on maintaining his power despite serious military setbacks and an increasingly difficult internal situation. He played on the interest of the United States to prevent the collapse of the Nationalist regime and to promote the unification of military forces on the Chinese territory.[136]

Stilwell's growing tensions with Chiang Kai-shek created increasing pressure on the U.S. government to remove him. In October 1944, Stilwell was recalled to Washington and replaced by General Albert Wedemeyer. To smooth over the differences between the Nationalists and the communists, Roosevelt sent Patrick J. Hurley to China as his special envoy. Hurley, later ambassador to the Nationalist government, was convinced that he would be able to reconcile the positions of both sides, whose differences he considered similar to those between ruling and opposition parties in Western countries. On 7 November, he flew to Yan'an, where he had intensive talks with Mao and Zhou. The resulting five-point agreement reiterated the communist concept of national unification under a coalition government that would include all parties, groups, and politically influential persons, regardless of their affiliation. It also endorsed the communist demands for democratic political reforms and for a united command structure under which all forces opposing the Japanese occupation would be regrouped and armed.[137]

In the eyes of the CCP leadership, Hurley's signing of such an agreement represented an official U.S. endorsement. They saw it as a document that put the relations between the United States and the two Chinese parties on an equal footing. Zhou, who returned with Hurley to Chongqing on 10 November, began to launch a public relations offensive, his specialty, to spread communist demands for an end to one-party rule and the establishment of a coalition government. To convince people from all walks of life and political leanings of the validity of these concepts, he personally met with as many people as possible. He entertained American reporters, through whom he hoped to spread his ideas to the outside world. However, Chiang Kai-shek, whom he met on 22 November, flatly rejected the agreement and made a counterproposal casting aside the idea of a coalition government and emphasizing that recognition of the CCP would require that Yan'an armed forces be reorganized as a part of the Nationalist army. After the reshuffle, the CCP would be allowed to send representatives to the Military Commission of the Nationalist government. Zhou's reaction to these proposals was guarded. Hurley's signature on the agreement was, to say the least, an indication of American support for the communist position that Chiang Kai-shek could not entirely ignore. But Hurley backed out of the agreement and tried to persuade Zhou to accept participation in the Nationalist government. Zhou's response was that the CCP would not play the role of "guests without any authority in the government." Clearly biased in favor of Chiang Kai-shek, Hurley responded that the CCP could not expect U.S. military and political support until it had reached a compromise with Chiang. But Zhou refused to yield on the issues of a coalition government and on the official recognition of the CCP-controlled areas. The negotiations reached a stalemate, and Zhou returned to Yan'an for consultation.

In an exchange of letters with Zhou Enlai during the following weeks, Hurley suggested that neither the five-point agreement nor Chiang's counterproposal should be considered the final word in the negotiations. Rather, they should be seen as the basis for further negotiations. In his letter dated 20 January 1945, he asked Zhou to return to Chongqing to resume talks.[138] Before Zhou set out for Chongqing on the twenty-fourth, he made a public statement laying down the conditions under which he was ready to continue negotiations, including preparations for the establishment of a coalition government by a meeting of all parties—the GMD, the CCP, the Democratic League—and of public figures without any party affiliation. He demanded the suspension of all secret service activities, the withdrawal of all special agents, and the removal of all government troops surrounding communist areas, the Eighth Route Army, and the New Fourth Army. He also insisted on full recognition of the legal status of these armies and of the governments elected by the people in the "liberated" areas. Zhou was not ready to submit Communist troops to a reorganization under GMD command as long as the one-party rule of the GMD was still in effect. On 13 February, he and Chiang met in Hurley's presence. On that occasion Zhou reiterated his demand for a national conference to pave the way for a coalition government. But Chiang was adamant in his refusal on this point. As he told Zhou, he was convinced that the CCP wanted a coalition government "because you want to overthrow the government; you want to convene a conference of all parties to divide the spoils!"[139] Chiang's rejection of the agreement was corroborated by Hurley himself. During the spring of 1945, he made several statements that clearly favored the Nationalist position. In a press conference he declared that the U.S. government would not extend official aid to armed political parties or warlords in China. Mao expressed his anger at Hurley's inconsistencies in two articles issued by the Xinhua News Agency on 10 and 12 July. They condemned Hurley for working hand in glove with Chiang Kai-shek against the communists and warned that the policy of the United States toward China was conducive to creating conditions for a civil war in the country.[140]

In August 1945, events moved at a startling pace. On 6 and 8 August, respectively, the United States dropped atomic bombs on Hiroshima and Nagasaki. On the eighth, the Soviet Union entered the war in Asia, launching a large-scale offensive on the Japanese Kuantung Army along a 4,000-km battle line in Manchuria. On the fourteenth, Japan's emperor formally accepted unconditional surrender. The same day, the Sino-Soviet Treaty of Friendship and Alliance was signed. In it Stalin recognized the Nationalist government and promised it moral support and military aid. On the same day, a cable from Chiang Kai-shek reached Yan'an to invite Mao Zedong to Chongqing to discuss outstanding issues between them. A cable from Stalin also reached Yan'an on the twenty-second or twenty-third, urging the CCP to do anything possible to avoid the risk of a civil war, which, according to the Soviet leader, might lead to the annihilation of the Chinese nation.[141]

By the end of the war, the CCP had greatly changed from what it had been in 1937. Mao claimed that it commanded military forces totaling 910,000 troops and 2.2 million militia, counted 1.2 million members, and established itself at the rear of the Japanese-occupied zones in "liberated" areas, with a total population of 95 million.[142]

In view of the forthcoming negotiations, Zhou drafted a six-point "declaration on the current situation," which the Central Committee adopted on 23 August. The declaration called for peace, democracy, and unity and reiterated the basic communist demands: recognition of CCP governance in the areas it controlled and of its armed forces as independent. It also repeated the call for a coalition government based on a political consultative conference representing all parties and nonpartisan leaders. Mao drafted a circular informing the entire Party on 26 August that he and Zhou were heading to Chongqing to negotiate. The circular suggested that the negotiations might lead to conditional recognition of the CCP by the Nationalist government. The CCP was prepared to make concessions to this end, such as ceding "liberated areas" in the south to Nationalist control. Those were areas where, in fact, communist control was relatively weak. Communist strength lay in northern China and in the areas north of the Longhai river to Inner Mongolia, where communist troops were expected to maintain their control.[143]

Accompanied by Zhou and P.J. Hurley, the U.S. ambassador to China, Mao flew to Chongqing on 28 August 1945. Mao's personal security during his stay in Chongqing was one of Zhou's major concerns. An assassination attempt by Chiang Kai-shek's secret agents or his detention, as had been happened to General Zhang Xueliang, could not be discounted. Mao was well aware of this and had left instructions with Liu Shaoqi and other leaders who had remained in Yan'an that the Red Army should take action if Chiang detained him.

To ensure Mao's comfort and safety, before leaving Yan'an, Zhou sent detailed instructions to his Chongqing office concerning Mao's daily habits, his accommodations, and his security needs. He personally checked the plane Mao was going to take. In Chongqing, Chiang Kai-shek turned over one of his own private residences, Linyuan (Forest Gardens), to Mao. Mao and Zhou stayed there for two days before moving to General Zhang Zhizong's house, Guiyuan (Laurel Garden). Courtesy prompted them to accept these lodgings, but within their beautiful surroundings, they were separated from their staff, which both Mao and Zhou found increasingly inconvenient. Mao decided to move to the building of the Eighth Route Army, where he was surrounded by his own staff. With Zhou in a room next to his, Mao felt assured. Later Mao was invited to stay at a house belonging to Lin Sen, the former chairman of the Nationalist government. Before accepting the invitation, Zhou sent his security experts to the house to thoroughly examine it. But this did not satisfy him, so he personally looked over the place, especially the room where Mao was to stay. Only when he was assured that there would be no traps did Zhou allow Mao to enter the room.

Whenever Mao went out, Zhou accompanied him. Anxious to build up Mao's image, Zhou was concerned that Mao, who had been far removed from city life, would act properly and would impress the outside world not only as a Party leader but also as a national statesman and a capable and forceful rival to Chiang. The two communist leaders went together to receptions, banquets, and other public gatherings, and Zhou introduced him to celebrities of all kinds, staying as close to him as a bodyguard.[144]

During the forty-three days of negotiations, Mao and Chiang met eleven times to discuss issues of a general nature. In the meantime, Zhou and his negotiating team were working out the details. The negotiations did not resolve any of the controversial issues. The government refused to recognize the communist-led governments in the base areas, the Shaan-Gan-Ning Border Region, or the provinces of Rehe, Hebei, Chahar, Shandong, and Shanxi. The CCP resisted the reorganization of its army and its incorporation into the Nationalist army. Chiang Kai-shek persisted with his principle of "unifying military command and government administration" and refused to move even an inch on these questions. Zhou's offer to withdraw communist troops from base areas in a number of southern provinces (Guangdong, Zhejiang, southern Jiangsu, southern Anhui, Hunan, Hubei, and Henan) also fell on deaf ears. Hurley, who acted as a mediator, reported to Zhou that Chiang was ready to accept twenty divisions of communist troops if the communists would give up their demand for governorship of the five northern provinces. The only option for the communists, according to him, was either to accept unification under the Nationalist government or allow the talks to end. Mao could return to Yan'an at any time, with or without agreement, he added.[145]

Zhou deeply resented Hurley's ultimatum. When Mao learned about it, he demanded to meet the U.S. ambassador without delay. At their meeting, Mao told Hurley that the CCP had great patience; it would neither accept Chiang's conditions nor adjourn the talks.[146]

On 10 October an agreement was finally signed that recorded the differences as well as the agreements, pertaining mainly to the convocation of a political consultative conference. The two parties accepted the principle of peace and national reconstruction, the equal and legal status of the various political parties, and democratic rights for the people. The communists abandoned their demand for the formation of a coalition government while the government, in return, agreed with the CCP to convene a political consultative conference. Although Zhou remained in Chongqing to sort out the details of the agreement, many key issues remained unresolved.

While the leaders were engaged in negotiations, the communist and Nationalist armies engaged in a competitive race to seize territories in northeastern China. Under the terms of the Japanese surrender, General Douglas MacArthur, the Commanding General of the U.S. Armed Forces in the Far East USAFFE, had authorized the Nationalist government to accept the Japanese surrender in China, on Taiwan, and in northern Indochina. Chiang Kai-shek, on 12 August, ordered the communist forces to maintain their positions. But Mao ordered Zhu De to start an offensive on key Japanese positions and communication lines. In September 1945

Yan'an issued a strategic directive concerning the "development of the north and the defense of the south." Its main target was to gain complete control over Rehe and Chahar and the provinces in northeastern China. To achieve this purpose, twenty thousand cadres—including ten members and ten alternates of the Central Committee, among them four members of the Politburo—and 110,000 troops were dispatched to these regions. Mao commanded his troops to move there as quickly as possible. Their rush to the area was not to be hampered by matériel and weapons, which Mao ordered to leave behind. The solders were told that there would be enough military equipment left behind by the Japanese that they would be able to salvage. All they had to do was to reach the area ahead of the Nationalist troops.[147]

The Nationalist government took countermeasures. On 23 August, the commander-in-chief of the government forces, General He Yingqin, issued an order to the Japanese military leadership in China to defend their positions against communist assaults, pending the takeover by government troops. Between late August and end of September, numerous clashes took place between communist and Japanese forces acting on behalf of the Nationalist government.[148]

In September 1945, the CCP established the Northeast China Bureau of the Central Committee in Shenyang, headed by Peng Zhen. This was followed by the founding of the Northeast Democratic Allied Army, the precursor to the Fourth Field Army of the People's Liberation Army (PLA). The troops had been assembled from the base areas of northern China and Shandong. They were joined by others who had been operating in the northeast during the war of resistance. By the end of 1945, 280,000 communist troops under Lin Biao's command were stationed in the northeast.[149]

Manchuria was controlled by Soviet forces under General Rodion Yakovlevich Malinovsky. During the three months of Soviet occupation of the northeast, the communists took advantage of their presence in the area to seize large quantities of arms and equipment from the surrendering Japanese troops. The Soviet forces also adopted delaying tactics at a number of points to prevent the landing of U.S. troops at ports in the area. To counteract the distinct disadvantage of the Nationalist forces in that area, the United States transported a total of 540,000 GMD troops by air and by sea to northern China, Manchuria, and Taiwan between September 1945 and June 1946.

With the action shifting more and more to the battlefield, negotiations became pointless. Zhou, who had remained in Chongqing, finally returned to Yan'an, and Hurley, on 27 November, announced his resignation, accusing some members of the U.S. embassy of undermining his mediation efforts by favoring the communist side.[150]

In the United States, Harry S. Truman had succeeded Roosevelt as president upon his death in mid-1945. On 15 December, Truman nominated General George Marshall as his special envoy to China, charged with helping to broker a ceasefire between the CCP and the Nationalists and to ensure the implementation of the Chongqing agreement signed by Mao and Chiang. A communiqué issued at a meeting in Moscow in late December 1945 between U.S., British, and Soviet foreign ministers called upon the rival parties to seek a negotiated solution and promised to abstain from intervening in China. Despite the pledges not to interfere, U.S. forces continued to transport Nationalist troops to the northeast while the Soviet troops maintained their clandestine transfer of Japanese military equipment to communist troops in the area.

Zhou viewed this kind of U.S. military aid, involving direct intervention of the U.S. air force and navy, as a change in U.S. policy toward China. During the war against Japan, the United States had recognized the efforts of the CCP and had followed the principle of "supporting Chiang while utilizing the communists" (*fu Chiang yong gong*). After the war, U.S. policy had become one of "supporting Chiang while suppressing the communists" (*fu Chiang ya gong*). He had no illusions that the new administration would also support the Nationalist government. Concerning CCP policy toward the GMD, Zhou stated that the basic aim was to maintain peace and democracy and that the CCP intended to implement a policy that was militarily defensive and politically offensive. In other words, the CCP, despite its official support for peace and democracy, would defend its position toward the Nationalist government by any means necessary. With respect to the United States, CCP policy would be "to neutralize the United States, but not to provoke it, though it would criticize its erroneous policies. In particular, it would strongly react against any eventual armed intervention in Chinese internal affairs. In such a case, it was ready for 'resolute resistance to an armed attack'."[151]

Zhou's statement reflected the disillusionment of the Chinese communist leadership about U.S. policy toward the CCP. They nonetheless viewed Marshall's nomination as a positive development, reflecting what they called the failure of Hurley policies. Zhou and other communist leaders hoped that Marshall would be a more open-minded interlocuteur than Hurley had been. Zhou left Yan'an to greet Marshall upon his arrival at Chongqing airport on 22 December. The following day, he paid him a visit. In their talk, Zhou agreed with the U.S. envoy that hostilities in China should cease after the eight-year-long war against Japan, which had caused great losses. He also agreed with Marshall about the need for political reforms and presented again the communist position to call a political consultative conference of all parties and political forces to prepare a constitution and to reform the government. Praising the achievements of the United States, he said that China could learn much from the Washingtonian spirit of national independence, from Lincoln's concept of a government for and by the people, the concept of freedom fostered by Roosevelt, and the example for China of American agricultural and industrial policies.[152]

The first phase of talks between the CCP and the GMD—mediated by Marshall—went comparatively smoothly. In January 1946, an agreement was reached to cease hostilities and to reorganize the two armies on the principle of separating the army from the political party. Marshall persuaded Zhou to introduce this rule, based on the Western tradition of nonintervention of the military in politics. Zhou accepted this, stating that the CCP would no longer give orders to the Red Army, with the full knowledge that Chinese conditions would not allow it to be implemented either by the GMD or by the CCP. Chiang Kai-shek, for his part, agreed to convene a political consultative conference on 10 January 1946. Following a proposal of Marshall's, a tripartite committee consisting of Marshall, Zhou Enlai, and Zhang Qun (who was later replaced by Zhang Zhizhong) was established and mandated to implement the ceasefire and related matters. An executive headquarters, where the three parties were represented, was established in Beiping to supervise the implementation of the agreements.

During the opening meeting of the political consultative conference on 10 January 1946, Chiang delivered a speech promising to guarantee the freedom of all people, equal status of all political parties, local autonomy, general elections, and the release of political prisoners. In his remarks Zhou welcomed Chiang's statement and expressed his opposition to civil war. The same day, he and Zhang Qun, on behalf of the CCP and the GMD respectively, signed a truce. The two sides issued an armistice order effective at midnight on 13 January. The armistice, significantly, did not apply to northeastern China, where the communist forces were striving to take control. It was also agreed that the military would no longer come under Party control. By 31 January, the final day of the meeting, the conference had adopted an agreement on government organization, a program for peace and national reconstruction, an agreement on military affairs, on a national assembly, and on a draft constitution.[153]

The prospects for internal peace and reconstruction created an optimistic mood among the CCP leaders, who regarded the agreement as a significant breakthrough. In their view, it signaled the beginning of the "destruction of the one-party dictatorship" and "the advance of our Party, the armed forces, and the base areas" toward a "new stage of peace and democracy."[154] On 27 January, the CCP Secretariat appointed eight leaders, including Mao Zedong, Liu Shaoqi, Zhou Enlai, and Zhu De, to participate in the future government. It was suggested that Zhou be nominated as vice president of the executive branch of the government. Mao was so impressed by Marshall's attitude that he asked Zhou to transmit his gratitude to the U.S. envoy for his help in bringing about the truce. Mao hoped that Marshall would be able to keep Chiang Kai-shek in line and to play a constructive role and even expressed his desire to visit the United States. Zhou received instructions to manipulate Marshall with the aim of advancing the peace process. To this end, he was to avoid anything that might irritate the U.S. envoy.[155]

Despite the optimistic mood prevailing in Chongqing, negotiations soon began to falter about the usual discrepancies among the two parties with respect to the northeast and the reorganization of the troops. Clearly, the CCP was not ready to give up any of the advantages it had gained during years of struggle against the government. It welcomed peace because the popular mood demanded it and because it created opportunities for the consolidation of its position and the recognition of its status both in China and abroad. General Marshall, in several talks with Zhou, attempted to explain the Western tradition of separating the military from politics. Although aware that such separation did not correspond to Chinese realities, Zhou diplomatically expressed his agreement with that principle. But he took offense at the suggestion that the nationalization of the troops had to be completed before democratic reforms of government were effected. The lengthy discussions between Zhou and Marshall about the methods of reform and cooperation remained fruitless. The political targets of the communists did not change.

They remained adamant about maintaining the independence of their troops and the self-government of the areas under their control, while the Nationalists remained equally adamant in their refusal to accept this. This became even more evident after the tripartite committee preliminarily agreed that the army should first be reduced to fifty Nationalist divisions and ten communist divisions. Then, in a second phase, the armies would be merged into a unified national force. Mao, who clearly wanted to maintain the independence of the communist forces, instructed Zhou not to commit himself to the second phase.[156] Zhou, however, was not particularly worried about this issue. Later that year, he explained to the leadership in Yan'an that, although the ratio of fifty to ten divisions and its integration into the Nationalist army were intended to restrict and to control communist forces, these stipulations were of no importance. The agreements between the CCP and the GMD allowed for local self-government, which, in turn, permitted the stationing of its own forces. This meant, said Zhou, that communist troops in CCP-controlled areas would remain free of Nationalist interference.[157]

## Civil War

After the preliminary agreement on the reorganization of the armies was adopted, the fate of northeastern China became a central issue. Since the communist leadership had no intention of relinquishing these areas, military clashes between Nationalist and communist armies became increasingly frequent during the spring and summer of 1946. Communist forces had to retreat in a few major battles fought in northern China and on the Central Plains while government troops accelerated their attacks on communist base areas in eastern, northeastern, and southern China.[158]

On 3 May 1946, Zhou and his wife left Chongqing for Nanjing, once more the country's capital. There he continued his talks with Marshall and Zhang Zhizhong in a changed, more hostile atmosphere. In a telegram to Mao on 3 June, Zhou expressed his disappointment in Marshall's mediation, which, he said, was increasingly biased in favor of the Nationalists. Zhou reported that, especially on the question of northeastern China, Marshall demanded concessions from the communists but not from the government.[159]

With the escalation of the war, Zhou's relations with Marshall deteriorated even further. At the end of August, the United States agreed to turn over to the government all available war matériel. Zhou repeatedly protested this. On 2 September, Zhou sent a cable to Yan'an in which he stated that the United States and the GMD agreed on all major issues and that he considered it urgent "to expose the American fraud." Based on Mao's instructions, Zhou informed Marshall on 9 October that he no longer had the confidence of the CCP and that he should withdraw from the mediation. Two days later, government forces seized Zhangjiakou, a key city held by the CCP in northern China. On the same day, Chiang Kai-shek, confident of his ability to wipe out all communist troops, called the legislature into session, and ordered it to draw up a constitution. The National Assembly opened its session on 15 November without the participation of the CCP. The following day, Zhou held a press conference to condemn the GMD for "tearing up the agreements from the political consultative conference." On 19 November 1946, Zhou and the entire CCP delegation left Nanjing for Yan'an.[160]

After his return to Yan'an and the outbreak of the civil war, Zhou turned his focus from diplomacy to military affairs. At Mao's side as his chief aide, as vice chairman of the Military Commission of the Central Committee and as general chief of staff, he directed military operations at CCP headquarters. At the same time, as the head of the Urban Work Committee of the Central Committee in charge of work in GMD-controlled areas, he continued to direct underground activities.

At the beginning of the civil war, the CCP leadership predicted that communist forces would defeat Chiang's armies within five years. In fact, it took only three years to force a much larger and better-equipped army into retreat and to conquer the entire territory with the exception of a few areas. The bulk of the war was fought on the barren land of the northwestern loess plateau. Other significant theaters of war were located in the northeast, where Lin Biao was in command, and in Shandong province, where communist forces operated under the command of Chen Yi. All commanders were in constant communication with Mao and Zhou, who refused to remain in remote headquarters controlling military operations from a blackboard. From their highly mobile Red Army headquarters they directed all battle plans and troop movements.

Those communist-held cities and towns became the target of the Nationalist offensive launched in July 1946. From June 1946 to June 1947, the Nationalist strategy was successful in winning virtually all the cities and towns in the northeast, in taking over large portions of the northern provinces, and in regaining control over major communication lines north of the Yangtze River. In most of the battlefields, though,

Nationalist troops failed to capture communist forces, who, when confronted with an enemy superior in numbers and equipment, preferred to withdraw in order to remain intact. Communist forces, which had been renamed the PLA in July 1946, stayed largely on the defensive, engaging in strategic withdrawal to the countryside. As a result, by the spring of 1947, government forces were thinly spread across vast areas and unable to gain more ground.[161]

In early 1947, roughly 250,000 government troops besieged the Shaan-Gan-Ning Border Region. Confronting them was the communist Northwest Field Army under General Peng Dehuai, which had fewer than thirty thousand troops. As government troops were planning to close in, Xiong Xianghui informed Zhou about Hu Zongnan's plans to seize Yan'an and to wipe out the main communist forces in northern Shaanxi.

Xiong reported to Zhou in early March that General Peng planned to use fifteen brigades, about a hundred and fifty thousand men, to strike the communist forces in the area. Xiong was able to supply details about the distribution, strength, and positions of the forces and the air cover that would be provided to them. The attack was planned to begin on 13 March.[162]

Zhou prepared the evacuation of the border region. In view of the overwhelming strength of the enemy, he saw this as a strategic retreat, based on the principle of "leaving nothing to the enemy and hiding the stores of grain" (*jianbi qingye*). Party files and other materials, the elderly, the weak, the ill or disabled, and the children were the first to be evacuated toward areas around Wayaobao, northeast of Yan'an. From there, they proceeded across the Yellow River to the "liberated" areas in Shanxi and Suiyuan. Party and regional government organizations, schools, and other institutions also moved out. Zhou personally took charge of tasks, including the organization of a team responsible for the transportation of important files of the Central Committee and the Military Commission to the Shanxi-Suiyuan sub-office of the Central Committee. Together with Liao Chengzhi, the director of the Xinhua News Agency, he worked out a plan to move the communist radio station to a place safe enough to ensure continuity of broadcasting. He supervised the move of the Urban Work and the Social Departments, two key departments under the Central Committee in charge of mass organizations and intelligence in GMD-controlled areas. Two of his top assistants, Tong Xiaopeng and Luo Qingchang, were put in charge of the safety of these departments, which were fitted with additional radio equipment, decoders, and operators. He organized his foreign affairs team to be transferred to a safe place in Shanxi. Once established in Shanxi, the Foreign Affairs Group, as it was then named, was led by Yang Shangkun (in the 1980s, president of the People's Republic). Its members—including Wang Bingnan, Zhang Wentian, Ke Bainian, Wang Guangmei, and Chen Hao—had experience in foreign affairs, rare among personnel in the communist hinterland; they formed the nucleus of what became the Ministry of Foreign Affairs.[163]

The large-scale exodus from Yan'an began on 8 March 1947. Eleven days later, Nationalist armies approached the town. With their superior strength, they hoped to encounter and overwhelm the main force of the communist troops defending Yan'an and to annihilate it, but they found an empty town. The occupation of Yan'an and the Shaan-Gan-Ning Border Region was nonetheless hailed as a major Nationalist victory although, in fact, it had only limited military significance. Moreover, General Hu's decision to pursue the enemy led him into a trap. The communist general Peng Dehuai, thanks to Xiong's intelligence, was aware of Hu's operational planning and thus was able to defeat many Nationalist troops and to capture several of its high-ranking GMD officers.

Mao and Zhou were among the last to withdraw from Yan'an, leaving at dusk on 18 March, when advance units of the government troops were closing in on the city. Heading northeastward, they progressed through the night, camped at dawn, and slept for much of the next day. Under Mao's and Zhou's leadership, several hundred people comprising the Politburo and the military headquarters were to walk through the loess plateau of northwestern China for more than a year, covering more than a thousand kilometers They were sometimes near and sometimes far from the main force commanded by Peng Dehuai.[164]

On 28 March 1947, Mao and Zhou arrived at Zaolingou, a small village about ninety kilometers northeast of Yan'an. Their plan was to stay in the area as decoys to draw attention away from the CCP leadership, whom Hu Zongnan's troops were all too eager to capture. Mao argued that the mountainous terrain, friendly relations with the local residents, and a lot of room to maneuver created favorable conditions for playing hide and seek with the enemy. But, as a precautionary measure, he insisted on dividing the CCP Central Committee. Three members of the Secretariat, Mao, Zhou and Ren Bishi, formed the Front Committee, which was to direct military operations. A Central Working Committee headed by Liu Shaoqi and Zhu De, the other two members of the Secretariat, were to cross the Yellow River toward northeastern Shanxi to ensure the successful completion of the tasks of the Central Committee. A Rear Committee formed by Ye Jianying, Yang Shangkun, Li Weihan, and Deng Yingchao was also to go to Shanxi, accompanied by the majority of the staff of the Central Committee, to ensure the continuous functioning of the CCP apparatus in case Mao or any other important leader were killed or captured by enemy forces.

A staff of about three hundred, which Mao named the Kunlun Detachment, was assigned to the Front Committee. Their security was assured by additional troops of four companies from the Central Guards Regiment (numbering about four hundred). Zhou divided the Kunlun Detachment into four groups in charge of military affairs, intelligence, radio communications, and the Xinhua News Agency. About ten people who served as attendants to the leaders were added to the first team. The group in charge of radio communications, which was to ensure contacts with all field armies throughout the country, became the nerve center of the command structure.[165]

The Kunlun Detachment and its leaders were constantly on the move. A high degree of mobility was essential to mislead the enemy and conceal their whereabouts. Showing great physical stamina, Zhou traveled back and forth on horseback between the two Central Committees to maintain communication between them and the Front Committee. In April 1947, the Front Committee settled down for fifty-six days at Wangjiawan, a small village in a deep valley in Ansai county about a hundred kilometers northwest of Yan'an. As was the case elsewhere in northern Shaanxi, residents of the village for generations lived not in houses but in caves that had been dug into the hills. From those caves, via radio transmitters, Mao and Zhou continued to direct military operations in all major war theaters in the country.

To compensate for their inferiority in numbers and equipment, communist forces employed tactics of deception, misleading enemy forces, and, whenever possible, drawing them into traps where they could destroy a maximum of their forces and capture their military equipment. The following example illustrates this kind of maneuvering. While government troops continued to search for the main communist forces in the northwest, Peng Dehuai, the communist commander in the region, waited for the right opportunity to ensnare them. It arrived on 14 April, when he was ambushed and defeated a brigade totaling 4,700 men.

Pleased about this victory, Mao spread the news to communist troops in other war theaters. "Our policy is to continue our former method," he wrote in a telegram to Peng, praising him for his victory. It is "to keep the enemy on the run in this area for a time (about another month). The purpose is to tire him out completely, reduce his food supply drastically, and then look for an opportunity to destroy him."[166] These "tactics of wear and tear," as Mao called them, proved successful. Government troops were unable to engage an evasive enemy that continually disappeared into the mountains. In their attempt to seek battles with the communist troops, GMD army units were ambushed and wiped out. By February 1948, when the last battle was fought in northwestern Shaanxi, more than half the government troops in the area were either defeated or exhausted.[167]

While Mao and Zhou stayed at Wangjiawan and Peng Dehuai's troops were stationed at Wayaobao, Chiang Kai-shek received information telling him the CCP headquarters and its main force were in an area about 200 kilometers from Wangjiawan in Suide county, northeastern Shaanxi. Nine brigades of Hu Zongnan's troops were ordered to proceed to Suide. Only one brigade was left behind to guard an important supply depot at Panlongzhen. On 4 May, Peng attacked and defeated the isolated brigade, arrested its commander, and captured food reserves, 40,000 army uniforms, and more than a million pieces of artillery.

The communist forces successfully continued their evasive tactics. Hu Zongnan, increasingly tired of chasing an army that was never where he expected it to be, considered withdrawing his troops from Yan'an. This did not fit in with Mao's plans, which were to tie down Hu's troops in the Yan'an area to stop them from operating elsewhere. To keep the enemy in the area, the CCP leaders staged a public appearance in the village of Zhenwudong, about 45 kilometers from Yan'an. On 14 May, they organized a mass rally to celebrate the victories of the Northwest Field Army. In the presence of Peng Dehuai, Lin Boqu, and Xu Zhongxun, Zhou Enlai delivered a speech to congratulate the communist forces. He made a point of mentioning that Chairman Mao and the CCP headquarters were still in northwestern Shaanxi. The communist radio station broadcast the news, which, in due course, reached Chiang Kai-shek in Xian. Chiang's radio surveillance team equipped with powerful American receivers traced its origins to Wangjiawan, which they took as an indication that the CCP headquarters was also located there. On 6 June, a reconnaissance plane appeared above Wangjiawan, alerting the communists to an impending attack. The following day, more than twenty thousand GMD troops advanced on the village. That evening, in torrential rain and lightning, Mao, Zhou, Ren, and the Kunlun Detachment (now renamed the Third Detachment) left the area, luring the enemy to follow but never catch up.[168]

Though continuously on the march, Mao and Zhou directed communist military operations within the entire country. From 21 to 23 July 1947, they assembled all available military leaders from different war theaters at the village of Xiaohe to review the military tactics of the previous year and to plan their future actions. In his report about the war situation, Zhou pointed out that, during the first year of the war (June 1946–July 1947), the communist forces had succeeded in wiping out about a third of government troops. During the first few months of confrontation, the Nationalist army, spread out thinly over vast territory, had seized 104 cities in the base areas. As a result, in March 1947, Chiang Kai-shek had to change tactics from an all-around offensive to attacks on certain key areas in northern Shaanxi and Shandong. The communist forces, which had been on the defensive before, started their own offensive in many areas and recovered sixty-two cities, Zhou reported, made possible by the expansion of the communist armed forces to more 1.9 million troops. This expansion, he added, would permit them to carry the war into GMD areas during the next phase (July 1947–July 1948).[169]

A few months later, in December, Zhou was able to report to a similar gathering that the PLA had changed its strategy from defensive to offensive warfare on all battlefields. The area and population under CCP control, he said, covered 32 percent of the country, while the PLA had grown to more than 2.2 million troops, almost reaching the strength of the GMD, which had 2.56 million. In the northeast, government forces were on the defensive. In northern China, troops under the command of General Fu Zuoyi were barricaded inside the cities and unable to take any initiatives. Chiang Kai-shek could now depend only on troops in the south. In the rural areas of Guangdong, Fujian, Zhejiang, and Anhui, the Nationalist government was threatened by vigorously growing guerrilla warfare, he announced. Moreover, student and worker movements against the Chiang regime in Nationalist-controlled areas had become increasingly stronger. This was a "second front," Zhou said, bringing together people who were embracing the communist cause not on the battlefield but in civil life in the cities.[170]

At the outbreak of the civil war, a movement for peace and democracy and of protest against the government started at the universities of Kunming in Yunnan province. The assassination of two university professors who took an active part in the movement sparked a nationwide protest. This was compounded by the outrage over the rape of a female student at Beijing University by U.S. soldiers, which triggered further demonstrations against the presence of U.S. troops in China and the government that had invited them. On 31 December 1946, Zhou took advantage of the atmosphere on campuses to issue a directive to underground Party organizations ordering them to mobilize students and others in support of the indignant Beijing students. He demanded that the U.S. soldiers involved in the incident be brought to trial in a Chinese court, that all U.S. troops withdraw from China, that the U.S. government stop interfering in China's internal affairs by providing the Nationalist government with weapons and loans. In January 1947, half a million students in Tianjin, Shanghai, Nanjing, Hangzhou, Wuhan, Chongqing, Kunming, Guangzhou, and other cities responded to Zhou's call. Although clandestine Party branches existed on many campuses since the breakdown of the second united front, Zhou was pleasantly surprised by the strength of the discontent, which he intended to channel toward the communist cause.[171] He started to readjust the system of urban work of the Party by ordering the Shanghai, Hong Kong, and North China Bureaus to direct the student and workers movement in their areas. In a directive of 7 March 1947, he instructed Party members to avoid provocation and confrontation with the authorities. Students should be encouraged to use petitions and appeals within the scope of the law. The Party should focus on economic issues that were of direct interest to students and workers. In accordance with Zhou's recommendations, the Shanghai Bureau presented demands for a fair rationing system for government bureaucrats, teachers, and workers, greater stipends for students, and an increase in funds for education and called for a boycott of classes and for opposition to foreign loans financing the civil war.[172]

However, the students did not allow themselves to be restrained from staging large-scale demonstrations against the civil war. Zhou, from Wangjiawan, changed his instructions to the CCP Shanghai Bureau asking it "to pay close attention to the development of the situation and pursue Party policies of fully arousing the masses to oppose U.S. imperialism and Chiang Kai-shek." On 15 May, students in Nanjing, Tianjin, and Beipjing clashed with the police while demonstrating against the deteriorating conditions of education. On 20 May, students from several other cities arrived in Nanjing to join demonstrations against hunger, civil war, and political persecution. Police and troops intervened, wounding more than a hundred students while trying to repress the demonstrations. This event, termed the "May Twentieth Incident" provoked further mass rallies in about sixty cities in areas controlled by the GMD. On 23 May, Zhou instructed the underground Party to open "a second front" using the same slogans and using flexible tactics combining overt with covert work and legal with illegal struggle in order to destabilize the GMD wherever possible. On 1 June, armed soldiers and police attacked students at Wuhan University, killing three of them. This incident gave rise to further demonstrations and protests in other areas of the country.[173]

Workers were equally discontent. Strikes started in Shanghai in February 1947. The subsequent effort to put down the strikes left 3 workers dead and more than 60 others injured. During 1947, 1.2 million workers went on strike in major cities. Poverty-stricken and famished people attacked rice depots. "The Chiang Kai-shek government is besieged by the whole people," Mao wrote in his cave at Wangjiawan. In his view, there were two battlefronts in China: a military front and the front created by the student movement for "food, peace, and freedom" directed "against hunger, civil war, and persecution." For the communist leadership, "events in China progressed much faster than expected."

In the course of their wanderings, Mao, Zhou, and Ren Bishi reached Xibaipo in April 1948. That small village was to house their military and Party headquarters during the last phase of the civil war. Situated on the north bank of the Hutuo river in a well-developed area close to Shijiazhuang, the provincial capital of Hebei province, it comprised seventy to eighty households. Living conditions in the village were better than in northern Shaanxi. Liu Shaoqi, Zhu De, and other leaders had already settled down there. From this peaceful place, the CCP leadership directed the largest campaigns of the civil war, involving millions of soldiers on both sides.

The decisive phase of the civil war began in the autumn of 1948. By that time the PLA had grown to an army of 2.8 million men, about half of which was made up of field armies equipped with modern weapons seized from the GMD. Many of the troops had been recruited from militia units and through large-scale military campaigns that took place at the same time as land reform in the rural areas. Others were captured enemy soldiers ready to fight for the communists.[174]

Between the fall of 1948 and to the spring of 1949, the communists launched three major campaigns. The first was the Liaoxi-Shenyang campaign in northeastern China, which involved 700,000 troops under the command of Lin Biao. This gave them numerical superiority over government forces facing them that totaled 550,000. Between September and November 1948, this campaign—with Mao and Zhou in command—wiped out 470,000 government troops and put northeastern China under communist control.

The second was the Huaihai campaign fought between November 1948 and January 1949 over a large territory centering on Xuzhou in northern Anhui. The field commanders were Liu Bocheng, Deng Xiaoping, and Chen Yi. Although the government forces (800,000) outnumbered the communists (600,000), the GMD were defeated, losing 550,000 troops in the battle.[175]

Parallel to this campaign, a third battle was fought from November 1948 to January 1949 for the conquest of Beiping and Tianjin. One million PLA troops under the command of Lin Biao, Luo Ronghuan, and Nie Rongzhen confronted the Nationalist forces numbering 520,000. Within two months, their troops were either wiped out or joined the PLA. Tianjin was captured by force. Surrounded and outnumbered, the commander of the Nationalist forces in Beiping negotiated a settlement. On 22 January, he agreed to withdraw all his troops and to surrender the city. The PLA entered the city on 31 January without firing a single shot.[176]

By the end of 1948, having lost his main force, Chiang Kai-shek was no longer in a position to continue the war. On 1 January, in his New Year's message to the nation, he proposed peace talks with the CCP. "If only peace can be realized," he said, "I certainly do not care whether I remain in office or retire, but will abide by the common will of the people."[177] In a last attempt to reach a settlement with the communists, Chiang pleaded with the United States, Britain, and the Soviet Union to mediate. Stalin offered to do so under conditions that he spelled out in telegrams to Mao on 10 and 11 January 1949. The CCP leadership, in a telegram drafted in Zhou's polite and diplomatic style, turned down Moscow's instructions on how the CCP should respond to the GMD. Instead, the telegram suggested to Stalin what the Soviet response to Chiang should be. It made clear that the Chinese communists rejected all other attempts at Great Power mediation as duplicitous and biased in favor of the GMD. The Soviet authorities relented and, in accordance with this suggestion, responded to the GMD that "the restoration of China's integrity as a democratic peace-loving state is the affair of the Chinese people itself and that this integrity could probably be best achieved by the direct negotiations between the internal forces of China, without foreign interference."[178]

The communist leaders must have taken great satisfaction in this exchange of telegrams with Stalin, which came only a few months after Stalin had rejected Mao's proposal to report to him personally about the revolutionary situation in China. Stalin had refused to receive him on the grounds that Mao should not leave China at a time when the revolution, albeit approaching victory, had not yet been entirely victorious. Stalin suggested sending a member of the Politburo to China to be instructed about the Chinese views.

When the Soviet envoy, A.I. Mikoyan, arrived at Xibaipo village on 31 January 1949, the situation was much clearer. As he declared from the outset, Mikoyan had come merely to listen, not to hold discussions. Mao, Zhou, Liu, Zhu, and Ren took turns informing him about the war situation. But it was Zhou Enlai, soon to be appointed prime minister of the new government, who took charge of detailed briefings on the reconstruction of a country that was in shambles after decades of conflict.[179]

On the 21 January, Chiang stepped down as president of the Nationalist government. He left Nanjing for Xikou, his hometown in Zhejiang province. Vice President Li Zongren took over as acting president. He was ready to negotiate with the CCP on the basis of terms that Mao had laid down on 14 January, which amounted to unconditional military and political surrender, demanding—among other things— punishment of war criminals (Chiang Kai-shek was considered "number one") and the abolition of the national constitution, which was considered bogus.

The peace negotiations began on 1 April between a six-member CCP delegation led by Zhou Enlai and a delegation of an equal number of representatives from Nanjing, headed by Zhang Zhizong. For the first time in the decades of negotiations with the GMD, Zhou found himself in a superior position. Chiang had never recognized that there was a civil war in China. For him, the purpose of military operations was the suppression of bandits, led by Zhou. This time everything was different. The negotiations were between the conqueror and the conquered.

Leaving aside his usual charming manner, Zhou opened the talks by asking Zhang sternly: "Why did you go to Xikou to see Chiang Kai-shek before leaving Nanjing?" Zhang explained that at that point Chiang still held power although he had officially retired. His consent would be needed to seal any agreement reached during the negotiations. Zhou said that the CCP would not accept a bogus peace dictated by Chiang Kai-shek. He asked the government representatives whether they had come with the necessary credentials to implement the terms proposed by the CCP. Zhang replied that the government had no specific plans, but it was ready to listen. After ten days of negotiations, Zhou produced a "draft agreement for internal peace." After more negotiations, on 15 April, Zhou produced the "final version" of the document. Zhang asked, "When you talk about the final version of the document, do you mean it is an ultimatum? Are we allowed to say only 'yes' or 'no'?" Zhou replied, "The document represents our final position."[180] The Nanjing government was given five days to respond. Zhou made it clear that the PLA would wait until 20 April before crossing the Yangtze River to march on Nanjing.

An envoy was sent to Nanjing to transmit the draft agreement to the authorities while the other government delegates stayed in Beiping to wait for the government's decision. On 20 April, Chiang Kai-shek and Li Zongren rejected the CCP plan. The following day, Mao Zedong and Zhu De issued an "order to the army for country-wide advance." The PLA crossed the Yangtze River to the south, capturing Nanjing on the twenty-third. Both Chiang and Li fled, the former to Taiwan and the latter to the United States. After twenty-two years in power, the Nationalist government had collapsed.

# II

# YEARS IN POWER

# 3

# Nation Building (1949–1966)

## The Imperial Palace

In March 1949, Mao Zedong, Zhou Enlai, and other leaders of the Chinese Communist Party (CCP) abandoned the village of Xibeipo in Pingshan county, where, a year earlier, they had established their headquarters and began their march toward the capital. They were approaching the goal for which all of them had fought for the major part of their lives: the conquest of their country. The leaders were in high spirits. Mao told Zhou that he felt as if they were going to the capital to take the imperial examinations. In that case, Zhou replied, they should aim for the highest possible marks. At this historic moment, Zhou recalled the fate of Li Zicheng, the leader of a peasant uprising at the end of the Ming dynasty, who, in 1644, had overthrown the emperor and captured the capital. After years of battle, Li, his prime minister, and generals were so infatuated by their success and so taken with the luxuries of city life that they ignored the dangers brewing in the north. There, a Ming general had forged an alliance with the Manchus. Together they confronted the new and totally unprepared powerholders in Beijing and defeated them within a month. Thereafter, the Manchus ruled the country for more than two hundred and fifty years. As far as Zhou was concerned, such a setback could not be allowed to happen to the communists. "There can be no turning back," he remarked. In complete agreement, Mao proclaimed: "We shall never be like Li Zicheng!"[1]

The convoy, with its eleven jeeps and ten trucks, wound its way to Zhuoxian—a county with a railway station roughly fifty kilometers south of Beijing—from where the travelers continued their journey by train towards Beiping. But the leaders did not settle down in the future capital. For security reasons Mao, Zhou, and their aides established their headquarters in the Fragrant Hills, a charming scenic spot in the western suburbs where modest but comfortable quarters had been prepared for them. Hidden away from the bustle of the city and provided with anti-aircraft shelters, the area was well protected and allowed the leaders to prepare for the final takeover of the capital in a serene environment.

Zhou soon found commuting from the Fragrant Hills to the city too cumbersome and time-consuming. In May 1949, he moved to Beijing. He and other high-ranking Party leaders established the seat of the Party center in the western part of the imperial city at Zhongnanhai, the Middle and the Southern Lake area. Adjacent to the imperial palace, Zhongnanhai was surrounded by high vermilion walls. On the eastern bank of the South Lake stand mansions and pavilions, among them Yingtai, where the formidable Empress Dowager Ci Xi had imprisoned the emperor Guangxu (1875–1908) for having attempted to introduce political reforms to China. During the civil war, most of these buildings had been occupied by the GMD army and used as its headquarters. Zhou installed his office and living quarters in a courtyard called Juxiang Shuwu (the Study of Chrysanthemum Fragrance). It was an enchanting place surrounded by the Garden of Prosperity and Grace (Fengze Yuan). Zhou did not use this courtyard, which was considered the most beautiful in Zhongnanhai, for any length of time. As soon as Mao decided to move to Zhongnanhai as well, Zhou turned it over to him, moving to Xihuating (the Western Flower Hall), claiming that he was very attracted to the blossoming Chinese crabapple tree in its courtyard.

Xihuating is a relatively recent building, constructed in 1910 as an office for Prince Chun, the father and prince regent of the last emperor, Pu Yi. But the 1911 Revolution ended the Qing dynasty before Prince Chun had a chance to use the building. Located in the northwestern corner of Zhongnanhai, it consists of two courtyards. The main hall in the front courtyard was used to receive foreign dignitaries. The rooms on the two sides of the hall were offices of Zhou's secretaries and service staff. Zhou and his wife, Deng Yingchao, then vice chairwoman of the National Women's Federation and an alternate member of the Central Committee, lived and worked in the rear courtyard, where both had offices, bedrooms, and a sitting room. Corridors linked the main hall with the living rooms.[2]

When Zhou moved into Xihuating, the buildings were in disrepair. The floors, paved with bricks that were cold in the rugged Beijing winter, added to the dampness on rainy days and emitted an unpleasant odor of mildew. The walls were covered with flaking paint and the wood, a major ingredient of traditional Chinese houses, was splintering. While the main hall, to be used for official purposes, was being renovated, Zhou insisted that he could make do with the rest of the courtyard. It was, as he said, much better than the Yan'an caves. He argued that the limited resources of the country should be used for productive purposes, rather than for improvement of the leadership's living conditions. Only after ten years was he prepared to allow some renovation of his increasingly uncomfortable living quarters. While he was absent from Beijing for two months, the bricks on the floor were replaced by wood and covered with beautiful carpets. Crevices at the doors and windows were filled, splintered and rotten beams were replaced, and the entire dwelling was repainted. New furniture and new curtains completed the work. But Zhou was angry about these improvements. When he returned, his face sank at their sight. "What happened?" he asked his secretary, who had been in charge of the renovations and who had done what he thought would please the premier. "Who authorized you to do all this? ... How much money have you spent? Why, this is extravagant!" Zhou exclaimed.[3] Declaring that he would not enter the house until it was restored to its original condition, he left in anger to stay at the Diaoyutai Guesthouse. Later, he calmed down, admitting that the original condition of the house could not be restored without squandering even more money. But he was determined to return to his living quarters only after all the new furnishings had been removed. The matter did not rest there. He brought the issue to the State Council, where he declared that his house had been renovated in a way of which he did not approve. He felt uneasy about the expenditure involved. He was responsible for the waste, he told his colleagues, inviting them to visit the house. By making so much of the matter, Zhou intended to offer an object lesson. A few years after entering Beijing, Party and government officials had began to vie with one another over improvement of their living conditions. Zhou, who was notoriously frugal and acutely aware of the poor state of his country's finances, strongly disapproved of such expenditures.[4]

Not only was Zhou extremely thrifty when it came to state expenditure, but he was also exceedingly sensitive to anything smacking of corruption, whether in official or family matters. Party discipline required the strict subordination of the family to political requirements. Moreover, with its strong emphasis on family political background, the Party expected its members to disavow their families if they did not belong to the laboring classes. This way of thinking was far removed from the Confucian outlook—still deep-rooted in China—which regarded filial duty and respect for elders as one of the prime duties of a son. Zhou, who came from a mandarin family, clearly had an undesirable family background. This background must have reinforced his determination—at an early stage of his involvement with the revolution—to subordinate his personal life entirely to Party discipline. In the 1920s he severed his relations with his family. But in 1939, he returned to his ancestral home to pay his respects to the tombs of his ancestors and to add his name to the tablets representing the Zhou family tree. This demonstration of filial duty clearly had political motives. China was in the early period of war against the Japanese when the CCP and the Nationalist Party (Guomindang, GMD) were in a phase of cooperation. Zhou's visit to his ancestral home was meant to contradict the Nationalist propaganda asserting that communists showed no respect for their families.

Throughout his life, he permitted political priorities to prevail over all other considerations. Despite his Confucian upbringing, Zhou's attitude toward his family remained contingent to Party policies. Only within this framework did he allow members of his family to approach him and allow himself to deal with them. While working in Chongqing during World War II, he took care of his father, Zhou Shaogang, for several years. Realizing that his father was unable to make a living for himself, Zhou invited him to live with him, and his father remained until his death in 1942.[5]

After the founding of the People's Republic, Zhou, who had many relatives from both his mother's and father's families, was extremely careful to avoid nepotism and favoritism. He profoundly disapproved of such practices, which had been rampant in traditional Chinese society and under GMD rule. He discouraged his relatives from coming to Beijing to see him, and he strictly forbade his nieces and nephews to reveal their relationship with him. In fact, family affiliations and the private life of important leaders were considered state secrets. Zhou also refused to return to his hometown of Huai'an and issued strict instructions to the local authorities not to transform his house into a memorial and not to keep up the Zhou family tombs.[6] His admonitions were respected during his lifetime, but today his family home and the traditional family school that he attended as a child have been restored and are visited by a large number of tourists every year. In celebration of the hundredth anniversary of his birth in 1998, his hometown opened a vast commemorative park with a museum dedicated to his life and a reproduction of Xihuating, his living and working quarters in Beijing.

Zhou's youngest brother, Enshou, who was forty-five years old in 1949, lived in Tianjin, supporting his wife and six children on a minimal salary. At the end of that year, having found a job at the Ministry of Internal Affairs, he moved to Beijing. Zhou, who wanted to avoid any suggestion of nepotism, instructed the minister to see to it that his brother was employed at the lowest level and lowest wage.[7] Since such a salary was not enough to maintain his large family, Zhou supplemented his brother's income by 120 yuan per month. When Zhou Enshou began to suffer from an ulcer and could not work regularly, Zhou asked him to retire, arguing that, under the circumstances, he should not draw full pay. At the same time, he increased his brother's allowance to 200 yuan per month.

Zhou Enlai and Deng Yingchao did not have any children of their own. Since his brother had difficulty earning enough to take care of his children, Zhou invited three of his brother's children to live with him and his wife in Zhongnanhai. The first to move to their uncle's home was his eldest niece, Zhou Bingde, who arrived at Zhongnanhai in the summer of 1949. The twelve-year-old girl found several other girls her age living there, for example, Mao's daughters Li Min by his second wife He Zizhen and Li Na by Jiang Qing, the two daughters of Mao's secretary and Zhu De's granddaughter. Bingde was soon joined by her younger sister and brother, but of the three she who remained the longest with Zhou and Deng. When she reached the age of twenty-five, her mother and Deng Yingchao began to worry about her marriage prospects. Bingde, who did not have a boyfriend, was introduced to three young men who were considered suitable, since they had been students in the Soviet Union. But Bingde was not interested in any of them, and shortly thereafter she found the right partner without the help of her concerned family. He was the grandson of Shen Junru, the president of the Supreme Court. They married the following year. Bingde remained one of the few close relatives with whom Zhou and his wife maintained a life-long relationship.

Another woman with a close tie to Zhou and Deng was Sun Weishi, whom they had adopted after her father was killed by Chiang Kai-shek's secret police in 1927. In the 1920s her father, Sun Bingwen, had been recruited by Zhou Enlai to join the CCP in Germany, and they later worked together in the underground in Guangzhou.

Weishe, as mentioned in Chapter 2, accompanied Zhou when he went to Moscow for medical treatment in the summer of 1939. She was to enroll at the Moscow Northeast University and later at the Moscow Academy of Drama, and remained in the Soviet Union for more than six years. After returning to China, she became a director of the Chinese Youth Artistic Drama Theater in Beijing and married Jin Shan, a well-known actor and director.

Li Peng was another orphaned child of a revolutionary whom Zhou and his wife took into their home. Born in 1928, he was the son of Li Shuoxun, the political commissar of the Twentieth Division, which was involved in the Nanchang Uprising. Li Shuoxin died in 1931 after being seized by the GMD authorities. In 1939 Zhou brought Li Peng to Chongqing and enrolled him in middle school there. Two years later, when Li Peng was twelve, Zhou sent him to Yan'an, where he studied until 1945. Later he went to Moscow to study hydraulic engineering, a field in which he worked continuously until he became prime minister in 1987.[8]

*         *         *         *

On the afternoon of October 1, Mao stood on the balcony above the grand Gate of Heavenly Peace. Surrounded by important leaders of the CCP and its allies, he proclaimed the People's Republic of China. "We, the Chinese people have stood up and our future is infinitely bright," he shouted to the cheering crowd crammed into the square below.

Zhou Enlai was premier of that newly established state and would remain in that post for more than twenty-six years, from October 1949 until his death on 8 January 1976. Few have held the position of prime minister for such a long time, in China or elsewhere. Zhou combined many of the complex prerequisites necessary for this accomplishment. His unquestioning loyalty towards Mao and his devotion to duty helped him to survive politically where others had failed. His way of dealing with people made him widely popular with many but also generated fears in others. One of his long-standing secretaries describes Zhou as a jovial man capable of relieving tension and making people feel at ease. When he met with people who were awed in the presence of such a high-level and prestigious leader, he usually succeeded in drawing out people with his simple friendliness. He always showed great sympathy and kindness to his secretaries, who spent their waking and sleeping hours at Zhongnanhai—always at his disposition. Although he was extremely demanding and invariably noticed the slightest slip in anyone's performance, he was never impolite in his rebuff but, rather, acted like a father figure making people learn from their mistakes.[9] Other witnesses report a less beneficent view. Subordinates who did not belong to Zhou's inner circle were awed by him. Some report that Zhou often arrived at meetings with the stern face of a traditional schoolmaster beginning the meeting with a roll call. Since his knowledge of dossiers was usually detailed, he gave the impression that he was capable of detecting the slightest flaw in the reasoning of his subordinate. But he treated all other people whom he met in the exercise of his duty in the most charming and friendly manner.[10]

Although Zhou was premier of the most populous country in the world, his office staff, compared with that of other world leaders in comparable positions, was relatively small. It consisted of a director, his deputy, and a number of secretaries, organized in five sections: general affairs; foreign affairs; military affairs; financial, economic, and administrative affairs; and communication, transportation, agriculture, and forestry. In the mid-1950s, as many as eighteen secretaries worked at the premier's office. Their number was cut drastically in late 1957 and early 1958, when some of them were transferred to various cultural and educational departments to replace leading cadres who had been labeled "rightists" and sent to labor camps.[11]

Zhou's working hours, and therefore those of his staff, were closely modeled after Mao's. This meant that they worked throughout the night. Zhou's day began at about 11 A.M. After awakening, Zhou spent about an hour in the bathroom while reading the four most important daily newspapers: *Renmin ribao* (People's Daily), *Guangming ribao* (Guangming Daily), *Jiefang ribao* (Liberation Army Daily), and the Shanghai *Wenhuibao*. He also received urgent reports delivered by his secretaries and even sometimes by vice premiers and ministers, while sitting on the toilet. This uninhibited habit was very common in the Chinese countryside, where veteran revolutionaries had lived for decades without the slightest comfort. It became an embarrassing situation only when Chen Hao, his female secretary in charge of foreign affairs in the 1950s, had urgent matters to report. She would than ask a male secretary to do the reporting on her behalf.

## The Rise of a Nation

With the proclamation of the PRC, the CCP had been able to achieve a long-held goal, which had been a recurring theme throughout Chinese history: national unification. This feat had provided the Party and its leadership with a high degree of legitimacy. However, despite the victorious marches of the People's Liberation Army (PLA), the communist presence and policies had not penetrated evenly into Chinese society, which continued to be dominated by its traditional parochialism.

Mao was well aware of this. He was determined to rally as much support as possible for his regime. In his famous article "On the People's Democratic Dictatorship," published on 30 June 1949, he proclaimed a "new democracy," based on an alliance between workers, peasants, and the urban bourgeoisie. The new government should therefore include all parties and public figures sympathetic to the communist revolution. They would all participate in the Chinese People's Political Consultative Conference (CPPCC), which would include the CCP, various democratic parties, civic organizations, regional representatives, the PLA, minority nationalities, overseas Chinese, and well-known public figures. As a "people's dictatorship," the alliance would be dominated by the CCP.[12]

Beginning early in his official mandate, Zhou showed a unique capacity for rallying and mobilization, gaining the confidence of those who were skeptical, and bringing noncommunists into the government—tasks that Mao probably could not accomplished. His ability to do so differentiated Zhou from other visible Chinese leaders of the time.

Zhou launched a year-long campaign to diffuse suspicions, to create a conciliatory atmosphere, and to bring people together who were ready to work for "New China." He approached some well-known public figures who had not joined the communist cause, including representatives of the GMD. One of his first targets was the GMD peace delegation with whom he had "negotiated" in the spring of 1949 and whom he had forced to accept his surrender terms. One by one, he visited the delegates at the Beijing Hotel. He suggested to its leader, Zhang Zhizong, that, having accepted the CCP peace proposals, he might put his personal security at risk if he returned to the south. Zhou reminded him of General Zhang Xueliang's fate after the Xian Incident. Suggesting that Zhang break with Chiang Kai-shek, he offered him a position in the new government. Zhang, concerned about the fate of his family in Nanjing, hesitated to accept Zhou's offer, but he came around after Zhou, through his underground network in the south, was able to bring the general's family to Beijing. Zhang remained in Beijing as did all the other members of his delegation, whom Zhou approached with the same suggestion.

In early 1949, Zhou sent his wife to Shanghai with a letter from Mao to invite Song Qingling to join the alliance. Estranged from her family and opposed to GMD policies for many years, Song readily accepted. Huang Yanpei, a well-known personage in industry and commerce then seventy-two years old, was another person whom Zhou approached. For decades, Huang had refused all offers of an official post, but Zhou convinced him to accept a position as vice premier of the new government. Also approached was General Fu Zuoyi, the commander of the GMD forces in northern China, who had avoided bloodshed by peacefully surrendering Beijing to the Red Army. Zhou persuaded him to join the PLA and, aware of Fu's expertise in water resource management, appointed him minister of water conservancy in the new government, a post that he retained for many years.[13]

The new government indeed faced many tasks. Tackling them would require the participation of all qualified personnel possible. Economic reconstruction was high on the agenda. China, a poor agrarian country even before the war, emerged economically ruined from eight years of struggle against the Japanese occupation and more than three years of civil war. Between 1936 and 1949, its production of basic food grains had considerably decreased while its population had grown. Famine was widespread in many rural areas. Output of coal, iron, steel, and cotton, already inadequate for the country's needs in 1936, had fallen to alarmingly low levels. Per capita income in 1949/50 amounted to half the level in India.[14] The financial system, or what was left of it after the defeat of the GMD, had completely collapsed; inflation had reached unprecedented levels. One of the first measures of the new government was to introduce monetary reforms in which the old Chinese silver dollar, now virtually worthless, was replaced by the *renminbi* (lit. "people's currency," RMB). The reform went rather smoothly in the north, where the RMB was first introduced. Major obstacles remained, however, in southern China and especially in major cities such as Shanghai, where merchants refused to accept the *renminbi* for trade and financial speculation inflated the silver dollar against the new currency.

Land reform was another pressing issue, as were social reforms, such as a new marriage law and abolition of opium addiction and prostitution. The building of institutions to handle these problems was perhaps the most urgent task of the new government, but personnel both qualified and true to the communist cause to staff these institutions were in short supply.

To relieve this shortage, Zhou began a campaign to recruit Chinese intellectuals and professionals not only in China but also abroad to fill the positions in the new government. Many Chinese living abroad responded enthusiastically and returned to China to help in reconstruction efforts.

The inaugural meeting of the CPPCC, numbering 662 members, met from 21 to 30 September in Beijing and formed the Government Administrative Council (Zhengwuyuan, later renamed Guowuyuan [State Council]), whose composition Mao and Zhou had established in advance. Mao Zedong was the chairman; and Zhu De, Liu Shaoqi, Gao Gang, Song Qingling, Li Jishen, and Zhang Lan were vice-chairpersons. Among the six vice-chairpersons, three (Song; Li, who had been chairman of the GMD left-wing Revolutionary Committee; and Zhang Lan, chairman of the Chinese Democratic League) were not communists. The council declared Beijing the capital of the new republic and nominated Zhou Enlai as premier and foreign minister.

Noncommunists occupied a number of positions at the government level as well. Of four of the vice premiers, two were not members of the CCP. Out of the 109 leading posts at the Government Administrative Council, 49 were occupied by noncommunists. At ministerial level, ten ministers were members of parties other than the CCP or did not have any party affiliation.[15]

The Government Administrative Council had under its overall jurisdiction twenty-one ministries, three commissions, four bureaus, and a Secretariat. Four committees under the premier were responsible for the coordination and direction of more than thirty institutions. The Finance and Economic Committee under Chen Yun and Bo Yibo, for example, supervised fifteen ministries dealing with economic and financial affairs and the Bank of China. The Committee on Culture and Education was in charge of the Ministry of Culture, the Ministry of Education, the Bureaus of Information and Publications, and the Academy of Sciences. Most of the activity in those areas was handled directly by the committees, which referred only major issues to the premier. Zhou was directly in charge of the Ministry of Foreign Affairs, the Ministry of the Interior, the Commission of Overseas Chinese, and the Secretariat.[16]

Among the many institutions that had to be reestablished was the Foreign Ministry for which Zhou showed deep personal interest, and for which he involved himself more intensely than in any other institution.

Throughout his tenure as premier, Zhou played a significant role in Chinese foreign policy, and he was clearly the CCP's foremost specialist in foreign relations. From 1949 to 1958, he acted as both premier and foreign minister. Zhou's influence over Chinese diplomacy was undiminished even after the post of foreign minister was transferred to Marshal Chen Yi in 1958. Although Mao—as in all other important political issues—formulated the general principles of foreign policy and made the final decisions, he was well aware of Zhou's superior diplomatic abilities. "Zhou Enlai is very talented," Mao once stated in a conversation with the Soviet leader Nikita Khrushchev. "He is better than me in international activities" because "he is dexterous at solving problems."[17] Indeed, Zhou's detailed knowledge of dossiers, his skill at negotiation and organization, and his ability to mediate in the most complicated situations were vital to the implementation of Chinese foreign policy goals and earned him the respect of many politicians and diplomats around the world.

As discussed in Chapter 2, Zhou's experience in foreign affairs dated to the 1920s, when, as a representative of the CCP, he began to deal with the Comintern and the Soviet Union. Early in the anti-Japanese war, in 1937, he established the first office dealing with external problems—the International Information Section—in the Wuhan Office of the CCP-led Eighth Route Army. A year later, in 1938, the Wuhan office moved to Chongqing, the wartime capital, where Zhou replaced the International Information Section with a Foreign Affairs Office. In Chongqing, Zhou maintained extensive contacts with foreign diplomats, military men and journalists.

After his retreat to Yan'an, Zhou's interaction with the outside world was limited to contacts with the American envoy Patrick J. Hurley and the Dixie mission. George Marshall's mediation between the CCP and the GMD government concerning the shape of China after the end of World War II again put Zhou into the forefront of diplomatic activity. The Foreign Affairs Office was transferred to Nanjing to assist him in his negotiations. After the failure of these negotiations and the outbreak of the civil war, he interrupted his diplomatic activities to concentrate on military affairs. He resumed his duties as the Party's chief spokesman on foreign affairs at the CCP headquarters in Xibaipo in Hebei province.

On 8 November, Zhou opened the Ministry of Foreign Affairs, located in a prestigious and historic building at Waijiaobu (Foreign Ministry) Street in the eastern part of the city, which was the first

Western-style mansion in Beijing, built by British architects in the late Qing dynasty. At that time, it was known as the Zongli geguo shiwu yamen (Board for the General Management of the Affairs of All Countries). In 1912 it became the Foreign Ministry of the northern warlord government under Yuan Shikai.[18]

Zhou's imprint marked the Foreign Ministry more than any other State Council institution. When World War II came to a close, while Zhou was still in Yan'an, he pondered the question of who would comprise a diplomatic staff for the CCP—people who would be able to handle diplomatic affairs in the future government. At that time, he drew up a list of those who had been involved in one aspect or another of foreign affairs, either in Chongqing or in Nanjing, or who had worked with the teams supervising ceasefires in various localities.

Unlike other ministries or official departments, where, under the rubric of implementing the principle of "new democracy," people who belonged to democratic parties or had no party affiliation were employed in official positions, the Foreign Ministry employed only CCP members. Zhou believed that foreign affairs were a politically sensitive area, like military affairs, and therefore required the strict discipline and ideological correctness. For him the only difference between foreign and military matters in this respect was that the army fought with guns while diplomats fought with words.[19]

However, the lack of expertise in certain areas made it necessary to make exceptions to the principle of employing only communists. To staff the Department of Treaty and Law at the Foreign Ministry, for example, Zhou fell back on former employees of the GMD government whom he hired not as regular staff but as advisers. The assignment to the Legal Department of Mei Ruao, a well-known grand judge who had represented China at the trial of Japanese war criminals in Tokyo, was an example of such an exception.

Clearly, Zhou handpicked an elite group to work at the Foreign Ministry. He appointed three deputy vice ministers from the Ministry who were close to him and who had had exposure to foreign affairs. The most highly placed was Wang Jiaxiang, a life-long friend of Zhou's, who served as ambassador to the Soviet Union. The second was Li Kenong, who had worked with Zhou as intelligence office in GMD-dominated areas in the 1930s and 1940s. The third was Zhang Hanfu, who had been—under Zhou's direction—editor of the CCP newspaper *Xinhua ribao* (New China Daily) in Chongqing. Other high-level positions in the ministry were occupied by Zhou's most trusted followers, such as Wang Bingnan, Qiao Guanhua, Chen Jiakang, Ke Bainian, and Gong Peng. Huang Hua and Zhang Wenjin, two close associates, who had been appointed to head the offices of foreign affairs in Nanjing and Tianjin in early 1949, also joined in the ranks of New China's diplomats.

Ambassadors to the few countries with which China had established diplomatic relations had been chosen mostly from among PLA generals, who had gained some experience in diplomacy during negotiations with the GMD and the U.S. mediators. They included Ji Pengfei, who represented China in the German Democratic Republic; Huang Zhen, who went to Hungary; Geng Biao, envoy to Sweden; Yuan Zhongxian, who represented China in India; and Wang Yuping, the ambassador to Romania.

The junior staff was recruited at different universities where students had some language training and had acquired an impeccable political record either in the underground party or as participants in progressive student movements. Zhou took a keen interest in their training and in their personal lives, often keeping himself informed at Saturday night dances held by the ministry on its premises or at the Beijing Hotel, which Zhou frequented. Under his guidance, the Foreign Ministry staff gained increasing expertise and experience and soon could be relied on to provide credible analysis on foreign countries. The staff expanded gradually, growing from an initial 170 to some two thousand by the mid-1960s.[20]

## First Steps in Foreign Policy

Among the earliest tasks Zhou assigned to the Foreign Ministry was the implementation of the principle of "making a fresh start." This principle, which became one of the most important guidelines of foreign policy at that time, regulated the establishment of new diplomatic relations and the status of foreign establishments and personnel left over from the GMD period. It implied that diplomatic relations established with the GMD government were now null and void. Zhou took no chances in the implementation of this policy. After the takeover of Nanjing—the seat of the GMD government—he issued specific instructions to the field armies in the area that the PLA, the military control commission, and the municipal government of the city should shun official contacts with foreign embassies and legations. Anything that might convey the impression that their status as foreign representations was recognized was to be strictly avoided.

On 1 October, Zhou Enlai notified all governments that any country wishing to establish diplomatic ties with the People's Republic had first to break relations with Taiwan and express support for the PRC's claim to Taiwan's seat at the United Nations. This, he told his colleagues at the Foreign Ministry with some excitement, was the first foreign policy document issued by the new government. Moscow was the first to respond, breaking its relations with the GMD and recognizing the new Chinese government within a day of its establishment. The countries of Eastern Europe, North Korea, and North Vietnam followed suit. In October and November, diplomatic relations were established and ambassadors were exchanged with eleven communist countries.[21]

In December 1949 and January 1950, thirteen non-communist countries (Burma, India, Pakistan, Great Britain, Ceylon [later called Sri Lanka], Norway, Denmark, Israel, Indonesia, Afghanistan, Finland, Sweden, and Switzerland) also recognized the People's Republic, the first among them, being the Burmese foreign minister, who cabled Zhou Enlai on 16 December. The Burmese government was ready to cancel its obligations toward Taiwan, demand the expulsion of its representatives from the United Nations, and transfer ownership of Taiwanese property in Burma to the People's Republic. Zhou regarded this agreement as a model for further negotiations on the establishment of diplomatic relations. But, aside from Burma, only six others (India, Indonesia, Finland, Sweden, Switzerland, and Denmark) were ready to accept the Chinese conditions. Talks with Great Britain, Norway, and others were unsuccessful. As for the United States, Zhou had authorized contacts between Huang Hua, the director of the Office of Foreign Affairs of the Nanjing Military Control Commission, and Leighton Stuart, the U.S. ambassador to China. After some initial discussion between May and August 1949, it became clear that the Chinese and U.S. positions were so far apart that it was impossible to reach an agreement. The U.S. ambassador was recalled and left China on 2 August. His departure was underscored by an angry article called "Farewell, Leighton Stuart!" written by Mao and published by the official press in the middle of August. Sino-American relations would not recover for over twenty years.[22]

Foreign encroachment on China's territory and the humiliations felt by the Chinese had generated such profound resentment that the elimination of all foreign influence became a major objective of foreign policy. Apart from the work related to the reestablishment of diplomatic relations, the principle of "cleaning the house before entertaining new guests" (*dasao ganjin wuzi zai qingke*) implied the abolition of all privileges enjoyed by foreign countries and thus became a major task for Foreign Ministry officials.[23] Starting with the Legation Quarter in the eastern part of Beijing, where most foreign consulates and foreign barracks were concentrated, the ministry posted a notice signed by the Beijing Military Control Commission on the walls of the U.S., British, French, and Dutch consulates. It announced that the land on which the buildings stood was to be taken over by the government and that all barracks and their affiliated edifices on that land were confiscated for military use. After some token negotiations between the Beijing Office of Foreign Affairs, the Western European Department of the Ministry of Foreign Affairs, and foreign representatives, the Military Control Commission seized American, French, Dutch, and British properties in Beijing, American and British buildings in Tianjin, and French buildings in Shanghai.

Foreign property in China, if not already withdrawn, quickly became the second target. In 1949 some seventeen hundred foreign enterprises were in operation, representing a total investment of $860 million. Foreign capital controlled a majority of the supplies of electricity, natural gas, and oil and most of the water supply in Shanghai. The American Department and the Western European Department of the Foreign Ministry were ordered to rid the country of these enterprises after Zhou had devised measures to abolish them by means of confiscation, appropriation, forced purchase, or simply taking control.

Christian missions and schools established and funded by Western countries did not fare much better. About twelve thousand missionaries, about half of them foreigners, were working in China in 1949. Regarded as vehicles of imperialist "cultural aggression," the schools and missions were quickly dismantled. The new government refused to recognize their property rights and transferred their holdings to Chinese churches. When the Korean War broke out in 1950, the communist government cut all relations between Chinese and foreign churches and reinforced its hold over the churches by insisting on a policy of "self-administration, self-support, and self-propagation of the Gospel".

In 1949, China had more than twenty universities, including Yanjing University and Furen University in Beijing and Jinling University in

Shanghai. Seventeen of them received subsidies from the United States, which also funded more than two hundred hospitals and more than seventeen hundred primary and middle schools. In December 1950 the Government Administrative Council, under Zhou's direction, took over some of them while others were allowed to function on the condition that they ceased to receiving foreign subsidies.[24] Deprived of their financial resources, little by little they closed.

Other foreign activities were equally curtailed. The "American Information Service" was ordered to halt all activities, while the British Council was confined to its premises. Foreigners were no longer allowed to publish newspapers or journals in China. Foreign news agencies and journalists from countries that did not have diplomatic relations with China were ordered to cease operations.

As a result of this policy, diplomats, businessmen, missionaries, teachers, doctors, journalists, and other professionals of various nationalities left China. The U.S. blockade after the Korean War increased China's isolation even further. The door to the outside world—with the exception of a few countries—gradually closed.

In June 1949, Mao announced his policy of "leaning to one side" By which he meant that China's foreign relations should focus on the Soviet Union and its allies. The modus vivendi with the United States that Zhou had attempted to negotiate in 1949 was thwarted by the negative response of the U.S. government and its obvious preference for Taiwan. By 1949 a cold war had developed between the United States and the Soviet Union, with each acting out the conflict through cohorts in Europe and elsewhere. In Asia and the Pacific the United States anchored its regional influence in Japan, then still under U.S. postwar occupation. To avoid isolation, China had an immediate self-interest in establishing an alliance with the Soviet Union. Mao and Zhou believed that such an alliance would provide a counterbalance to the United States, create a basis for China's security, and provide it with technical and economic aid in reconstruction. As the year of 1949 drew to a close, the Soviet Union became the destination of Mao's first trip outside China. Accompanied by two of his secretaries, Chen Boda and Ye Zilong, his security officer Wang Dongxing, and his interpreter and adviser Shi Zhe, he traveled to Moscow to meet Stalin. It was the first face-to-face meeting between the two communist leaders.

The official occasion for Mao's journey was the celebration of Stalin's seventieth birthday on 21 December. But Mao had three problems on his mind. The first was the Sino-Soviet treaty that Stalin had signed with Chiang Kai-shek in 1945 and that the Chinese communist leaders considered obsolete. Mao was wanted the 1945 treaty to be revoked and a new treaty of friendship and alliance to be signed with the Soviet Union. Through such a treaty he hoped to obtain security guarantees against a potential attack by the United States or its clients and Soviet support for economic reconstruction, including trade and credits. The Chinese leadership was by no means sure about Stalin's attitude toward these matters. It had therefore been decided that Zhou would join Mao in Moscow only if Stalin indicated that he was willing to negotiate on these issues.

On the day of his arrival on 16 December, Mao raised the issue of the treaty in his first meeting with Stalin. Stalin was evasive, pointing out that the 1945 treaty had been signed within the framework of the Yalta agreement involving the United States and Great Britain; thus any changes in the treaty could affect positions agreed upon with these two countries.[25] In the following weeks Stalin showed no interest in further talks with Mao. But the Chinese leader—determined to reach an agreement with Stalin—remained in Moscow after the birthday celebrations were over and other delegations had left the Soviet capital. However, he soon became impatient, complaining to the Kremlin's liaison official that "he had nothing to do except eat, sleep and shit."[26] Wang Jiaxiang, the Chinese ambassador to the Soviet Union, tried to exert pressure on the Soviet Foreign Ministry with respect to the treaty. But nothing happened until 2 January, when Vyacheslav Mikhailovich Molotov and Anastas Ivanovich Mikoyan, both members of the Soviet Politburo, appeared at Mao's dacha to inform him that Stalin was ready to talk. Although it was not clear whether Stalin was ready to agree to Chinese conditions, Mao immediately sent a telegram to Beijing asking Zhou to join him in Moscow.[27]

Stalin was willing to negotiate, but it still was not clear on what basis. Only at his meeting with Mao and Zhou on 22 January did he indicate that he was ready to discard the 1945 treaty for a new document. "To hell with the Yalta agreements," he told them.[28] It is not known what brought about this change of mind. It might have been due to a new element in U.S. foreign policy that was to exercise strong influence on the Sino-Soviet talks. The U.S. secretary of state, Dean Acheson, in a speech on developments in Asia on 12 January, had stated that the Soviet Union intended to annex parts of China, a "process that is complete in Outer

Mongolia ... [and] nearly complete in Manchuria." This American attempt to drive a wedge between China and the Soviet Union was perhaps intolerable to Stalin, who aimed to sharpen the divisions between China and the West.

After Zhou arrived in Moscow on 20 January, he became the driving force of the agenda. While Mao distanced himself from the practical deliberations once the general principles governing the treaty had been laid down, Zhou, working with newly appointed the Soviet foreign minister Andrey Yanuaryevich Vyshinski, designed the language of the agreement, mulling over Soviet proposals, making counterproposals and toiling over every detail with his usual thoroughness. The central document, called the Treaty of Friendship, Alliance, and Mutual Assistance, was signed on 14 February. Its basic aim was to "prevent jointly, by strengthening friendship and cooperation, ... the revival of Japanese imperialism and the resumption of aggression on the part of Japan or any other state that may collaborate in any way with Japan in acts of aggression"; "any other state" clearly hinted at the United States.

During the 1940s, the Soviet Union had established a presence in Manchuria. Although it had become an ally, the principle of "cleaning house" would have to apply to it as well, though in this particular case Zhou was ready to compromise. In a separate and secret protocol, he and his Soviet counterpart dealt with the problems of the Chinese Changchun Railroad, of Lushunkou (Port Arthur) and Dalian. The agreement allowed for an extension of Soviet control over Lushun and the Chinese Changchun Railroad until 1952. China would take over the administration of Dalian, which had been given the status of a free port under the Yalta agreements. China was expected to reimburse the Soviet Union for expenses related to reconstructing Lushun after the war. It was also agreed that the Soviet government would transfer to the Chinese government all property acquired from the Japanese without compensation. This, however, was symbolic, since most of the property and equipment captured from the Japanese had already been removed to the Soviet Union. The restitution to the Chinese government of "Cossack Town," near the old Russian embassy in Beijing, was another important element in the policy of "cleaning house." Cossack Town had been built by the Tsarist government and continued to be used as a military compound with extraterritoriality rights held by the Soviet government.[29]

Zhou obtained some agreement from the Soviet leaders on every issue important to him. The treaty finally concluded was undoubtedly one of the most important accords of that time, forging a strategic alliance—directed against the West—between the two communist giants. But on many issues Stalin remained noncommittal. Moreover, the withdrawal of Soviet military forces from Lushun was delayed until 1955 because of the Korean War. Soviet insistence on remaining in Manchuria and Xinjiang and establishing Sino-Soviet companies in Xinjiang—secured in secret additional agreements—must have given Zhou the impression that Stalin wanted to exert some sort of strategic control over these areas. Stalin's actions laid the foundation for fundamental disagreements between China and the Soviet Union, which gradually came to a head in the 1950s.

## The Korean War

Mao's "new democracy," conceived to convert people to his cause and embrace all those who were not openly opposed to the regime, was soon overshadowed by two political movements carried out on a nationwide scale in the early 1950s: land reform and the suppression of "counterrevolutionaries." The suppression of "counterrevolutionaries" was a far cry from the tolerance that the new regime had professed to practice. It suspected that more than two million people still adhered to the premises of the old society. As such, they were viewed as "political bandits, local tyrants, enemy agents, backbone members of reactionary parties, heads of secret societies" and other "counterrevolutionary" groups considered hostile to the new government and suspected of sabotage. The task of ferreting them out was left to local authorities, a policy that left ample room for waging personal vendettas. By the fall of 1953, half a million people had been imprisoned on such charges and about the same number had been executed. Land reform, aimed at eliminating the landlord class and redistributing land among the peasants, was implemented on a massive scale in the newly liberated areas and involved more than three hundred million people. Liu Shaoqi directed the program from the center. To these movements was added a third: the campaign to resist U.S. aggression and aid Korea in the Korean War, a war that was to become Zhou's major concern during that period.

The Chinese government and military, although aware that the North Korean leader Kim Il Sung was making preparations for the invasion of the south, had not been informed of Kim's precise intentions and the timing of his attack. In Moscow in April 1950, Kim secured Stalin's support for his policy to unify Korea under his authority. Although Stalin saw great strategic advantages in the unification of the Korean peninsula under a communist regime, he refused to become directly involved in the scheme. Instead, he advised Kim to enlist Chinese aid for his plan. During talks in May 1950 in Beijing, Mao endorsed Kim's plan. He could not have done otherwise since he had just achieved his own goal of reuniting China and wanted to draw Tibet and Taiwan into the realm of the People's Republic.

When the Korean War broke out on 25 June 1950, Zhou was in the process of implementing a Central Committee decision to demobilize half of the PLA forces of 5.6 million. Since he did not foresee direct involvement in the war, Zhou continued with the demobilization plan. But he insisted on maintaining closer contact with the North Korean authorities by establishing Chinese representation in the North Korean capital of Pyongyang. For this delicate mission, he chose Chai Chengwen, an intelligence officer of the general chief of staff, who was considered an expert on the military situation on the Korean peninsula.[30]

While the North Korean People's Army was fast advancing on South Korean territory, Kim, exhilarated by his success, was planning to end the war in August. Mao and Zhou were more cautious. In their talk with Kim in May, they had warned him about a possible U.S. intervention on behalf of South Korea, an admonition Kim refused to take seriously.[31] They proved to have been right. Contrary to Kim's expectations, the reaction of the Truman administration was swift and efficient. First, in the absence of the Soviet delegation at the UN Security Council, the U.S. government pushed through a resolution condemning the aggression. Second, on 27 June, the Truman administration ordered air and naval support for South Korea. Third, on 7 July, the Security Council adopted a resolution to constitute unified military forces under the auspices of the United Nations and under the command of General Douglas MacArthur. Fourth, the U.S. Seventh Fleet was ordered to "neutralize" the Taiwan strait by cruising in its waters and thus blocking any Chinese attempt to invade Taiwan. Zhou Enlai, in a statement delivered on 28 June, criticized the United Nations and the American initiatives as an "armed aggression on Chinese territory."[32]

In view of the U.S. military presence in the area, Zhou had growing doubts that the war would end as quickly as Kim expected. He was expected a protracted war, even though the North Korean troops had penetrated deeply into the south. In his opinion, the U.S. commitment to South Korea had tilted the odds. On 2 July Zhou called N.V. Roshchin, the Soviet ambassador, to Zhongnanhai. He was concerned about the indifference with which the North Koreans had discarded Mao's warning about a likely U.S. intervention, he told the ambassador. He also informed him that China was ready to deploy nine divisions on the border between China and Korea. If U.S. troops crossed the Thirty-eighth Parallel dividing northern and southern Korea, Chinese troops might have to enter North Korean territory, he said. In that case, China hoped that the Soviet government would provide air cover for the Chinese troops.

Stalin endorsed the Chinese plan to reinforce its armed forces along the Yalu river and promised to provide them with air cover whenever needed. The Soviet air division stationed near Shanghai could be used for that purpose. Stalin suggested that if needed, he would be able to provide more aircraft. In July, Zhou ordered the deployment of 260,000 men along the Yalu river, thus establishing the Northeastern Frontier Guards under the command of Gao Gang. To prepare for eventual military activities in Korea, Zhou ordered Chai Chengwen to conduct a topographic survey of the Korean peninsula. In late July, the Korean People's Army (KPA) reached the Naktong river pushing the U.S. and South Korean troops toward Pusan. Kim Il Sung was so pleased that he broadcast a speech threatening that, by the end of August, the U.S. troops would be forced into the sea.[33]

While the North Korean forces were engaged at the southern tip of the peninsula, Lei Yingfu, Zhou's military adviser and deputy director of the Central Military Commission's Operations Department, analyzed the military situation in Korea. He drew attention to some danger signals. First, thirteen U.S. and South Korean divisions—entrenched in a triangle close to the Naktong river—were trying to pin down the KPA there. Second, the KPA had moved so far into the south that its supply lines stretched out for 400 to 500 kilometers. Interruption of these lines would deal a fatal blow to the KPA. Third, the United States was stationing forces in Japan that would be ready to intervene at short notice. Large numbers of British and American warships were converging in the Sea of Japan. Fourth, studies of the topography of the peninsula disclosed ideal terrain for landing operations, an opportunity that General MacArthur, known for his formidable military skills, would certainly not let pass, since he had absolute air control. Lei concluded that MacArthur would be planning to land to the rear of the North Korean army. Although MacArthur had several options, Lei said, it was most likely that he would land at Inchon was the greatest, because it was the best site for cutting off the KPA's strategic link with supply lines from the north and encircling North Korean troops. Convinced by Lei's reasoning, Zhou insisted that he present his arguments to Mao, who also was immediately persuaded by the logic of Lei's analysis. They decided to hasten the deployment of the Northeastern Frontier Force (NFF) along the Yalu river and to notify the Soviet and the North Korean leaders about the possibility that U.S. naval forces might land to the rear of the KPA.[34]

Zhou watched the turn of events and their implications for China with growing concern. In a speech on national defense on 26 August, he pointed out that the chances for a quick North Korean victory were diminishing, while the likelihood that U.S. forces would land at Inchon was becoming greater. Since he no longer excluded the possibility that China might have to fight a war against the United States in Korea, he issued instructions to the general chief of staff to prepare for such an eventuality. The NFF was reinforced by several army units.[35]

Zhou was greatly concerned about the difficulties that Chinese troops would face if they entered Korea. Chai Chengwen, whom he recalled to Beijing in September, confirmed his worst fears. "The biggest problems," according to Chai, "will be caused by inadequate means of transportation. Rail transport is not secure. Highways are in bad shape and too narrow. Moreover, it will be impossible [for our troops] to acquire local supplies because food or munitions are not available. Nor can we seize enough from the enemy to sustain large-scale operations."[36]

The question of whether China should become involved militarily on Korean territory became a major topic of discussion at the Politburo. The Chinese leaders were concerned that an American victory on the Korean peninsula would seriously threaten China's security. But Mao cautioned against any open Chinese military intervention to confront the United States, proposing that China should assist Korea by sending volunteers. Zhou echoed Mao's views, saying that the American imperialists would become unscrupulous if they succeeded in their military mission in Korea. The problem should be approached from the long-term point of view, Zhou said. If Kim was to achieve victory, "the weight of China must be thrown into the balance."[37] On 26 August, Zhou, striving to be prepared for any contingency, met with the commanders of the Northeast Frontier Force (NFF) to discuss possible military intervention in Korea.

While reinforcements were proceeding toward the Korean border, Party leaders in Beijing continued to discuss whether China should get involved in a military confrontation with the United States. Lin Biao, the commander of the famous Fourth Field Army, who had many military accomplishments to his credit, expressed anxiety about possible devastation if the "imperialists" used atomic weapons against Korea or China. Others held the view that the PLA and the country needed a period of rest to recuperate from the long years of fighting. Nie Rongzhen recalls that Mao, too, had been pondering the question "to fight or not to fight … for a long time and from different angles."[38]

As the Chinese strategists had predicted, MacArthur's troops landed at Inchon. On 15 September, seventy thousand troops under the UN flag disembarked from more than 260 ships to begin a massive amphibious landing on Inchon's beaches. They met no resistance. On 18 September, Stalin dispatched General M.V. Zakharov to Korea to order Kim Il Sung to halt the offensive along the Pusan perimeter and to redeploy his forces to defend Seoul. He also directed Ambassador Roshchin to solicit the Chinese government's views on the situation. Zhou Enlai, who met the Soviet ambassador that day, advised him that communications with the North Korean government were very poor regarding military matters and the Chinese government was totally ignorant of the KPA's operational plans. As for Roshchin's question about the course of action the KPA should take, Zhou suggested that the North Koreans, if they had reserves of about a hundred thousand men, should use them to eliminate the enemy's forces at Inchon. If they lacked such forces, they should withdraw to the north.[39]

On 25 September, Seoul fell back into South Korean hands. Air raids caused heavy losses to the KPA, destroying most of its tanks and much of its artillery. Troops in the south, instead of retreating to the north, rapidly disintegrated, leaving Pyongyang vulnerable. On 27 September, Stalin convened an emergency session of the Politburo, where he condemned the incompetence of the KPA command and held the Soviet military advisers responsible for all these blunders.

On 29 September, General MacArthur restored the government of the Republic of Korea under Syngman Rhee. The Chinese leadership, albeit prepared for the American strategy, was taken aback by the speedy reversal. On 30 September, Zhou Enlai issued a warning to the United States, declaring that "the Chinese people will not tolerate foreign aggression, nor will they supinely tolerate seeing their neighbors being savagely invaded by imperialists."[40] Through the Chinese envoy to Pyongyang, he advised Kim on how to react to the American encirclement that had trapped eight North Korean divisions. His counsel was reminiscent of his own military experiences in which relatively weak forces had engaged against a superior enemy. Four divisions, according to Zhou, should destroy all their heavy weapons and split into many small detachments. This should enable them to slip through the enemy lines to an area north of the Thirty-eighth Parallel. The other four detachments should also divide up and remain in the south to fight a guerrilla war. If they did so, he said, "there will still be hope for victory."[41]

October 1, the first anniversary of the founding of the People's Republic of China, marked a turning point in the war. On that day, South Korean troops, with the backing of the United States, crossed the Thirty-eighth Parallel. MacArthur made a statement demanded the KPA's unconditional surrender. The Soviet ambassador forwarded a telegram from Stalin to Mao and Zhou asking them to send five to six divisions to the Thirty-eighth Parallel to help the North Koreans to build up their reserves. Kim Il Sung sent frantic appeals to Mao to request the intervention of the NFF. In the meantime, Stalin had made it clear to the Chinese leadership that he would not intervene. His major concern was avoiding a direct military confrontation with the United States. The CCP leaders met again to discuss the situation. Mao's major preoccupation was national security. In his view, the intervention was necessary to stop the United States from gaining a stronghold in the area. At the meeting, Zhou reported the superior military equipment of the U.S. army on the ground but especially in the air, where the United State had completely total control. In spite of this, Mao believed that China should enter the war, bringing into play the abundance of its manpower and its advantageous logistical position. He was convinced that the Chinese forces could confront the South Korean army and even the U.S. troops if the gaps in equipment and air force could be filled by the Soviet Union.

On 2 October, while the people were still celebrating the People's Republic's first National Day, China's leaders were holding emergency meetings at Zhongnanhai to continue the debate on whether to send Chinese troops to Korea. There was considerable hesitation among the leadership, including the military, on confronting the United States in Korea. The meetings did not reach a final decision on that day. In response to Stalin's request on 1 October to send troops to Korea, Mao told Stalin through the Soviet envoy:

> We originally planned to move several volunteer divisions to North Korea to render assistance to the Korean comrades when the enemy advanced north of the Thirty-eighth Parallel. However, having thought this over thoroughly, we

now consider that such actions may entail extremely serious consequences. In the first place, it is very difficult to solve the Korean question with a few divisions.... In the second place, it is most likely that this will provoke an open conflict between the United States and China, as a consequence of which the Soviet Union can also be dragged into the war, and the question would thus become extremely large.[42]

This wording represented the majority view of the Politburo and the Central Military Commission, but not that of Mao. At that time Mao, although still officially seeking consensus among the leadership, refused to budge after he had formed his own opinion. He thus added to the telegram that the final decision of the Politburo was still pending. Further discussions would clarify the issue. Thus, he left the door open to intervention.

On the heels of the South Korean troops, the U.S. Army was also approaching the Thirty-eighth Parallel. Zhou Enlai, alarmed by these developments, summoned K.M. Pannikar, the Indian ambassador to China, to his office in the early hours of 3 October, asking him to transmit a message to the United States. The somewhat cryptic message was that "we would take matters into our hands" ("*women yao guan*") if U.S. troops crossed the Thirty-eighth Parallel.[43] This could be understood to imply that, in such an event, China would intervene in Korea.

The Politburo discussed the issue further on 4 and 5 October. Some members continued to voice reservations, if not outright opposition, to China's interference in the war, arguing that the enormous tasks of reconstruction and reform in China required vast resources and the energetic attention of the people at all levels. They also stressed the lack of adequate equipment for the Chinese troops. But Mao remained unshaken in his assessment that there was no other way. "Your arguments are based on good reasons," he said. "But all the same, once another socialist nation is in a crisis, we would feel bad if we stood idly by."[44]

Zhou Enlai was one of the few firm supporters of Mao's position. Others, for example, Lin Biao, had serious reservations about engaging China in such an uncertain venture at that time. He refused Mao's offer to direct military operations in Korea, pleading bad health. This prompted Mao to call Peng Dehuai to Beijing to hear his views. Peng, whose prestige as a military leader matched that of Lin Biao, arrived from northwestern China on the afternoon of the fourth, in time to listen to the debates. After weighing the pros and cons of the argument overnight, he came out in Mao's defense the following day. Mao's single-minded determination and Peng's firm endorsement of Mao's position changed the atmosphere of the meeting, which finally agreed to the intervention. The following day, Zhou began to make organizational arrangements with the Military Commission. Now, he said, the question was no longer whether China should fight a war in Korea, but that the United States was forcing it to fight. It had become a matter of self-defense. He also stressed that China could not refuse assistance to the Korean government and to its leader, Kim Il Sung, who had repeatedly requested it.

But China could not go it alone. To enlist Stalin's support in the war effort, Zhou traveled to Stalin's summer resort on the Black Sea on 10 October to brief Stalin on the CCP Politburo's discussions. Beijing would face enormous difficulty in intervening in Korea, he told Stalin. An intervention would be possible only if the Soviet Union provided air cover as well as military equipment and ammunition for the Chinese troops. Stalin's response was two-pronged. He said he was ready to provide the Chinese army with military equipment and weapons but could not deliver air cover because the Soviet air force needed two to three months to prepare for such operations. If Beijing had difficulty in sending troops to North Korea, Stalin said, then it should not send them. Socialist countries will not perish, he continued. China would not perish if North Korea were lost.[45]

Zhou reported his conversation with Stalin to Mao the same day. On 13 October, an emergency meeting of the Politburo, which again discussed the issue, was held in Beijing. Later that day Zhou received a cable from Mao informing him that "the Politburo had come to the unanimous conclusion that it is in our interest to send our army to Korea." Notwithstanding Stalin's refusal to provide air support, Mao had made his final decision with the Politburo's agreement.[46] The cable instructed Zhou to transmit this information to Stalin. In his next meeting with Zhou, Stalin informed him that the Soviet government would be willing to supply military equipment only on a credit basis. He planned to send a total of sixteen air force regiments to China, but they would be allowed to operate exclusively on Chinese territory north of the Yalu river, not to cover the operations of the Chinese volunteers in Korea. It was not clear when the Soviet air force would be available. The Soviet promise to provide air cover for Chinese operations in Korea had taken on a quite different meaning and was far from Chinese expectations. Stalin's strategic objective was to counterbalance the United States in Korea—if possible through the Chinese—but not to confront it directly. Not only did he want the Chinese to do his dirty work, but he had no intention of bearing any of the costs of operations. But only after the Chinese leadership was already committed to the defense of North Korea did Stalin make it clear that he expected repayment of all military and other assistance that he rendered to the Chinese war effort.

Immediately upon his return to Beijing on 18 October, Zhou met with Mao, Peng Dehuai, and Gao Gang. They ordered two hundred thousand Chinese troops to cross the Yalu river under the cover of darkness the following night. Up to this point the entire debate had taken place in the utmost secrecy and at the top leadership level—now the entire country had to be informed. Speaking before the Standing Committee of the CPPCC, Zhou explained the reasons for China's entry into the Korean War. He argued that the security of northeastern China, where half the country's heavy industry was located, would be jeopardized if the United States subjugated North Korea. The area would not be assured of its normal development if it remained within the range of American bombers. He pointed out that it would be in China's immediate interest to enter the battle in North Korea itself, rather than establish a defense perimeter against an American military threat in the area. Such a defense would require the renovation of at least eight airfields, the stationing of a large number of frontier guards along the 500-kilometer-long border and the relocation inland of several key industries.[47] To rally popular support for the intervention in Korea, the CCP launched a nationwide propaganda campaign to "resist American aggression and aid Korea."

After consultation with Stalin, Mao, on 13 November, appointed Zhou general commander of the Chinese forces in Korea. Kim Il Sung, Peng Dehuai, and Gao Gang were informed after Stalin had expressed his agreement. With Mao in charge of general strategy, Zhou as overall commander and coordinator and Peng as field commander, the three acted as a team as they had done in 1947 and 1948 during the war against the GMD in northern Shaanxi, using the same operational methods. Zhou became the nexus of military operations, and all communications passed through his office. It was his responsibility to refer issues to Mao if he believed that they required Mao's personal attention. He handled all problems of "secondary" importance so that Mao could concentrate on the most critical issues. Mao signed cables that Zhou considered of prime importance. Those drafted by Zhou were delivered in the name of the Central Military Commission.[48]

Under the name of "Chinese People's Volunteers to fight the United

States and its lackey Syngman Rhee" (CPV), the Chinese armies crossed the Yalu river on 25 October. General MacArthur's goal was to end the war by Thanksgiving Day, an objective that seemed within reach because his troops were fast approaching the Yalu river. In the first encounter between the Chinese volunteers and the Korean forces, Peng Dehuai, in a vigorous campaign, pushed the South Korean army back to the south of the Yalu river. Between 24 November and 24 December, the CPV confronted U.S. troops and succeeded in recovering the entire area north of the Thirty-eighth Parallel. MacArthur, who had extended his goal to ending the war by Christmas, had to change his timing again. Between 31 December and 8 January, a third campaign allowed the CPV to cross the Thirty-eighth Parallel. A poor and weak country that had been the victim of foreign aggression for more than a hundred years had been able to push back the troops of the most powerful country in the world from the Yalu river to the Thirty-eighth Parallel: The victory was celebrated with pride.

The battle had been won at a very heavy price. The Chinese armies encountered enormous problems in their confrontations with the UN forces, which enjoyed far superior firepower. Though superior in numbers, the Chinese troops had to cope with deficient military equipment and serious logistical problems. Their communication and supply lines stretched over long distances within northeastern China and within Korea from the Yalu river to the Thirty-eighth Parallel. They were constantly threatened by U.S. air defenses and bombing. The situation became so critical that, in November 1951, Zhou called a logistics conference at Shenyang, the headquarters of the Northeast Military Region. At the meeting it was decided to accelerate the construction of railways and airfields in the area, to provide a larger number of trucks to the army, and to improve air defenses by any means available, but these measures did not address the problems.

In the months that followed, Peng Dehuai went to Beijing several times to brief Mao and Zhou about the heavy casualties suffered by the troops and the increasing difficulty in keeping the front lines supplied with basic necessities. Peng was convinced that the war would be long and drawn out and that no easy victory was in sight. Under the circumstances, the outcome would depend heavily on proper solutions to logistical problems. On 24 February 1952, the Central Military Commission, presided over by Zhou, discussed these problems with representatives from various government departments involved in the war effort. All of them emphasized their difficulty in meeting the demands of the war. Their complaints did not convince Peng, who, in an angry outburst, shouted: "You have this and that problem.... You should go to the front and see with your own eyes what food and clothing the soldiers have! Not to speak of the casualties! For what are they giving their lives? We have no aircraft. We have only a few guns. Transports are not protected. More and more soldiers are dying of starvation. Can't you overcome some of your difficulties?" The atmosphere at the conference became so tense that Zhou was forced to adjourn it. Subsequently, Zhou called a series of meetings, where it was decided to divide the PLA into three groups, to be dispatched to Korea in shifts; to accelerate the training of Chinese pilots; to provide more anti-aircraft guns to the army at the front lines; to buy more military equipment and ammunition from the Soviet Union; to provide the army with more food and clothing; and to transfer the responsibility for supplies from the Northeast Administrative Area to the central government.[49]

On 1 March 1951, in a cable to Stalin, Mao emphasized the difficulties of the Chinese forces in Korea and the urgent need for air cover of the supply lines. Apparently impressed by the Chinese efforts in Korea, he finally promised to provide two air force and three anti-aircraft divisions, as well as six thousand trucks. Even this did not solve the acute logistical problems created by the sheer number of Chinese troops in Korea, which, by April, had totaled more than a million. In late April, Peng sent his deputy, Hong Xuezhi, to Beijing to report to Zhou about the situation. What his soldiers feared, he said, was not the enemy, but that they had nothing to eat, no bullets to shoot, and no trucks to transport them to the rear when they were wounded. Zhou replied that the Soviet air force, despite Stalin's promises, had not yet arrived, but that more anti-aircraft guns would be made available. At the same time a massive training program for air defense was carried out within the entire army, which allowed the Chinese air force to take part in the war from September onward.

Between 22 April and 1 June, another campaign was fought between the Chinese and the U.S. forces, ending in a stalemate at the Thirty-eighth Parallel. The two sides agreed to negotiate an armistice on the basis of the status quo on the battlefield. On the Chinese side, Zhou directed the truce talks, which began on 10 July 1951. Li Kenong, Zhou's long-standing collaborator in the secret services, and Qiao Guanghua, who became foreign minister in the 1970s, headed the negotiation team. A group of experts from the Foreign Ministry and the Xinhua News Agency assisted them. Behind the scenes, Mao and Zhou issued instructions on all important issues as they did on military matters. The negotiations staggered on for two years. While the talks proceeded, several major military campaigns were fought, but neither side made any significant breakthrough. In November 1952 a new president was elected in the United States, Dwight D. Eisenhower, and he was wary of the war. So was the Soviet leadership after Stalin's death in March 1953, not to mention the Chinese leadership, which was simultaneously coping with a problematic national reconstruction effort and social reforms. Finally, in July 1953, a ceasefire was signed at Panmunjom.[50]

The decision to enter the Korean War was made at a moment of uncertainty and risk. China was militarily confronting the most powerful country in the world at a time when it had not yet consolidated its own new regime and when the leadership was divided about the issue of entering the war. But Mao was ready to take great risks because he believed that a confrontation between the United States and China had become inevitable after the U.S. Army stepped onto Korean territory and began marching toward the Yalu river. And he decided to enter the war not to save North Korea or to please the Soviet Union, but to save China. A second motive that Mao mentioned several times in later years was his desire to demonstrate to Stalin his spirit of internationalism. Mao believed that Stalin regarded him as a nationalist, as another Tito (Marshal Tito, the leader of Yugoslavia), and that Stalin's perception of him changed only after the CPV entered the Korean War. This act, Mao thought, proved to Stalin that the CCP was a truly Marxist party.[51]

China emerged from the Korean War more united than before by national pride, despite the war's enormous cost. The Chinese people were made to believe that aggression was initiated by the United States and South Korea, not by the fraternal communist state to the north. After having been humiliated by Western powers and Japan for more than a century, China had proved to the world that it could stand up militarily to the strongest power in the world. The Chinese army, although poorly equipped, had forced it into retreat and provoked a military stalemate. Mao, Zhou, and Peng Dehuai had shown themselves to be great leaders. In counterpoint to the triumphant sentiments strongly encouraged by official propaganda, the Korean War had some negative ramifications for China. One direct consequence was the consolidation of Chiang Kai-shek's regime on Taiwan and its security guarantee by the United States.

A second was the tremendous cost of the war for a country still recovering from years of civil strife.

The Korean War was Zhou Enlai's last military assignment. He had been in charge of the Central Military Commission since 1947. In July 1952, Peng Dehuai succeeded him in managing the day-to-day business of the commission. After the eighth Party congress, in 1956, Zhou focused increasingly on the work of the Standing Committee and the State Council and on foreign affairs, relinquishing his post as vice chairman of the Central Military Commission.

## Upswing in Foreign Policy

A major consequence of the Chinese intervention in Korea was further isolation. Condemned by the United Nations as an aggressor, unable to obtain Taiwan's seat in that organization, and diplomatically cut off from the majority of UN member states, Beijing's image outside its borders was negative. The United States was in a process to actively pursue its policy of containing communist states by forging military alliances with countries surrounding them. The problem was compounded by the CCP's policy of supporting revolutionary movements in Asian countries with large ethnic Chinese populations. Oppressive domestic policies tarnished China's image even further.

Zhou Enlai was increasingly concerned about China's isolation, the negative perception the outside world held of his country, and the American efforts to surround China with military bases. The realization of the ambitious plans for economic reconstruction, in his view, required a "peaceful international environment" and improvement in China's image abroad. This required the formulation of a new foreign policy framework, away from exclusive orientation toward the Soviet Union and the communist bloc. Central to this framework, which Zhou outlined in the early 1950s, was the formation of an anti-imperialist and anti-colonial united front of Third World countries. These countries, which were not aligned with either superpower, could counterbalance them both. Zhou's most significant foreign policy initiative was the promotion of the Five Principles of Peaceful Coexistence, based on the concept that countries with different social systems could live side by side peaceably. More important than their social systems was a joint effort internationally—in which China, as a developing country, would also take part—to combat imperialism and foreign intervention in the Third World. His approach to the Third World was highly pragmatic and guided by geopolitical rather than ideological considerations. In his quest for China's security and international prestige, he sought to develop a sense of common interests and solidarity. Flexibility, negotiation, and personal diplomacy were the tools that Zhou employed to achieve his goals. His first target was China's immediate neighborhood, where he wanted to decrease tensions. The peace agreements concerning Korea had to be consolidated, and Indochina, where France and the Vietcong militarily supported by Beijing—were at odds, had to be pacified. The Soviet government supported Zhou's endeavors by proposing to France, Great Britain, and the United States the convocation of a meeting, which China would attend, on Indochina and Korea.[52]

## The Geneva Conference

Attending the Geneva conference gave Zhou Enlai his first significant exposure to the world outside China as the prime minister. He took great care to prepare thoroughly for the confrontations with the world powers. Drawing on Soviet experience in world politics, he discussed the relevant issues with the Khrushchev and Molotov on three visits to Moscow. He took with him a staff of about two hundred, so that they could gain experience in international affairs and diplomatic negotiations at the conference. Although Zhou made it a point of insisting on a modest life-style at home, he took up residence at Grand Mont-Fleury, an estate in Versoix, a small town seven kilometers outside Geneva. He had priceless furnishings and antiques shipped from China to add the already stately rooms where Zhou entertained statesmen, diplomats, and prestigious guests with Chinese banquets. A newcomer to the non-communist world, Zhou was observed closely by the Western press, which was soon taken with his elegant manners and his eloquence. In negotiations, however, his counterparts found in him a tough but not intransigent negotiator, adept at the art of conciliation.

The Geneva conference to resolve, among other matters, the Korean question began on 26 April 1954. Zhou had arrived at the conference fully aware that there could be no agreement on Korea—a position he had already laid down before his departure in a memorandum to the CCP Central Committee. The gap between the positions of the United States and China was indeed so wide that, even after fifteen meetings between late April and the middle of June, the stalemate could not be broken. Zhou

Enlai's principal antagonist at the conference was U.S. secretary of state John Foster Dulles, and the principal issue separating them was that China refused to recognize the United Nations as an agency of collective security in Korea as long as its seat was occupied by Taiwan. While Zhou was in favor of a commission of neutral countries to supervise elections in Korea, U.S. foreign policy was focused on support of Taiwan and South Korea and building military alliances against the communists. The relationship between Zhou and Dulles was by no means pleasant, either officially or personally; neither would budge an inch on the Korean problem. Even so, Zhou did not expect Dulles to refuse to shake his outstretched hand. His rude and condescending behavior would rankle for decades afterward. Wang Bingnan, the general secretary of the Chinese delegation, denied that the encounter between Zhou and Dulles had even taken place.

Negotiations on the Indochina question, which began on 8 May, were equally complicated but, in the end, more fruitful. On this issue, Zhou's objective was to counter U.S. intervention in the area, and thus the internationalization of the Indochina conflict, with the formation of a "Southeast Asian military bloc" that would use Asians to fight Asians."[53] Zhou employed all his diplomatic talents and flexibility at the conference, playing the United States, Great Britain, and France against one another. Believing that because the United States had its own strategic interests in Southeast Asia it was not interested in finding solutions at the Geneva conference, he tried to establish contacts with England and France to "open new ways for solving international disputes through big power consultation."[54]

The British government was not particularly anxious to be drawn into a multinational military alliance in Asia. Knowing this, Zhou used every opportunity at the conference to improve bilateral relations with the British. Diplomatic relations were established at the level of chargé d'affaires, and policies were decided that improved trade relations. Clearly, Zhou and the Chinese delegates left a favorable impression on the British. Sir Anthony Eden, the British representative, wrote in his memoirs: "Zhou is poised and firm in negotiations. He works for the fine points, even by the standard of his country."[55] According to Humphrey Trevelyan, the British representative in Beijing, discussions with the Chinese took place at several levels and were relaxed, pleasant, and friendly.[56]

Before the conference, Zhou, Ho Chi Minh, the leader of the communist movement in Vietnam, and Khrushchev had agreed on a common position: that a truce between the Vietcong and France was desirable and that the Sixteenth Parallel should be used as the border to demark the areas respectively controlled by northern and southern Vietnam.

The day before the negotiations on Indochina were scheduled to begin, news reached Geneva that Vietcong troops—commanded by the Chinese general Wei Guoqing and with the support of Chinese artillery—in a vigorous battle against the French colonial troops had taken over the city of Dien Bien Phu. This victory, ironically, caused sharp differences to surface between the Chinese and Vietnamese communists who had cooperated on the battlefield. Pham Van Dong, the premier of the north Vietnamese regime and its chief delegate to the conference, reconsidered the concept of a demarcation line and contemplated the possibility of an immediate ceasefire with some minor adjustments that would allow the Vietcong to keep the areas that it controlled in the south. He placed his hopes on a general election, which, in his view, would finally settle the Vietnam problem He also hoped for a solution that would consolidate north Vietnamese military positions in Laos and Cambodia.

Zhou, however, continued to prefer a demarcation line between the north and the south. He argued that an immediate ceasefire would exclude from north Vietnamese territory the rich Red river delta and such important cities as Hanoi and Haiphong. He also was not convinced that the Western powers would agree to general elections. Moreover, the French defeat and the Vietcong military presence in Laos and Cambodia increased his concern about possible U.S. involvement in South Vietnam. He was therefore ready to search for compromise on these matters.

When, at the end of May, the conference turned to the issue of Laos and Cambodia, the Vietcong refused to admit its military presence in those countries, thus creating an immediate deadlock. It was expected that the negotiations would break down completely on 16 June. On the evening before, Zhou, Molotov, and Pham Van Dong discussed the situation once more. Zhou emphasized the importance of reaching an agreement with France and thereby preventing U.S. involvement in Indochina. He pointed out that the refusal of northern Vietnam to admit the existence of its forces in Lao and Cambodia would lead not only to a total breakdown of negotiations on these countries but also to the failure of the Geneva conference as a whole, thus ruling out a solution to the Vietnam problem. Molotov strongly supported Zhou's suggestion that Vietcong forces should withdraw from these countries. Under heavy pressure from China and the Soviet Union, Pham Van Dong finally agreed that Zhou should act as the mediator between Vietnam and the Western governments.

While the conference adjourned for three weeks beginning in late June, Zhou left Geneva for India and Burma, though his major preoccupation was to meet Ho Chi Minh to iron things out concerning the strategy to follow in Indochina. When the two leaders met from 3 to 5 July in Liuzhou, southern China, Zhou reiterated the dangers of an U.S. intervention in Vietnam and the advantages of coming to terms with the French, who, Zhou believed, were under heavy domestic pressure to end the war. The two men reached a consensus on their position for the next phase of the conference: They would accept a ceasefire in Vietnam based on a "temporary" division of the country in two at the Sixteenth Parallel. Zhou told Ho that, after French troops withdrew, it would take no more that two years before all of Vietnam would fall under Vietcong rule. On the Cambodia question, Zhou and Ho agreed to find a political settlement, and on the Laos problem they were willing to accept the designation of an area near the border with Vietnam, where pro-communist Laotian forces would be allowed to remain.[57]

The final stages of the conference were clearly marked by Zhou's diplomacy. After his return to Geneva on 12 July, he visited the newly elected French prime minister, Pierre Mendès-France, to find out about France's intentions in Indochina. The discussions, dominated by Zhou, confirmed his impression that the French government was ready to withdraw from Indochina and was concerned about the negotiation deadlock with Vietnam. When Mendès France inquired about Ho Chi Minh's current thinking on the matter, Zhou said: "Each side would need to step toward the other.... Which is not to say that each has an equal number of steps to make."[58] He agreed to intervene again with the north Vietnamese to speed things up. In another effort to find a compromise, Zhou insisted that north Vietnam accept the French proposal to use the Seventeenth Parallel as the demarcation line between north and south Vietnam. In his view this would be a small price to pay for the withdrawal of the French troops. On 16 July, he informed the conference that the Vietminh would accept partition at the Seventeenth Parallel. The first Indochina conflict ended with the signing of an agreement on 21 July.

Ultimately Zhou's diplomacy at the Geneva conference did not halt the U.S. move toward a collective security system in Asia. Considering the Geneva results "catastrophic," Washington and its allies, on 8 September, founded the South-East Asian Treaty Organization (SEATO) in Manila. This was followed by a mutual defense treaty with Chiang Kai-shek, signed in Washington on 2 December, which Zhou immediately condemned as a "treaty of naked aggression."[59] Two years later, the second Indochina war broke out—which lasted until the mid-1970s.

## The Kashmir Princess Incident

As China' premier, Zhou was asked to represent China at the Afro-Asian conference at the Afro-Asian conference held in Bandung, Indonesia, in April 1955. The conference was in some measure overshadowed by an attempt on Zhou's life as he traveled to the site of the conference. The Chinese government had chartered an Air India passenger plane, called the Kashmir Princess, to transport the delegation from Hong Kong to Jakarta on 11 April. En route the plane crashed into the sea, killing all eleven passengers on board. Only three crewmembers survived. Because he (and other high-level members of the delegation, including Vice-Premier Chen Yi) was not on board, Zhou was not among the victims.

The crash was not accidental, but deliberately caused in an attempt to assassinate Zhou Enlai. A GMD intelligence organization operating in Hong Kong had sabotaged the plane. There appears to be little doubt that Zhou had been aware of the plot beforehand; his own intelligence operating in Hong Kong had been able to warn him in time. Those who perished were low-level cadres, mainly journalists (one each from North Vietnam, Poland, and Austria). Why did Zhou decline to act to prevent the crash? He could have cancelled the flight or chosen a different route. But in his estimation the lives of the victims were dispensable, so he used them as bait to alert the British authorities to the operations of GMD intelligence in Hong Kong; the British, he believed, would then be motivated to use their power to disable it. Immediately after the crash, Zhou told the British authorities that they could count on his support in their investigations, if they were willing to cooperate in the destruction of the espionage network. Politically, this would improve relations between Great Britain and China, building on the progress made in Geneva.[60]

Representatives of twenty-nine Asian and African countries attended the conference. Most of those countries had no diplomatic relations with China, and many of them, aware of Chinese support for worldwide revolutionary movements, harbored suspicions about Beijing's policies. In Zhou's view, the conference offered an ideal opportunity for dispelling those fears, declaring China's peaceful intentions to the world, especially to neighboring countries, reducing China's isolation, and expanding its diplomatic, economic, and cultural exchanges.

However, the conference did not unfold as he had hoped. Convened to find common ground against Western colonialism and imperialism, the conference threatened to turn into an attack on communism when the Iraqi delegate declared that communism as one of the three forces threatening world peace—the two other being "old colonialism" and "Jewish imperialism." He claimed that "colonialism of a new type has been bred by communist parties." Other speakers picked up the thread. The prime minister of Pakistan stated that, while the old colonialism was on the wane, newly independent countries in Africa and Asia should be careful not to open their doors to a new kind of imperialism that promoted itself as a movement of emancipation but was, in fact, more vicious. The foreign minister of the Philippines praised the good intentions of the United States in his speech and attacked the submission of certain countries to other big powers (meaning the Soviet Union) where only one party was allowed to rule. This was a rebirth of the worst features of old colonialism, in which freedom was only a phantom. The prince of Thailand made a frontal attack on China. He expressed his concern about three things that he believed threatened the stability of his country: 1. that the Chinese government was organizing ethnic Thais in Yunnan province, on Thailand's northern border, to win them over to communism; 2. that there were 3 million ethnic Chinese in Thailand with dual citizenship whose loyalty to Thailand was questionable, and 500,000 Vietnamese in northeastern Thailand, who also could not be trusted; 3. that Vietcong troops had approached the Thai border twice in the previous two years on their way to Laos. These three elements were threatening the stability of his country. In addition, several pro-Western delegates, such as Turkey, defended their alliance with the United States.[61]

Zhou Enlai could not let the remarks critical of China go unanswered, but he feared intensifying the existing apprehension, distrust, and hostility toward China. Such a development would prevent the conference from achieving anything substantive and cause it to end in controversy, neither of which was in China's interest. All eyes were on Zhou and how he responded, because most delegates realized that the outcome of the conference was at stake. Zhou was scheduled to speak a few hours later during the same day. Concluding that the speech he had prepared would not meet the needs of the situation, he decided to distribute it rather than deliver it. Over lunch he quickly scribbled a new statement to answer to the charges of a communist threat that had been raised. When he mounted the rostrum to address the conference, he neither dodged nor counterattacked previous speakers but, instead, declared: "The Chinese delegation has come for the purpose of seeking unity, not of picking quarrels." Sidestepping frontal attacks from pro-Western delegates who condemned communist imperialism, he said, "We Communists never disclaim our belief in communism nor do we deny that socialism is a good system. Nevertheless there is no point for anyone to delve upon one's ideology or political system, since such differences do exist among us." And he announced that the Chinese delegation was in Bandung to "seek common ground while reserving differences" (*quitong cunyi*), a strategy that was to become the practical foundation of the Five Principles of Peaceful Coexistence. He believed there was a basis for finding a community of views "because most of the countries in Asia and Africa have been through periods of misfortune and suffering, and continue to experience such, thanks to colonialism." "If we seek common ground and remove the misfortune and suffering imposed on us by colonialism, then it will be easy for us to understand and respect each other, to be sympathetic and helpful to each other, not to be suspicious and afraid of each other, not to be repulsive and antagonistic toward each other," he declared.[62]

Zhou's conciliatory speech won the support of the leaders of the the sponsors of the conference, and many other delegates. Thus spared from entanglement in disputes that would lead nowhere, the delegates reached agreement on a number of proposals, in particular, a statement on world peace and cooperation Zhou had sponsored on the basis of the Five Principles.

The Bandung conference gave Zhou ample opportunity for bilateral exchanges with a large number of Third World leaders. He had intensive discussions with the Egyptian leader Gamal Abdel Nasser, and he negotiated with the Indonesian prime minister Ali Sastroamidjojo on the status of Chinese nationals in Indonesia with dual nationality. Meeting with as many delegates as possible, he tried to reassure them that China was a poor country that had its hands full with national reconstruction and would not engage in any subversive activities in other countries. At the conclusion of the conference, the Taiwan question was raised. Zhou's position was that Taiwan was a part of China and an internal matter, but he took the opportunity presented by the conference to make a conciliatory announcement to the United States: "The Chinese and

American people are friendly with one another," he said. "The Chinese people do not want war with the United States. The government of China is ready to sit down with the government of the United States to discuss ... the question of relaxing tensions in the area."[63] He thus considered "tension in the Taiwan area" an international issue that could be discussed.

Zhou believed that the Bandung conference emphasized the potential value of the Third World as a bulwark against the polarization of the world by the two superpowers. Thus he provided the basis for later Chinese analyses of world affairs, culminating in the Three Worlds Theory expounded by Deng Xiaoping at the United Nations in April 1974.

After the Bandung conference, the number of Asian and African countries that had formal relations with China increased. As part of his continuing efforts to improve China's image abroad, from November 1956 to February 1957, Zhou led a Chinese delegation on a goodwill mission to Cambodia, India, Burma, Pakistan, Afghanistan, Nepal, and Ceylon. His purpose was to convince their leadership of Beijing's peaceful intentions in the area and of a Chinese foreign policy based on the Five Principles of Peaceful Coexistence.

However, China's neighbors had some lingering concerns: (1) unresolved border problems; (2) complications relating to the role of ethnic Chinese in some of the countries; and (3) Chinese support for revolutionary movements, which created serious apprehensions. Prince Norodom Sihanouk of Cambodia was particularly concerned about subversive activities among ethnic Chinese in his country. Zhou tried to allay his fears, saying that Chinese policy was to encourage ethnic Chinese to acquire Cambodian citizenship. He promised that the CCP would not foment revolution in the ethnic Chinese community. Any ethnic Chinese who wished to join the Communist Party had to do so in China. Chinese with Cambodian citizenship would not be accepted in the local associations of fellow provincials or townsmen or any similar organizations that were widespread among overseas Chinese.[64]

In Burma, where Zhou was received with traditional Asian ceremony, he reiterated this sentiment in his talks with the prime minister. Zhou's efforts to reassure the leaders of these countries about Chinese sincerity in its adherence to the Five Principles met with a positive response. His diplomatic forays not only succeeded in thwarting U.S. plans to create a viable military alliance system in Asia, but also reduced the feeling of insecurity that generally pervaded the area in the 1950s.[65]

During Zhou's visits the question arose as to how to reconcile Chinese official assurances of noninterference in other countries' internal affairs with its aid to other Asian communist parties. Zhou argued that the Chinese government had always differentiated between foreign affairs, on one hand, and revolution in a given country, on the other: The former was a matter of state-to-state relations while the latter is an internal matter. Echoing Mao, Zhou stressed that revolution was not for export. In any given country it had to depend on its people. The CCP, he said, gave "only" moral support to revolutionary movements in other countries, while the Chinese government refrained from interfering their internal affairs.[66] Zhou's words were not convincing. Although the State Council under his leadership did not deal with communist parties in other countries, the Liaison Department under the CCP Central Committee did. A major office under the jurisdiction of the Central Committee, it handled relations with and aid to communist parties outside China, in cooperation with the PLA general chief of staff.

## Development Models, 1953–1956

Despite the costs incurred in the Korean War, the economy was slowly recovering. Controlling rampant inflation was the new government's greatest achievement. The positive effect of this on industrial and agricultural output in 1952 was clearly visible: and wages of workers and peasants increased in real terms Nonetheless, China, with the largest population in the world, remained one of the poorest countries. The method and pace of economic development and the construction of socialism remained a major theme of debate among the Chinese leadership for years to come. In particular, the course of action with regard to "socialist construction," as it was called, became a subject of heated ideological controversy.

Zhou, relieved of military duties, launched into the problems of urban and industrial economics, in which he had no experience. Urban affairs— as industrialization was called—would become a priority of policy-making. Zhou believed that, given some time, a centralized economy, managed through vigorous five-year plans, would transform China into a prosperous country. But as his expertise in managing a modern economy was negligible, he followed the only model of industrialization available to him, which was that of the Soviet Union. Under his direction, and with Chen Yun as his deputy, a group of six men began to draft the first five-year plan (1953–1957), which was expected to lay the foundations for industrialization. But they needed the assistance of China's "Soviet Big Brother" for both material and expertise. In August 1952, with a plan drafted, Zhou led a delegation of more than a hundred, including government officials, economists, and experts from various sectors, to Moscow to negotiate an agreement on economic and technological assistance with the Soviet government. He was well aware that his cadres were skilled at revolution but not necessarily at managing economic planning. Therefore he had decided that those who would be responsible for implementation of the plan should receive basic training in Moscow. Moreover, after he had settled the major principles of the agreement with the Soviet Union, his negotiating team was to remain there for as long as necessary to iron out the details.[67]

On 20 August, Zhou discussed the draft five-year plan with Stalin. The plan emphasized the development of heavy industry, which the Chinese leadership considered the foundation of modern industry and a strong national defense. The overall target for industrial growth was 20 percent a year while agriculture was expected to grow 8.9 percent a year.

To reach this target, Zhou, Chen, and others had drawn up a list of 151 industrial enterprises to be established during the subsequent five years. This would not only require the material and technical assistance from the Soviet Union, but also Soviet help in training Chinese workers and specialists. In a separate agenda, Zhou specified China's needs for military industry. He asked for Soviet help in manufacturing airplanes, artillery, tanks, radar equipment, and cars. Zhou told Stalin that for every Chinese shell fired on the Korean battlefield, the U.S. forces responded with nine shells of their own.

The discussion between Stalin and Zhou clearly was not one of equals. Stalin assumed the role of the knowledgeable teacher pointing out the flaws in Zhou's plans. He criticized the Chinese plan for failing to provide a margin for error and for failing to include military spending in its annual growth rate targets. According to Stalin, a margin for error was necessary to account for unforeseen events that might affect overall growth rates. Since military procurement depends on industrial development, Stalin also advised integrating military spending into the overall plan. Stalin also asked for a detailed list of items that the Chinese government expected the Soviet Union to provide.

"Let's say that in 1953 we provide weapons for 10–15 divisions," Stalin said. "We need to know how much steel and other materials will be needed to fulfill this order. During that same year, 1953, we must supply a certain amount of equipment for the civilian sector. This must also be calculated. Then both sums, the civilian and the military, must be combined to determine whether we will be able to supply the entire amount. This is how a plan must be drafted for each and every year. Perhaps our Chinese comrades believe that all these weapons are lying around somewhere in a warehouse. No, they must be produced."

Respectfully, Zhou acknowledged that the Chinese planners lacked expertise and agreed that it was difficult for them to perceive the overall situation. In an attempt to justify the annual growth rate of 20 percent, he explained that Chinese economic potential had been underestimated during the first three years after liberation. Chinese planners had projected allocating 7.7 billion rubles and 4.5 billion rubles for civil and military industrialization, respectively. Mao would like to know, Zhou asked, whether this would be a suitable ratio. Stalin considered this "very unbalanced," a judgment that he quickly reversed after Zhou gave him more detailed information about the military expenditures planned by the Chinese. Korean War costs accounted for 44 percent of the state budget in 1950. In 1951, military expenditures increased further, to 52 percent. With the beginning of armistice negotiations in 1952, they fell to 27.9 percent. Zhou reckoned that yearly investment in military industry in the five-year plan would total 12–13 percent of all industrial investment. Stalin was finally convinced that this was an acceptable ratio. An important aspect of the negotiations pertained to the need for Soviet specialists in various areas. From 1953 onward, Zhou said, China would need additional specialists in the following fields: 190 experts on financial and economic matters; 417 military experts; and 140 medical and paramedical instructors. The number of specialists needed for the military industry was still under study. Stalin's answer to these requests was noncommittal. The Soviet Union would send experts to China, he said, but, at this point, it was difficult to say how many could be made available.

The discussion then turned to the financing of goods and services sent from the Soviet Union to China. Zhou suggested three ways of financing the Chinese trade deficit with the Soviet Union: (1) increase Chinese exports to the Soviet Union; China could supply cattle, leathers, fur, wool, silk, mineral resources, beans, fats, and tea; (2) payments in foreign currency; or (3) credit. He asked which of the three options was most acceptable. Stalin said that it would be necessary to make use of all three. He was particularly interested in natural rubber, of which he was ready to import 15,000 to 20,000 tons a year. In addition, Stalin wanted increased supplies of lead, tungsten, tin, and antimony. This would, however, not cover the costs of goods and services delivered by the Soviet Union. Zhou therefore asked for a loan of 4 billion rubles. Stalin remained noncommittal. The Soviet Union would grant a loan, he said but 4 billion rubles was too much. The agreement finally reached stipulated that, within the next eight months, the Soviet Union would assist China in the construction of 150 industrial enterprises proposed for the period covered by the first five-year plan, among them 44 military enterprises, 20 metallurgical companies, 7 chemical plants, 24 mechanical processing plants, 52 energy enterprises, and 3 light industry factories. The loan that the Soviet government was willing to grant to China totaled 500 million rubles.

During Zhou's stay in Moscow, a number of other agreements were signed. The Chinese government extended the period that the Soviet Union would be allowed to use Port Arthur, while the Soviet government transferred administration of the Changchun Railroad to China and agreed to construct a railway between China and Mongolia, which would facilitate the transport of goods between the two countries. They also signed an agreement to cooperate on the technology of rubber production.

On 22 September, Zhou Enlai and Chen Yun returned to Beijing, leaving Li Fuchun and more than a hundred others to redraft the five-year plan and to iron out the details of the agreements with the relevant Soviet departments.[68]

## The Gao Gang Affair

The construction of a "New China" focused on the question of how to create an economically viable socialist state. This question dominated the Chinese leadership in the decades to come. And under the pretext of what economic model would lead to the best socialist society for China, the communist government's first major political crisis broke out in 1953. The crisis turned into a serious challenge to the political stature of Liu Shaoqi, the president of the People's Republic, and Zhou Enlai.

Originally, the power structure, which had taken shape in 1945, had placed Mao at the summit of the political hierarchy, with Liu Shaoqi as second in command, followed by Zhou Enlai, Zhu De, and Ren Bishi (after his death in 1950 Ren was replaced in this role by Chen Yun). This power structure was based on an alliance between Mao and Liu Shaoqi, which had been instrumental to Mao's establishment at the helm. The position of the five leaders remained unchanged after the establishment of the People's Republic. They formed the Secretariat of the Politburo, at that time the leading organ of the Party. Mao, at the pinnacle of power, dominated Party, army, and government, while Liu and Zhou, respectively, managed the Party and government systems. Under the central leadership, a regional structure divided the country into five areas, each of which was overseen by a leader who concentrated in his hands authority over Party, military, and administrative affairs. These five powerful men were Gao Gang (northeastern China), Rao Shushi (eastern China), Lin Biao (central China, an area later renamed south-central China), Peng Dehuai (northwestern China), and Deng Xiaoping (southwestern China).

In the course of 1952, a few important changes took place in the central administrative structures, all of which tended to restrict Zhou's jurisdiction. In mid-1952, Mao recalled Peng Dehuai from Korea to put him in charge of the Central Military Commission, which had hitherto been under Zhou's jurisdiction. From then on, Zhou was expected to focus his attention on Administrative Council Affairs, which had to handle an increasing workload as the administration expanded and economic development progressed. Some time later, Mao indicated that he was not satisfied with Zhou's management of state affairs. It is not clear what provoked his irritation, but he complained about "dissipation" of work of the Administrative Council. In late 1952 and early 1953, Mao initiated a reshuffle of the central Party and administrative system. He called several prominent provincial leaders—including Gao Gang, Rao Shushi, and Deng Xiaoping—to Beijing, appointing them to important positions in the central hierarchy. The most significant consequence of the reorganization was Gao Gang's designation as head of the State Planning Commission (SPC) and the placing of eight ministries formerly part of Zhou Enlai's Administrative Council under the jurisdiction of the SPC. Mao thus created an "economic cabinet" on equal footing with the Administrative Council, largely independent of the premier and in charge of the most important tasks faced by the country at the time. Zhou, who had been instrumental in designing the first five-year plan, was now removed from its implementation. Although he maintained his official rank as the third man in the central hierarchy, his position was considerably weakened.[69]

The reduction of Zhou's power was further compounded by disputes on ideological and fundamental policy issues between Gao Gang and Liu Shaoqi that led to a power struggle among the top leaders. Gao was a man of great competence and ambition, as well as a notorious womanizer. As one of the founders of the Red Army and the Red base area in northern Shaanxi, he had offered shelter to Mao and his battered troops after the Long March. He became a member of the Politburo in 1945, and he was appointed as a vice-chairman of the government in 1949. His real power base, however, was in northeastern China, which—apart from its traditional role as industrial center—had become a strategically important hinterland during the Korean War.

Gao's transfer to Beijing, while making him more controllable by the Party center, nonetheless catalyzed him to strive for further enhancement of his position. He saw himself as a major leader second only to Mao, which meant the elimination of Liu and Zhou. He used number of issues concerning the method and speed of socialization, which conflicted with Liu and Zhou. But he managed to win Mao's support for his concepts. But his main complaint was the appointment to high-level posts in the government of Party leaders, rather than of leaders of the army. He argued that the army had fought a protracted civil war for twenty-two years, a struggle that had sustained the Party and had allowed it to "grow out of the barrel of the gun." In his view, the victory of the communist movement was due mainly to the army—a fact that had not been properly recognized and had resulted in its underrepresentation in the government. Liu Shaoqi's experiences as a leader of the underground Party and labor unions in the white areas, he argued, could not compensate for his short and temporary association with the army. There was therefore no justification for Liu and his associates' promotion to the high positions they had acquired at the seventh Party congress in 1945 and after the founding of the People's Republic.[70]

Gao's objections to the distribution of leading positions in government and Party were caused at least partially by political differences that had developed between him and Liu Shaoqi. They emerged at the National Conference on Financial and Economic Work, which the Central Committee had convened in the summer of 1953 to assess financial and economic policies during the preceding four years. Since Mao himself had endorsed Gao's political concepts on several occasions, Gao—strongly supported by Rao Shushi, the head of the Central Committee Organization Department—used the conference to stir up resentment against Liu Shaoqi, who, he claimed, was politically immature, and Zhou Enlai, whom Gao believed was out of favor with Mao. It is possible that he was aiming to obtain the post of premier for himself. Immediately after the conference, Gao toured the eastern and southern provinces to discuss the issue with military leaders, such as Zhu De, Peng Dehuai, and Lin Biao. Later, it was claimed that he had been able to gain their support.[71] But he was unsuccessful in rallying to his cause other central leaders, such as Deng Xiaoping and Chen Yun. They reacted by reporting Gao's activities to Mao.[72]

Gao Gang and his supporters underestimated the strength of the alliance between Mao and Liu. If Gao Gang thought that Mao—despite disagreement with Liu on some issues and displeasure with Zhou's methods of handling certain government affairs—would support his attempts to eliminate Liu and Zhou, he seriously misjudged him. There was no question that both Liu and Zhou would adjust their views to align with those of Mao, who, at that time, was still relatively tolerant of different opinions. He was satisfied with the "unity" that the Party had achieved since the rectification campaign in Yan'an, and he had no intention of changing the basic power structure established at the 1945 Party congress. In fact, he resented Gao's attempts to rock the boat just when he was trying to lead the country from the stage of "new democracy" to socialism. If he disagreed with Liu and Zhou on certain policy issues, he differed even more with Gao's views on the role of the military during the revolution, which he considered overinflated. Mao clearly favored the principle that the Party should "always command the gun."[73] If Gao's views had prevailed, they would have required a reassessment of Party history, which in effect would have led to a reappraisal of the Yan'an "Resolution on Certain Questions in the History of the Party." The resolution which was passed by the Central Committee in April 1945 consolidated Mao's version of the CCP's historical evolution and thus of Mao's own position at the apex of leadership. In December 1953, Mao called a meeting of the Politburo to discuss Gao's case. His position was clear. "There were two headquarters in Beijing," he said. "The first one, headed by me, stirred up an open wind and lit an open fire. The second, headed by others, stirred up a sinister wind and lit a sinister fire, it operated underground." He condemned Gao for having formed "an anti-Party alliance,"[74] thus pronouncing his political death sentence.

In February 1954 the fourth plenum of the seventh Central Committee went further into the issue. Liu Shaoqi, Zhou Enlai, Deng

Xiaoping, and others accused Gao, Rao, and their supporters of having formed an alliance with the intention of splitting the Party. In mid-February, Zhou chaired a meeting to deal with Gao Gang, where he repudiated Gao's theory of the relationship between the Party and the army and reiterated Mao's theory that "the gun must never be allowed to command the Party." He deplored Gao's sectarian activities and his attempts to spread "rumors" to attack Liu Shaoqi and other leaders. His aim, said Zhou, was to sow discord in order to usurp the power of the Party and the state. Finally, he denounced Gao's dissolute life. The accusations against Gao were so devastating that he committed suicide in 1954, before he was officially expelled from the Party in 1955. Rao, who was also purged, was jailed and remained so until his death in 1975.[75]

## Opposition to "Rash Advance"

Zhou's diplomatic accomplishments ensured him a reputation as a polished and talented representative of New China on the international scene. Domestically, the fall of Gao Gang considerably improved Zhou's political position, which was also enhanced by the change in status of the State Planning Commission—from then on directed by Li Fuchun—from an independent "economic cabinet" to an agency under Zhou's jurisdiction. Zhou and Li cooperated closely in the process of industrialization, while maintaining good working relations with Chen Yun and Bo Yibo, who headed the Finance Commission and the Economic Commission, respectively. But differences among the leaders about the modus and pace of socialist construction surfaced again. It was generally accepted that it would require three five-year plans, or fifteen years, to achieve the transformation of the agricultural sector and the change in individual handicrafts in urban areas from the private to the collective system. The same amount of time was allocated for the nationalization of private industry, which would go through a period of joint state and private ownership before it could be finalized.

Mao, however, was increasingly impatient with the pace of economic progress projected by his colleagues, who were, as he said in July 1955, "tottering along like a woman on bound feet." He was particularly critical of Deng Zihui, the vice-premier in charge of agriculture, who had argued that cooperatives should be implemented gradually. Agreeing with Deng, Zhou also warned of impetuosity in the rural sector. But Mao's claim that caution was equivalent to conservative right-wing ideas prevailed and, in

October 1955, the Central Committee, including Zhou, accepted Mao's decision to accelerate rural collectivization.[76]

By the end of 1955, 63.3 percent of all rural households had joined cooperatives, and by November 1956, 96 percent. With self-satisfaction the proud leadership announced that the fifteen-year plan of socialist transformation in the agricultural sector had been realized in four years.[77] This boosted Mao's determination to use similar procedures in other sectors. As a result, socialization of handicrafts, industry, and commerce also began to gather momentum. Mao, Zhou, Chen Yun, Chen Yi, and others held separate meetings with representatives of private industry and commerce to urge them to accept the transformation. Under great pressure from the government, most owners of enterprises and commercial business yielded immediately. By the end of 1956, a system of joint private and state management was established in 99 percent of private industry and 82 percent of private commerce. The same occurred in the handicraft sector, where, by the end of 1956, 92 percent of the workers had joined cooperatives.[78]

The dramatic speed of transformation in these sectors led Mao to believe that an acceleration of industrialization was also possible. The 1956 plan for the national economy—which had been approved in October 1955—was revised; its targets in all important sectors were considerably increased. The immediate result of this policy was a sharp uptick of employment in state-owned industries by 2.3 million and a budget deficit of 3 billion yuan. Moreover, all items not directly needed for industrialization and capital construction were in short supply.

Zhou was well aware of Mao's quest for accelerated industrialization. But he was convinced that the projected fifteen-year period for the industrialization process was more realistic, and he was concerned about the possible negative effects of the new policy, which might overheat the economy. His dilemma became apparent on several occasions when he attempted to pay heed to Mao's ideas while, at the same time, warning against being unrealistic and "drawing up plans which are blindly impetuous" and calling for a revision of the inflated targets. In February 1956, he cautioned the State Council against the tendency "to move too fast." While "enthusiasm for socialism should on no account be dampened," he insisted that "tasks that depart from Chinese realities" should not be set, nor should the country try "to go beyond its capacities, or speed up development haphazardly."[79] Two days later, when he presided over a meeting discussing the 1956 national economic plan, he cut rather than raised the targets for the annual growth rate of some major items such as capital investment and the production of steel, coal, grain, and cotton. In April he visited the northeastern and northern regions of China, where he examined the prospects for steel production. He returned convinced that, even in regions where steel industry had been implanted for decades, there was no economic basis for sustaining accelerated growth. Problems not limited to inadequacy of capital, building material, mechanical equipment, and mismanagement were rampant; and output was produced to achieve certain quantitative targets while quality was grossly neglected. At the State Council and the Politburo, Zhou proposed cutting government expenditure, decreasing the rate of capital investment, and reducing production targets. If he was eloquent enough to convince his colleagues, none of them was ready to contradict Mao openly. The Politburo thus adopted Mao's principle of "opposing conservatism" in economics and, at the same time, Zhou's idea of "opposing impetuosity." An editorial drafted for the *People's Daily* that emphasized caution and "opposition to rash advance" in economic activities was submitted to Mao, who, as he later stated, returned it unread.[80]

Zhou, with Chen Yun, Li Xiannian, and Bo Yibo, started to work on the revision of the second five-year plan (1958–1962), reducing targets for major agricultural and industrial production and cutting expenditures. The slogan "to achieve greater, faster, better, and more economic results in building socialism," which Mao favored, was deleted from key passages of the economic plan. In his report to the Eighth National Congress of the CCP in September 1956, Zhou emphasized that a reasonable growth rate and realistic targets, combined with balanced and proportionate development, should be the guidelines for economic policy. Such a policy will not work if it is established without taking into account the country's resources in material and manpower, he said. In November, at the second plenum of the eighth Central Committee, Zhou went a step further, arguing that China's industrialization would take more than fifteen years to accomplish and insisting that it might not materialize at all unless a proper balance between the different sectors of the economy—requiring a slowdown in the growth of heavy industry—could be achieved.[81]

Although dissatisfied with Zhou's pronouncements, Mao abstained from interfering in economic matters for a while. In 1956, he was preoccupied with the Eighth National Congress of the CCP, the Twentieth Congress of the Communist Party of the Soviet Union (CPSU), with its condemnations of Stalin, and the subsequent crises of the communist movements of Hungary and Poland. In 1957 he launched the "Hundred Flowers" movement, which generated serious criticism of Party policies. Many intellectuals—among them many well-known noncommunists—supported Zhou's circumspect approach to the economy and expressed disapproval of the leadership's "craving for greatness and success" and search for "quick achievement and instant benefit" from the development of the economy at excessive cost and great waste. But in October 1957 Mao began to criticize all policies moderating output targets on the grounds that they had led to the dampening of the revolutionary spirit necessary to "promote progress." "Bourgeois rightist opposition" to socialism had been promoted instead. Those who had acclaimed such policies, Mao said, were "only 50 meters from the right."[82] These statements ushered in a complete change of the political atmosphere. No further criticism against rash advance in economics was made public, while right conservatism was again condemned in the official press. In Moscow, where Mao attended the celebration of the fortieth anniversary of the October Revolution, he was so impressed by the launching of the Soviet *Sputnik* and Soviet claims of catching up with the United States fifteen years hence that he pledged to catch up with Britain in fifteen years. Shortly thereafter, he devoted an entire conference, held in Nanning in southwestern China, to the criticism of "economic conservatism." He claimed that "opposition to rash advance" had become a political issue and that the term "rash advance" was so inappropriate that it should never be used again. At the same conference he revealed that he had never read the *People's Daily* editorial of 20 June 1956, which the Politburo had submitted to him prior to publication. "Why should I have read something that is directed squarely against me?" he asked his audience. Then he ordered the distribution, as negative examples, of the editorial, of parts of Li Xiannian's report to the National People's Congress and of Zhou's report on the 1957 five-year plan, all of which supported a cautious approach to economic planning and socialization.[83] Local Party leaders like Ke Qingshi and Wang Renchong, the Party secretaries of Shanghai and Hubei province, respectively, received high praise for their enthusiasm in accelerating socialist construction. Ke, who had submitted a report entitled "Braving the Storm and Accelerating the Process of Construction of a Socialist New Shanghai," became Mao's favorite: Ke's report was imbued with lofty targets and high aspirations to such an extent that he ordered it to be reprinted in all major newspapers. Then Mao confronted Zhou directly and in the presence of many others, waving Ke's paper at him and asking, "Comrade Enlai, you are the premier, can you write a report like this?" Zhou answered that he could not. The humiliation did not stop there. "Shanghai is an important base of the Chinese working class," Mao continued. "One would not be able to write a good paper like this unless one had strong aspirations for the building of socialism." Addressing Zhou again, he asked, "Are you opposing 'rash advance' (*fan maojin*)? I am opposing opposition to 'rash advance' (*fan fan maojin*)!" Zhou—usually ready to confront even the most problematic situation—seemed to be at a complete loss and incapable of uttering a word in response. At the conference, he admitted that he had made a mistake by opposing the "rash advance." He accused himself of having committed "a mistake in principle," which originated in his failure to realize that the change in the ownership of the means of production could not but entail much faster development of the economy. He also accepted full responsibility for having exaggerated the importance of specific minor shortcomings in the development process; and he apologized for having carried out a retrogressive policy where Chairman Mao had expected a progressive one.

Mao, however, was not satisfied with Zhou's self-accusations. In March 1958, at a conference in Chengdu, he made a number of speeches criticizing all attempts to curb "rash advance," saying that "rash advance" was "Marxist" and opposing it was "non-Marxist." Again he reproached Zhou of having thrown cold water on the enthusiasm of the people and of having encouraged rightists to attack the Party. Again Zhou believed that he had to respond with self-accusations—however degrading this might have appeared to him. Yet he hesitated to do so immediately. On 19 March he delivered a report on foreign affairs. On 23 March he briefed the conference about a project to construct a dam at the Three Gorges of the Yangtze River, of which he was in charge, and, finally, on 25 March he made another self-criticism about his economic policy. Instead of promoting a policy of "getting greater, faster, better, and more results" (*duo, kuai, hao, sheng*) in building socialism, he had implemented a policy of "getting smaller, slower, poorer, and more expensive results" (*shao, man, cha, fei*). If he had finally come to realize his mistakes, he said, it was due to Chairman Mao's teachings.[84]

The dilemma for Zhou and other members of the State Council who supported Zhou's views was that Mao's repeated and public denunciations made it impossible to defend their positions. After Mao, whom they all accepted as their supreme leader, had established a political line, the margins for political discussion diminished considerably. In a private talk with the Chairman, Zhou once again apologized for his "mistakes" and explicitly accepted Mao's criticism. But Mao was still not satisfied. He had decided to launch a second surge of his own brand of socialism by calling for a "Great Leap Forward," through which he expected the mobilized masses—in a spirit of storming heaven—to work with their bare hands to achieve huge increases in agricultural and industrial output. If he wanted to implement a movement of such a scale, doubts among the rest of the leadership could not be tolerated. He convened a session of the eighth Party congress, a forum large enough to publicize his intentions. In Mao's view, the congress would also provide the right audience to listen to Zhou's self-criticism, which had only been heard by a limited number of central and provincial leaders.

For Zhou, preparing yet another self-criticism, to be read to more than a thousand delegates at the Party congress was humiliating. Many years later, Fan Ruoyi, his political secretary who had prepared many of Zhou's official statements, described the mental contortions Zhou had gone through to prepare his statement. He and Fan started to work on the text at midnight. Zhou had decided to dictate his statement to Fan, but the normally eloquent premier was halting and inefficient in his dictation, often interrupting himself and gazing at the ceiling for several minutes. He obviously was not convinced that his political views were wrong and could not bring himself to formulate a statement that went against his innermost convictions. Fan finally suggested leaving Zhou alone to sort out his thoughts. Two hours later, Deng Yingchao went to Fan's office to tell him that the premier was staring blankly at the walls. Together they finally persuaded him to give the general idea of his statement to Fan, who would then write the text for him.[85]

Zhou's self-criticism was an important event at the congress. It served Mao not only to humiliate the premier, who had expressed a different opinion on a core policy issue, but also to air his own views and to assert his own position as the paramount leader. Zhou began his speech by praising the congress which Mao had destined to inaugurate the Great Leap Forward as an occasion for "ideological liberation." He declared that China had come to an era in which "in one day, changes were taking place that normally would take twenty years.... The miracles that the process of national economic reconstruction had provoked," he said had convinced him of "the correctness of Chairman Mao's line" and of the "seriousness of the error of opposition to 'rash advance,'" for which, he told his audience, he bore "the brunt of responsibility." Proposing a detailed analysis of the errors involved so that the proper lessons could be drawn, Zhou pointed out that two different lines of socialist construction had confronted each other: Mao's correct line, asserting that faster development was necessary and feasible, and his own opposition to it. He regretted that he had failed to recognize "that the building of socialism could attain such a scope and speed." Without realizing its harmful effects, he had formulated the concept of "rash advance," Zhou said. He thanked Mao for his timely intervention and correct guidance. Without it, he said, more serious consequences would have been inevitable.

An analysis of the ideological causes of political errors was considered a necessary part of any serious self-criticism. Zhou therefore proceeded to accuse his "natural inclination toward pragmatism on some issues and toward dogmatism on others" of being a major reason for his tendency to misjudge political situations. He terminated his speech by emphasizing the necessity of "learning from Chairman Mao." "On the one hand," he declared, "my errors have shown that if one departs from or goes against his guidance and instructions, one always goes astray and commits mistakes. On the other hand, if we do things correctly, it is due to Chairman Mao's leadership and thought."[86]

Zhou was not the only leader whom Mao expected to deliver this type of submissive declaration. Others, like Chen Yun, Li Xiannian, and Bo Yibo, also made formal statements expressing their deep regret about their opposition to Mao's views of rapid industrialization. The effect was such that the congress became an oath-taking rally on behalf of the entire Party to economically "catch up with Britain in seven years (instead of in fifteen as previously declared) and with the United States in another eight to ten years." Mao called on the entire nation to "do away with blind faith and to display the creative spirit of daring to think, speak and act," a call to which the congress responded with a standing ovation.

Mao's attempt at manipulating the Party had worked. The leaders, who, in fact, disagreed with him, disavowed their own much more realistic convictions and supported him publicly, thus reinforcing Mao's position and contributing considerably to the further development of the Chairman's personality cult. Although he preceded others with his public declarations of guilt, Zhou was nonetheless deeply depressed by the turn of events. His state of mind was not improved by rumors that Mao was considering replacing him with Ke Qingshi. He asked the Standing Committee of the Politburo to decide "whether it would be appropriate for him to continue as premier of the State Council." But Mao, if he ever had intended to dismiss Zhou, had changed his mind, and on 9 June, an enlarged meeting of the Standing Committee confirmed Zhou in his position.[87]

## Intellectuals and Thought Reform

During the early years of the People's Republic, the political status of China's intellectuals became controversial. Zhou's considerable efforts to rally China's talented people to the task of economic and social reconstruction were thwarted by the deep mistrust of intellectuals harbored by many other leaders. In the early 1950s there were few intellectuals—a loosely defined term used during the years of revolution to differentiate Party members who had some education from peasants and workers who had none. After 1949 it received a broader connotation, referring to scholars, professors, writers, artists, teachers at all levels, doctors, engineers, journalists, and functionaries. In most cases, their education was a blend of traditional Chinese and some elements of Western culture. About two million people belonged to this category, totaling 0.37 percent of a population of 540 million.[88] Since they were associated chiefly with the class of landlords and the bourgeoisie economically and politically, the Communist Party mistrusted them, considering them alien to their cause. The Party leadership was convinced that intellectuals needed to be ideologically remolded before they could be useful in the building of socialism.

During the Korean War, a movement of ideological remolding was started. The moment was purposely chosen as an occasion to eliminate pro-American sentiments, which, it was assumed, many intellectuals were harboring. The rectification of pro-American feelings, circumscribed as "liking America, fearing America, and worshiping America" (*qinmei, kongmei, chongmei sixiang*) became the major objective of the campaign.

Zhou officially launched the thought reform in the autumn of 1951 with a speech that he delivered on 29 September to a group of teachers from universities and colleges in Beijing and Tianjin. He declared: "Most of the intellectuals of our country come from landlord or bourgeois families … so we cannot expect them to take the side of the working class all at once." In Zhou's view, if Chinese intellectuals were to be acceptable and useful members of the new society, they had to be prepared to serve the revolutionary cause. It was therefore inevitable that they had to go through a process of ideological remolding, which would resolve the question of "where they stood" (*lichang wenti*). As a first step in the right direction, they had to learn to be true patriots. From there they would proceed to a stage of service to the people (*renmin de lichang*). Only after that would they be able to reach the highest level and obtain the status of "working class" (*gongren jieji de lichang*). "It is not easy to acquire a firm working-class stand," Zhou told his listeners. "It takes a long period of trial and study and of tempering in struggle." But it was possible to achieve this transformation, he assured the intellectuals, if they engaged in study and revolutionary practice and went to the countryside and the factories to become aware of peasants and workers lives.

In his five-hour-long speech, he talked about his own experience in ideological remolding. His origins, a bankrupt feudal family, had necessarily influenced his own reasoning and outlook, he said. His political thinking was at first nationalistic or patriotic, but through study and practice, he ended up as a communist. He emphasized the importance of criticism and self-criticism as instrumental to ideological remolding.[89]

The process of this remolding had its own method. To increase ideological awareness, the participants took part in study sessions where they read Party documentation or Mao's works. These "studies" were expected to enlighten them about discrepancies between their own political thinking and that of the working class. After they understood their errors, it was expected that they would be able to correct them through self-criticism in front of others and by listening to the criticism of others.

Special meetings were held to examine certain specific attitudes. Some were geared to condemn supporters of U.S. imperialism. Others attacked such traditional Confucian concepts as loyalty, filial piety, and the doctrine of the mean and of benevolence and humanity. Western concepts of liberty and democracy also became a focal point of repudiation. Remarkable means of propaganda were employed to degrade famous works of literature and art produced by "bourgeois" intellectuals.

Zhou Enlai was relatively passive in these campaigns. He did, however, join Mao in his criticism of Liang Shuming, a noted scholar of Chinese philosophy, ethics, and politics, and a leading member of the Chinese Democratic League. Liang Shuming had made considerable efforts to mediate between the GMD government and the CCP after the anti-Japanese war. As a mediator, he had earned a reputation for impartiality. As a person, he was known for his frankness and honesty, but also for his stubbornness. Both Mao and Zhou knew him well. After the founding of the People's Republic, though Liang declined an invitation to join the government, he became a member of the CPPCC.

In September 1953, Liang became embroiled in a public controversy with Mao about the plight of Chinese peasants, arguing that after "liberation," Chinese peasants remained impoverished. Cadres in the rural areas were qualitatively and quantitatively below standard. He emphasized the differences of living standards between peasants and workers. They were so substantial that "workers were in ninth heaven, whereas peasants were down in ninth hell." He concluded that it was inappropriate for the CCP to ignore the plight of the peasants.

Mao disagreed with Liang's assessment and accused him of opposing Party policies. But, instead of bowing to Mao's views, Liang challenged him. This kind of open defiance was unprecedented, and Mao considered it a serious affront that he was not prepared to tolerate.[90]

Zhou took charge of Liang's official repudiation. On 17 September, he delivered a long speech that reviewed the different stages of Liang's life, all riddled with political errors. To begin with, in his youth, Liang had been a true believer in Confucius. He had started his career in the early 1920s as a professor of Indian philosophy at Beijing University. Before the war against the Japanese invaders, he had spread the view that China could be saved only by promoting education in the countryside. He had often declared that society should change through reforms, rather than through class struggle. After the war, while attempting to mediate between the GMD and the CCP, he had pretended to be impartial, but, during critical junctures, he had, in fact, backed the position of the GMD. In Zhou's speech, the most important events in Liang's life became damaging pieces of evidence of his reactionary stand and his hostility to the Communist Party.

Zhou's speech was repeatedly interrupted by Mao, making bitter and sharp remarks concerning Liang Shuming. The omnipotent Chairman seemed to have lost all self-control in his anger over the powerless intellectual, who had merely stated an opinion. Mao accused Liang of being "a man without a sense of shame, … an ambitious schemer, … a hypocrite, … a man not to be trusted, and an assassin who killed people with his pen."[91]

It is not known whether Zhou gave this speech out of his own initiative or on orders from Mao. Whatever his motives, they do not change the fact that he betrayed a friend in order to please Mao. Although his life was spared, Liang was discredited and humiliated as a "living specimen (*huo biaoben*) of the die-hard reactionaries still existing in China." His works disappeared from the public until the 1980s, when they were again viewed as treasures of Chinese literature.

In 1955, the official witch hunt of intellectuals came to a temporary halt. The movements of ideological remolding and of elimination of counterrevolutionaries among the intellectuals were expected to have either eliminated or changed those who had expressed opposition to Party policies. It is impossible to establish how many people actually changed their outlook as a result of the remolding process. But most of those who went through the process emerged with a clear idea about what they could say openly and what they should keep to themselves if they wanted to avoid political problems.

As the leadership again realized the need for technically capable people to participate in China's development, the question of improving working and living conditions of intellectuals was again on the agenda of the Politburo. A committee under the direction of Zhou Enlai began to assess the situation of intellectuals at the national level.

The committee found that, sixteen years after the founding of the People's Republic, the number of Chinese intellectuals had increased from 2 million to about 5 million, mostly because of a strong influx of graduates from colleges, universities, high schools, and professional middle schools in the first half of the 1950s. Within this group, 2 percent—about a hundred thousand—were considered high-level intellectuals. The committee estimated that 40 percent of them were politically "progressive and sincere supporters of the Party." Another 40 percent were "middle of the road," which implies that they were politically inactive. The remainder was divided in two: half were "backward" and "ideologically opposed to socialism"; the other half were believed to be "counterrevolutionaries" and "bad elements," both hostile to the new regime.[92] This analysis of the political stance of intellectuals was to provide the basis for the Party's decision concerning their participation in the construction of socialism in the country.

The committee furthermore observed that intellectuals had not been used to their best advantage mainly because of unsuitable work assignments that often had nothing to do with the training that they had received. Mistrust of intellectuals led to absurd practices forbidding engineers and technicians to visit factories or depriving them of information vital to their work. Some were moved into positions but were denied the powers necessary to do their jobs. Others spent a disproportionate amount of time in political study sessions and other unproductive political meetings.

In January 1956, Zhou Enlai addressed these issues in a speech to high-ranking government and Party leaders stressing the importance of intellectuals in national development. He emphasized that they were workers in the service of the nation who were indispensable to the process of modernization. To fully mobilize the intellectuals and to develop their potential for the national construction program, he called upon Party and government institutions at all levels to "improve the arrangements for using their skills efficiently." He also demanded that Party leaders at all levels "try to understand them, to have confidence in them, and to give them the support they deserve so that they can work with enthusiasm." In this context, he recommended that appropriate working conditions and material benefits be provided to them.[93]

Many Chinese intellectuals, who had long suffered from having a reputation for harboring pernicious thoughts and for being useless to the working class, were pleased to learn that they had become an accepted part of the working class. Zhou's statement gave them the impression that they were needed. Although they continued to be subject to ideological remolding, their situation seemed to have changed for the better. Further improvement appeared to surface with the Hundred Flowers movement, which created an exceptionally free atmosphere in cultural activities. Intellectuals felt as if they could breathe more freely. In 1957, when they were invited to participate in the Party's rectification campaign and to "help the Party to overcome its shortcomings," many responded actively and honestly. For many of them, the campaign against "rightists" that followed only a few months later came like a bolt out of the blue. More than half a million intellectuals were accused of having attacked the Party and were labeled as anti-Party and anti-Socialist rightists. In 1957 and 1958, labor camps were filled with such "enemies of the people." His earlier efforts to improve the conditions of intellectuals responsible for "right deviation" notwithstanding, Zhou followed Mao's repressive policy against them.

## The Great Leap Forward

Criticism of economic pragmatism and its branding as "opposition to rash advance" and "right deviation" comprised the ideological foundation for the Great Leap Forward. It introduced a clear break with Soviet-style socialism—a break that Mao made explicit in March 1958 at the conference in Chengdu, where he had warned against "dogmatic and superstitious" copying of the Soviet model. He observed that, although it may have been necessary to follow the Soviet model in the early days of the People's Republic, China was now ready to achieve greater results by following its own economic path. Under the guidance of the "General Line of building socialism by going all out, aiming high," it would be able to "achieve greater, faster, better, and more economic results in socialist construction," as Mao had formulated.

The imperative of the General Line was speed. In the official formulation, speed was its "key" and its "very soul."[94] Many leaders other than Mao also believed that the Chinese economy could develop by leaps and bounds if the "enthusiasm of the people for the General Line were fully mobilized." Output of steel and grain was taken as a key indicator of economic progress. In his draft of the second five-year plan (1958–1962), Zhou had suggested that the output of steel should more than double within five years and that the output of food grain would increase from 185 to 250 million tons between 1957 and 1962.[95] In fact, he considered these estimates overly optimistic, but some of the leaders believed that they were able to achieve much more. During the spring of 1958, targets were revised upward several times. Rivalry between the central planning authorities and regional economic planners contributed to this escalation. Li Fuchun, for example, came up with a number that multiplied several times Zhou's assessments of production possibilities, while Wang Heshou, minister of metallurgy, expressed the conviction that steel output for 1958 should be twice as high as in 1957, thus reaching the level of about 11 million tons planned for 1962. Mao was clearly seduced by these figures. At an enlarged meeting of the Politburo, held in August 1958 at Beidaihe, he declared that output of major industrial items would exceed comparable British levels within two to three years. These targets were officially accepted, and Zhou was formally outvoted.[96] He never disclosed his private thoughts about these figures, though it can be assumed that he must have had serious reservations about them. But Mao had announced his decision, and, as so often before, Party discipline and Zhou's instinct for political survival guided his decision to comply with Mao's utopian desires.

In the first eight months of 1958, only 4 million of the more than 10 million tons of steel planned were actually produced. This should have dampened the leadership's enthusiasm. But Chen Yun noted at the Politburo meeting that Soviet leader Nikita Khrushchev did not have confidence in the Chinese targets. Such statements stoked indignation among Party members and drove national pride as a significant factor in support of Mao's utopia. Mao, who believed that miracles could be achieved by mobilizing the people, did not consider readjusting the target for that year. Ninety million people were sent to the mountains to cut down trees for fuel, mine coal with their bare hands, and search for iron ore in order to fuel the more than one million backyard furnaces that had sprung up practically overnight, inspired by Mao's exhortations. Many people, caught up in the excitement and fervor promoted by official propaganda, argued that they were simply emulating methods of iron-making used by their ancestors a thousand years earlier. Zhou watched these developments with mixed feelings. In his public speeches, he felt obliged to extol the "excellent situation," but privately maintained strong misgivings. After receiving a report from Henan province stating that, in one of its counties, one million tons of pig iron would be produced by the end of the year, he requested the opinion of an expert metallurgist. The expert informed him that the production of one ton of pig iron would require more than 10 tons of raw material (iron ore, coal, coke, limestone, etc.). Raw material of that kind was not available in the county in question, nor did it have the means of transporting it to the production site from elsewhere. Zhou sent one of his secretaries to the province to bring him samples of the iron made by the backyard furnaces there. The secretary returned with something that was, as Zhou discovered to his dismay, "not iron at all." He explained to the premier that he had observed the peasants roaming the mountains and collecting black stones that they believed was iron ore. Since Zhou could not halt the drive after it had been officially launched, however absurd it might have appeared to him, he sent chemistry students to the countryside to help the peasants. But the 23,000 students who went to the countryside were too few to give effective support to a movement involving 90 million people.[97] The attempts to produce steel were a waste of money, material, and manpower. Moreover, it caused serious and widespread destruction of the environment. It is not known how many trees were cut down and burned in the furnaces. Deforestation was widespread.

The agricultural sector was the other focus of Mao's utopian goals. Under his direction, output targets for food grain were revised several times. The target of 250 million tons of grain for 1962 that Zhou had suggested was increased first to 350 million tons. A few months later, the target was established at the extravagant figure of 750 million tons. But Mao and others were so confident about their ability to reach these targets that they asked themselves what should be done with the abundance of subsequent harvests.[98]

These optimistic expectations were paralleled by an upsurge in the socialization of the agricultural sector. In rural areas, the then-existing 740,000 cooperatives were merged into 26,000 people's communes. Believing that people's communes would be "the best organization for building socialism and for the gradual transition to communism," Mao and the Party center forcefully encouraged this radical transformation. It took only the summer months of 1958 to achieve this major change, which was accompanied by an indiscriminate transfer of manpower, land, draft animals, farm implements, and financial resources.

The consequences of this policy were disastrous. Peasants quickly found the overcentralization and the egalitarianism practiced by the communes overwhelming. Morale among the peasants was greatly undermined by the rule that peasant families were no longer allowed to make food for themselves. Their cooking utensils were either melted down in furnaces or confiscated for the use of communal canteens, and they were deprived of their tools and private plots. The negative effects on agricultural productivity were tremendous. The enthusiasm of local cadres, driven by their desire to overfulfill production quotas, compounded the problem. It became common to order peasants to plant seeds much more densely than normal. It was vainly hoped that doing so would increase grain output many times over. Such absurdities, rather than furthering Mao's goals, contributed to the debacle that followed the Great Leap Forward.

Soon the acute strain on finances and on the supply of raw material, food, and daily necessities became apparent. A few months after the Beidaihe conference, Mao began to reconsider his lofty goals for the economy. He called a number of meetings in the first half of 1959, which, in view of the problems created by the Great Leap Forward, lowered the targets for the 1959 economic plan. Measures were taken to control the overenthusiastic local cadres, who had strained local resources. Mao admitted that he, too, was liable to make mistakes and that the people, including himself, needed to rein in their enthusiasm. This was no time for mutual reproach, he said to an enlarged Politburo meeting at Zhongnanhai in June 1959 but, rather, a time to draw lessons from past mistakes.[99]

The following month, Mao called an enlarged Politburo meeting of central and provincial leaders at Lushan in Jiangxi province to review the experiences and results of the previous year's economic program. Mao expected that holding the meeting in such a scenic spot would help the leaders to relax and to engage in a free discussion. This "forum of free discussion" (*shenxian hui*) would, in Mao's view, contribute to a common understanding of the situation and to an agreement on specific issues.

In his speeches Mao emphasized the "the great achievements over the past year and the great prospects" (for the future), but he also mentioned the continued existence of numerous problems. He reiterated the views that he had expressed during the previous few months, stressing the necessity of balanced economic growth and proportionate development of the different economic sectors. In smaller circles he went even further. Despite his sharp condemnation of opposition to "rash advance" a year earlier, Mao declared in the presence of his political secretaries Hu Qiaomu, Li Rui, and Tian Jiajing, and a few others that the Lushan meeting was "in essence to oppose rash advance." He saw himself as "the ringleader of opposition to rash advance," seemingly forgetting that, a few months earlier, he had come out as the "ringleader of rash advance."[100]

Zhou delivered the underpinnings to the new direction Mao's views had taken. In his speech on 6 July, he reviewed the situation along Mao's lines and emphasized the great achievements of 1958. The General Line for socialist construction, which Mao had formulated, continued to be absolutely correct, he pointed out. The shortcomings that had emerged were due not to the Line itself but to the fact that production targets had been set too high and that an imbalance among the different sectors of the economy had developed. Another mistake had been that too much power had been delegated to local authorities. In later speeches before the conference, he talked about more specific problems, like the huge budget deficit and the serious shortage of major raw materials.[101]

Peng Dehuai, defense minister and member of the Politburo, took a position very similar to that of Zhou Enlai. In a private letter to Mao on 14 July, he stated that most of the problems of the Great Leap Forward were essentially due to "petty-bourgeois fanaticism," by which he meant that people had been overly enthusiastic and unrealistic in their attempt to "make the leap."[102] The letter caused a controversy after Mao ordered its distribution to those who attended the meeting. Some leaders openly supported Peng's views, while others expressed their disagreement. Zhou did not find anything noteworthy about the letter.

Mao, however, took serious offense. Launching a vehement attack on what he called a "frantic offensive from the right," he refused to accept Peng's remarks concerning "petty-bourgeois fanaticism," which, in his view, actually represented enthusiasm among the socialist masses. Some people had stood firmly with the Party, Mao said, while some had vacillated when confronted with difficulties, and still others had opposed the "three red banners."[103] Turning toward Zhou, he said, "Premier, the last time you opposed 'rash advance,' but this time you stood firmly." He thus clearly differentiated between Zhou's attitude and that of Peng, whom he accused of "bourgeois vacillation" and "right opportunism."

The change from criticism of "left" errors to "right deviation" directed against one of the leading figures of the Chinese revolution completely transformed the spirit of the meeting. The relaxed mood, which Mao had intended to create, gave way to a tense atmosphere concerned mainly with the purge of Peng Dehuai. Mao delivered a speech listing all of his differences with Peng over the previous thirty years. Lin Biao condemned Peng as a "careerist, a conspirator, and a hypocrite." Zhou changed his attitude to follow suit, now calling Peng's letter a rightist attack on the General Line. Peng, he said, was too proud and therefore prone "to insubordination." Peng therefore should adopt an attitude of "docility" and should remold himself through "thorough ideological transformation."

On 4 August, with the growing political tide against Peng Dehuai becoming evident, Zhou escalated his attacks on Peng, pointing out that his letter was a planned and well-prepared action with ulterior motives directed against the Party, the General Line, and against Chairman Mao. Naming Peng as "the main representative of the dangerous right opportunism," Zhou said that the main task of the plenum was to defend the General Line and to oppose any attempt to split the Party.[104]

After the Lushan conference concluded on 16 August, criticism of Peng and his supporters continued at the Central Military Commission in Beijing. Zhou joined in the process, focusing on the issue that Mao had launched concerning Peng Dehuai's effective cooperation with him over the preceding thirty years: he divided Peng's military career into fifteen periods, starting with his "joining the Party for speculative purposes" during the early years. Over the course of his membership in the Party, Peng had followed four erroneous political lines and, though he had "ostensibly supported Chairman Mao," he had "in reality opposed him after the Zunyi conference" until 1959, when he openly attempted to usurp Party and military power. Altogether, he had cooperated with Mao for about ten years, Zhou said, while, the rest of the time he had been uncooperative. He further pointed out that Peng had been an important member of Gao Gang's anti-Party clique who hitherto had escaped undetected. All these elements proved that Peng was "a careerist, a conspirator, and a hypocrite" who had hidden in the Party for decades. This episode demonstrates yet another instance in which Zhou not only remained on the right side of Mao, but also contributed to Mao's personality cult, which, in view of Mao's failures, was sorely in need of bolstering.

A resolution adopted by the Central Committee officially condemned Peng Dehuai and some of his supporters for having formed an anti-Party clique. They were labeled "right opportunists" and deprived of their posts. A large-scale campaign was launched within the Party itself, in which more than 3.6 million cadres were subjected to investigation and many were labeled right opportunists.[105] The main ramification of Peng's purge was the continuation of Great Leap policies, which led to one of the nation's most serious economic crises. A sharp decline in the production of major agricultural and animal products created food shortages and, in some areas, famine. About 30 million peasants entered the already crowded cities to work for state-owned enterprises. Net food producers now became net food consumers. Inflated capital construction led to grave imbalances in the development of other sectors of the economy, to the detriment of housing, schools, hospitals, and light industry providing for daily necessities.[106]

## The Road to Cataclysm

Mao's criticism of Zhou's relatively moderate economic programs paved the way for the Great Leap Forward. But after the calamitous aftermath of the "leap" policies came to light, Zhou had responsibility for repairing the damage. By 1960, the agricultural crisis had reached the point that it could no longer be ignored. Zhou was fully aware of this, but was unable to propose a remedy until Mao allowed a change in the direction of the economy. But Mao allowed for no change. The purge of the alleged anti-Party group around Peng Dehuai and the subsequent campaign against right opportunism completely overshadowed all attempts to put the economy back on course.

Food was so scarce after the ill-fated experiment of the Great Leap Forward that hunger was rampant. Reports on food shortages poured into the State Council offices from all parts of the country. In May 1960 Zhou was informed that grain stocks were at a critically low level in such major cities as Tianjin, Shanghai, and even in the capital.[107]

In the countryside, the situation was even worse. The Gansu Provincial Party Committee, for example, reported that a large number of people had died from hunger and dropsy. The root of the disaster, according to the committee, was political, provoked by "egalitarianism, indiscriminate transfer of resources, and an awesome 'communist wind'" dominating the political atmosphere.[108] This clearly indicated that the Party committee blamed the collectivization policies of people's communes for the calamities.

From the same province came another alarming report concerning the normally disciplined soldiers of the PLA. One of its famished elite units stationed in Gansu province, assigned to the trial launching of rockets in desert areas, had destroyed a 30-kilometer-long windbreak forest in order to mix leaves with grain. Zhou informed the commanders of the military regions, then meeting in Beijing, about the problem and asked them to find grain for the starving soldiers at the rocket base. This was not easy, because everyone had similar problems, but upon Zhou's insistence they were sent a wagon of grain.[109]

Mao waited until June 1960 before finally acknowledging that mistakes had been made and should be corrected.[110] His admission of failure opened the way for a shift in policies. An "emergency directive on current policies for rural people's communes" drafted under Zhou Enlai's direction inaugurated the change in November 1960. The directive aimed to end the premature establishment of collective ownership in rural areas, which—as the Gansu report had already suggested—was considered the root of "destructive egalitarianism and indiscriminate transfer of resources."[111] This premature collectivization and the arrogant and arbitrary demeanor of many rural cadres toward subordinates, compounded by widespread exaggeration of production targets and real output and food waste in communal mess halls, all contributed to the serious damage suffered by the rural sector. The damage prompted Mao to ask all leading members of the Party to carry out their own investigations of the situation in the countryside. Mao was particularly concerned about the peasants' reactions to the communal mess canteens that he had so strongly advocated.

Zhou Enlai was one of the first leaders to go on a fact-finding mission, touring villages in Hebei province for a few weeks in the spring of 1961. In his meetings with the peasants assembled to discuss their problems, none of them dared to speak up. Zhou's attempts to encourage them to talk by addressing them individually only created embarrassment. With self-conscious giggles, they assured him that the mess canteens were very good. Finally he managed to thaw the atmosphere when he succeeded in encouraging a middle-aged peasant to pour out his reservations about a number of problems. In the mess canteen system, the peasant said, food had become increasingly scarce for them because village cadres twisted the system to their own advantage. "Life has become much more difficult in recent years," the peasant said, and, pointing his finger at Zhou, he added abruptly: "If things are allowed to continue like this, even you will starve to death." Impressed with the man's honesty, Zhou asked him: "How can that be?" "Because we will take care of ourselves" was the answer. "We will stop selling grain. You will not be able to buy anything from us. So you will not have anything to eat." Zhou informed Mao by telephone that all commune members he had seen demanded to eat at home and wanted the mess canteen system to be dissolved. Most of them resented the egalitarian system of free supply and demanded a return to the precommunal assessment of their work by points gained on the basis of performance, so that the principle of "more work, more pay" could be implemented. The pressure was so significant that the communal dining system was abandoned.[112]

Zhou was racking his brain to find a solution to the famine. Together with vice premiers Li Fuchun, Li Xiannian, Tan Zhenlin, and Xu Zhongxun, he set up a "food substitution group" (*guacaidai lingdao xiaozu*), which he directed himself. Its mission was to encourage the population to find substitutes for grain, such as maize and algae. Urban dwellers were also encouraged to grow vegetables at home and raise rabbits and chickens to supplement their food supply.[113]

In early 1961 the level of food grain stocks fell to a new low. Examining avenues of relief, Zhou concluded that reserves were indeed minimal and should not be touched. Purchases of grain from the countryside could not be increased because, in some areas, people were already starving. Even the two traditional grain producing areas of Sichuan and Heilongjiang suffered from supply shortages for the current year. A further cutback in food rationing for urban residents could not be considered because the ration amount was already so low. Given the considerable deterioration in relations with the Soviet Union, Zhou refused to consider an offer from Moscow to lend China a million tons of wheat. At the same time, the Chinese government had to fulfill international obligations, which consisted of providing 60,000 tons and 160,000 tons to Albania and East Germany, respectively. To cover the most urgent needs, the Central Committee, in March 1961, decided to import 5 million tons of grain per annum from Canada and Australia for the next four years. Yet all this was inadequate. On an inspection tour to the northeast, Zhou found that the area was so short of grain that he finally accepted an offer of 200,000 tons from the Soviet Far East to feed China's northeast. It was later repaid with imported grain.[114]

Another measure that Zhou took was to extract as much grain as possible from provinces with comparatively higher yields and to redistribute it to the poorer regions. In many cases the Ministry of Grain under the State Council, which was in charge of implementing this policy, was unable to overcome the resistance of the better-off provinces to deliver their produce for redistribution. Zhou had to deploy all his sagacity and skills in meeting emergencies and solving thorny problems related to this situation. Chen Guodong, the Party secretary at the Ministry of Grain, recalled how Zhou tackled the problem. Chen and the vice-minister in charge of grain distribution went to Zhongnanhai several times a week to work with Zhou. During these meetings, which always took place at night, they made detailed calculations of monthly purchases, sales, transportation, distribution, and storage of grain. Zhou was meticulous in checking all estimates and calculations and questioning anything that might have given rise to the slightest doubt.[115] No detail escaped him, and he insisted on being provided with the most up-to-date and precise information about the grain situation throughout the country. To monitor grain flows in the country, he devised a food allocation table. Using his abacus, he checked calculations himself. This also enabled him to correct exaggerated and bogus figures on grain production. His general assistant, a young woman named Zhang Shuyun, asked him once why he, the premier, would not leave such trivia to others. Zhou answered that he could not leave this work to others: "You must understand that this concerns millions of lives.... How can I know the real situation if I do not make the calculations myself?"[116]

In addition to the food shortage, Zhou had to deal with the scanty supply of coal, China's main source of energy. Miners needed proper nourishment if they were to ensure normal production. In order to guarantee efficient distribution of coal, enough trains for transportation had to be provided. These were not minor problems. To tackle the emergency, Zhou established a ten-member coal group at the State Council. The group, headed by Vice Premier Gu Mu, met daily to make decisions about the production, distribution, and transportation of coal. One of Zhou's secretaries participated in the group's meetings, so he was kept informed about the situation in this sector.

The kind of problems that were Zhou's daily concern during the three years of crisis also had a personal dimension. During the worst period of famine, in 1960 and 1961, he stopped eating meat and eggs. He also had to deal with a family situation when his nephew, Zhou Erhui, and his new wife visited him at Zhongnanhai. After her marriage, the young bride moved from her hometown of Huai'an to Beijing, where her husband worked at the Institute of Iron and Steel. At a time when it was official government policy to resettle urban dwellers from the large cities to the provinces, it was surprising that the local authorities had given her permission to move to the capital. Zhou was immediately convinced that this had been done because she had married the nephew of the premier. Zhou insisted that she return to Huai'an. Unlike many other husbands and wives whose professional circumstances forced them to live separately, the young couple was not ready to do so. Together they left Beijing and settled down in Huai'an.[117]

The harsh realities began to sober even Mao. In January 1961 he remarked at the ninth plenum of the Central Committee that "socialist construction should not be carried out in haste; it should take half a century [and] must go slowly for a few years."[118] His changing attitude enabled the Central Committee to make a "readjustment" in industrial policy to replace the principle of "leaping forward." Under Zhou's direction, the readjustment consisted mainly of cuts in production targets in the major sectors of the economy. The plan submitted to a Central Working Conference at Lushan in August–September 1961 recommended the reduction of production targets for steel from 19 million to 8.5 million tons in 1961 and to 7.5 million tons the following year. Mao, at the Lushan conference, was ambivalent. Speaking on 23 August, he cautioned against optimism and called upon his audience to be prepared for "further setbacks," yet he also warned against pessimism, saying that "there is nothing extraordinary about the few mistakes [we have made]." He told his audience that "we reached a bottom line, [so] we can only go up."[119]

Mao's admission of mistakes was an unusual gesture that concealed considerable uneasiness about the political disturbances created by the Great Leap Forward. His awareness that the controversies accompanying "leap" policies from their very outset had only deepened in the course of the preceding few years made him concerned about Party unity. By the end of 1961 agriculture showed signs of revival and the industrial decline was halted. This was the right time, Mao believed, to face the Party and the people. He called an unusually large conference of more than seven thousand, representing the central authorities, the regional bureaus of the Central Committee, the provinces, the prefectures, the counties, and a number of industrial enterprises. The "Seven Thousand Cadres Conference, as it became known, met in January and February 1962 in Beijing. Its major purpose was to reach a common understanding of the domestic situation among the cadres at various levels and to discuss the readjustment of economic policies. In spite of the deep crisis, the central Party leaders—apprehensive of widespread discontent at lower levels and as desirous as Mao to maintain the unity of the Party—stood behind the chairman, going out of their way to uphold Mao's prestige and to defend the authority of the Party, which Mao symbolized.

Liu Shaoqi set the tone in a major report, which offered a joint appraisal of the situation by a twenty-one-member committee of high-ranking Party leaders selected by the Central Committee and presented a laudatory review of the Party's record from 1949 to 1958. This was followed by a positive appraisal of the three catastrophic years, announcing that "a series of new achievements were scored in socialist construction." The report mentioned neither the economic crisis nor the widespread famine and the death of millions of people. The few "shortcomings" that were summed up were considered secondary. Liu attributed them mainly to natural calamities and to the lack of experience of the center—by which he meant the Politburo, the Central Secretariat, the Central Committee and its departments, the State Council, and the ministries. The leaders of the provinces should also bear some responsibility. As to Mao, he paid tribute by reminding the attendees that Mao had been the first to perceive and point out the mistakes. As early as November 1958, Liu said, the Chairman had suggested taking measures to check the tendency toward premature transition to communism and to rectify the mistakes of egalitarianism. As for industry, Mao had denounced inadequate planning and the excessively high production targets fixed in recent years.[120]

The report, which was meant to ensure the support of a presumably unified Party, provoked significant dissent in closed group sessions. Questions were raised as to the precise nature of mistakes committed and the causes of the serious crisis engulfing the country since 1958. If natural calamities—which should have affected mainly agriculture—were the major cause of the problems, then why were other sectors of the economy such as finance, industry, and transportation equally touched; why did the disastrous economic situation spread across the country while natural calamities occurred only in parts of the country? With respect to human mistakes, which Liu had presented as errors of implementation, questions were asked as to why the entire country had made the same mistakes if they had not been a result of a general policy line.[121]

On 30 January, Mao, in an extraordinary gesture, admitted that he, too, was capable of error. "Any mistakes that the center has made ought to be my direct responsibility, and I have an indirect share in the blame because I am the Chairman of the Central Committee," he said. But he also blamed Party leaders at various levels for their shortcomings, insisting that the leadership's "knowledge of socialist construction is extremely inadequate." Ignoring the problems that the country was facing, Mao spoke about democratic socialism and the need to promote democracy within the Party, where, in his view, "one-man tyranny" in the person of the secretary of the Party committee prevailed. "Whatever the secretary says goes," Mao said. He emphasized that cadres should listen to different opinions and that the present conference should be a forum for airing complaints about superiors from their subordinates. To drive home his point, he cited numerous examples from Chinese history.[122]

All the other leaders who took the floor raised their voice in defense of Mao and the Party. Lin Biao and Zhou's statements were characteristic of the two men. Both of them, in different ways, contributed to the cult of Mao's person that had become rampant at the time. Lin Biao devoted his speech to praising the Chairman and Mao Zedong Thought. In his view, all failures of the past were due to departures from Mao's instructions. "In times of trouble," he said, "we must rely even more on the leadership of the center, on the leadership of Chairman Mao, and trust Chairman Mao's leadership even more. If we do that, it will be even easier to overcome our problems. Facts prove that these troubles come precisely from our failure … to act according to Chairman Mao's instruction. If we proceed according to Chairman Mao's directives, if we listen to his word, then our troubles will be very much smaller, and there will be fewer curves on the road."[123]

Zhou Enlai spoke twice in the same vein, offering encomiums about Mao. At a group meeting of representatives of Fujian province, he also stressed the importance of following "Chairman Mao's instructions on the necessity to seek truth from facts" and criticized the "tendency to boast and tell lies" that had surfaced among Party leaders in the recent years.[124] His speech to the Plenum paid tribute to Mao while taking personal responsibility for the debacles of the Leap. "We were not in accordance with Chairman Mao's directives to take reality as the starting point, to take agriculture as the basis, to arrange appropriate proportions between agriculture, light industry and heavy industry, to put emphasis on producing a variety of goods and on their quality, to achieve an overall balance, and to leave room for maneuver. Instead, we disobeyed Chairman Mao's directives and objective laws, worked from a subjective viewpoint, stressed quantity and speed, did not leave room for maneuver, allowed gaps (in the economic plans) to expand; neglected variety and quality, and solely and one-sidedly sought figures and high targets. In organizing production and work, we messed things up, blindly issuing directives ..." He continued with the confession that he had "mistakenly and one-sidedly laid down that industry and agriculture should increase production at Leap Forward pace each year."[125] He took responsibility for having allowed excessive procurement and consumption of grain, the introduction of inflated targets, the spread of inflated production figures, and disproportionate transfers of grain from the countryside to the cities and excessive exports. He also blamed himself for decentralizing economic decisions in the drive to create regions with relatively complete industrial systems. To achieve this goal, control over 98.5 percent of light industry and 76 percent of heavy industry was handed down to lower levels of government. In fact, Zhou's self-criticism, in a tortuous way, deflected Mao's ruinous policies from Mao onto himself. He had opposed those policies—albeit not openly—and had tried to reduce their negative effects on the economy. Yet, when confronted by Mao's overbearing demands to take great leaps, he had followed his orders. Zhou's claim that disasters had occurred because of his failure to follow Mao's instructions represented a degree of prostration to the Chairman to which no leader other than Lin Biao would submit.

The Seven Thousand Cadres Conference was followed by a series of other meetings meant to "let off steam" or to "cool down" (*lengjingxialai*). They convened at different levels of the Party hierarchy to denounce the blunders committed since 1958 and to openly criticize leaders responsible for them. Policies of the Great Leap Forward were abandoned. The resulting atmosphere of relaxation had a particularly beneficial effect on intellectuals, who, for the first time since the establishment of the People's Republic, were allowed to play a role in discussions of the problems of society.

By 1961 Zhou had articulated a new direction of official Party policy toward intellectuals. Mao's formulation at the Seven Thousand Cadres Conference in early 1962 on the issue of 'broadening democratic life' allowed a further step towards the improvement of the status of intellectuals. In his famous speech "On the Question of Intellectuals" presented in Guangdong on 2 March 1962, Zhou dealt with a wide range of questions about the role of intellectuals in Chinese society. Since that society was divided into various classes, the question of what class intellectuals belonged to was the key issue of his speech. As he pointed out to his audience—composed of leading cadres from the world of science and literature—"intellectuals are not an independent class but a social stratum composed of mental workers." Under the old regime they served the ruling class, he said. At that time, all intellectuals could be considered bourgeois intellectuals. At present, according to Zhou, that conclusion no longer holds. He quoted Lenin, who stated that "the dictatorship of the proletariat is a specific form of class alliance between the proletariat, the vanguard of the working people, and the numerous nonproletarian strata of the working people [petty bourgeoisie, small proprietors, the peasantry, the intelligentsia, etc.]." From this he concluded that Lenin included the intellectuals in the "nonproletarian strata of the working class." He then proceeded to address the question of "how to unite with the intellectuals," advocating trust and improvement of living conditions.[126]

Chen Yi, vice premier and foreign minister, also addressed the conference. While reiterating Zhou's views, he spoke in a style that was very different from Zhou's. He was far less cautious about the political consequences of his declarations. His language was vivid, humorous, and sharp, his statements full of candor. The audience responded to him with laughter and spontaneous applause—a rare occurrence in Chinese politics. He bluntly stated that he considered relations between the Party and intellectuals "very abnormal" (*hen bu zhengchang*). He condemned Party leaders for their lack of insight, which dictated their mistrust of China's intellectuals. "Workers, peasants, and intellectuals are the three components of our nation's working people," he declared. "After having gone through a process of ideological remolding and many tests for twelve years, they should no longer be classified as bourgeois intellectuals." He ended his speech with a statement that touched his audience deeply: "Today, I bow to you to remove your cap [as bourgeois intellectuals]."[127] With these words, Chen Yi bowed deeply to his audience.

In his "Report of the Government" to the National People's Congress on 28 March, Zhou addressed the issue again, stressing that, since the founding of the People's Republic, intellectuals had fundamentally changed. A large number of young intellectuals had been trained, and crucial changes had taken place in the ideological and political outlook of those who had been educated in the old society. In his view, they had undoubtedly become "the working people's intellectuals."[128]

Zhou's statements at the Guangdong Conference sparked controversy among senior Party leaders. Lu Dingyi, a member of the Central Secretariat and director of the Central Propaganda Department, declared sarcastically that there were either bourgeois intellectuals or proletarian intellectuals, but he had never heard of "working people's intellectuals." At a meeting of the Central Secretariat, he expressed reservations on behalf of officials engaged in ideological work at various levels about Zhou's definition of intellectuals. Chen Yi's tribute to them raised even more eyebrows. Ke Qingshi, the radical mayor of Shanghai, simply refused to transmit Chen Yi's speech to Party organizations under his jurisdiction.[129]

Facing a storm of criticism, Zhou believed that he needed Mao's support on this matter. But when he approached him, the Chairman did not utter a word. He persisted in his misgivings about intellectuals. His mistrust came out into the open at the Beidaihe conference in August 1962, which discussed the question of the rehabilitation of intellectuals. Mao declared that "some of them did come over [to us] outwardly, but not inwardly. Some did not even come over outwardly." He also disapproved of Chen Yi's remarks at the Guangdong conference. "They had their motives when they wanted you to make a speech," Mao told him. Zhou, who sensed that his own remarks did not correspond to Mao's present political mood, began to defend himself. He explained that it had not been his intention to blur class distinctions when he referred to intellectuals as belonging to the working class. When he had presented his report on the work of the government, he had done so on behalf of the Party, which had approved it, he said, adding that it was therefore not his own report. He found a supporter in the person of Deng Xiaoping, who declared that there was nothing wrong with the premier's views on intellectuals. The relevant parts of Zhou's report should be taken as the standard since they had been approved by the Center. Deng ordered their distribution to all Party organizations.[130] This put a temporary end to the controversy.

The moderation of Party policies toward intellectuals once more proved short-lived. Mao was increasingly obsessed with the notion of class struggle in the areas occupied by men of learning. Science, literature, art, publishing, and education became subjects of his profound mistrust. In his view, "very little has been achieved in terms of socialist transformation" in these areas. His incapacity for tolerating independent thinkers led him to believe that such people were "still dominated by the dead," implying that old bourgeois thinking had not yet died. A nationwide campaign of criticism in literary circles and in social sciences that was soon carried out once more aborted all attempts to improve the conditions of intellectuals in society.

## Class Struggle

After the Seven Thousand Cadres Conference, Mao retreated to the south, leaving his colleagues to handle economic affairs. From 21 to 23 February, the Standing Committee meeting at Xilou (Western Building) at Zhongnanhai discussed the 1962 state budget and the revival of the economy. Contrary to the estimates made at the Seven Thousand Cadres Conference, the leaders found themselves confronted with a budget deficit of 5 billion yuan for 1962 as well as with soaring prices. In view of the largely unreliable statistics on which they had based their earlier appraisal, they instructed the Ministry of Finance to carefully check the figures and to present them with a realistic assessment of the economic situation. The ministry produced figures showing large budget deficits for the previous five years and a high potential for inflation for the current year.[131] The assessment at the Seven Thousand Cadres Conference that "the most difficult period had already passed" could no longer be sustained. As Liu Shaoqi pointed out, the country was in fact "in a state of emergency" and urgent measures were needed to steer the economy onto a healthier course. Chen Yun proposed introducing a period of "readjustment and recovery" in major sectors of the national economy and, in the process, to give agriculture priority. On 24 February, Zhou, accompanied by Liu Shaoqi and Deng Xiaoping, flew to Wuhan to report to Mao about their discussion. Mao had received mainly optimistic estimates on the economic situation from local leaders in the south. In their view, the economic situation in 1961 was better than that in 1960, and there were signs that it would improve still further in 1962. Although Mao felt optimistic and encouraged about the prospects, he approved the deep cuts in the 1962 plan proposed by Liu, Zhou, and Deng.

The Standing Committee on 7 and 8 March again discussed problems of economic readjustment. Its members were unanimous that the 1962 annual plan should be corrected by introducing drastic cuts in targets for heavy industry and capital construction while giving priority to agriculture and to daily necessities of urban residents.[132] Zhou, in his speech on 8 March, focused on the general situation. "The current financial and economic difficulties are serious," he said. Furthermore, "there might be problems we have not yet been able to perceive." He emphasized the importance of agriculture and of the needs of the market. In his view, they had to be given top priority in economic planning.[133]

On 28 March, Zhou delivered the Report on the Work of the Government to the plenum of the National People's Congress at the Great Hall of the People. In his report to the larger audience, he did not mention famine, inflation, shortages of daily necessities, or other calamities. Instead, he talked about "imbalances" that had "occurred in many areas" as a result of the "enormous development" and the "rapid progress of the past few years." To "correct these imbalances, consolidate our achievements, and pave the way for further vigorous development," Zhou said that the Party had decided to implement "a policy of readjustment, consolidation, filling in gaps and raising standards" (*tiaozheng, gonggu, chongshi, tigao*).

Zhou's report gave agriculture priority. "The decline in agricultural production is the chief factor responsible for the imbalances in the economy," he asserted. To redress the imbalances, growth rates in heavy industry had to fall drastically and quotas for industrial products, which were not in urgent demand or for which there was not enough raw and semifinished material, had to be reduced. Enterprises that produced such material should be reduced in size or merged with others. A number of capital construction projects thus would have to be postponed. Zhou emphasized that the experience of the previous few years had enabled the Party finally to realize that industry cannot develop beyond the possibilities provided by agriculture in terms of necessary supplies of marketable grain, industrial raw materials, and other kinds of farm and sideline products. Nor should enterprises recruit too many laborers since they would be needed in agriculture. "We must … place agriculture at the top of the agenda in our drive to develop the economy," Zhou concluded.[134]

In April, Zhou replaced the ailing Chen Yun as head of the Central Financial and Economic Group, which had been reestablished after the Xilou conference in February. Under his direction, the group worked out a new economic plan for 1962, which the Standing Committee discussed between 7 and 11 May. The plan proposed deep cuts in various sectors of the economy, in particular, reduction of capital investment from 12.33 billion yuan in 1961 to 6.76 billion yuan in 1962; closure of industrial enterprises or their merger with other production units; decrease in the number of workers and staff of state enterprises by 8.5 million and of the urban population by 10 million from January to August. In his speech on the eleventh, Zhou said that, in the short run, it would not be possible to readjust the economic imbalances "caused by our own mistakes." It might take place during the third five-year plan or even later. Again, he emphasized the importance of agriculture.[135]

The revival of agriculture and the structure of agricultural production remained the major issues. Immediately after the Seven Thousand Cadres Conference concluded in February 1962, the Central Committee issued a directive establishing production teams as the basic unit of accounting within people's communes, thus giving more responsibilities to the smaller units.[136] Mao accepted this system although he considered it a retrogression from the degree of socialization already achieved. But the peasants in some areas went further than that. Dividing up the communal land and engaging in independent operation (*dang'an*), they used the household as the basis for linking work, output, and income.

The system, generally known as "fixing farm output quotas for each household" (*baochan daohu*), became popular among the peasants. Sometimes with official blessings, sometimes spontaneously, it spread to many localities. It was estimated that 80 percent of the peasant households in Anhui province, 74 percent in the area of Linxia in Gansu province, nd 40 percent in Guizhou province had adopted the system. It was also practiced in Guangxi, Fujian, Guangdong, Hunan, Hebei, and the northeast. In July 1962, the assessment was that about 20 to 30 percent of all households in the countryside had adopted the system. Wherever it was practiced, agricultural production increased.[137]

The *baochan daohu* system became a heated topic of discussion at the leadership level. Its effectiveness won support from a number of high officials. Mao's secretary, Tian Jiaying, whom Mao had sent to investigate in early 1962, had originally opposed the system. He changed his mind after observing the realities in the countryside. Chen Yun was clearly in favor of *baochan daohu*, encouraging Tian in his assessment. Returning to Beijing at the end of June, Tian reported to Liu Shaoqi about his findings in the countryside and argued for the formal introduction of a system of farming based on the household. Liu was in favor of legalizing and of popularizing the system.[138] Deng Xiaoping's views on the subject were also clear. As his well-known remark goes: "It does not matter if the cat is white or black, as long as it catches mice."[139]

To Mao, however, efficiency in agricultural production was not the issue. His preoccupation was the establishment of his own view of socialist forms of production in rural areas. "According to you," he asked Tian, "which will be the main form of economy in the countryside: collective economy or private economy?"[140] To Chen Yun, he remarked that "to divide land and to operate independently comes to disintegrating the collective economy. It is revisionism." Chen, feeling uneasy about being at odds with Mao, asked for sick leave and immediately left Beijing.[141] Zhou Enlai, for the time being, was not caught up in the controversy, since he had not voiced an opinion on the issue—although in private, he had agreed with Chen Yun.[142]

The issue was a major contributing factor behind Mao's radicalization and his alienation from the rest of the leadership. This became apparent at the Central Work Conference meeting at Beidaihe from 25 July to 24 August 1962. In his keynote speech, Mao attacked what he called "the three winds": the wind of excessive pessimism (*hei'an feng*), the wind of "going it alone" (*dang'an feng*) in the countryside, and the wind of reversing correct verdicts (*fan'an feng*) on rightists and counterrevolutionaries. "We have been discussing difficulties and darkness for two years now; it has become illegal to discuss brightness," he said sarcastically. In contrast to the results reached by the Standing Committee in February and May, Mao emphasized that, despite numerous problems, "our achievements are great. The future is bright." Those who believed that there was no future or who had lost confidence he berated as ideologically confused and wrong. As for himself, he added: "I am not particularly pessimistic with regard to the problem of the current situation. It is not all gloom." Referring to the *baochan daohu* system and "going it alone," he said, people believe "that only by doing that will there be more grain; there is no other way out for agriculture." He was convinced that "going it alone" should not be allowed to compete with collective agriculture. "In the final analysis," Mao asked, "are we going to take the socialist road or the capitalist road? Do we want rural cooperatives or don't we? Should we have *baochan daohu* or collectivization?"[143]

The survival of collective ownership in the rural areas was of vital importance to him, while a responsibility system based on households or independent activities in the rural sector would engender the collapse of his vision of rural socialism in China. "The peasants want freedom, but we want socialism," Mao had stated.[144] Faced with Mao's categorical denunciation of the new system, Liu Shaoqi was the first to change his stand. Zhou Enlai followed suit. In his speech on 17 August, he paid tribute to the Chairman for having in a timely way and "unequivocally put forward three questions of tremendous importance." "Class struggle is a long-term problem that existed in all historical periods," he said. Having experienced class struggle for decades, Zhou said, people are now confused, thinking no more of it. He considered it a serious problem that peasants were in favor of independent operations, that they wanted "to go it alone." As for Mao's criticism of what he considered to be an overstatement of the difficulties faced by the rural sector, Zhou said, "We have talked a little bit too much about difficulties recently, thus producing negative effects on the Party." He began to stress Mao's point that "there are difficulties, yet the situation is not all dark." As for the *baochan daohu* system, Zhou said, "Once the Chairman pointed it out, the question has become clear. We have been able to see things clearer."[145] This was the end of the rural responsibility system. Not until the 1980s would it be revived and legalized when Deng Xiaoping gave it the green light within the framework of his reform policy.

In the wake of the Beidaihe conference, the tenth plenary session of the eighth Central Committee was convened in Beijing from 24 to 27 September 1962. Speaking at the opening session, Mao plunged into a discussion of class and class struggle. Focusing on the danger of Khrushchevian revisionism in China, he emphasized the importance of opposing revisionism abroad and preventing it at home.

> Now then, do classes exist in socialist countries? Does class struggle exist? We can now affirm that classes do exist in socialist countries and that class struggle undoubtedly exist.... We must acknowledge that classes will

continue to exist for a long time. We must also acknowledge the existence of a struggle of class against class, and admit the possibility of the restoration of reactionary classes.... Therefore, from now on we must talk about this every year, every month, every day.[146]

The emphasis on class struggle heralded the Cultural Revolution. Class struggle was to provide the ideological basis for purging most major leaders. On 26 September, Zhou spoke in support of the Chairman, emphasizing that the issues Mao had raised were "very much to the point," "very timely," and "very important." He reiterated that the Standing Committee had overestimated the difficulties, creating undesirable effects on the cadres at various levels, and criticized the practice of *baochan daohu*. During the current period of readjustment, Zhou said, there were achievements as well as mistakes. Some mistakes that the Chairman called attention to had been made because of misunderstanding, but some were due to an erroneous orientation. Zhou pledged to correct them at once, now that the Chairman had identified them.[147]

## Downturn in Foreign Relations

The distressing internal situation in the early 1960s was reflected by the deterioration in China's foreign relations. Foremost was the transformation of relations between China and the Soviet Union from one of privilege to outright hostility. It had been germinating since the mid 1950s and reached a peak in the early 1960s, when the ideological differences between their respective communist parties could no longer be papered over. The Chinese policy of "leaning to one side" had begun to wane by February 1956, when serious differences surfaced as a consequence of the twentieth congress of the CPSU in Moscow. At the congress Khrushchev shocked the communist world with his criticism of Stalin—the great leader of communist revolution—and of Stalin's personality cult, which had been systematically promoted during Stalin's lifetime. The Chinese communists were particularly astonished by these remarks, referring to Khrushchev's statements as his "secret report," because foreign delegations were kept away from the session in which Khrushchev made them. Actually, the Chinese learned of his statements only after the meeting had concluded, when an emissary of the Soviet Politburo read them excerpts of Khrushchev's speech in Russian which the Chinese delegates did not understand.

Zhou and other CCP leaders in Beijing obtained the full text of Khrushchev's report not from the Soviet Union, but from a Xinhua News Agency's translation into Chinese of a *New York Times* translation into English, published on 10 March. When Mao, on 17 March, called a meeting to discuss the situation, he had barely had the time to take note of the "secret report." Participants at the meeting also complained that the document translated into Chinese and that they had not been able to fully comprehend its meaning. Most important, Zhou and all other CCP leaders—realizing the tremendous impact that Khrushchev's denunciation of the world's leading communist figure would have on the international communist movement—were deeply disturbed by the lack of prior consultation with "fraternal parties" on such an important matter. Mao set the tone for the reaction to Khrushchev's actions by declaring that the Soviet leader had "disclosed [Stalin's] mistakes" (*jiele gaizi*) but, at the same time, had "made a mess of things" (*tongle louzi*).

The Politburo discussed the matter a number of times before releasing an editorial in the *People's Daily*, a document drafted by a team of writers under the direction of Chen Boda, Mao's senior aide on ideological questions, and carefully revised by Mao himself. The *People's Daily* editorial, published on 5 April, supported criticism of Stalin's mistakes "in principle," but disagreed with Khrushchev's complete rejection of the Soviet leader. But the implications behind the careful wording of the article were much deeper. It was time "to think things out for ourselves" (*duli sikao*), Mao said at the 4 April meeting of the Central Secretariat. He added that the Chinese communists should no longer depend on anyone else and should go their own way. They had already affirmed their independence during the revolutionary period. They should also do so in the times of socialist construction. Mao said he had been thinking about these questions for a few years. China should go its own way in socialist construction, rather than following the Soviet Union. "Thanks to Khrushchev's disclosure of [Stalin's] mistakes, we shall learn to do things entirely according to Chinese circumstances," he declared.... "We shall find our own way of building socialism in China."[148] With this, he indicated a new direction for Sino-Soviet relations, with serious implications for the international communist movement.

Zhou Enlai, in a briefing at the Foreign Ministry addressed to Chinese ambassadors, translated Mao's statement in foreign policy terms. The Chinese and the Soviet communist parties held different views on the correct way to criticize Stalin, he said. While it was necessary to disclose Stalin's mistakes and to do away with "blind faith" in him, Khrushchev's criticism was not "impartial (*bu quanmian*) and his methods were questionable." He held that "Stalin was a great Marxist-Leninist, who unconsciously had made mistakes," but "he and his achievements should not be completely negated." Regarding future relations with the Soviet Union, he told the Chinese diplomats that "although the Soviet leaders can show positive results in some areas, they are too intransigent in other aspects." Instead of asking the Chinese ambassadors "to learn from the Soviet big brothers," as he had frequently done in the past, he urged them to "think things out for themselves," not to copy things indiscriminately from the Soviet Union and to be vigilant about arrogance and big power chauvinism, which characterized so much Soviet diplomacy.[149]

The twentieth Party congress had a strong impact not only on the Chinese Communist Party but also on the international communist movement. In Eastern Europe, Khrushchev's de-Stalinization conveyed a sense of liberation to the communist parties in power, spawning revolt against Soviet interference in their affairs. In Poland and Hungary, people took to the street to protest Soviet domination of their country. The rumblings of discontent in both countries focused world attention on the region. The Chinese leaders were deeply concerned about events in those two countries, which, they were certain, would have serious repercussions for the entire socialist camp. The night of 21 October, Mao called a meeting of the Standing Committee to discuss a cable from the CPSU informing them of the Soviet government's intention to suppress the Polish revolt with armed force and asking for Chinese political support. Mao—fully aware of the urgency of the matter—responded that suppressing the Polish revolt would be a typical case of "the recalcitrant son and a father who wants to beat him with a big stick.... A big socialist state wants to invade a neighboring socialist state," he added. "This is big power chauvinism and should not be allowed." Zhou and other CCP leaders supported this view, so the meeting decided to express strong objection to Soviet actions. At one o'clock in the morning of 22 October, Pavel Yudin, the Soviet ambassador, was called to Zhongnanhai, where Mao, Zhou, and others informed him that the CCP Politburo would consider Soviet armed intervention in Poland a violation of the principles of proletarian internationalism. "If you dare to do so in defiance of the will of the peoples of the world," Mao told him, "we will condemn you publicly." He asked Yudin to transmit this message to Khrushchev without delay. Later that day, Deng Xiaoping and Liu Shaoqi led a Chinese delegation to Moscow to discuss the issue with the Soviet leadership. Zhou maintained daily communications with the Chinese envoys.[150]

The Hungarian revolt against the communist regime at the end of October engendered quite different reactions in Moscow and Beijing. The Soviet leadership was divided over the issue of whether to intervene in Hungary. By 30 October, they had decided to forgo intervention and to seek a solution to the crisis by following a "peaceful path." The Chinese leadership, however, considered the Hungarian situation far more dangerous than the one in Poland. Seeking greater autonomy from the CPSU, as the Poles had done, was one thing; attempting to abolish one-party rule, forming a coalition with other parties, proclaiming neutrality, and renouncing all obligations under the Warsaw Pact—as the Hungarians had done—was a different matter. It meant opting out of the communist bloc and thus required a different reaction. Liu and Deng, who were scheduled to leave Moscow on 31 October, were instructed to inform the Soviet leaders of the Chinese position demanding the suppression of the "counterrevolutionary riots" in Hungary. It appears that they did not have the opportunity to do so. While they were waiting at the airport to catch their flight back to Beijing, a high-level Soviet delegation arrived at the airport to bid them farewell and, more significantly, inform them that the Soviet Presidium had changed its position adopted only a day earlier and was now supporting military intervention in Budapest.[151]

On 1 November, the Chinese government issued an official statement on the events, which Zhou had carefully revised. While giving support to the Polish and Hungarian people's demands for democracy, independence, equality, and improvement of material conditions, it warned against "the danger of attempts by reactionaries to sabotage people's democracy and the unity among socialist countries." But the statement also blamed the Soviet Union and its autocratic foreign policy for the disturbances in Eastern Europe. Without mentioning the Soviet Union by name, Zhou condemned the "mistakes of big power chauvinism," which had seriously damaged the common cause of the socialist countries.[152]

The question of how to regain socialist unity remained on the agenda. But the issue was riddled with difficulties. Khrushchev, apparently worried about the increasingly sharp criticism voiced in Beijing, thought that Zhou's personal intervention might help to calm the waters. He issued an invitation to the Chinese premier to come to Moscow, which Zhou received on 30 November while he was in India. This was followed, a few days later, by a Polish request to visit Warsaw. Zhou postponed a planned visit to Afghanistan and returned to Beijing on 3 January to prepare himself for his delicate mission. He left for Moscow on 7 January, accompanied by Marshal He Long, the vice chairman of the CCP Military Commission; Wang Jiaxiang, the vice foreign minister; and Liu Xiao, China's ambassador to the USSR.[153]

In Moscow, Zhou had three meetings with Khrushchev and the Soviet Politburo, where he emphasized the differences between the Polish and the Hungarian situations. Condemning the original Soviet attitude in the Polish case as "big power chauvinism," he pointed out that the principles guiding relations among fraternal countries are incompatible with the movement of Soviet troops toward Warsaw and the imposition of military pressure on Poland. Although he considered it imperative to forcefully suppress what he had come to see as subversive imperialistic activities in Budapest, Zhou charged that the Soviet Union, at the beginning of the Hungarian crisis, had adopted a "capitulationist" attitude. Regarding the lessons to be drawn concerning relations among socialist states, he emphasized the principle of equality between them. In his speech at the banquet given in his honor at the Kremlin, Zhou stressed the need for "genuine discussion and amiable consultation" and the adoption of the Five Principles as guidelines in the relations between socialist countries. No one should be allowed to think of himself as being "a head taller than others," he said, adding that with respect to relations between fraternal parties, a big party, no matter how big it was, still remained an equal partner that should not be allowed to impose its ideas on others.[154]

Khrushchev politely thanked Zhou for his efforts to appease the Poles and for his support in the Hungarian case, but was deeply disturbed by Zhou's criticism of Soviet chauvinism. At some point in the discussion, Khrushchev became more agitated, declaring that he had not expected Zhou to lecture him about how to deal with other countries. When the Soviet leader complained about the endless requests for aid from East European leaders, Zhou interrupted him impatiently, asking him to consider all that the Soviet Union had extracted from East European countries over the years. On this and several other occasions the discussions descended into a scorching diatribe. By telephone, Zhou informed Mao in detail about his talks with Khrushchev, including the bitter acrimony that spoiled the atmosphere between the two leaders. Mao approved of Zhou's attitude toward the Soviet leader and told him to "give him advice; if he refuses to listen, then leave him alone."[155]

Despite their discord, Khrushchev was eager for Zhou to travel to Poland and Hungary and thus continue his efforts at appeasement. Janos Kadar, the head of the new Hungarian government installed in Budapest with the support of Soviet tanks, was called to Moscow for consultations with Zhou and the Soviet leadership. On 10 January 1957, they discussed the text of the joint Sino-Hungarian communiqué to be issued after Zhou's visit to Budapest. It stressed solidarity within the socialist camp, the need to suppress the "subversive activities of the imperialists in socialist Hungary," and the importance of strengthening the proletarian dictatorship.[156]

Between 11 and 16 January, Zhou was in Poland. In his talks with Wladyslav Gomulka, first secretary of the polish communist party, and others, he was struck by the strong anti-Soviet sentiment harbored by the Polish leadership. He tried to temper it by stressing the contributions the Soviet Union had made to the cause of communism. In his view, this was of primary importance, while the inequality of relations between the Soviet Union and other socialist countries, of which he thoroughly disapproved, was of secondary importance and could therefore be corrected. Zhou held that it was essential for socialist countries to improve their solidarity at a time when enemies were trying to exploit the mistakes made by the communist movement. Despite the differences between the Soviet and the Chinese communist parties over the preceding decades, he said that the CCP continued to follow the road opened up by the October Revolution. Solidarity within the international communist movement, with the Soviet party at its core, he repeated, was still of the utmost importance. Striving for peaceful coexistence with other countries was not the same as conveying an impression of weakness to imperialist countries, and correcting internal errors was not the same as negating the achievements of socialism. Gomulka replied that Zhou's views would be carefully studied.[157]

In his one-day visit to Hungary on 17 January, Zhou made public speeches before five different groups of people and talked with the leadership for seven hours, saying that China supported the Soviet efforts "to smash the counterrevolution" since the nature of the Hungarian situation was different from the Polish one. Hungary would certainly have been lost to the West had the Soviet Union not intervened militarily. He gave assurances of Chinese support for the new government as long as it did not impair "the unity of the socialist camp" and the cohesion of the Warsaw Pact. And he insisted that socialist countries should seek solutions on the basis of consultation between equals.[158]

Zhou returned to Moscow from Hungary and then proceeded on to Afghanistan and New Delhi, where he arrived on 24 January for talks with India's prime minister, Jawaharlal Nehru. From Delhi, he reported his impressions of the Soviet leadership to Mao. In his talks with the Polish and Hungarian representatives, he had stressed the need for socialist unity under Soviet leadership, but he believed that, in fact, the Soviet leaders always placed their own interests above those of other fraternal parties. The Soviet Union would certainly repeat past mistakes, Zhou said. There were significant differences between the Soviet and the Chinese parties. With respect to the international situation, the Soviet leaders were preoccupied with immediate and short-term problems and did not assess the world situation with a long-term perspective. "We have to bring their attention to the problem," Zhou suggested, "but with patience."[159]

In the years that followed, Sino-Soviet differences continued to grow. A host of issues were being debated, many of them dealing with relations within the socialist camp and leadership of the socialist revolution in the Third World. Khrushchev had voiced criticism of the Great Leap Forward, greatly angering Mao. But the crux of the matter was the issue of war and peace in a world of nuclear weapons. Whereas, in the Chinese view, war was unavoidable, Khrushchev warned against the dangers of a nuclear confrontation, which, he believed, had to be avoided at all costs. In an open letter to the CCP, the CPSU pointed out that "the atom bomb does not distinguish between imperialists and working people, it strikes at areas, so that millions of workers would be killed for every monopolist destroyed.... Apparently those who describe the thermonuclear weapon as a 'paper tiger' [as Mao had repeatedly done] are not fully aware of its destructive power," the letter said.[160] The Soviet leader, perceiving Mao's discounting of the danger of nuclear weapons as a serious threat, cancelled his defense agreement with China and his promise to supply the Chinese with a sample atom bomb. Zhou, for his part, concluded that the Soviet Union, by refusing to fulfill its agreement with China, was trying to maintain a Soviet-American monopoly on nuclear weapons. The Soviet insistence on peaceful coexistence with the United States and the conclusion of a test ban treaty between the two countries further validated Zhou's perception.

Clashes between India and China over border disputes in August 1959 also contributed to the deterioration of relations between China and the Soviet Union. The Soviet news agency, TASS, issued a statement expressing regret over the clashes but not support for China. Zhou angrily pointed out that Khrushchev was allowing the ideological disputes between the two communist parties to affect state-to-state relations. When Khrushchev went to China at the end of September 1959, after a visit to the United States, the Sino-Indian border disputes became a bone of contention during his talks with Mao and other Chinese leaders. Khrushchev complained that the Chinese had pushed Nehru toward the West over no more than a piece of barren land. Zhou interrupted him to defend the Chinese position. Khrushchev showed no interest in Zhou's elaboration on the border question, but said to Mao, "You sent Zhou Enlai to Moscow in 1957 to lecture us on how to handle relations with other socialist countries." Zhou retorted that he had not "lectured" anyone but had only pointed out problems as they really existed.[161]

On 20 April 1960, *Hongqi* (Red Flag) published an editorial titled "Long Live Leninism": it placed Sino-Soviet ideological polemics openly on display. At this point, an increasing number of Chinese leaders were involved in relations with the USSR. Being in charge of state-to-state relations, Zhou was not directly involved in the ideological disputes. They were handled by Liu Shaoqi and the Central Secretariat under Deng Xiaoping, who called upon the best writers of the Party to form a writing group engaged in fighting with the pen.[162] From an orthodox and doctrinaire Marxist point of view, the Chinese made vigorous attacks on Khrushchev and other Soviet leaders, accusing them of attempting to revise Marxism-Leninism, capitulate to imperialism, and betray the interests of the revolutionary people of the world.

In October 1961, Zhou led a CCP delegation to attend the twenty-second CPSU congress in Moscow. At the congress, ideological disputes flared up with such vehemence that Zhou left Moscow in protest before the congress concluded. In October 1964, Khrushchev was overthrown. The Chinese leaders were jubilant about the fall of the "chieftain of modern revisionism." They were convinced that the new Party leadership under Leonid Brezhnev could only improve the ideological situation in the Soviet Union. In order to explore to what extent the CPSU would return to the path of Marxism-Leninism, Zhou Enlai and He Long were sent to Moscow with a delegation to participate in the activities marking the forty-seventh anniversary of the Russian Revolution. To his great disappointment, Brezhnev informed Zhou that the CPSU would not change any of the views expressed in the polemics with the CCP and that its China policy would remain the same as under Khrushchev. Even more galling to the Chinese was Soviet defense minister Marshal Rodion Yakovlevich Malinovsky's remarks about China and Mao, which he freely expressed to He Long. Malinowsky suggested that, since the Soviet leaders had succeeded in removing Khrushchev, the Chinese leaders should follow their example and overthrow Mao. He made it clear to He Long that friendly relations between the two countries could be restored if that happened. Informed about these remarks, Zhou lodged a vigorous protest with Brezhnev, who apologized and assured Zhou that Malinowsky's remarks did not represent the official views of the CPSU. But the incident deepened Chinese resentment against the Soviet Union and the rift between the two parties.[163]

Zhou Enlai's last official contact with the Soviet leadership before the Cultural Revolution began in 1966 was a meeting in Beijing with Soviet prime minister Alexei Kosygin in February 1965, when the latter was on his way to Vietnam. In their talks Zhou proposed the improvement of trade relations, the completion of the projects the Soviet Union had contracted with China before the polemics had started, the development of cultural cooperation, the implementation of a banking agreement that had been concluded in the 1950s, and student exchanges, but no progress was made in any of these areas.[164]

The repercussions of the Sino-Soviet dispute were not confined to the socialist camp. Both China and the Soviet Union tried to build up support for their positions among Third World countries, where Chinese leaders believed that national independence movements were strongly allied to revolutionary movements. Moreover, after many African countries won independence in the early 1960s, the withdrawal of the Western colonial powers had left a power vacuum, which, in the Chinese view, might be used by the two superpowers establish some form of neocolonialism. From December 1963 to February 1964, Zhou led a delegation to thirteen Middle Eastern, African, and Asian countries to demonstrate China's willingness to develop friendly relations with these countries, to support movements for national independence in these areas, and to clarify misunderstandings about China's domestic and foreign policies. Although Zhou Enlai impressed many of his hosts with his personal charm and some of his charges against the superpowers fell on sympathetic ears, he failed to find solid allies because many of the countries he visited remained dependent on Soviet or American economic assistance.[165]

## Strategic Decisions

The development of nuclear weapons had been on Zhou's agenda since the mid 1950s. On 14 January 1955, Zhou invited Li Siguang and Qian Sanqiang, respectively China's top geologist and physicist, to his office at Zhongnanhai. For three hours the two scientists—both educated in the West—explained to the Premier their work in the field of exploration of uranium and nuclear technology. The next day they were invited to talk to an enlarged meeting of the Central Committee Secretariat—presided over by Mao himself—about the basics of atomic energy. Shortly thereafter, Mao decided that Chinese scientists should begin research on atomic power.

With the deterioration of the relations between the Soviet Union and China it became increasingly clear that the Soviet Union was unwilling to keep its commitment to transfer nuclear technology to China. As a result, the Chinese leadership attributed even higher priority to the development of atomic weapons. Zhou Enlai was determined to "just ignore [the Soviets] and to do it ourselves" while Chen Yi declared the he "could not quite straighten his back as a foreign minister if we don't have the missile and atomic bomb."[166]

Zhou, as most leaders realized, was the only person capable of efficiently building up a project of such complexity. He had the organizational talent needed for this kind of intricate problem, the power to make major decisions and to cut through cumbersome procedures which might hamper many essential issues. Mao agreed. Under the code name "project 596," a group of western educated scientists set to work. They were assured of the cooperation and the infrastructural support of more than twenty ministries, an equal number of provinces and more than 900 factories, scientific research institutes and universities. In November 1962, a Special Committee of fifteen persons with Zhou as its chairman was created to organize the teamwork.[167]

The work proceeded smoothly despite of a large number of technical problems that required solutions and massive mobilization of manpower for the project. In the early 1960s, while the country was still in the grips of famine, a great number of scientists, technicians, workers and military began to converge to the atomic test base that had been established in the desert of Lop Nor (Luobubo) in west China. To ensure adequate living conditions—especially food—for them required astute solutions. Zhou himself took charge of the food supply. He instructed the Ministry of Commerce and the PLA logistics department to establish a special supply station—whose performance he monitored himself—to cater to the needs of the test base.

In January 1964 Zhou was informed that enriched uranium, vital for the making of the bomb, had been developed—undoubtedly an important breakthrough. On 11 April, Zhou called the Special Committee to discuss suitable dates for the explosion. By October all preparations were finished; and the first atomic bomb was detonated on 16 October 1964 at the Lop Nor test facility. It was the day when Khrushchev was overthrown. Seven months later, on 14 May 1965, a second bomb was tested in an aerial drop. On that occasion, Zhou made explained to the Central Military Committee why Mao had chosen this particular date for the explosion which coincided with the Afro-Asian Solidarity Conference. The date was chosen to give the participants of the conference a chance to voice their reservations about the Chinese atomic tests. But, more importantly, Zhou declared that it would give the Chinese representatives at the conference the opportunity to justify the tests in front of the Third World delegates.[168] For Zhou and his country these were days of great triumph and considerable increase in self-confidence. In defiance of all odds and in spite of their increasing isolation, they had finally achieved a major goal they had set for themselves.

The increasingly hostile relations between China and the Soviet Union, between China and India, as well as the escalation of the war in Vietnam with growing American involvement gave rise to a series of other strategic decisions by the Chinese leadership. They were based on a report by the PLA General-Chief-of-Staff that strongly influenced Mao's assessment of the international situation. The report suggested that the greatest threat to China emanated not from the United States but from the Soviet Union. Therefore, China's major cities, its industries, its communication lines, energy and water supplies would be vulnerable to an attack from the north and the northeast. Mao also became convinced that there was great danger of another world war into which China might be drawn. In an era of atomic weapons, Mao said, China needed strategic rear areas. He proposed classifying China's regions into three different sectors according to their vulnerability. Strategic exposure decreased as one moved from the northeast and the coastal areas towards the provinces of southwest and northwest China. These territories could be developed into "third line areas" where enterprises of strategic importance could be safely implanted. The first priority, according to Mao, should be given to infrastructural projects such as railways and iron and steel works which should be established in Sichuan and Gansu, and military industries should be implanted in or moved to Sichuan or Gansu. In August 1964, the Central Committee adopted Mao's proposal. This implied a revision of the Third Five Year Plan (1966–1970)—where Zhou had given priority to "providing people with food, clothing and daily necessities" through the promotion of agriculture and light industry. Preference was now given to the building up of extravagant projects of national defense.[169]

Third line construction—as the new policy was referred to—required a rapid revision of the Third Five Year Plan. For this purpose Mao ordered the establishment of a planning group under Zhou's direct responsibility and made it clear that none of the vice premiers were allowed to interfere with its work. According to Mao's instructions Zhou formulated the so-called "four guarantees" (*sige baozheng*) that the Chairman wanted to see as the basis for the Third Five Year Plan: to guarantee the completion of the requirements for war preparedness; to guarantee aid to foreign countries (this was most important for Vietnam); to guarantee the resources for the third-line construction and for the key projects associated with it. A Central Working Conference held in Beijing from 18 September to 12 October formally adopted these guidelines.[170] A year later, however, Mao appeared no longer to attach much importance to all this. He was preparing the Cultural Revolution which would cancel all previous economic plans and policies.

### The Vietnam War

At a time when relations between China and the outside world were becoming increasingly conflictual, it launched a campaign of socialist solidarity with North Vietnam, then engaged in an escalating conflict with the United States.

The agreement reached at the 1954 Geneva Conference regarding Indochina did not produce the unified Vietnam Zhou had hoped for. After the French withdrawal of France in the aftermath of a military defeat in Dien Bien Phu, the United States had stepped in to support the Ngo Dinh Diem regime in South Vietnam. From that point on there was no going back. Under the presidencies of John F. Kennedy and Lyndon

Johnson, U.S. military involvement was continuously escalated from 700 U.S. military advisers to a peak of 542,000 armed personnel in 1969.[171]

The United States became embroiled in Vietnam just when China's foreign policy, because of the Sino-Soviet split, was becoming increasingly militant. Zhou's Five Principles of Peaceful Coexistence in international relations were gradually replaced by a growing emphasis on the support of nationalist and revolutionary movements. The discrepancy between traditional and new radical foreign policy became evident in the early 1960s, when Wang Jiaxiang, the head of the International Liaison Department of the Central Committee, suggested that should China focus its attention on overcoming its own growing economic difficulties. He argued in favor of a more conciliatory stand in foreign policy in order to avoid any crisis with the United States, the Soviet Union, and India. Also, he recommended a decrease of Chinese expenditures in foreign aid. Mao derided Wang's proposals as "three reconciliations and the one reduction" (*san he yi shao*), by which he meant that they were tantamount to a reconciliation with imperialists, revisionists, and such reactionaries as the "Indian ruling clique."[172] The Chairman insisted that in the face of Soviet revisionism, China should become the mainstay of the worldwide revolutionary movement, which, he believed, was on the upsurge at that time. In Mao's mind, there was, therefore, no question of reducing aid to revolutionary movements in the world. Though Zhou may not have agreed with this view, he, as was usually his wont, submitted to Mao's analysis. In the case of Vietnam, however, he proceeded wholeheartedly to operationlize a firm policy of supporting the Vietcong in their struggle against American imperialism.

The Chinese government vigorously protested every step Washington took to increase its involvement in South Vietnam. The creation of a U.S. military command structure in the South Vietnamese capital of Saigon generated a firm response from Beijing. On 27 August 1962, Zhou Enlai flew to Guangzhou to meet with North Vietnam's premier, Pham Van Dong, where he made the commitment to supply the Vietcong with enough weapons to arm 230 infantry battalions, free of charge.[173] He invited the leaders of the communist parties of Vietnam, Laos, and Indonesia to talks in Guangdong province in September 1963. In a strong statement, Zhou assessed the future U.S. strategy in Vietnam. He thought it likely that the United States would intervene directly in Vietnam, but was not troubled by this prospect since he did not believe in the efficacy of such an intervention. In his view, U.S. forces were too dispersed throughout the world to be able to crack down effectively on the revolutionary movement in Vietnam. It was as if the United States were stretching out ten fingers to catch ten fleas at the same time. He believed that the United States was doomed to fail if it became involved in a war in Indochina. But, he insisted that the American imperialists could be defeated only if the Southeast Asian people persisted in their struggle and remained firm in their belief that they would prevail. Southeast Asia, he argued, was one of the areas where all major contradictions of the world were centered. While the imperialists and the colonialists were deeply involved there, the rule of the local regimes was weak in this area. The communist parties, for their part, were privileged by a solid position through the support of a politically conscious people, and their rich experience in fighting reactionaries. He assured the participants at the meeting that China would serve as a reliable rear area for the revolutionary movement in Southeast Asia. China took it as its most solemn and just duty to give them its utmost support in their struggle against imperialism.

As U.S. involvement amplified during the Johnson administration, the communist leaders of the region gathered at another strategic meeting, held in Hanoi from 5 to 8 July 1964. Zhou presented two scenarios: either the United States would intensify its "special warfare" in the south or wage a "limited war," sending U.S. troops to South Vietnam and Laos and bombing North Vietnam. Regardless of what happened, Zhou promised that the CCP would give its full support to its Vietnamese and Laotian comrades. In view of the vast military and economic superiority of the United States, he believed that the best strategy for the Vietnamese would be to engage in protracted warfare, to pin down the Americans in the jungles of Indochina and to exhaust them in a struggle that might last up to five years or even longer. It would be of course preferable if the war remained limited to its present scope, but China, he said, would be prepared to meet any expansion toward its border. If the United States engaged in further escalation, China would do the same, adding, that "if the United States sends troops to fight a war in Indochina, China will also send troops to fight against it."[174]

Clearly, there were strong indications that China was ready to "fight a Korean-type war with the United States." This was reinforced in August 1964, after the Golf of Tonkin incident where North Vietnamese gun boats attacked American vessels in international waters, leading the U.S. government to order air strikes against North Vietnam. In protest, Zhou approved a Central Committee directive to organize mass demonstration in major Chinese cities. He took part in a mass rally of 100,000 people in Beijing on 8 August. All over China, 20 million people demonstrated in support of North Vietnam. In February 1965, after communist guerrillas attacked U.S. Army barracks at Pleiku, President Johnson sanctioned unlimited air cover over South Vietnam and ordered the deployment of two battalions of marines at Da Nang. Beijing reacted with official condemnation, and Zhou organized a mass rally at the Tiananmen Square to demonstrate solidarity with the Vietnamese people in which 1.5 million people participated.[175]

During 1965, China continued to send messages to the United States threatening to send troops to fight side by side with the Vietnamese if the United States escalated the war; this was echoed in an editorial carried by the *People's Daily* on 25 March. In response, the U.S. ambassador, Walter Stoessel, stated at Sino-American ambassadorial talks in Warsaw—the only forum where direct communications between the U.S. and Chinese officials took place—that his government had no intention of fighting a war with China and that bombardments would be confined to North Vietnam. Zhou mistrusted that statement, viewing it as an attempt to divide China and Vietnam. He asked the President Ayub Khan of Pakistan to pass a message to the United States that consisted of three points: (1) that China would not provoke a war with the United States; (2) that China meant what it said and would act in accordance with all its international obligations (a replica of a warning that Zhou had issued before U.S. troops crossed the thirty-eighth parallel in Korea, which the U.S. government had ignored); and (3) that China was prepared for a war if the United States made the first strike.

Later Zhou added another point to his message: that if war broke out, it would have no boundaries, by which he meant that an attack on China from the air and by sea would lead to a ground war. The United States alone would not be able to decide how such a war would proceed. If the United States attacked China from the air, China would strike back at places of its own choosing.

In the course of 1965, Zhou and the North Vietnamese government and army developed an elaborate program of military assistance covering military and economic affairs, engineering, communications, and logistics. To implement it, Zhou established the "Aid Vietnam

Leading Group of the Central Committee," headed by Luo Ruiqing, and the "Aid Vietnam Working Group of the State Council," headed by Yang Chengwu as the executive organ of the Leading Group.[176]

The Chinese air force had permanent instructions to keep a close watch on the U.S. aircraft encroaching on Chinese air space. On 9 April, Zhou authorized the Chinese air force to open fire on U.S. aircraft entering the air space over Hainan island and the mainland. The following day, the Central Committee stepped up war preparations, issuing a directive that the war in Vietnam had become a serious threat to China's security and called upon all Party members, the army, and all people to brace themselves for the worse.[177]

Before Chinese troops entered Vietnamese territory in June 1965, Zhou issued another protest note, condemning the direct participation of U.S. troops in combat operations in South Vietnam. Once established on Vietnamese territory, the Chinese troops began operations with the establishment of outposts on the islands along the coast of North Vietnam. The aim was to prevent U.S. troops from replicating landing maneuvers at Inchon during the Korean War. PLA surface-to-air missile units and anti-aircraft units took over air defense from the North Vietnamese, who concentrated on the ground war. The construction of roads, railways, and bridges was taken over by the Chinese engineering troops and North Vietnamese railway construction battalions. Chinese logistical units supplied food and ammunition. At the peak, there were 170,000 Chinese troops in North Vietnam, including minesweeper units. Between 1965 and 1968, a total of 320,000 Chinese troops were involved in the Vietnam war effort. They constructed 1,200 kilometers of highway, more than 300 bridges, and more than 100 kilometers of railroads. Chinese troops engaged in numerous air-defense operations. During the three years they were in North Vietnam, they suffered more than 6,000 casualties.

Perhaps the greatest Chinese contribution was the construction of the Ho Chi Minh Trail, a path winding through the jungles from the border of Yunnan province to South Vietnam, thus greatly reducing the effectiveness of U.S. bombing. Zhou was directly involved in its planning and construction. Using bicycles, handcarts, or wheelbarrows as transportation vehicles, it supplied food and ammunition through the jungles from China to the guerrillas in South Vietnam.[178]

The Chinese decision to confront the United States in Vietnam was clearly a consensual option, but the modalities of its operation were probably Zhou's. The Chinese intervention in Vietnam, is once again another classic example of his great acumen of rigorously implementing decisions, and of confronting his diplomatic adversaries with remarkable agility.

# 4

# Cultural Revolution (1966–1976)

The last ten years of Zhou Enlai's life were perhaps the most difficult and the most tragic. They coincided with the Cultural Revolution, a political movement that produced unprecedented social division, mass mobilization, hysteria, upheavals, arbitrary cruelty, torture, killings, and even civil war. All this occurred under the instigation and the patronage of Mao Zedong, who by that time had turned into one of the most tyrannical despots of the twentieth century.

Zhou was deeply affected by these developments. The Cultural Revolution released the monster that he and the rest of the Chinese leadership had helped to create, and that now raised its head to devour them. All of them had contributed to the establishment of a hierarchical structure with Mao at the undisputed pinnacle, a position that they had reinforced with a devout personality cult vigorously promoted by Lin Biao. On his initiative, the "little red book" of Mao's quotations was published in millions of copies spreading Mao worship throughout the entire nation.

Zhou made his own contribution to lift Mao's deification to a new height by producing a song and dance performance entitled: "March forward under the banner of Mao Zedong Thought." He used the well known folksong "The East is Red" that had appeared in the 1940s as a keynote for a collection of patriotic and revolutionary songs of the past four decades.[1] It was accompanied by dances and dialogues describing the history of the Chinese Communist Party and the People's Republic. Zhou was intensely committed to the production of the show, dedicating so much of his time to the theme, composition, plot, scenery, choice of songs and dances, dialogues, lightening, make-up and rehearsals that he became its de facto director. Mao occupied the most prominent place in all the scenes. All dances, songs and dialogues gave credit to Mao's shaping of a victorious revolutionary strategy. Many scenes were revised several times before Zhou was satisfied. He ordered the inclusion of three of Mao's poems: "Jinggangshan," "The Long March" and "The PLA occupies Nanjing" in the performance. He adapted historical realities to his need to herald Mao's accomplishments. In short, he conveyed the notion that only Mao had been capable of leading the Chinese revolution to a victory.[2]

On 2 October 1964, "The East is Red" was performed by 2,000 artists accompanied by a 1,000-person chorus made up by university students. All Chinese leaders, including Mao, watched the performance. It was staged repeatedly in Beijing to ensure that all citizens would be able to see it. Then it was made into a film that was shown all over China. It had become Zhou's masterpiece. According to Edgar Snow who saw the stage performance in Beijing:

> In the four-hour revolutionary pageant of dance and song ..., Mao was the only hero. As a climax in that performance—presented with a cast for the visiting king and queen of Afghanistan, accompanied by their host, Chairman Liu Shaoqi—I saw a portrait copied from a photograph taken by myself in 1963, blown up to about thirty feet high. It gave me a mixed feeling of pride of craftsmanship and an uneasy recollection of similar extravagance of worship of Joseph Stalin seen during wartime years in Russia.[3]

Despite the unrelenting homage to Mao, the demi-god, virtually all leaders, irrespective of rank, fell victim to Mao's manipulations. While Mao proceeded with his purge, they, the leading cadres, veteran revolutionaries, and old comrades-in-arms, observed the downfall of their peers without demurral. Did any of them ever wonder whether he would be the next to be dismissed, imprisoned, and even killed?

Only once, in February 1967, did members of the Politburo dare to raise their heads and express strong reservations about Cultural Revolution policies. Zhou remained neutral in the dispute. And none of the leaders questioned Mao, who promptly quelled their revolt, the immediate consequence of which was the intensification of the madness of the Cultural Revolution.

Citizens from all walks of life were also deeply affected by the Machiavellian aberrations of the Cultural Revolution. There are no reliable statistics about the number of those who died during that period, or about those who were physically or mentally tortured, but their number arguably runs into millions. People were driven into factionalism, leading to mutual recriminations among colleagues, neighbors, friends, and families. The cases of broken marriages and shattered professional lives, and the sensation of disillusionment with the revolution and the society, for which many had worked all their lives, have never been assessed. Nor have the repercussions of this era on young people been investigated. Driven into the Red Guard movement, they were abused and incited to act on their cruelest instincts. They were encouraged to practice vandalism and hooliganism and penalized if they hesitated to comply. Their minds were clouded with senseless propaganda, they were deprived of education and family life, and finally, when their usefulness as Mao's temporary pawns faded, they were exiled to remote labor camps. Stalin's victims were sent to labor camps in Siberia and elsewhere, and Hitler's victims were transported to concentration camps, but none of them believed that they were going there to serve their country. In China they did. The youth of China, exiled to the northeastern provinces, to the deserts of Mongolia, and to remote areas in central and western China, went there voluntarily, with smiles on their faces and a belief in their hearts that they were serving Chairman Mao's "great and justified cause."

Although at times Zhou tried to circumvent some of Mao's most radical policies, his loyalty to the Chairman overshadowed all other considerations. He remained a willing servant of the despot, who, in his eyes, represented the Chinese Communist Party (CCP) and the cause for which so many communists had sacrificed their lives. And the party could not be wrong. This attitude also helped him to survive politically. He was the only one of the highest-ranking leaders to survive the turmoil without being purged. For this he was willing to close his eyes to the injustices against his closest colleagues, to deal with clamorous Red Guards and their irrational demands, and to face the most ruthless infighting at the apex of the Party hierarchy, where he had to cope with a group of arrogant leftists promoted by Mao, and where a false step could lead to personal disaster.

During most of the period, Zhou's position—navigating the frequent political vacillations characteristic of this period—remained hazardous. In the initial stages of the Cultural Revolution, Mao did not inform him of his far-reaching intentions but used him to serve his immediate needs. After the Cultural Revolution was in full swing, Zhou was constantly maneuvering between his own convictions and the need to adjust to the radical policies promoted by Mao and his coterie. After the purge of most of the senior leaders of the Party, the government, and administration, he developed an iron self-discipline and seemingly limitless work ethic, managing the country almost single-handedly—a task already exacting under normal circumstances but gargantuan in the chaos generated by the Cultural Revolution. His efforts to maintain a minimum of administration and to avoid a spill-over of the Cultural Revolution into certain sectors, such as the economy and foreign affairs, attracted criticism and, in some cases, virulent attacks. As a result, many of his efforts were doomed to fail.

## From Poetry to Politics

Reflecting on post-1949 China, Mao concluded that the revolution had failed to eliminate the bourgeois class in Chinese society; that "bourgeoisie" was still prominent and still struggling against the proletariat and its socialist achievements. Most important, in Mao's perception, the Party itself had lost much of its revolutionary spirit, and many of its leaders had become representatives of the bourgeoisie and of capitalism. He referred to them as "bourgeois elements" and "capitalist roaders" who had to be eliminated.[4]

With the benefit of hindsight it is clear that Mao intended to carry out a major purge of the Party establishment. Proceeding step by step—a tactic he called "peeling the bamboo shoot"—he gradually shifted his attacks to the highest echelons of the Party hierarchy.[5] He did not reveal his designs, but to carry them out, he used a group of leftists to light the flames of mass insurrection. Because, at the start of the Cultural Revolution, they were outsiders without legitimacy, Mao also needed Zhou, clearly an efficient and capable administrator with the authority and the ability to implement Mao's instructions that, at that stage, the leftists did not possess.

As his first target, Mao singled out the literary establishment of Beijing. His initial move, launched in Shanghai in the autumn of 1965, was the publication of an article by Yao Wenyuan, a left-wing intellectual, under the title "Commenting on the Historical Play 'Hai Rui Dismissed from Office.'" It strongly criticized a play written in by Wu Han, then a vice-mayor of Beijing and noted historian of the Ming dynasty. The play commended Hai Rui, an official at the Ming court, for having confronted the emperor over the issue of returning to peasants land confiscated by local despots. It is worth noting that it was Mao's long-time secretary, Hu Qiaomu, who had originally commissioned Wu Han to write the play, the underlying objective of which was to encourage subordinates to report honestly about the results of the Great Leap Forward. Hu had evidently acted on Mao's orders. But now Mao ordered Wu Han's play to be criticized because he perceived it as a condemnation of his own Great Leap policies and of his dismissal of Peng Dehuai.

Criticism of Wu Han's play in 1965 was clearly a prelude to Mao's offensive against the party leadership in Beijing. Peng Zhen, mayor of Beijing, was a powerful leader not only in Beijing but also in the central Party hierarchy, in which he was second only to Deng Xiaoping, the general secretary of the Party. Peng was in charge of the cultural activities in Beijing and, as such, had strong influence on those activities throughout China. As Wu Han's superior, he refused to cooperate in the plot against his friend.

Zhou and the Beijing leadership were unaware that Mao had instigated Yao's article. The unexpected attack on Wu Han therefore came as a surprise, causing considerable irritation at the Beijing municipality and the Central Propaganda Department.[6] Things became much clearer when Mao instructed Zhou, then in Shanghai to celebrate the eightieth birthday of the American writer Anna Louise Strong, to see to it that the Beijing newspapers reprinted Yao's article without delay. Zhou had a long-standing relationship with Wu Han. He had encouraged him to join the CCP and knew that Wu Han had been a faithful supporter of the communist cause since the 1940s; moreover, he was aware that Wu had written his play at Mao's behest.[7] Nevertheless Zhou's unquestioning loyalty to Mao drove him to act upon Mao's instructions. He telephoned Peng Zhen to convey the Chairman's wishes. Realizing that such a publication would mean the end of Wu Han's career, Peng said, "Premier, you know Wu Han very well. In the present situation, what do you think we should do?" Zhou promptly replied, "This is not the time to inquire about my views; the point is to carry out the Chairman's decision. There is no alternative but to reprint the article."[8]

Public criticism of Wu Han's play then took off. It became the center of heated debates at political meetings, where people examined the negative lessons to be drawn from the play. Zhou believed that the increasingly tense atmosphere had become so potentially harmful to Wu Han that he advised him to leave the city. In late February 1966, Zhou made arrangements for Wu to hide in a people's commune near Beijing. But less than a month later, Wu was recalled to the capital and turned over to university Red Guards to be "struggled against." Incarcerated in March 1968, he died in October of that year.[9]

Attacks now were shifted to Peng Zhen. In early March, Zhou invited Peng to his residence in Zhongnanhai to prepare him for what was to come. Peng still found Wu's condemnation difficult to accept. But Zhou told him "not to repeat what you have said just now to anybody. As of today you have to keep quiet!" Peng, who had not yet grasped the full implications of Mao's actions, asked Zhou why he had to be silent about Wu Han's case. "Because that [Wu Han's opposition to the party] is Chairman Mao's view. You, I, and all comrades in the Politburo should respect Chairman Mao's views." He urged Peng to be patient and not to try to explain everything because it might take years for matters to be cleared up.[10]

But Zhou's advice came too late. From Hangzhou, Mao accused the Beijing Municipal Party Committee and the Propaganda Department of the Central Committee of shielding undesirables and of refusing support to the left. He criticized Wu Han and others no longer by innuendo but by name, claiming that they were "antiparty and antisocialist elements."[1] In mid-April, the Secretariat of the Central Committee held meetings to criticize Peng Zhen. In late April, he was deprived of all his posts. All the frontline leaders, such as Liu Shaoqi, Zhou Enlai, Zhu De, and Deng Xiaoping, who had supported Peng's policies, now abandoned him and went along with Mao. Peng's purge was the first serious blow Mao dealt to the Party establishment. But none of them seemed to understand the implications of Mao's actions, nor did they imagine that they could be his next victims.

Luo Ruiqing, linked to the military establishment, was another target. As general secretary of the Central Military Commission, general chief of staff of the People's Liberation Army (PLA), member of the Central Committee Secretariat, and vice-premier of the State Council, he was another "bamboo shoot peel." His downfall was the result of a power struggle between him and Lin Biao, who felt threatened by Luo's growing influence over the armed forces. In addition, he had clashed with Lin Biao over methods of military training, which Lin believed required political indoctrination. Lin, a member of Mao's left-wing coterie, convinced Mao that Luo harbored an ambition to gain total control of the army.[11] Between 8 and 15 December 1965, a number of Party and army leaders were hastily summoned to Shanghai. No one but Mao, Lin, and Zhou was aware of the purpose of the gathering. On 11 December, Luo was called to Shanghai from Kunming in Yunnan province, where he was on a military inspection tour. Upon his arrival in Shanghai, he was escorted to a house where Zhou informed him that his "political problems" had been a subject of discussion at the highest level. According to the reminiscences of Luo's wife, all this was completely unexpected. It had never even occurred to Luo that he might have committed "political mistakes." After Zhou left, she asked her husband what was going on. "There is a meeting," he answered. "I am being accused of opposing Lin Biao, of refusing to give priority to politics in my work and of having wild ambitions in the army."[12] He and his wife were both placed under house arrest. Zhou and Deng went to see them once more, this time to convey a message from Mao that if Luo was innocent of the accusations (opposition to Lin Biao, refusal to give priority to politics in the army, and possession of wild military ambitions), then he should begin to examine his other problems. But Luo did not understand what problems Mao was referring to.

In early March 1966, when Luo was allowed to return to Beijing, the Standing Committee of the Central Military Commission, on Mao's orders, escalated the attack on him. Now, he was accused of opposing the Party, the Chairman, and Mao Zedong Thought. In desperation, Luo telephoned Zhou to ask him to arrange a meeting with Mao in the belief that he might be able to convince the Chairman of his innocence. But Zhou, knowing that there would be no hope of justice from Mao, told him that he was "too naive."[13] A few days later, on 18 March, Luo attempted to kill himself by jumping from the top of a building, but he only broke his legs. His suicide attempt made matters worse. He was accused of being a "diehard counterrevolutionary" who intended to throw the onus of his "ignominious death" on the Party. Along with Peng Zhen and two other high-ranking leaders, Luo was officially purged at an enlarged meeting of the Politburo held in Beijing from 4 to 26 May 1966.[14] On 16 May, the Politburo issued a circular calling on all Party members to thoroughly expose all reactionary and bourgeois ideas.[15] It also established a Central Cultural Revolution Group (CCRG), which gave legitimacy to Mao's left-wing coterie, dominated by his wife, Jiang Qing.

After Luo's disgrace, rumors began to circulate about a military coup threatening Beijing, probably started by Lin Biao. Mao took them seriously and instructed Zhou to make special security arrangements for the capital. Zhou transferred three army divisions to the city to reinforce the Beijing Garrison and to ensure the protection of Party and government installations. In a speech to the Politburo on 21 May, Zhou warned of a "counterrevolutionary coup" and, at the same time, applauded the inculpation of Peng, Luo, and others as "a victory for Mao Zedong Thought."[16]

In spite of his ability to adjust to new situations, Zhou remained outside of Mao's intimate circle of radicals as represented by the newly established CCRG. As a result, he was often in the dark about the Chairman's latest thinking, leading him to make a series of "mistakes," for which he then had to apologize. He did not, for example, immediately understand Mao's scheme for mobilizing the masses against the establishment. It was Kang Sheng—adviser to the CCRG and Mao's evil genius—who was instrumental in encouraging a mass movement at Beijing University (often abbreviated as "Beida"). On 25 May, a poster appeared on campus criticizing its president and an official of the Beijing Party committee in charge of education for alleged attempts to restrict or sabotage the Cultural Revolution. Before this point, public attacks on high-ranking officials by those who were below them hierarchically had not occurred, so the poster created a sensation. Zhou was shocked by the event and sent his representatives to Beida to investigate the situation. He insisted that all differences with the leadership at Beida were a matter of internal Party policy that should not be publicized on posters. But this kind of publicity was precisely what Mao wanted. In fact, he was so satisfied with the poster that he ordered its immediate broadcast nationwide. Zhou was even more stunned when he was informed of Mao's intentions only minutes before the poster was put on the air.[17]

The excitement over the poster encouraged students at Beida and other universities to criticize professors and university officials for failure to follow Mao's directives concerning the Cultural Revolution. Middle-school students began to organize a Red Guard movement that pledged to safeguard Mao's revolutionary line. The situation soon spiraled out of control to the point that school authorities desperately sought help from the Party center to restore order. The Standing Committee, presided over by Liu Shaoqi, discussed the situation in early June and decided to send the "work teams" to universities and high schools to bring the situation under control.[18] Zhou supported this decision, and more than a thousand cadres from Party and government institutions were dispatched to the schools. The confrontations, initiated by students against their teachers and school officials, were quickly contained, and a number of students were singled out as "sham leftists but real rightists." The first signs of chaotic indiscipline at places of learning had thus been quelled.

When Mao finally returned to Beijing after an absence of nearly eight months, he overturned the Party leadership's attempt to rein in the confrontation in Beijing's educational institutions. He sharply condemned Liu's and Deng's efforts to maintain order, emphasizing that the work teams had rendered a "disservice" to the Cultural Revolution by suppressing radical students. He ordered their immediate withdrawal and the organization of a rally of ten thousand students and teachers to announce his decision. Zhou, Liu, and Deng appeared at the rally to make public self-criticisms of their policies.[19]

Mao accelerated the movement in August. At the eleventh plenum of the Central Committee, he once more criticized the leadership's work team policy and, in an unusual gesture, himself wrote a poster "Bombard the Headquarters ...," condemning Liu and Deng for having "adopted the reactionary stand of the bourgeoisie, enforced a bourgeois dictatorship, and struck down the surging movement of the Great Proletarian Cultural Revolution." To sharpen the effect of his attack on Liu and Deng, Mao referred to the rightist deviation in 1962 and to policies, "leftist in form but rightist in essence," practiced in 1964.[20]

Zhou's views were identical to those of Deng and Liu; but to find himself cast in the same mold as them was embarrassing and undoubtedly complicated his position vis-à-vis Mao. To foreclose any risk of an attack he made a self-criticism at the plenum in August to underline his "poor understanding" of the Cultural Revolution. He admitted that he was inclined to "treat the new revolution, the new movement with old methods and with an old frame of mind," reproaching himself for his failure to "follow the developments closely" and pledging to mend himself by "throwing himself with enthusiasm into the battle" of the movement.[21]

By playing safe and by distancing himself from other party leaders, Zhou managed to maintain his previous position as number three in Mao's new and radical reshuffle, while Lin Biao was promoted to second place in the party hierarchy and Liu Shaoqi was demoted to the eighth rank. After his mea culpa, he was entrusted with the direction of the Politburo, a task that had hitherto been part of Liu Shaoqi's responsibilities. Put in charge of both the government and the party, Zhou now officially moved to the center of political action. But his power was severely reduced, because he had to share it with the CCRG, which participated in all Politburo meetings.[22]

## *Red Guards and Rebels on the Move*

Continuing his campaign to radicalize the situation, Mao encouraged the middle-school students attached to Qinghua University to "revolt against reactionaries." In a letter of 1 August 1966, he expressed his "warm support" to the young rebels. This gave the Red Guard movement at schools and universities a serious boost. To celebrate the launching of the Cultural Revolution, he appeared two weeks later on the rostrum at the south gate of the Imperial Palace to "receive" one million students and teachers who had assembled at Tiananmen Square. Mao did not utter a word, but Lin Biao called on the students "to smash those persons in power who are traveling the capitalist road, the bourgeois reactionary authorities, and all royalists of the bourgeoisie." He also urged them to destroy the "four olds," that is, old culture, old ideas, old customs, and old habits of the exploiting class. This was indeed a landmark event to which the Red Guards responded eagerly. From 19 August to the end of September, they beat to death seventeen hundred people in Beijing alone and chased from the capital some eighty-five thousand people whom they considered representatives of the "five black categories," namely, former landlords, rich peasants, counterrevolutionaries, bad elements, and rightists. Many cities were under siege and became targets of "red terror."[23]

Zhou was caught on the horns of a dilemma. Clearly, it was out of character for him to endorse such brutal actions; at the same time, he could not challenge them since Mao had encouraged the revolt. Zhou tried to find a safe formula: while demonstrating his solidarity with the Chairman, he attempted to restrain the Red Guards from committing outrageously wayward acts that were undermining the stability of society. So what did he do? First, he openly demonstrated his solidarity with Mao and the CCRG, publicly praising the Red Guards' killing and vandalism. "You have smashed the 'four olds'," he said in a speech, "and you have established the 'four news' of the proletariat. You have completely smashed what was left of the old world and thus made a great contribution to the Great Proletarian Cultural Revolution in our country."[24] At the same time, he tried to keep the Red Guards from going too far. For this purpose, he established a "General Liaison Station of Beijing University and Middle-School Red Guards," with responsibility for maintaining regular contacts with the Red Guards and advising them on their activities. The Red Guards, however, bluntly refused to listen, making the effectiveness of the station questionable. Thus Zhou had to become personally involved in numerous discussions and negotiations with the Red Guards. From the date of the establishment of the liaison station on 24 August 1966 until the end of the year, he was present at forty large meetings with Red Guards and many smaller ones. In all these encounters, he urged the Red Guards to refrain from violence and emphasized that the majority of cadres at all levels were basically good and that only a small number of them deserved to be attacked. Ransacking houses and chasing people out of the cities, he told them, did not serve the purpose of the Cultural Revolution. To reach out to the restive rebels psychologically, he also had to engage in banal discussions such as those on women's hairstyles, which at any other time would have been considered trivial. Some Red Guards complained that Song Qingling (Sun Yat-sen's widow) was still making up her hair in a chignon, a symbol of feudalism. Zhou warned them against any improper action against her or any other well-known non-communists who had made a valuable contribution to the Chinese revolution. He also discussed the problem of girls' wearing their hair long and suggested that, at least, short braids should be permitted. On another occasion, when Red Guards suggested outlawing Islam, Zhou cautioned them against any such action and reminded them that there were many countries in the world with a large Muslim population.[25] Although Zhou was not completely successful in convincing the Red Guards, he did save the Imperial Palace, which was on the brink of being destroyed as part of the movement to abolish the "four olds." Zhou ordered it closed, and so it remained for the entire period of the Cultural Revolution.

Mao further compounded the ongoing chaos. In June, while still sojourning in Hangzhou, he declared that students from all over China should be allowed to travel to Beijing "to create havoc there."[26] When Mao "received" more than a million and a half Red Guards at Tiananmen Square on 31 August, Zhou moderated Mao's radical call by encouraging students to come to the capital in stages and in groups. This was confirmed by a Central Committee and State Council document issued on 5 September. At the same time, the CCRG sent students from Beijing to other cities to recount their rebellious experiences to the others and to kindle the flames of radicalism in the provinces. This massive phenomenon of exchanging "revolutionary experiences" created serious logistical problems. From September until the end of the year, providing transportation for the millions on the move became one of Zhou's major concerns. He spent endless hours with officials at the Ministry of

Railways to draw up plans to accommodate the travelers and thus to ensure the implementation of Mao's idea while avoiding a total breakdown. Since he was also responsible for lodging and feeding the students who arrived in the capital, he instructed the city's work units to host the students. He took the lead by arranging for some of them to stay at Zhongnanhai.

In October 1966, Mao further accelerated the campaign against the "bourgeois reactionary line" of Liu Shaoqi and Deng Xiaoping, contending that they had oppressed revolutionary students at the beginning of the Cultural Revolution, whereas the correct line should have been to "trust and rely on the revolutionary masses." Their target of attack, insisted Mao, should have been the "handful of Party members in power taking the capitalist road." The Liu-Deng line, he said, was "hitting hard at many to protect a few," instead of "hitting hard at a few to protect many."[27]

Lin Biao reiterated Mao's reasoning in a major speech on 1 October, Chinese National Day, and the campaign reached a climax with a *Red Flag* editorial published the following day.[28] The campaign against the Liu-Deng line was now officially launched with a focus on their decision of dispatching work teams to rein in the chaos at schools and universities. Liu and Deng made self-criticism in October at a central work conference, attended by delegates from all over China. The forum provided widespread publicity of their disgrace. But Zhou, who had supported Liu's and Deng's policies, was not persecuted. He had been on an official visit to Romania, Albania, and Pakistan when the campaign to restore order was in full force. This was taken as an indication that he was not involved in the actual implementation of these policies. In fact, Mao, aware of Zhou's organizational efficiency, had no intention of purging him along with the other major leaders. He also was sure of Zhou's loyalty and needed his help in carrying forward his Cultural Revolution.

In the wake of the conference, Zhou was confronted with a host of problems created by Red Guards. First, the work of the State Council under his jurisdiction was seriously hampered by fulminations against the Liu-Deng line, which mainly affected former work team leaders of ministerial rank. The university students demanded revenge. They wanted former work team leaders to return to their schools and submit to "struggle sessions." During those sessions, the officials, among them many of ministerial rank, were cruelly humiliated. They were often held prisoner and sometimes even tortured to death. The authorities were reluctant to let work team leaders return to the places where they had operated. But the students were hardly deterred by this; they forced their way into the ministries to capture those whom they wished. Equally important for them was to lay their hands on the dossiers the work teams had compiled about them; they feared that these files might contain information detrimental to their future careers and lives. Nearly all ministries were broken into, including the Ministry of Foreign Affairs, where students penetrated the Political Department and removed several bags full of dossiers that had been collected on them. Groups of Red Guards also penetrated the Ministry of Geology four times, remaining on the premises for fifteen days and in the end abducting two vice-ministers. Others staged a twenty-eight-day sit-in at the gate of the National Commission for Defense Science to demand that one of the department directors of the commission be handed over to them.[29] Even Lin Biao's military establishment was not spared. Riotous students from military schools broke into its offices to claim Li Tianyu, the deputy general chief of staff, accusing him of having disciplined students at military academies.[30] Constant harassment thus obstructed the functioning of the government, putting Zhou under considerable strain to ensure its day-to-day work.

Another source of disorder was the emergence of factionalism among the Red Guards. Aggressive radical organizations and more conservative groupings both claimed to follow Mao's political line and tried to win the support of the CCRG, which had the power to decide who was radical and who was conservative.

Zhou devoted much of his time and patience to mediating between the factions. While the CCRG did not hesitate to decide who were revolutionaries and who were conservatives, Zhou was vaguer. In his view, both factions were "revolutionary mass organizations"—the difference between them was that the conservatives had come to realize the importance of criticizing the Liu-Deng line only after some delay. The radicals, he argued, should help them in their understanding and unite with them.[31]

It is interesting to note that conservative Red Guards generally were the offspring of high cadres then under attack. One of the conservative organizations, the Western City Pickets of Red Guards, for example, operated under the leadership of the son of Foreign Minister Chen Yi, who was under investigation by the radical faction of the Foreign Affairs System. The Western City Pickets strongly opposed the radical Red

Guards' attacks on their parents. Zhou, while verbally supporting the radicals, extended a helping hand to this conservative group, providing them with offices, telephones, vehicles, and printers.[32]

Zhou Enlai's sympathies for the conservatives made him vulnerable to pressures from the CCRG and other radicals. In the fall of 1966, some radicals accused him of "muddling along without a clear distinction between the revolutionaries and the conservatives."[33] This was the first of a series of leftist attacks Zhou had to endure during the months to come.

## Repercussions on the Economy

In its early stages, the Cultural Revolution was perceived as a political purge in the areas of culture and academia or, in Mao's terms, the superstructure of society. Clearly, this excluded the economic sector. But, by June 1966, the situation had changed; disturbing signs of frenzy also began to appear in the industrial and the transportation sectors. To nip the agitation in the bud, the Central Committee and the State Council, with Mao's agreement, issued a joint circular reminding enterprises that they had to fulfill state quotas and that production should not be interrupted by the Cultural Revolution. This also applied to the rural sector, where the people's communes were expected to continue to function normally.[34]

But this was hardly possible. The escalating Cultural Revolution soon engulfed all sectors, including the economic sector. The counties directly involved in management of the agricultural sector were particularly targeted by Red Guards from the cities, who had ostensibly come to help their local counterparts to "make revolution" and to uncover "capitalist roaders" in Party and administrative organs. In one county in Heilongjiang province, for example, aside from the Party secretary and the county magistrate, eleven out of twenty-one heads of the agricultural communes were subjected to "struggle sessions." In the late summer and the autumn of 1966, the spillover of the Cultural Revolution into the rural sector became even more evident; and as the harvest season approached, it became imperative to limit the negative effects of the movement on food production, on which the entire country depended.[35]

In the industrial sector, too, workers began to rebel. A large number of contract and temporary workers, feeling disadvantaged in comparison with full-time workers, went on strike. Zhou had now to face the additional danger of economic disruption. While publicly continuing to emphasize the great historical significance of the Cultural Revolution, he privately confided to close aides his concern that all the agitation might damage the economy even more than the Great Leap Forward had. "Should the economic bases be destroyed," he said, "the situation will be uncontrollable." In order to avoid such an eventuality, he tried to increase his own control over the economic sector by appointing to the State Council—with Mao's approval—two renowned economists, Gu Mu and Yu Qiuli, to act as his aides in economic affairs, each in charge of ten ministries.[36] At a mass rally on 15 September, he emphasized the importance of a well-functioning economy, which, in his view, should not be a target of the Cultural Revolution. "The aim of the Great Proletarian Cultural Revolution," he said, "is to revolutionize people's ideology and, as a consequence, to achieve greater, faster, better, and more economic results in our country's industrial and agricultural production." According to Mao's instructions, he said, people should "take a firm hold of the revolution with one hand and press production forward with the other." He asked workers and peasants to remain at their jobs and implored Red Guards and students to abstain from "going to the factories and enterprises, to Party, government, and public institutions at the county level and below, and to the people's communes, in order to establish revolutionary ties." Instead, the students should help with the harvest.[37]

Zhou then issued two circulars to reiterate the previous directives concerning revolutionary activities in the economic sector. A third one prohibited the establishment of Red Guard organizations in enterprises and government institutions dealing with economic issues; those that had already been established were ordered to be dissolved.[38]

Despite these precautions, the Cultural Revolution continued to gain momentum and to spill over into the economic sector. In November, the CCRG countered Zhou's policies with its own twelve-point regulation stipulating that workers should establish their own revolutionary organizations and that students and Red Guards should be admitted to factories to "exchange revolutionary experiences" with the workers.[39]

In early December, Lin Biao joined the fray. Presiding over an enlarged meeting of the Politburo, he declared that promotion of the Cultural Revolution in all areas was inevitable: "let it engulf every field and penetrate every field."[40] He thus proposed his own definition of the Cultural Revolution: a "movement to criticize, examine, and educate cadres in a big way." The CCRG followed suit, denouncing what it regarded as the State Council's attempt to "starve the revolution" under the pretext of "grasping production."[41] A new version of the regulations on industry was adopted, stipulating that the Cultural Revolution should unfold not only in the industrial and transportation sectors but in rural areas below the county level, a decision directly involving the people's communes.[42] The whole economy thus had become a target of agitation.

Once again Zhou found himself in a difficult situation. After having expressed doubts about the premise that "once revolution was grasped, production will develop automatically," he was now confronted with Mao's changed attitude and the overwhelming victory of the radical faction; and once again, he adjusted his own attitude to match Mao's. In a speech to the Politburo, he accused all those who had expressed concern about the adverse effects of the movement on the economy of having "demonstrated a poor understanding of the Cultural Revolution." All his attempts to persuade them of the contrary, he said, had met with failure. With this approach, he identified himself with Lin Biao and the CCRG. But, at the State Council, he developed a more subtle approach, telling his ministers that the situation at the moment was irreversible and therefore the only way to survive was to go with the tide. "We will drown if we go against it," he said.[43] Indeed, shortly thereafter, the *People's Daily* of 26 December carried an editorial welcoming the "upsurge of the Great Proletarian Cultural Revolution in industrial and mining enterprises," complicating Zhou's task even further.

When the Cultural Revolution was officially launched in 1966, Zhou had pledged to involve himself fully in the movement. But as the year was drawing to a close, he was becoming increasingly doubtful about its value. No longer did he hide his concern from his trusted colleagues. But to oppose Mao's policies openly would have risked his political and perhaps his physical survival. Besides, the Cultural Revolution demanded such a commitment that, even for the adroit and elusive Zhou, it became increasingly difficult to remain aloof. He had to embrace the movement, but to do so would mean, as he confided to his colleagues at the State Council, "to go into the inferno." "If I do not go through the inferno," he asked, "then who will go?"[44]

The new year began ominously. Workers' organizations in Shanghai rebelled and seized power in the local and municipal Party committees, throwing out "the handful of Party members in power taking the capitalist road." In no other communist-ruled country had a leader of the Communist Party ever called upon the people to seize power from the Party officials. But this was precisely what Mao did. Not only did he welcome developments in Shanghai, he elevated them to the status of official policy to be emulated elsewhere. "This is a great revolution in which one class overthrows the other," he declared and added with great satisfaction that "since the revolutionary forces in Shanghai have risen, there is hope for all of China."[45] Mao was determined to regain the power that he believed had been lost to his political foes. He was determined to renew the Party and state establishment by replacing the current structures with tripartite revolutionary committees based on the participation of the masses. In practical terms, this new policy led to the establishment of "rebel" organizations in enterprises and government institutions at all levels that mirrored the Red Guard organizations at schools and universities.

Mao expected Zhou to guide this new policy, and so he did.[46] While playing up to the radicals, he wanted to control the process of seizing power, by raising a series of leading questions: did power seizure mean that all leading cadres were suspected of being "Party members in power" and were thus to be removed from their positions? On what basis can one decide whether a person was "traveling the capitalist road"? Who had the right to seize power? And what form should it take?

Zhou gave his own definition of "Party members in power" by declaring that they were those who had supervisory responsibilities. Clearly, this widened the category of "power holders" considerably, since anyone holding the rank of Party branch secretary (the basic unit in the Party structure) or section chief (the basic unit of government administration) would fit into this classification. In Zhou's estimation, not all power holders were traveling the capitalist road. However, since it would take too much time to determine who did and who did not, power should be seized as quickly as possible; and the question as to who is a capitalist roader would have to be answered later. Zhou emphasized that, while power should be seized in the provinces and municipalities, the Center, meaning the Politburo, should be untouched.[47]

There was something paradoxical in Zhou's approach, which unavoidably led to some confusion. While emphasizing the official policy line that power seizure should take place in all leading institutions at provincial and government levels, he tried to retain as many leading cadres as possible, mostly ministers and vice-ministers, to run the government administration on the grounds that most cadres were politically acceptable and thus should be allowed to work. However, he authorized immediate power seizure in practically all Party and government units, regardless of whether or not its leading cadres were "traveling the capitalist road."

As the Cultural Revolution gathered momentum, the confusion deepened. Zhou was unable to keep his ministers and vice-ministers at their posts; the majority of them were either "overthrown" or had to submit to "examinations." Normal government functioning became impossible. Even worse was the impasse generated by factional infighting among the rank and file over their share of power. In the face of such paralysis, Zhou had no alternative but to turn to Mao and Lin Biao. In May 1967, he reported to them that factional conflicts in most of the State Council institutions had reached the point that he felt compelled to introduce military control to ensure the functioning of the ministries. Mao accepted Zhou's suggestion. Military representatives became active in most government institutions, with some exceptions, particularly the Foreign Ministry, where Zhou had already agreed to the establishment of a strong rebel organization.

Zhou's problems at the central government were mirrored at the provincial level, where leaders were seriously threatened by Red Guards and rebels. About thirty provincial Party leaders were forced to leave their hometowns for Beijing, where they were given safe haven at a guesthouse of the Central Committee. But before long Red Guards and rebels from the provinces complained to the CCRG that the Beijing authorities were providing shelter to local Party leaders responsible for carrying out Liu Shaoqi's policies suppressing the student movement. Their emissaries arrived in Beijing to search for the leaders and to return them to the provinces, where they were to be "struggled against." The situation became critical in the summer of 1967, when Zhou, under pressure from the radicals, allowed Red Guards from Sichuan to take Li Jingquan, the secretary of the Southwest China Bureau of the Central Committee, and Liao Zhigao, provincial Party secretary for Sichuan, from the guesthouse to attend a "struggle meeting." Zhou had agreed, on condition that they would be returned promptly. However, after the guesthouse was penetrated by Red Guards, it was no longer safe, so Zhou acted with Fu Chongbi, the commander of the Beijing Garrison, to hide the leaders in PLA barracks in Beijing's suburbs. Jiang Qing, who wanted them to return to their home provinces, demanded to be informed about their hiding place. Zhou tried to avoid arguing with her, but Fu was pressured to reveal the whereabouts of the leaders. He was saved by a telephone call summoning him to Mao, to whom he explained the problem. Mao decided that they could remain in Beijing for a while, giving them a respite.[48]

While Zhou was reorganizing the activities of the ministries, in accordance with the requirements of the rebels' power seizures, his own position was endangered. The premier had experienced some challenges earlier, but they had been sporadic and did not present a serious threat. He continued to be regarded as the "general chief-of-staff of the proletarian headquarters of Mao Zedong." But in February 1967, Zhou's political position was seriously threatened by the "February Countercurrent"—an event that was in effect a revolt of senior leaders against the Cultural Revolution. It took the form of a serious confrontation between State Council members and veteran revolutionaries on the one hand, and the CCRG on the other. On two occasions—at a meeting of the Central Military Commission on 19 and 20 January and at a meeting of the Politburo on 11 and 16 February—they clashed regarding the way the Cultural Revolution had so far proceeded.[49]

The confrontation centered around three issues: (1) What role did the Party play in the Cultural Revolution? Was its leadership of the movement undesirable? (2) Should all veteran cadres be regarded as capitalist roaders and thus be removed? (3) Could the stability of the army be maintained while its leaders were under attack by students from the military academies and by the rank and file military staff?[50]

These questions indeed were crucial, for they centered on the role of the Party and the army, the two major institutions of the Chinese political system. In a concerted attack on the Cultural Revolution, these high-ranking leaders accused the CCRG of depriving the Party of its traditional leadership, of destroying the stability of the army, and persecuting veteran cadres who, for decades, had proved their worth to the revolution and the republic. Although there had already been a number of inner-party conflicts, the leaders emphasized that the struggle against them was the cruelest in the Party's history.[51]

Zhou presided over the Politburo meetings, with his characteristic caution. Although he abstained from restraining the veteran cadres from their confrontation with the CCRG, he also avoided joining them.

When Mao heard about the outburst of the senior leadership, he flew into a rage, asserting that the CCRG, whose "mistakes amounted to 1, 2, or 3 percent" was basically correct in the implementation of his policies. He made it clear that there could be "no way to overthrow the Cultural Revolution" and warned that outbursts by state and Party leaders, in effect, meant that "Liu and Deng should come back." If this were the case, he warned, he and Lin Biao, along with Lin's wife, Ye Qun, would return to Jinggangshan (the red base area in the 1920s) to engage in another guerrilla war.[52] This was a strong declaration: decisive, uncompromising, and belligerent. Mao ordered that those who had been involved in this challenge be criticized at enlarged Politburo meetings, by which he meant the participation of the CCRG. He instructed Zhou to preside over these meetings. Once again, since Mao had taken an unequivocal position against the old guard revolutionaries, Zhou immediately sought protective cover by criticizing himself, conceding that he had been "dull and slow in awareness" of the present struggle and thus had failed to prevent the occurrence of the "two upheavals." But if Mao avoided criticizing Zhou directly, Jiang Qing did not hesitate to do so. In a frontal attack, she accused him of wavering in his support of the Cultural Revolution. Once again, Zhou found himself with his back to the wall. His only way out was to act just as he always did in such situations: denigrate himself, condemn those who were under attack, and go along with Mao. Between 25 February and 18 March, he chaired a number of meetings that forcefully attacked all those involved in the "February Countercurrent" events.[53]

The major consequence of all this was the strengthening of the political position of the CCRG to the detriment of the traditional leadership. The Politburo stopped functioning. Its tasks were taken over by the CCRG assembling in "routine meetings" presided over by Zhou. To further disgrace the veteran leadership, the CCRG leaked classified material about the February events to its own partisans among Red Guard leaders, who immediately started a "counterattack on the February Countercurrent," characterizing it as "capitalist restoration."[54]

Zhou was now overshadowed by Jiang Qing, who had accumulated increasing popularity as Mao's "good student" and the zealous leader of the "revolutionary left." Radical students began to accuse Zhou of having acted as the "the backstage boss of the February Countercurrent." Word was spread that the Cultural Revolution had entered a new phase: the phase of a struggle between the "old administration" (headed by Zhou) and the new one under the CCRG.[55] Denunciations of this kind, though still by innuendo, became increasingly frequent. Mao stopped all this to avoid any diversion from his focused strategy of lambasting Liu Shaoqi. He therefore instructed Chen Boda, his former secretary and the head of the CCRG, to make a public statement to come to Zhou's rescue. In late

May, Chen told Red Guards that "Premier Zhou is respected abroad as well as at home.... He is in the responsible position of carrying out Chairman Mao's and Vice Chairman Lin Biao's policies. No one, under any circumstances, is allowed to find fault with Premier Zhou."[56] The attacks against Zhou came to a halt.

Mao had thus saved Zhou from the radicals, largely because he needed him to manage the country and to faithfully carry out Mao's wishes without being challenged. No one in Mao's entourage had Zhou's capacity for running the affairs of state. However, while wanting Zhou to be at the helm under his control, Mao introduced a radical institutional change after the February events that was shifting the balance of power in favor of the CCRG. The Standing Committee of the Politburo, emblematic of traditional state power, had been dethroned, while the CCRG was increasingly asserting itself, with Mao's support and encouragement.

## Relations with the New Power Elite

For Zhou all this was paradoxical and tragic. He was assigned the task of running the country in close cooperation with the CCRG, over which he hardly had any control. In his subtle, prudent, and low-key way, he maintained a relationship with the CCRG. He identified himself with the radical group on all major issues, working closely with its members in support of the Red Guard movement, in criticizing Liu's and Deng's bourgeois line, and in the campaign to seize power. Although he frequently disagreed with the CCRG, he avoided open confrontation. In fact, when differences surfaced, he tended to hold back, changing his stand when it was clear that conflicts with the CCRG could only create political problems for him.

In early 1967, for example, Kang Sheng and Jiang Qing launched a campaign to "ferret out renegades" among high-ranking Party officials who had been imprisoned by the Guomindang in the 1930s and then released on the eve of the anti-Japanese war. These officials were now suddenly accused of complicity with the Guomindang to obtain their release. In a letter to Mao, Zhou tried to defend the old guard, stating that some of them had indeed made confessions to obtain their release. But, he reminded Mao, this had been done in compliance with a decision of the Party leadership in Yan'an encouraging them to employ such a strategy. Moreover, he emphasized, this question had already been reexamined in

the past by the seventh and eighth congresses of the CCP and that, in his
view, there was no reason to reopen their cases, since it had already been
established that they could not be considered renegades.[57]

Mao paid no heed to Zhou's reminder and did not object to the
renewal of the accusations. Sixty-one high-ranking and hitherto highly
respected Party officials were therefore purged. Since Mao supported the
purge, Zhou ceded. As he had on many other occasions, he changed his
position on the issue and, in public speeches, joined in the condemnation
of the "sixty-one-renegade group."

Zhou, weakened within the institutional framework, was eager to
develop good relations with the new dignitaries not only on major issues
but also on a personal level. On many occasions, he therefore expressed
his respect for Kang Sheng, knowing that Mao trusted him. In addition,
he often invited Chen Boda to accompany him to meetings with foreign
visitors, usually presenting him as the "best assistant to Chairman Mao
and vice chairman Lin" and the "outstanding theoretician of our Party
who has excelled in the interpretation of Mao Zedong Thought."[58]

Managing Jiang Qing, Mao's powerful and ill-tempered wife, was
more difficult. Her views, moods and outbursts were universally dreaded,
and no one, not even Kang Sheng and Chen Boda, could afford to ignore
them. It therefore required the most meticulous care even from the
naturally cautious and diplomatic premier. Zhou's relationship with Jiang
Qing dated back to the 1940s in Yan'an, where she had become Mao's
wife. Whenever Jiang Qing quarreled with her husband, she would come
to Zhou complaining, sometimes even crying, and Zhou would mediate
between the couple. After the 1949 Revolution Zhou boosted her status.
Since Jiang Qing had had a career as a film actress in the 1930s, Zhou
appointed her to the Commission of Film Censorship. And, in 1956, he
suggested to the Standing Committee that she be nominated as one of
Mao's five political secretaries, with the rank of vice minister, an official
position she held before the outbreak of the Cultural Revolution.[59]

In the early phases of the Cultural Revolution, Jiang Qing had
developed more self-assurance. She was not only Mao's wife and senior
secretary but also one of his most trusted aides and most authoritative
spokeswoman, who faithfully assisted him in launching the new political
movement. Zhou understood the political weight she carried at the time
and treated her accordingly.

Among the members of the CCRG, Jiang Qing was perhaps the only
one who dared to confront Zhou when differences emerged. Zhou

handled such situations with self-restraint and patience. At the same time, he played on her vanity, seizing every opportunity to publicly praise her and to emphasize the importance of her role in the revolution. One such occasion was during the campaign against Liu Shaoqi's "bourgeois reactionary line" in the fall of 1966, when Zhou declared that the campaign "could not be separated from the leading role of comrade Jiang Qing." Another occasion was during the stand-off between conservatives and radicals in the late summer of 1967, when he paid public tribute to Jiang Qing for her speeches against ultraleftism.

Perhaps the most important service that he rendered Jiang Qing was the timely help he extended to her when hostile Red Guards tried to uncover her past. During the 1930s, newspapers had given her romances a great deal of publicity; no one paid much attention then, but resuscitating them now could prove extremely damaging to her image as a "proletarian revolutionary" of the Cultural Revolution. A group of Red Guard organizations hostile to her and the CCRG was trying to do precisely this: unearth her past. The most troublesome event was the circumstances of her release from a Guomindang prison, where she was held for revolutionary activities in Shanghai, and of her relationship with Cui Wanqiu, a special agent of the Guomindang. It was alleged that she had confessed and betrayed the Party before her release.[60] These accusations made her vulnerable in the campaign to "ferret out renegades" that she had helped to initiate.

Again in the summer of 1967, Zhou came to her rescue. A number of bags containing material about Jiang Qing's past were delivered to the Beijing garrison. Fu Chongbi, fearing Jiang Qing's reaction if she learned that he possessed such material, sought Zhou's advice on the matter. Zhou considered it important to give her assurances that no one had read the material, so he ordered the bags to be sealed in the presence of Xie Fuzhi, minister of public security; Wang Dongxing, director of the Central Committee General Office; Wu Faxian, commander of the air force; and Fu. He then informed Jiang Qing about the matter, and, with her consent, the bags were burned in the presence of the same witnesses.[61] To prevent any further investigations into Jiang Qing's past, Zhou made a public statement criticizing those who had engaged in collecting material about her and emphasized that any attempt to destroy her in this way would be in vain. He assured his audience that Jiang Qing's history was "red" (revolutionary), and not "black" (counter-revolutionary).[62]

Zhou amplified his public adoration after Mao's comments that Jiang's revolutionary activities in the 1930s led him to "discover more about Jiang Qing's character." In a public speech, he emphasized that her career had always been characterized by militancy for the Communist Party. Confronted with persecution from renegades and Guomindang reactionaries when she was very young, she had shown great courage in fighting back. The articles she wrote in the 1930s were full of revolutionary fervor from which all could learn. Therefore, those who had collected slanderous material against her had identified themselves with the "black gang." After reaching Yan'an at the beginning of the war of resistance against the Japanese, she became Chairman Mao's diligent student and close comrade-in-arms and later took part in the liberation war. After the war, Zhou continued, she had been persecuted by Liu Shaoqi, Deng Xiaoping, Peng Zhen, Luo Ruiqing, Lu Dingyi, and others whom Zhou mentioned and who, in the meantime, had been politically purged. But Jiang Qing, Zhou said, had stood up against them. Then he praised her great contributions to the reform of Beijing opera and to the cause of the Cultural Revolution. He concluded by emphasizing Jiang Qing's virtues, such as her strictness toward herself as well as others, which prompted her to measure every comrade with the yardstick of Mao Zedong Thought and enabled her to make the right distinction "between us and our enemies." Always ready to help her comrades, she was also relentless against the enemy. Those characteristics, Zhou concluded, were worth learning from.

In return for such accolades, Jiang Qing, at least for a time, showed due respect to Zhou both in public and in private. In her talks with the American writer Roxane Witke, for example, she made frequent friendly references to him. Nonetheless, a measure of tension existed between Zhou and Jiang Qing's friends in the CCRG, a tension that was particularly obvious during the first two years of the Cultural Revolution and reached a new peak during the final years of Zhou Enlai's life.

Zhou also had to reckon with Lin Biao's power center. Lin had succeeded in establishing a position of strength after purging a number of powerful military leaders. Although relations between Lin and Zhou dated back to the 1920s, they had little personal contact before they arrived at Yan'an after the Long March. Born in 1906, Lin was eight years younger than Zhou and was his student at the Huangpu Military Academy. After his graduation, he became a brilliant military leader, closely associated with Mao during the wars against the Guomindang and Japan.

Lin's meteoric rise to power began in 1959, when Lin replaced Peng Dehuai as defense minister after Peng's disgrace at the Lushan conference. Promoted to a position as the only vice-chairman of the Party and Mao's heir apparent at the eleventh plenum of the Central Committee in August 1966, Lin became the most powerful leader after Mao. He was his comrade-in-arms in command of the army and his first lieutenant in launching the Cultural Revolution. It was Lin, not Zhou, who was Mao's spokesman in the promulgation of this movement. Since Mao had a habit of making only short utterances about his intentions, it was Lin who interpreted the Chairman's remarks to the public. During the first years of the Cultural Revolution, Lin's speeches were therefore issued as authoritative Party documents to be studied and followed by all its members. In May 1966, Lin elaborated on his theory of a coup d'état to legitimize the launching of the Cultural Revolution. In August, he gave impetus to the Red Guard movement by calling on the guards to carry out the campaign to destroy the "four olds." In October, he started a systematic attack on Liu Shaoqi's bourgeois reactionary line at a mass rally at Tiananmen Square and at a central work conference. He led a vigorous crusade for Mao's strategy of creating "great disorder under heaven."[63]

It was therefore imperative that Zhou openly demonstrate his full agreement with Mao's decision to choose Lin as his heir and clearly show that he harbored no ambitions to higher leadership for himself. He displayed this conviction both in public and in private by extolling Mao's wisdom and by extending his utmost respect to Lin. In a long speech in August 1967, he compared Liu Shaoqi's and Lin Biao's behavior from a historical point of view. While systematically repudiating Liu—even though Liu had been the most vigorous proponent of Mao Zedong Thought in the early 1940s—Zhou stated that Lin was "the first holder of the great banner of Mao Zedong Thought' and a tested leader of the Party whose present high position should be legitimized by law.[64]

While flattery appeared to provide Zhou with a modicum of security, it nonetheless contained elements of danger to Lin's position. Excessive praise of anyone other than Mao could be damaging, something that Lin was well aware of. At the ninth Party congress, Zhou pronounced his most eloquent and comprehensive accolades for Lin Biao, devoting about two-thirds of his remarks to Lin. He reached back to the past to stress that, forty years earlier, Lin had become Mao's close comrade-in-arms when, as a "glorious representative" of the Nanchang uprising, he had led a group of insurrectionary forces to Jinggangshan to join Mao. Zhou clearly exaggerated Lin's importance, since at the time he was only a company leader in a regiment led by General Chen Yi. But Zhou contended that, "from this time on, Lin Biao always kept in step with Chairman Mao" and "made outstanding contributions to the Chinese people's revolutionary struggle and cause." Zhou suggested that Lin had always firmly sided with Mao in the inner-party struggles against Wang Ming, Gao Gang, Peng Dehuai, Peng Zhen, Luo Ruiqing, and Liu Shaoqi. He had developed Mao's thinking on the political education and role of the army. Zhou underlined that, in propagating Mao Zedong Thought, Lin had "come up with a complete set of effective and practical popular methods for the study of Mao Zedong Thought." Zhou expressed his appreciation for Lin's initiative to edit the "little red book" containing quotations from Mao. He also enumerated Lin Biao's contributions to the Cultural Revolution, emphasizing that Lin's designation as "Mao's close comrade-in-arms and successor" could only be "the most correct conclusion that can be naturally deduced from comrade Lin Biao's more than forty years of revolutionary fighting."[65]

Lin Biao felt embarrassed by this praise, not so much because he was innately modest, but because he feared the anger it might fuel in Mao, who did not tolerate "a second sun in the sky." So Lin immediately rose to make an extemporaneous speech to demonstrate his modesty. He had remained in step with Mao during the Jinggangshan period not because of far-sight, as the premier said, but because of the simple belief that "Chairman Mao was a distinguished leader who deserved my support." He emphasized that he owed everything to Mao and added that he was not as brilliant as Zhou had claimed, because, without the Chairman, there would be no Lin Biao.[66]

Although relations between Zhou and Lin on the whole were not antagonistic, some conflict did arise in March 1967, when Zhou bypassed Lin to suggest directly to Mao that a commander-level meeting should be convened to discuss problems emanating from the Chairman's order to the army to "support the left." Although the suggestion was approved, yet Jiang Qing, Kang Sheng, and Ye Qun reproached Zhou for having circumvented Lin by approaching Mao directly on military matters and persuaded Lin that if he did not react he would become a figurehead. Subsequently, they all approached Mao to complain about Zhou's actions. Mao also agreed that Zhou should have talked to Lin before bringing the question to him. As soon as Zhou was informed about the matter, he wrote an apologetic letter to Lin, expressing his regret for what he had done—calling it an "unforgivable mistake"—and his readiness to accept Mao's and Lin's criticism.[67]

## Further Escalation

In the first half of 1967, the frenzy of the Cultural Revolution spilled over to the armed forces. An official decision that Mao had instigated, and that was jointly signed by the Central Committee, the State Council, the Military Commission, and the CCRG, instructed the PLA to support the "revolutionary left."[68] The order generated even greater confusion since there was no definition of who represented the "revolutionary left." While the CCRG regarded radical Red Guards and rebels as the "left," the military authorities in the provinces, with their strong proclivity for order and discipline, suppressed the often extreme and excessive actions of the radicals and gave their support to the conservatives, who were moderate and tended to cooperate with them. The question as to who was to seize power in the provinces thus remained largely unsolved; and, instead of establishing the "great alliance of revolutionary masses," which was Mao's goal, rival factions resorted to violence. Where a faction was supported by the military, its opponents raided weapon depots to arm themselves. The escalating violence reached the point of civil war in many areas.

Mao decided to examine situation himself. In July, he started an inspection tour whose first stop was Wuhan. The city was in turmoil, having become the scene of military confrontation with several hundred thousand people fighting in the streets. Concerned for the Chairman's safety, Zhou flew to Wuhan in advance to make arrangements for Mao's arrival. First, he issued orders to the military authorities to prevent hostilities between the various factions, to evacuate their strongholds, and to seize all their weapons. Then, meeting with the military leaders of the region, he carefully listened to their arguments and reasons for supporting the conservatives. Whereas Zhou's preoccupation was the reestablishment of order in the chaotic city, Mao was focused on whether the military had supported the "revolutionary left." He reached the conclusion that they had not. After receiving orders from the Chairman to convey his decision to the military, Zhou demanded that they admit their mistakes and make a public self-criticism.[69]

Zhou's words were in turn transmitted to a group of radicals by Xie

Fuzhi, the radical minister of public security, and Wang Li, member of the CCRG. On 20 July, the radicals, jubilant at being recognized as the "revolutionary left," paraded in the street to celebrate their victory and to disparage the conservatives. The latter—supported by military leaders— also took to the streets to denounce Xie Fuzhi and Wang Li. The balance clearly tilted in favor of the conservative demonstrators, whose numbers swelled to the hundreds of thousands. At the height of the agitation, soldiers broke into the guesthouse where the representatives from Beijing were staying and abducted Wang Li.

Beijing was shocked. Lin Biao declared that the "July Twentieth Incident" amounted to a counterrevolutionary riot. Zhou was even more concerned than before about Mao's safety. He flew back to Wuhan to persuade him to leave. After Mao departed for Shanghai, Zhou, ever the troubleshooter, negotiated with the Wuhan military authorities to gain Wang Li's release.

The incident in Wuhan was revealing. It accelerated the trend toward radicalization, dramatically symbolized by a million-member rally in Tiananmen Square, where Zhou and other leaders welcomed the return of Wang Li and Xie Fuzhi. The leaders of the Wuhan military region were ordered to Beijing, where they had to submit to criticism by the enlarged Politburo.[70]

The army was no longer immune to events. Attacks on the military became more and more prevalent. The situation was further complicated by àn editorial in *Red Flag,* the mouthpiece of the CCRG, calling on the public to "drag out capitalist roaders" in the army, which officially sanctioned the assaults. While intensifying their offensive against the conservatives, the radicals spearheaded attacks on the military authorities throughout the country. Conservatives, backed by the military, fought back. As a result, large parts of China exploded into civil war.

### Was Zhou the Great Protector?

Many observers have argued that Zhou was a great protector of those who had become victims of the Cultural Revolution, that he hid them, and that he used his authority to rescue many people. Although this is certainly true in some cases, this image does not correspond to reality. To demonstrate his loyalty to Mao and to ensure his own safety, he identified himself with the radical members of the CCRG; in public speeches, he condemned all the national leaders who were his close comrades and who had been officially purged at different stages of the Cultural Revolution. While showing consideration and even kindness to some of his ministers in private, he was tough on others in public. He stopped one of his vice foreign ministers, Liu Xinquan, from working and ordered him to conduct a self-examination, because he was accused of having suppressed the student movement while acting as a work team leader at the Beijing Foreign Languages Institute. He ordered the arrest of a vice minister who had attempted to seize power at the Ministry of Finance in defiance of his instructions. He told a public audience that Xiao Wangdong, the acting minister of culture, Lu Zhengcao, the minister of railways, and Zhang Linzhi, the minister of coal industry, had persevered in carrying out Liu Shaoqi's reactionary line. Zhang Linzhi was tortured to death in January 1967.[71] During the radical campaign to seize power, Zhou had in fact widened the scope of persecution by announcing in a public speech that all cadres from the level of branch secretary in the Party system and of section chief in the government were "power holders" and thus open to attack. He also singled out Zhang Jingfu, Party secretary of the Chinese Academy of Sciences, and Han Guan, deputy director of the Science Commission, to be purged as "Party persons in power taking the capitalist road." Furthermore Zhou denounced Chen Jiakang, a vice foreign minister who had worked under him since the Chongqing days, as a "political clown," because he had made unfavorable remarks about Chen Yi. Chen Jiakang was sent to the ministry's May Seventh Cadre School in Hunan, where he died. He also denounced Yan Hongyan, Party secretary in Yunnan, who had committed suicide in despair over the absurdities of the Cultural Revolution, and then accused him of having "resisted Chairman Mao's revolutionary line" by killing himself. He joined in the purge and the condemnation of a number of high-ranking members of the military, and as the Cultural Revolution progressed, Zhou accused more and more senior Party and army cadres of political crimes.

In the first half of 1967 Zhou was appointed to examine high-ranking cadres at the Central Case Examination Group (CCEG; "Zhongyang zhuan'an shencha xiaozu"), and his record there is not praiseworthy. As the president of the organization, he had overall responsibility for scrutinizing the activities of the three offices created for the purpose, dealing with high-ranking Party leaders, PLA officers, and cadres from public security, and the judiciary.[72]

The statistics of the operation are impressive. According to Song Renqiong, the director of the Central Committee's Organization

Department, who reviewed the work of the cadres (on the eve of the Cultural Revolution), 1,011, or 81 percent, had been subject to persecution. Forty of them died under torture during interrogations. Many more were maimed.

The dimensions of the persecution can be seen in the fact that as many as 213 high-ranking revolutionary elders in Beijing were either jailed at the notorious Qincheng prison or remained in custody in various places outside the city. Among them were ten members of the Politburo, ten members of the Central Secretariat, seven vice prime ministers, and seventy-one members or alternates of the Central Committee. Innumerable "offenders" at various levels were kept under custody in their own work units, where special rooms were reserved for this purpose, or in labor camps that usually were called May Seventh Cadre Schools.[73]

It is important to note that, to cope with the large number of "offenders," the CCEG obtained the transfer of 789 PLA officers to assist its staff. Among them were the most brutal and ruthless professional interrogators. To meet the needs of the CCEG, torture was routinely used to extract "confessions"; and investigating officers were free to devise and inflict all types of physical and mental abuse on their victims, including severe beatings, forced consumption of drugs (including hallucinogens), sleep deprivation, and denial of medical treatment.[74]

As chairman of the CCEG, Zhou "involved himself in all of its activities." Clearly, once he took accepted a responsibility, Zhou always made sure to execute his duty with the utmost care. But significantly the CCEG replaced the spontaneity of Red Guards and rebels with methods comparable to those employed in Stalinist gulags in the Soviet Union.[75] From then on, Red Guards were manipulated by a system established under Zhou's direction. Although he still had conflicts with the CCRG, he and they appeared to have agreed that the Red Guard movement needed to be channeled, albeit not necessarily for the same reasons. While the CCRG was eager to use the guards to implement its own political agenda, Zhou wanted to control them to avoid turbulence and excesses. Zhou's role in this oppressive system, organized during the Cultural Revolution, was not laudatory, which is clear in the details of what happened to some of his colleagues.

## Wang Guangmei

Zhou's capacity for adaptation to current trends became evident in his changing attitude toward Liu Shaoqi's wife, Wang Guangmei, whom he first protected but later abandoned. When Red Guards from Qinghua University abducted her, Zhou immediately telephoned the head of the Red Guard organization and sent his secretary to the university to accompany Wang back to Zhongnanhai. But Wang's political situation became increasingly complicated, and she became a threat to those who supported her. In mid-December 1966, her past history was discussed at a CCRG briefing session. Wang, who had become an underground Party member as a student in Beijing, later served as an interpreter for the CCP during its discussions with the Marshall mission in the 1940s. After the talks broke down, she left Beijing with the CCP delegation to join the communist headquarters in Pingshan county, Hebei province, where she married Liu Shaoqi. Because of her past contacts with Americans, Jiang Qing and Kang Sheng considered her an American spy. In December 1966, to substantiate this accusation, the CCEG set up a "Wang Guangmei case group."

On the night of 16 January 1967, Zhou, aware of the danger Wang was in, telephoned her to urge her "to brace herself for whatever was to come." He neither specified what to expect nor tried to save her from being accused as a spy. The "proof" of her complicity—that she had been following orders from the U.S. secret service when she married Liu—is similar to that used against many others.

Wang had a friend who was the sister of Yuan Shaoying, the wife of a professor at Chinese People's University; she also had a brother, Yuan Shaowen, who lived in the United States, where he worked in the aviation industry. According to Jiang Qing's and Kang Sheng's logic, working in such a sensitive area could be possible for a Chinese only if he was recruited by the Central Intelligence Agency. Here was the link to Wang Guangmei's espionage activities. Since she was visiting Yuan's home in Beijing, her only purpose could have been to exchange information with Yuan Shaowen through his sister.

In the summer of 1967, the professor and a colleague who vaguely knew Wang were arrested by the leaders of the case group. The interrogation of this colleague, who was seriously ill with cancer, was recorded as follows:

Q: Tell us about Wang Guangmei!

A: Wang Guangmei? I don't know anything.

Q: Tell us the little you know about her and her past!

A: Oh, … it is dangerous. With people like her, the country is in danger. This woman is not a simple woman. Wang Guangmei actually is a spy; but not an ordinary spy, she is a real spy. She is obviously a spy, a very serious, very tough spy.

Q: How do you know that she is a spy?

A: I ... I have a definite impression.

Q: Who told you that she is a spy?

A: I learned it from a letter.

Q: What letter?

A: It is not really a letter, it is a government bulletin.

This man died a few months after his inconclusive testimony, though it was not inconclusive for the investigators. The unfortunate university professor met with a similar fate. He was arrested and forced to confess that he was a spy working for the United States. During his interrogation, he was compelled to confirm Wang's spying activities. After torture, which made him critically ill, he declared that both he and Wang were employed by the "Strategic Information Bureau of the United States." He died in prison in 1970.[76] Thus the suspicions against Wang appeared to have been confirmed.

On 21 March 1967, Liu Shaoqi's "problematic past" was discussed at a meeting attended by Zhou, Mao, Lin Biao, Chen Boda, Kang Sheng, and a few others. Liu had been arrested by warlord governments in 1925 in Changsha and in 1929 in Mukden (Shenyang). On both occasions, it was alleged, he had confessed his membership in the CCP and, under pressure, had become a renegade. Zhou and the others decided that he should also be examined by "Group C," signing a document that Kang Sheng had drawn up to that effect. In May "Group C" was renamed the "Liu Shaoqi and Wang Guangmei case group," with the code name "Group 504." Jiang Qing and Kang Sheng, who were in charge of the proceedings of that group, immediately moved to arrest people considered capable of producing evidence to support their suspicions.[77] Zhou was aware of the infamous methods used to extract "confessions," but he did nothing to protect the victims.

In 1968, the so-called verdict condemning Wang Guangmei was publicized. At a mass meeting of a hundred thousand people, Jiang Qing announced that "Wang Guangmei is an important spy of the United States who collects strategic information!" Sitting next to her, Zhou echoed her words, shouting: "Down with the U.S. spy Wang Guangmei!" This, in turn, was echoed by the people in the rally. By shouting the slogan, Zhou drew a distinct line between himself and Wang, thus shielding himself from any accusation that he was on her side. In July 1970, when a death sentence was proposed, Zhou allegedly responded that she "deserved more than death." But Mao ruled this out, and Wang was instead imprisoned. She survived the ordeal and was rehabilitated after the Cultural Revolution.[78]

## Liu Shaoqi

Zhou's attitude toward Liu Shaoqi followed a similar pattern. During the campaign against the "February Countercurrent," many posters were put up in Beijing denouncing most of the top leaders. Even the government compound in Zhongnanhai did not escape the flood of incendiary posters. Liu, who could not avoid reading those posters, wrote to Zhou saying that he was "worried and upset" because not only he but also "a large number of senior comrades are regarded as enemies." He asked Zhou what he should do. Zhou replied that Liu should remain calm and take care of himself and informed him that he had reported his concerns to Mao.[79] This vague and noncommittal response was the last communication between Zhou and Liu, in spite of the fact that both lived at Zhongnanhai. On 1 April 1967, Liu was openly attacked as the "Number 1 Party member in power taking the capitalist road." On 7 April, his residence in the government compound was raided by rebels, and Zhou did nothing to stop them. During the summer, attacks on Liu reached a climax, with his subordinates interrogating him on his political attitude and physically abusing him in his own house. Zhou was the only one in Zhongnanhai who could have maintained some order in the government compound, but again he did nothing to prevent the violence and the abuse showered on Liu at the struggle sessions. Instead, in a long speech at a mass meeting, he castigated Liu for political "mistakes" he had committed between 1945 and 1966. Zhou enumerated how Liu had disappointed Mao, who had supported and helped him throughout the years, and about how right the Chairman had been to replace Liu with Lin Biao as his successor.

In October 1967, the eighth Central Committee condemned Liu as a "renegade, hidden traitor, and a scab" and expelled him from the Party "forever." Zhou, of course, raised his hand to endorse this decision. The ruthlessness of the attacks on Liu can be gauged from the fact that twenty-six thousand people were interrogated in connection with his "case." The death toll related to the Liu case is unknown. Liu was moved to Kaifeng in November 1969. Kept in solitary confinement and denied medical care, he died shortly thereafter.[80]

## Marshal He Long

He Long, commander of the Twenty-ninth Division of the Guomindang troops, had a long-standing relationship with Zhou, dating back to the Nanchang Uprising in 1927. Before the Cultural Revolution, He was in charge of day-to-day work at the Central Military Commission, often replacing Lin Biao, who, claiming poor health, was frequently unable to perform his duties. Frictions between the two military leaders had already surfaced before the Cultural Revolution, fueled by allegiances to different army corps within the Red Army. In addition, He Long had political and historical ties to Luo Ruiqing, whom Lin Biao had purged at the end of 1965.

Lin Biao had chosen He as his next target. Concocting a series of false accusations, Lin, with the support of the CCRG, fed Mao "evidence" about He's treacherous intention to usurp command of the air force. Rumors circulated about his alleged attempts to stage a mutiny. Red Guards were mobilized against him, and He's house in the old Legation Quarter in Beijing was raided. His new dwelling, a government guesthouse in another part of the city, became unsafe after a few days. On 9 January 1967, He and his wife went to Zhongnanhai to ask Zhou for advice and help. Zhou, who had no doubt about He's innocence, invited him to stay at his house in Zhongnanhai.

He and his wife remained there for ten days. But Mao's mood with regard to the old commander was already changing. He demanded that He Long be criticized by the Politburo. The official criticism of high-ranking leaders by this body required a special procedure, the first step of which was a "formal talk" with He Long. The Politburo had designated Zhou, Jiang Qing, and Li Fuchun, a high-ranking military leader, for this purpose.

Zhou's attitude then changed from that of a friendly supporter to that of an ominous interrogator. He solemnly declared, "Vice Chairman Lin told me that you have always talked viciously behind his back.... He is the vice chairman of the Party. The Party has principles. You should not make malicious remarks about him. You have no respect for him." When He Long, drawing continuously on his cigar, did not respond, Zhou continued, "Vice Chairman Lin told me that you poked your nose into many units of the navy, the air force, the engineering corps, the armored corps, the department of the general chief of staff and that you place your people there." He Long thereupon explained that his work at the Central Military Commission obliged him to maintain contacts with the different army units. But Zhou waved his hand to stop him and said that Wu Faxian, the commander of the air force, had reported to the Party that He had attempted to seize power in the air force. "Not only do you have no respect for Vice Chairman Lin," Zhou exclaimed, "you also have no respect for Chairman Mao. You never report to them or seek instructions from them. Like Deng Xiaoping, you have done nothing to spread Mao Zedong Thought." He Long tried to protest, but Zhou stopped him again. "Many people," he said, "in particular Vice Chairman Lin, have a negative opinion of you. He has raised a very serious question: The Chairman is still alive and healthy, but you meddle everywhere. After Chairman Mao, Lin Biao will head the Central Committee. He is afraid that you will not be obeisant to him and that you will make trouble." In tears, He Long asked: "Lin Biao said that? Premier, what do you say?" Zhou shook his head warily and said: "Let us stop here." He then told He that he had made arrangements for him and his wife to stay in the western suburbs, where they would be undisturbed.[81]

The next morning, He and his wife moved out of Zhou's house. Although they lived under the constant threat of renewed harassment, their life was relatively tolerable for the next nine months, since Zhou personally saw to their daily needs. But in September 1967, Mao approved a decision for He Long to be interrogated. This meant a change in He Long's status from a protected commander of the PLA to that of an offender who was to be investigated by the CCEG. The first consequence was a sharp deterioration in his living conditions. During the period of examination, He was not questioned but ordered to write confessions of his crimes. Although critically ill, he received only minimal medical treatment and was forced to live on prison food. In 1968, in a number of documents jointly issued by the Central Committee, the State Council, the Central Military Commission, and the CCRG, He was officially denounced as a renegade and a "counterrevolutionary revisionist." Zhou went along with the denunciation, signing all the documents and condemning He in his public speeches. He Long died on 9 June 1969, the day he was finally admitted to a hospital.[82]

## Chen Yi

Chen Yi's situation was somewhat different from the previous ones cited. Since Mao had decreed that Chen was to be criticized but not condemned as a counterrevolutionary, Zhou had more latitude in defending him against leftist attacks. Vice premier, member of the Politburo, and vice chairman of the Central Military Commission, Chen was another major target of persecution, despite being admired and respected for his ability to perform equally well as a soldier, diplomat, and poet. He was known for his humor, eloquence, and frankness.[83] The last of these, in particular, created serious political difficulties for him.

In June 1966, Chen Yi, like most of the other high-ranking leaders, was deeply involved in work team policies, having given his approval to send eight such teams to a number of units in the foreign affairs system,[84] including the foreign languages institutes, the Commission for Cultural Exchanges with Foreign Countries, and the Commission for Affairs of Overseas Chinese. Two of the work team leaders, Liu Xinquan, a vice minister of foreign affairs, and Zhang Yan, deputy chief of the Foreign Affairs Group of the State Council, had been particularly harsh with the rebellious groups in these institutions. After the reversal of these policies a few months later, they demanded their return to apologize and to make self-criticism. Liu and Zhang were reluctant to expose themselves to the vengeful young people and their predictably violent treatment. Chen Yi's attempts to mediate developed into a confrontation between him and the students. The problem was finally submitted to Zhou, who, on 3 December 1966, received a delegation of students from the Beijing Foreign Languages Institute to discuss the issue.

Complaining about the behavior of Liu Xinquan at their institute, the students referred to him as a "monster" (a term meaning counter-revolutionary).

Zhou Enlai (to the students): You are only twenty years old. Another forty years will pass before you become my age. Do you have any idea what kind of monsters you will encounter? Why do you describe Liu Xinquan in such a horrible fashion?

Student: Liu Xinquan is a counterrevolutionary revisionist.

Zhou (shaking his head): You cannot draw such a conclusion.

Student: We did.

Zhou: I haven't given you my approval.

Student (unyielding): Then we will reserve our views.

When the students continued to complain that the Cultural

Revolution was not actively implemented at the institutes of foreign languages and that left-wing students were still being suppressed, Zhou and the students had the following exchange.

Student: Comrade Chen Yi should bear the majority of the responsibility. He always tries to appease without differentiating between what is right and what is wrong.

Zhou: You accuse him of calming things down, but he has a good heart—he wants all of you to unite. Sometimes he goes a bit too far in his speech. We have been together for decades. He indeed has made a great contribution to the Party and to the revolution.

This exchange, like many others, did not change the course of events. Mao had decided that all leading cadres involved in work team policies had to make a public self-criticism before being reinstated to their positions. Zhou, eager for his colleagues from the State Council to resume their duties, succeeded in persuading Chen Yi, who did not comprehend what he had done wrong, to take the lead as the first vice premier to submit to this procedure. Chen Yi prepared a statement declaring that, in the early stages of the Cultural Revolution, he had followed a bourgeois reactionary line; that he had not immersed himself deeply enough in the study of Mao Zedong Thought, a fact that led to his failure to understand the significance and the direction of the Cultural Revolution; that some of his declarations, though made in good faith, had the effect of obstructing the Cultural Revolution; that he had been slow in correcting his erroneous attitude toward the "masses"; and, finally, that he had now realized his errors and was ready to correct himself.[85]

According to the established procedure, Chen's self-criticism was submitted to Mao for approval. Then, on 24 January, it had to be read at a meeting of ten thousand people at the Great Hall of the People. This was a pure formality—albeit a humiliating one—given the fact that the "masses" were aware of Mao's opinion on the issue and thus would readily accept Chen's declarations. Chen was then considered "liberated" and was allowed to resume his duties.

His self-criticism notwithstanding, Chen continued to disagree with the disorder and the absurdities of the Cultural Revolution, especially when it conflicted with the conduct of foreign affairs. An incident on Moscow's Red Square on 25 January 1967, when Chinese students recited quotations from Mao and laid wreaths on Lenin's and Stalin's tombs, was a case in point. The implicit, indirect criticism of the post-Stalinist leadership provoked the Soviet authorities, who ordered the students' forcible removal from Red Square. In spite of a strong official protest by China's Foreign Ministry against the manhandling of the students by the Moscow police, Chen Yi believed that the students had been out of line and—though claiming to defend Mao Zedong Thought— had merely "sought the limelight."[86] The distribution of propaganda material and of the "little red book" of quotations from Mao by Chinese embassies abroad also incited Chen Yi's indignation. He instructed the Chinese embassies to refrain from such activities, making it clear that the Cultural Revolution was not to be carried out by Chinese representatives abroad and that foreigners should not be pressured into accepting Mao badges or the "little red book."[87]

Chen Yi's "liberation" was short-lived. Within less than a month, he became involved in the February Countercurrent," once again jeopardizing his political position. Mao personally denounced him and gave him leave again to prepare a statement of self-criticism. Increasingly conscious of its own power, the CCRG was infuriated by Chen Yi's blunt disapproval of the Cultural Revolution and his palpable contempt for some members of the group. In a talk with a group of students returning from abroad, which took place only a few hours after the February confrontations between the Politburo and the CCRG, he emphasized the CCRG's responsibility for the unjustified ill treatment of old guard revolutionaries. "There are persons," he said, "who acted in bad style. They are trying to climb up by stepping on other people's bodies ... and by pushing ignorant youngsters ahead."[88]

When the CCRG conducted vigorous attacks on established cadres, Chen became a major target. Radicals regarded him as the "number one capitalist roader in the foreign affairs system" and "an antiparty, antisocialist, anti–Mao Zedong Thought element" ("three anti's," or *sanfan fenzi*). They issued numerous statements demanding that he be "smashed" and that he "come to the masses to submit to self-criticism."[89]

Self-criticism was by no means a spontaneous event. Mao had decided that Chen, like other Politburo members involved in the February events, had to follow a certain pre-established pattern. Zhou was responsible for implementation of the process. Since Chen Yi had already confessed to his "mistakes" in front of the Politburo, he was now expected to appear in front of the "masses" of the foreign affairs system.

The campaign against Chen Yi gave rise to arguments between Zhou and the radical rebels and Red Guards of the foreign affairs system. They had become increasingly suspicious that Zhou had deliberately delayed

Chen Yi's self-criticism in front of the masses. To compel Zhou to accelerate the process, they established a "liaison station to criticize Chen Yi" and, on 11 May, organized a mass rally calling for Chen to "come to the masses."

During the following night Zhou agreed to discuss Chen Yi's case again. Clearly, the frenzied atmosphere had made it unavoidable that Chen Yi had to confess to his "mistakes" once more. During the nightlong discussions, most rebels of the foreign affairs system agreed with the radical Red Guards that Chen Yi be treated as a "three-anti's element" and thus be "smashed." This attitude disappointed Zhou, who had hoped that the rebels—since they were government officials—would exercise a moderating influence on the Red Guards. He was eager for Chen's earliest possible reinstatement and thus refuted the accusations against the foreign minister, strongly arguing that Chen Yi, after having made a self-criticism, be free to work again.[90]

The next day, Red Guards again attempted to exercise pressure on Zhou regarding Chen Yi's case. Although they knew that Chen was at Zhongnanhai, they broke into the Foreign Ministry, declaring that they had come to abduct the foreign minister. Despite repeated attempts to force Zhou to bring Chen "to the masses," he procrastinated for more than two months. By the middle of July, this was no longer possible. Red Guards were camping outside the Foreign Ministry, boisterously calling for Chen Yi. Members of the CCRG also launched attacks on the foreign minister. At a mass rally staged in Beijing on 4 August, two of its prominent members, Guan Feng and Qi Benyu, declared that they fully supported the students and their demonstrations in front of the ministry, and that they regarded the students as representing the future hope of the foreign affairs system. This declaration, transmitted to the demonstrators by Yao Dengshan, a Foreign Ministry staff member considered to be a "red diplomat," made the students even more ecstatic.[91]

The question as to whether the foreign minister should be "smashed" or "liberated" became a major cause of division between the rebels in the ministry, who were far from a homogeneous group. The most important faction, in terms of numbers, was the Liaison Station of the Revolutionary Rebels, which grouped more than a thousand of about two thousand staff members who considered themselves radicals and demanded that Chen Yi be "smashed." In support of the radicals, the CCRG sent one of its prominent members, Wang Li, to talk to delegation of the Liaison Station. His talk on 7 August had several important consequences. It bolstered the morale of the radical faction and encouraged them to launch an attack on the more conservative groups, driving many of their members into hiding. The rebels took over the political department of the ministry, containing the personal files of the staff, which were of utmost importance for their future careers. This action was soon imitated by many other ministries of the central government. Finally, radical groups from the foreign language institutes, no longer satisfied with demonstrating outside its walls, penetrated the ministry, sealed the office of the Party committee, abducted two vice ministers (Ji Pengfei and Qiao Guanhua), and ordered them to sell Red Guard newspapers in the western part of the city.[92]

In the overheated atmosphere prevailing in Beijing, where the "revolutionary left" appeared to have won the day, public criticism of Chen Yi could no longer be postponed. Zhou had finally succeeded in extracting an agreement from the radicals concerning the procedure to be followed. The criticism sessions would begin on a small scale at the Foreign Ministry, attended by about a hundred people. This would be followed by a "medium-size" meeting convening about ten thousand staff members from the foreign affairs system to be held at the Great Hall of the People. Finally, the criticism session would close with a mass rally of about a hundred thousand people. On these occasions, Chen Yi was expected to listen to the participants' criticism and then make a self-criticism. After the satisfactory conclusion of this process, he would be "liberated" and reinstated to office.

There was, however, an additional problem for Zhou to resolve: who should chair the meetings? Zhou had tried to persuade the radicals and the conservatives to overcome their factionalism and to chair the meetings together. But the radical organizations were indignant about Zhou's intention to put the conservative faction, whom they believed were not in the mainstream of Mao's thinking, on par with themselves. Ultimately they refused to sit under the same roof with the conservatives. For the meeting planned at the Foreign Ministry, the question did not arise, because the radical Liaison Station held the majority there. But it did become an issue for the medium-size and the large-scale meetings. Zhou finally had to agree to organize two sessions, each chaired alternately by the radical and the conservative factions.[93]

The small meeting at the Foreign Ministry went as planned. Chen Yi, accompanied by Zhou, arrived at the small auditorium of the ministry to listen to the critical statements the rebels had prepared beforehand. Since there was not enough time for all of them to speak, it was decided that another small meeting should take place on 26 August.

On 12 August, a medium-size gathering of about ten thousand people took place at the Great Hall of the People. It was chaired by the radical Red Guards and rebels from the foreign affairs system. Chen Yi appeared, accompanied by Zhou Enlai and Xie Fuzhi, minister of public security, who wanted to ensure an orderly procedure. The second medium-size meeting, scheduled for 27 August under the chairmanship of the conservatives, never took place. The day before it was due to be held a large number of radicals stormed the Foreign Ministry, where the second small meeting was in session, in order to abduct Chen Yi and to deny the conservatives the right to hold their meeting. The Foreign Ministry Liaison Station, resenting the disturbance, interrupted their meeting, hid the foreign minister in an office inaccessible to the Red Guards and accompanied him back to Zhongnanhai in the evening. With this event, the process of criticizing Chen Yi came to an end. None of the planned large-scale meetings ever took place.

In early September the political atmosphere changed considerably. Tired of the anarchy rampant in the country, Mao blamed the "ultraleft" for the disorders. Chen Yi's "case," however, was never brought to the conclusion that Zhou had hoped to achieve. Since Mao had indicated that Chen should be criticized but not "smashed," Zhou used all the tactical maneuvering that he was capable of mustering to permit Chen's reinstatement as vice premier and foreign minister. But Zhou's maneuvers worked only halfway. Although Chen did not share the fate of many others, who were imprisoned or killed, he was not cleared and remained suspended from work. His duties at the Foreign Ministry were taken over by Ji Pengfei, who was nominated as acting foreign minister.

Chen did return to work for a short while in 1968, when Mao asked him to head a team of military experts to assess the world situation and China's strategy toward the Soviet Union and the United States. Under Chen's guidance, the team produced an analysis of the world situation that ultimately resulted in a rapprochement between China and the United States. It is noteworthy that it was not Zhou whom Mao asked to provide this kind of analysis, perhaps because Zhou was not the right person to formulate a broad policy framework despite his skill at creating operational policies. By contrast, Chen possessed that skill, though, in the end that did not save him: after having conducted his global analysis, he was once again ousted. Finally, in April 1969, at the ninth Party congress he was reelected to the Central Committee but not to the Politburo. A few months later, he was exiled to work in a factory in Hebei province. In August 1970, he took part in the Central Committee meeting at Lushan, where he again fell into political disgrace. Unaware of Mao's latest whims, he took a position different from Mao's and was condemned as a "sham Marxist" and an "antiparty careerist." Deeply depressed by his political setbacks, Chen Yi developed an intestinal cancer in early 1970 and he died in January 1972.[94]

## Ramifications for Foreign Relations

Since 1949, China had gone through myriad political gyrations, but none had any impact on the country's foreign policy. Zhou therefore presumed that this would also be the case for the Cultural Revolution, given the fact that both the party and the government had clearly ruled that "a clear distinction should be made between internal and external matters" (*bixu fenqing neiwai*).[95]

This position, however, could not be maintained. It became impossible to dissociate foreign policy from the Cultural Revolution, so its spillover into foreign relations became unavoidable. Two major factors contributed to this change: the first was the radicalization of Mao's thinking, which linked the Cultural Revolution to the international communist movement and laid claim to its leadership; and the second was the change in the configuration of internal forces with the emergence of the CCRG, which insisted on the global dissemination of Mao Zedong Thought.[96] Using the mass media under its control, it published numerous editorials intended as guidelines for foreign affairs. The group did not hesitate to circumvent Zhou and to issue instructions directly to the Foreign Ministry. Zhou's inviolable domain had been encroached upon.

The entire established foreign affairs system was considerably weakened. Zhou's own position had become vulnerable and Foreign Minister Chen Yi had become the main target of attack, repeatedly assaulted by the CCRG from above and by the Red Guards of the foreign affairs system from below. Zhou's deputies at the State Council Foreign Affairs Office—Liao Chengzhi, Zhang Yan, and others—were not allowed to function normally. Leading figures at the Foreign Ministry itself were also not spared. The first vice minister, Zhang Hanfu, had been taken into custody while Vice Ministers Ji Pengfei and Qiao Guanhua became major targets of attack because of their close association with Chen Yi. The two other vice ministers, Wang Bingnan and Chen Jiakang, were under investigation for their allegedly "bourgeois" lifestyle and work methods. The few other remaining vice ministers, who were not under political attack, had only narrow responsibilities. None was in a position to exercise effective leadership over the ministry. Even at the directorial level, many of its members had been forced to interrupt their professional activities and to "stand aside" (*kao bian zhan*).[97] And despite Zhou's explicit disapproval, Cultural Revolution activities in Chinese diplomatic missions took on proportions. Ambassadors and councilors at the embassies were accused by their own staff of having implemented Liu Shaoqi's bourgeois reactionary foreign policy. The situation, in fact, became so uncontrollable that Zhou called back almost all the ambassadors and staff to Beijing to take part in the Cultural Revolution at home.

Tumultuous incidents abounded everywhere. Just to give a few examples: a group of Beijing middle school students traveled to Hailar, a town on the border of Inner Mongolia where, in August 1966, they intercepted the Beijing-Moscow Express, entered the train, hung Mao's portrait on the cabin walls, and distributed anti-Soviet pamphlets to Soviet and Japanese travelers. Efforts by the Soviet crew to put an end to this activity ended in violence. The train was delayed for hours at the border. The following day, local Party leaders attempted to stop a recurrence. Unwilling to listen to local officials, the students insisted on telephoning Zhou. Employing his usual technique of going along with their "revolutionary spirit" while, at the same time, restraining their behavior, he discouraged the students from further misdeeds. He arranged for their return to Beijing by air and introduced them to Mao as "representatives of anti-Soviet heroes back from Hailar." These were extraordinary privileges. When the Soviet embassy complained about the incident, the Chinese Foreign Ministry denied any involvement.[98]

Even more damaging to China's image abroad was the incident of January 1967, when a group of sixty-nine Chinese students in Moscow marched to the tombs of Lenin and Stalin. After laying wreaths, they remained on the site, reciting quotations from Mao's "little red book" and proclaiming Stalin as the true friend of the Chinese people. The ensuing clashes with the Soviet police resulted in injuries, some of them serious, among the Chinese students.[99]

In Beijing, demonstrations at foreign embassies—including the Indian, Burmese, and Indonesian embassies and the British mission—proliferated, and Red Guards became uncontrollable. Zhou was worried about all this, but clearly had little choice. More often than not, the tactics that he had used earlier did not work. There was very little that he could do to fend off the popular fanaticism against foreign countries. Under the circumstances, he was forced to compromise on many proposals emanating from the domestic left-wingers and to sanction, one after another, suggestions from the rebel-dominated Foreign Ministry to lodge the "strongest and most vehement protests" against foreign countries after relatively minor incidents had occurred.

## The Hong Kong Riots

The chaos in foreign affairs spilled over to Hong Kong. Massive strikes erupted in the spring of 1967, provoked by a labor dispute that led to clashes with the police. Demonstrators marched to the office of the governor of Hong Kong to protest police actions and to plaster the walls of the governor's office building with posters and petitions. In spite of a series of injuries to the demonstrators, left-wingers decided to continue their struggle against the Hong Kong authorities. The Chinese-funded newspapers in Hong Kong published inflammatory articles, while loudspeakers installed at the top of the building of the Bank of China in downtown Victoria broadcast revolutionary slogans and songs. More violence occurred between the demonstrators and the police.

Initially, the Hong Kong events were spontaneous manifestations of social unrest that caught the State Council, its Hong Kong Office, and the Foreign Ministry by surprise. But the situation escalated rapidly into a serious crisis, as a labor dispute at a relatively insignificant factory developed into a confrontation between Great Britain and China, with the Chinese government insisting that the people of Hong Kong had the right to import the Cultural Revolution onto their territory and the British government refusing to concede any portion of its rule in the colony.

The Hong Kong affair intensified because of the direct intervention of mainland authorities. Led by a powerful network of CCP underground organizations, and supervised by the Hong Kong and Macao Working Committee, which operated under the guise of the Hong Kong branch of the Xinhua News Agency, protesters marched to the British governor's office, where they set up big-character posters denouncing the British. Further clashes with the riot police resulted in bloodshed.

Zhou was caught in a dilemma. While he felt obliged to support the leftists in their struggle against "British atrocities" in Hong Kong, he also knew that an open confrontation within the British colony could not be sustained. In line with his usual dual, contradictory tactics of both encouraging and restraining the unrest, he issued a series of contradictory and confusing instructions. On 15 May, he approved a Foreign Ministry statement demanding that the Hong Kong authorities punish the police involved in the reprisals against the demonstrators, apologize to the victims, and prevent the recurrence of similar incidents. Raising Sino-British tensions a notch further, he participated in a mass rally of a hundred thousand people opposing the Hong Kong authorities and sanctioned demonstrations in front of the British mission in Beijing, in which a million people paraded and shouted slogans for several days.[100] Hong Kong became a major issue on Zhou's already crowded agenda. He ordered the establishment of an ad hoc office on Hong Kong affairs at the Foreign Ministry with which he deliberated regularly. On the one hand, he criticized the spillover of the Cultural Revolution onto Hong Kong, which, he said, operated under conditions quite different from those in the mainland. On the other hand, he demanded that the ad hoc office produce a plan to defeat the colonial authorities. The office developed an agenda of strikes in the public sector that could eventually paralyze the colony. Zhou, albeit skeptical of its success, approved the plan, but after the first strike was launched in mid-June, it became evident that a continuous stream of financial support from China was needed to sustain the movement, and the Beijing authorities had no intention of committing themselves to financing a full-scale struggle in Hong Kong.

Nonetheless, the confrontation continued. In early July, Zhou even approved an operation by a group of Chinese militia, who, under cover by the PLA with heavy machine guns, crossed the border into the New Territories and attacked a border station, killing several police officers. Thrilled by the successful incursion, left-wingers in the Foreign Ministry's Hong Kong Office proposed more actions of the same kind. However, Zhou's restraining tactics pushed him to avoid any excessive confrontation with the British, because he knew that it would only be counterproductive. What he really wanted was to maintain the status quo in Hong Kong. In a private conversation with the commander of the Guangzhou Military Region, he therefore advised temperateness, explaining that the use of armed force was not in the interest of China's present Hong Kong policy and that all rashness should be avoided.[101]

Despite his own warnings against heedless actions, Zhou nonetheless approved a pompous note addressed to the British authorities. It was an ultimatum demanding the cancellation of a ban on the pro-communist newspapers in Hong Kong and the release, within forty-eight hours, of nineteen journalists imprisoned during the riots. The note—signed by Zhou—was delivered to the British chargé d'affaires on 20 August. Recalling this later, after the note led to a diplomatic disaster, Zhou said that, at the moment of signing it, he was too exhausted to give it any serious thought. The events may have been important enough to make them an issue for an ultimatum, but the Chinese position was too weak to enforce it.

The events now took their own course—in sum, a radical trajectory. When, on 22 August, the note was published, radical groups hastily established an organization called the Anti-Imperialist and Anti-Revisionist Liaison Station, charged with organizing demonstrations in front of the British mission. If the British did not concede to the ultimatum's demands within the established time frame, the offices of the British chargé d'affaires would be taken over.

Aware of the explosiveness of the situation, the municipal Party committee informed the Foreign Ministry and the Beijing Garrison of events. While troops were dispatched to protect the British mission, a number of Foreign Ministry officials went to the site to dissuade the rebel leaders from engaging in violence, to no effect. The emotionally charged demonstrators refused to listen. Zhou thereupon asked Chen Boda, who— as the head of the CCRG—wielded great influence over the radicals, to issue a statement asking the students to abstain from invading the grounds of the mission. Using loudspeakers on the site of the demonstration, Chen attempted to defuse the situation. However, in their state of excitement, the demonstrators ignored even Chen's appeal. The situation spiraled downward. As soon as the ultimatum deadline expired, the demonstrators broke into the building, ransacked the residence, set it on fire, and roughed up a few British diplomats, including the chargé d'affaires.[102]

That evening, Zhou summoned officers of the Beijing Garrison, Foreign Ministry officials, and Red Guard representatives to a briefing about the details of the attacks on the British mission. Zhou was indignant about the incident and criticized the Red Guards for their irresponsible actions and the Foreign Ministry officials for their failure to dissuade the students. It was evident to anyone with a minimal education, he said, that office buildings of a foreign mission were inviolable and that the host country was responsible for the personal security of diplomats. He criticized the Hong Kong Office for having issued the ultimatum. Mao was also disturbed by the incident, saying that the British mission had been burned either out of naïveté or by "bad people," referring to "class enemies" whose ulterior motive was to sabotage China's foreign relations.[103]

The failure of radical policy toward Hong Kong was perceived as a humiliation. Even Mao, who had encouraged revolutionary upheaval, was taken aback when he was confronted with the disasters created by his own policies. The blunders committed by radical policies ended in a complete loss of face, a result that Zhou fully recognized. After he was sure that Mao was thinking along the same lines, he used the Hong Kong events and the burning of the British mission in Beijing to change the official political direction. These events marked a turning point in the Cultural Revolution in the fall of 1967. Mao was no longer willing to allow the chaos of the summer to continue. Ultraleftists, he said, had abused the freedom of action that he had granted. They had to be restrained, if not eliminated. At the leadership level, two important members of the CCRG, Wang Li and Guan Feng, were accused of having instigated all the disorder and became convenient scapegoats. The radical Red Guards and rebels, who earlier had been praised for "carrying the banner of the great helmsman," were now condemned as ultraleftists and persecuted. Their usefulness as executors of the hitherto proclaimed disorder policies had come to an end.

## The Turning of the Tide

Mao had begun to show signs of weariness and concern over declining conditions in China. Several developments undoubtedly pushed him to think in terms of stemming the tidal wave of the Cultural Revolution. Chaos was gaining ground everywhere in the country. Evidence of confusion and violence mounted, and the center was increasingly unable to hold on to the reins of power. Following imperial traditions, Mao conducted an inspection tour to central China in July. In Wuhan, his first stop, he found that the city had become the scene of violent confrontation between conservatives and radicals. Mao stepped into the dispute by criticizing the regional military authorities for supporting the conservative factions and for having arrested a number of radical leaders. This, he declared, was a grave mistake.

In Beijing, too, the situation had become increasingly chaotic. Aware that Mao had left the capital, rebels and Red Guards by the thousands camped out at the government compound at Zhongnanhai, where Zhou had deliberately remained. He believed that his presence would stop the rebels and Red Guards from taking the compound by force. Indeed, they abstained from penetrating the premises. But using loudspeakers that were broadcasting day and night, the excited crowd demanded the presence of Liu Shaoqi and Deng Xiaoping at "struggle meetings." Their chants culminated in a rally of 5 million people at Tiananmen Square, where, with the CCRG in the forefront, Liu Shaoqi and Deng Xiaoping were condemned. Within Zhongnanhai, rebel groups composed of government staff were increasingly eager to contribute to the denunciation of Liu and Deng, exposing them to humiliation and mistreatment, which Zhou did nothing to check.[104] He was seriously threatened by the renewal of attacks against him by the CCRG, which once more enlisted the help of radical Red Guard and rebel organizations. In posters, mounted all over Beijing, they claimed that Zhou was the instigator of the "February Countercurrent," that he had betrayed the Cultural Revolution, and that he was "a shameful renegade of Maoism."

Having sensed Mao's mood of wariness and concern, Zhou, on 25 August, confided his grievances to Yang Chengwu, who had been appointed to act as liaison between Mao and Zhou. He talked about the worsening situation in the provinces, where armed fighting was rampant; about the siege of Zhongnanhai and the violence against Liu Shaoqi and Deng Xiaoping inside the compound; about the siege around the Foreign Ministry and the attempts to abduct the foreign minister; about Wang Li's inflammatory talk on 7 August and its possible impact on the foreign and other ministries. He described his unsuccessful efforts to prevent the attacks on the British mission and its diplomatic representatives. Finally, he told Yang that, under the present circumstances, attacks on the PLA were extremely dangerous since the army was the only institution capable of maintaining public order. Its prestige must remain intact.[105]

On the same day, Yang Chengwu flew to Shanghai, where, in a detailed report, he faithfully delivered Zhou's message to Mao. The Chairman listened but did not respond, waving Yang away without a word. It is not clear whether Mao saw the chaos for what it really was, namely, a manifestation of deep discontent in society and of disappointment with the Party and its hierarchical system and policies. But he did become seriously concerned by the report Zhou had transmitted through Yang. After reflecting for several hours, he summoned Yang back to his office and announced that serious steps would be taken to change the situation. "Wang Li's speech is very bad," he told Yang. "And the authors of the 1 August editorial demanding to uncover capitalist roaders in the army were disrupting the Cultural Revolution. They are bad people. Go back to Beijing and tell the premier to arrest them." Yang immediately left for the airport. But Mao once again called him back to give more detailed instructions. He was to tell Zhou that he had to arrest Wang Li and Guan Feng first. Qi Benyu was to be dealt with later.[106]

In early September, Zhou ordered the arrest of Wang Li and Guan Feng. The detention of two important members of the CCRG was a landmark, for it paved the way for a sudden change in the politics of the Cultural Revolution to which Zhou had eminently contributed, with his pivotal assessment of the situation. On 1 September, the change was officially announced at an enlarged meeting of the Standing Committee of the Beijing Municipal Revolutionary Committee. There, Jiang Qing and a number of other CCRG members officially reneged on some of the radical policies and actions they had earlier encouraged and, at times, provoked. They now condemned the call to unmask "capitalist roaders in the army," ignoring the fact that it was the CCRG that had initiated the call only a month earlier. They criticized factional fighting, which they earlier had encouraged, as well as the disturbances Red Guards and rebels had instigated in foreign relations. At the same time, they laid the groundwork for a new campaign—this time directed against the unruly radicals—by warning people to be vigilant about a recently emerged "sinister" group that allegedly planned to attack the "proletarian headquarters" and the PLA.

Zhou delivered the final speech of the meeting. He refuted the assessment made by some radicals that the Cultural Revolution had entered a new stage with a new tidal wave of struggle. In the second year of the revolution, he said, the focus was on the criticism of the Liu-Deng line, while the third year should conclude the Cultural Revolution. He emphasized that these were Chairman Mao's instructions, which "should be carried out resolutely, regardless of whether or not you understand them." He demanded that all factional fighting stop immediately so that "great alliances" of mass organizations could be established without delay. Then he complained about the sorry state of the economy, which was seriously disrupted by factional fighting and the paralysis of the transportation sector on both land and sea. Yet he repeated Lin Biao's words confirming the "achievements of the Cultural Revolution were very, very great" (*shouhuo henda, henda*) while "the losses were very, very small" (*sunshi henxiao, henxiao*).[107]

The country as a whole became aware of the change of direction on 5 September, when Jiang Qing and Kang Sheng—in contrast to their usual reaction—repeated Zhou's arguments at a meeting with mass organizations in Anhui province. The same day, Mao gave his official stamp of approval by intervening personally. He added a paragraph to an article published in *People's Daily*. In this addendum he blamed "a handful of counterrevolutionaries who are ... using slogans that sound 'leftist' but in essence are 'rightist'; they stirred up evil gusts of 'doubting everyone' while bombarding the proletarian headquarters and creating dissent and confusion." The "handful of counterrevolutionaries" was further described as the "16 May Group" (abbreviated as "516 Group"), whose organizers and manipulators made up the core of the "scheming counterrevolutionary gang." According to the article, "most of its members and leaders" were not yet fully identified, "since they sent their people to paste up wall posters in the middle of the night."[108]

## Revolutionary Committees

In his efforts to return the domestic situation to normal, Zhou concentrated much of his energy on the establishment of revolutionary committees in the provinces, a process that was considered vital to the passage from disorder to order. Mao had originally decreed that revolutionary committees—expected to replace the state system at provincial, municipal, and local levels—should be installed by the spring of 1968. They were to be composed of mass organizations, veteran cadres, and military representatives, thus establishing unity of the social strata. By the beginning of 1968, only twelve out of twenty-nine provinces, municipalities, and autonomous regions had been able to establish these committees. Although the military was powerful enough to impose its representatives on the committees, the delay had been caused by factional strife among mass organizations. Such strife had become so ingrained and internecine fighting had become so intense that little could be done to establish the committees. To accelerate the process, mass organizations from the provinces were summoned to Beijing, where they were forced to remain at the conference table until they were able to settle their disagreements. Zhou personally intervened in these negotiations and, in many cases, compelled the recalcitrant participants to bury their differences. In the fall of 1968, Zhou was able to pronounce the entire country "red," because "proletarian revolutionaries" had united "to seize power from the handful of party persons" who had chosen "the capitalist road." It was a "tremendous victory for the Great Proletarian Cultural Revolution," he declared.[109] Despite these declarations, Zhou was aware that differences among the factions had not ended but had only been papered over. Factionalism continued to thrive inside the committees rendering them ineffectual.[110]

## Purifying Class Ranks

The reversal of policies developed yet another dimension, taking the form of a campaign "to purify class ranks." It was really directed against rebels who were held responsible for the previous disorders. This entirely suited Zhou's disposition for promoting order and discipline. He therefore used any crack in the doors opened by Mao to commit himself in the campaign against leftist anarchy. Because Mao was adamant in his belief that the "battle against revisionism" was not over, and that ideological purification at the grass-roots level was necessary before socialism could take hold, Zhou joined the fray to direct the campaign and to rein in all excesses.

The new campaign created more victims and resulted in the death of more people than any previous campaign since the beginning of the Cultural Revolution. The majority of Western observers of China believed that the Cultural Revolution ended in April 1969 with the ninth Party congress, but the fact is that it only took a different form—one that was discreetly hidden behind closed doors, not visible to the public.

An experimental stage of the campaign was launched in the autumn of 1968 at Beijing and Qinghua Universities. Within roughly two months, it "uncovered" 280 class enemies among the faculty and administrative personnel. On the basis of this experience, the movement expanded to the rest of the country, culminating in the campaign "against the destructive activities of counterrevolutionaries" and the campaign against "corruption and theft of state property, against speculation and profiteering and against ostentation and waste."[111]

The perception of a threat from the Soviet Union also had repercussions for the campaign. On 30 January 1970 Zhou pointed out to Mao and Lin Biao that there were counterrevolutionaries trying to undermine war preparedness and the campaign had to be extended to target them.[112] Within the next ten months, 1,840,000 "counter-revolutionaries" were uncovered, of whom—according to incomplete statistics—284,000 were jailed because of "serious destructive activities." A conservative estimate claimed that several thousand "diehard counterrevolutionaries" were executed.[113]

## The Campaign against the May 16 Group

In the campaign to purify class ranks, the so-called May 16 Group (or 516 Group) was condemned as the culprit responsible for the chaos and destruction of the Cultural Revolution. Since Mao had decreed that this organization had to be "thoroughly exposed," Zhou again jumped into the fray to lead the campaign. In 1968, he described the 516 Group: It originated in the Department of Philosophy and Social Sciences at the Chinese Academy of Sciences. Its principal instigator was Pan Zinian, the elder brother of Pan Hannian, who had been Zhou Enlai's spy chief in the 1940s. During that period, Pan Zinian had also worked closely with Zhou on *New China Daily* in Chongqing. Zhou linked him and two other researchers at the Department of Philosophy and Social Sciences to the radicals Wang Li, Guan Feng, and Qi Benyu—by then removed from the CCRG. All were accused as Liu Shaoqi's henchmen and as "backstage bosses" of the 516 Group who, under cover of ultraleftism, engaged in counterrevolutionary activities. According to Zhou, the 516 Group had been able to infiltrate a large number of government institutions. Its activities were so subversive that those who participated in them had to be considered class enemies. Among many other things they were responsible for the fire that had damaged the British mission in 1967.[114]

In 1968, the CCEG established a "leading group to examine the 516 case," led by Chen Boda; Xie Fuzhi and Wu Faxian were among its most prominent members. Within the next few months, the ferreting out of "516 elements" was carried out on an experimental basis. Zhou drew the first conclusions from these experiments at a meeting of the Politburo on 24 March 1970. The 516 Group, he affirmed, is "an underground counterrevolutionary clique" manipulated by a number of high-ranking military (who had fallen into disgrace) and three former members of the CCRG.[115] All were described as counterrevolutionary double dealers of Liu Shaoqi's bourgeois headquarters." The Politburo issued a circular demanding the elimination of the group by thorough investigation while prohibiting forceful extraction of confessions. Ironically, the method used in the campaign amounted to precisely that, namely, forcing people to confess their membership in the 516 Group and to denounce others as members or supporters of that group.[116]

In September, Zhou began to restore order at the State Council. The Foreign Ministry became the focus of his attention. Offensively he announced that the leaders of the ministry's rebels had "direct or indirect" connections with the 516 Group. In effect, this was tantamount to accusing them of being accomplices in the group's criminal counterrevolutionary activities and to signing their political death sentence. For him it was an opportunity to punish the rebels—many of them young people he had selected and installed at that elite ministry and by whom he felt personally betrayed. In the winter of 1967/68, Zhou instigated a fierce campaign against rebels in the Foreign Ministry, denouncing them as ultraleftists, anarchists, and representatives of petty-bourgeois factionalism. The rebels, earlier admired as daring heroes of the Cultural Revolution, now became outcasts.[117]

Conservative groups at the Foreign Ministry picked up his signals. On 13 February 1969, a big-character poster appeared at the ministry with the flashy title "Expose the enemy and defeat him—criticize and repudiate the reactionary slogan 'Down with Chen Yi.'" Signed by ninety-one high-ranking ministry officials, among them a vice minister, several ambassadors, and directors of departments, it praised Chen Yi's revolutionary achievements, ignoring his involvement in the February Countercurrent and his various negative comments about the Cultural Revolution that had angered Mao. The high-ranking officials had apparently gone too far in their defense of Chen Yi. That this was indeed dangerous quickly became evident when Mao and the members of the Cultural Revolution Group promptly reacted by condemning the poster as a sign of "right deviation." Zhou, always on his guard, realized that the moment to acclaim Chen Yi was badly chosen. He identified himself with Mao and the CCRG, defending the Cultural Revolution against "right deviation" and putting a stop to these activities. On 24 February, he ordered his secretary in charge of liaison with the Foreign Ministry to inform authors of the poster that they had made a mistake and had rendered a disservice to Chen Yi. On 5 March, he reiterated his accusations against them and, at the same time, launched a campaign within the Foreign Ministry to "counterattack the right deviation that reversed verdicts."[118]

In May 1968, Zhou dispatched a group of military representatives to the ministry to lead the campaign. They established "516 case groups" at all levels of the ministry's hierarchy that quickly arrested a few dozen rebels who had been active at the Liaison Station of the Revolutionary Rebels. They were taken into custody on the premises in rooms specially reserved for that purpose and placed under twenty-four-hour surveillance, a service provided by their own colleagues. Under duress, a number of the detainees confessed their association with the 516 Group. Links were soon established between them and the Philosophical and Social Sciences Department at the Chinese Academy of Sciences and the Beijing Foreign Languages Institute—of which many of the Foreign Ministry staff were graduates. On the basis of enforced confessions, the outlines of an organizational network of 516 Group members began to emerge. However, Xie Fuzhi, the minister of public security, was dissatisfied with the campaign. In a report to Zhou Enlai, he complained that the military representatives at the Beijing Foreign Languages Institute were too lenient in their handling of the 516 Group. Zhou ordered their replacement with members of the military who would show less mercy toward "class enemies."[119]

In March 1970, the purge of "516 elements" at the Foreign Ministry deepened further. Zhou's military envoy reported that many confessed their guilt, and the ones who refused to confess were isolated. He came to the strange conclusion that those who confessed their membership in the 516 Group would be treated leniently while those who refused would be severely punished.[120]

In view of an increasing number of confessions, the policy of the "three not's" was introduced: those who had passed the interrogation satisfactorily would not be treated as "enemies of the people," would not be subjected to administrative sanctions, and their involvement in the 516 Group would not be recorded in their personal dossiers. While many continued to resist, many more chose to confess, having come to see the irony of the situation: if one admitted to being a member of the 516 Group, one would not be treated as one; but if one refused to admit such membership, one would be treated as one. The list of "516 elements" became increasingly long, including 1,500 out of 2,200 staff members in July 1970. Not only former rebels but also interrogators, not only average staff members but also department directors and vice ministers were branded as "516 elements." As the campaign reached a deadlock, Zhou, avoiding any comments about whether it was right or wrong, said that its emphasis should change. Instead of concentrating on the organization of the 516 Group, investigations should focus on the crimes committed by its members.[121]

Government institutions, universities, enterprises, and various organizations all experienced a situation similar to that of the Foreign Ministry: as much as 70 percent of their staff were accused of being members of the 516 Group. In Nanjing, for example, 270,000 "516 elements" were exposed. In the end, such "elements" numbered in millions. In many localities, the absurdities of the campaign had reached such proportions that it was declared null and void. This was the case, for example, at the Beijing Foreign Language Institute. But Mao insisted that the campaign should continue. Zhou declared that, as at the Foreign Ministry, the campaign should criticize some of the activities that had previously taken place such as camping outside Zhongnanhai, setting the British mission ablaze, and attempting to kidnap the foreign minister.

The campaign continued. In August 1970, Chen Boda, who was, in fact, heading the Special Case Group to investigate the 516 Group, fell into disgrace, and was accused of being the backstage boss of the imaginary 516 Group. His special case group dissolved and, in February 1971, Zhou replaced it with a "central united group examining the 516 case" headed by Wu De, a member of the Politburo and the head of the Beijing Municipal Revolutionary Committee.[122]

In September, Lin Biao's disappearance in a plane crash in the Mongolian desert put the campaign against the 516 Group on the back burner. His flight shook up the leadership, which quietly dropped the issue to focus on Lin Biao (for details on Lin's disappearance, see below). Only at the Foreign Ministry did it end somewhat differently. Zhou designated twenty ministry staff members to be officially sanctioned as "516 counterrevolutionary elements." Meetings were held to announce this decision but they did not provide evidence to corroborate the accusations. In addition, about eighty revolutionary rebels received administrative punishment and about 170 were required to make a self-criticism, because they were regarded as having made political mistakes during the Cultural Revolution. The roughly eight hundred people who had been members of the Liaison Station were dismissed from the ministry and reassigned to jobs in the provinces and in the Beijing municipal government. By October the hunt for the 516 Group at the Foreign Ministry officially came to an end.

Under the pretense of hunting for "516 elements," millions of people were wrongly accused and persecuted. Although the campaign was shelved after the Lin Biao affair (see below) in 1971, the central group examining the 516 case was disbanded only in December 1978. Most of the false accusations during the Cultural Revolution have been officially and openly redressed but not so in the case of the 516 Group. It had been so completely lacking in foundation that the twenty people Zhou labeled as "516 elements" were quietly rehabilitated in the late 1970s. But no mention was made of the other 516 Group cases, which had involved three-quarters of the ministry staff. The problems created to its alleged members by the official investigation of that group were simply ignored.[123]

## Lin Biao's Disappearance

When the ninth national congress of the CCP took place in April 1969, it established a three-group power structure represented by Jiang Qing's Cultural Revolution faction,[124] Lin Biao's military faction and — the weakest among the three — rehabilitated veteran cadres under Zhou Enlai's leadership.

The two former groups had cooperated since the beginning of the Cultural Revolution. But their relations began to deteriorate in 1968, mainly because of Jiang Qing's frequent interference in military affairs, which Lin Biao considered intolerable. Zhou, with his usual caution, maintained a neutral attitude toward the two groups. The palace intrigues between them increased in frequency and finally evolved into an open confrontation that broke out at the Central Committee plenum at Lushan in August and September 1970. As Mao arbitrated in favor of Jiang Qing, his mistrust toward Lin Biao developed in ever-greater proportions. Lin Biao, in the meantime, felt increasingly threatened.

On the evening of 12 September 1971, Zhou was in the Great Hall of the People presiding over a conference dealing with the draft of the government report to the forthcoming fourth National People's Congress. At ten o'clock, he received a telephone call from the general office of the Central Committee with a message from the 8,341 troops in charge of the security of important leaders. The message stated that Lin Biao's wife, Ye Qun, and son were trying to persuade Lin Biao to leave his summer residence at Beidaihe and to leave the country a *Trident* aircraft grounded at Shanhaiguan airport. It also stated that Lin Biao's daughter had delivered the information. She had been on bad terms with her mother for some time and was attempting to frustrate her mother's plans.

Zhou took immediate action, calling on his considerable organizational talents. First he ordered Wu Faxian, the commander of the air force, to verify the information about the aircraft. After Wu confirmed that the aircraft was indeed stationed at Shanhaiguan, Zhou issued instructions that the plane could not take off without a written order signed jointly by himself, Wu Faxian, Huang Yongsheng, the general chief of staff, and Li Zuopeng, commander of the navy and deputy chief of staff.

At 11:30 P.M., Ye Qun called Zhou to inform him that her husband was planning to leave Beidaihe for Dalian the next morning. When asked whether they had a plane at their disposal, Ye Qun said they did not. Zhou replied that he wanted her to wait so that he could consult with Wu Faxian. Then he gave a series of orders, all designed to neutralize Lin Biao's supporters. Wu Faxian was close to Lin. Suspicious that he might allow the plane to take off, Zhou asked his trusted aide Yang Dezhong to observe Wu Faxian's activities at Beijing's Western airport, where he was on duty. He dispatched Li Desheng, a member of the Politburo and the commander of the Beijing Military Region, to the headquarters of the air force to take command. He instructed Ji Dengkui, an alternate member of the Politburo and member of the administrative group of the Central Military Commission, to supervise command of the Beijing Military Region. Huang Yongsheng, also part of Lin's coterie, was ordered to remain with Zhou. Finally, he instructed Wu Faxian to make two planes ready for himself. He intended to fly to Beidaihe to dissuade Lin from leaving China.

However, none of his instructions led to the desired results. Before Zhou could take off for Beidaihe, he learned that Lin Biao's plane had already departed. Zhou then ordered the grounding of all planes throughout the country, unless they received a formal order jointly signed by Mao, Huang Yongsheng, Wu Faxian, Li Zuopeng, and himself.[125]

After issuing these orders, Zhou, accompanied by Ji Dengkui, rushed to Zhongnanhai to inform Mao about the situation. As Ji later recalled, when they arrived, Mao, apparently very calm, was sitting on the sofa in his study. Zhou asked him whether he wanted Lin's plane to be shot down while it was still within shooting range. Mao was deep in thought. After a while, he uttered a Chinese saying: "Nobody can help it if it is going to rain or if the widowed mother wants to get remarried" (*"Tian yao xia yu, niang yao gai jia"*), and he added: "Let him go."[126]

Shortly after three o'clock, Zhou convened the Politburo to tell its members about Lin Biao's flight. Then he transmitted the same information by telephone to the leaders of the military regions and the provinces. By that time, Zhou had not slept for more than thirty hours. When he was finally able to catch a bit of sleep, however, he was awakened by an emergency report from the Foreign Ministry, announcing that Xu Wenyi, the Chinese ambassador to Mongolia, had been summoned to the Mongolian Foreign Ministry at 8:30 P.M. on 14 September to hear a formal protest from a deputy foreign minister because an unauthorized Chinese military aircraft had entered Mongolian air space. The ambassador was informed that the plane had crashed near Undur Khan, killing everyone on board. The Mongolian authorities demanded an official explanation from the Chinese government. The Chinese ambassador promised to transmit the message to Beijing as soon as possible, relying on the Mongolian authorities for communication by telegram. The Mongolian telegram office informed him that, due to technical problems, it could not provide service for a few hours. Under the circumstances, the Chinese ambassador decided to reopen a direct telephone line connecting the embassy with the Foreign Ministry in Beijing, which, because of a deterioration in relations between the two countries, had been left unused for more than two years. At 12:20 A.M., he reported to Beijing about the plane crash.

Zhou telephoned the Foreign Ministry at 2 A.M., to transmit his compliments to Ambassador Xu Wenyi for his handling of the affair and to keep communications with the embassy in Ulan Bator top secret. He also issued instructions to Ambassador Xu to tell the Mongolian authorities that the plane had entered Mongolian air space because it had gone off course. The Chinese government expressed its regrets about the incident.

Zhou was eager to have his ambassador personally visit the crash site to investigate. After the Mongolian authorities granted permission, the Chinese ambassador and his three aides visited the area on 15 and 16 September. They found that the *Trident* 256 had crashed in a basin located about 70 kilometers northwest of Undur Khan.

The Chinese embassy took the same view as the Mongolian embassy had. Since the broken pieces of the plane were concentrated mainly in the burned area and the bodies were intact and not too heavily burned, the embassy concluded that the plane had caught fire while landing and then exploded. All these findings were reported to Zhou.[127]

But Zhou was not satisfied. He requested a detailed oral report about the events. The second secretary of the Chinese embassy in Ulan Bator, Sun Yixian, was dispatched to Beijing. He arrived on 21 September and Zhou received him at 11 P.M. During the three-hour meeting, Zhou inquired about all possible details. But since the cause of the plane crash remained unclear, he ordered Li Zhen, minister of public security, and Li Jitai, commander of the Beijing air force, to provide a detailed technical analysis of the accident. Their investigation, conducted from Beijing, found that the plane had been short of fuel, but at the time of the crash it still had enough fuel to fly for about half an hour; mysteriously, a landing had been attempted without activating landing gears and wing flaps.[128]

After Lin Biao's death, Zhou began to investigate the activities of the Lin Biao group and established a special case group for this purpose. On 24 September he announced to the Politburo that four of the highest-ranking military officers were suspended from duty and ordered to prepare statements confessing their ties with Lin Biao. The Central Military Commission was taken over by Ye Jianying. Ninety-three people suspected of having been Lin's followers were arrested, and a campaign to "criticize Lin and rectify the style of work" (*pi Lin zhengfeng*) was launched in Lin's military strongholds, the air force, the navy, and the PLA's General Logistics Department.[129]

The collapse of the Lin Biao group altered the power structure within the party. Of the five members of the Standing Committee of the Politburo, Lin Biao had died, Chen Boda had been purged, and Kang Sheng was critically ill, leaving only Mao and Zhou. In the Politburo and the Central Committee, the tripartite structure was replaced with a bipolar one in which the radicals were represented by Jiang Qing and the moderates by Zhou Enlai.

## Ultraleft or Ultraright?

The news of Lin Biao's death was communicated to the entire party in mid-October 1971 and to the general public a month later, and came as a great shock to most people. But Zhou could not have failed to notice that it was perhaps Mao who was the most disturbed by the incident. Despite his own role in driving Lin Biao to take desperate measures, the now seventy-seven-year-old Chairman had been traumatized by the entire affair. His health deteriorated rapidly, and he became deeply depressed. At the end of 1971, he fell seriously ill and in January 1972 suffered a stroke. He survived thanks to emergency treatment, but his condition remained unstable.[130]

Lin Biao's death caused Mao to become nostalgic about some of his other lifelong comrades-in-arms. On 14 November 1971, in Zhou's presence, he rehabilitated the veteran revolutionaries who had been demoted because of their involvement in the February Countercurrent, saying that their criticism at the time represented a concerted action against Lin Biao and other radicals. Mao's sudden decision, on 10 January 1972, to attend Chen Yi's funeral symbolized his changed attitude toward veteran cadres; Zhou immediately seized upon the occasion to improve Chen's status, even posthumously. Because Chen Yi had been stripped of his Politburo membership at the ninth Party congress, members of that organ were not expected to attend his funeral. But as soon as Zhou learned of Mao's intention to attend the funeral, he told all Politburo members to attend as well, thus transforming it into a political event that would lead to Chen Yi's rehabilitation. The gesture was of great importance to his family, which otherwise would have continued to suffer from discrimination. But it was also a means of reinforcing Zhou's own political position, which could only improve with the rehabilitation of the old guard.

Mao arrived in his nightshirt, over which he wore a heavy coat. At the funeral, he talked to Chen's widow, Zhang Qian, praising Chen's revolutionary past and his contribution to the Chinese and world revolutionary movement. Encouraged by Mao's words, Zhou suggested to Chen Yi's son that he publicize what the Chairman had said about his father to initiate the rehabilitation of other veteran cadres.[131]

At that time, Mao began to criticize various aspects of Lin Biao's policies, connecting him to "those leftists" who had set fire to the British mission in Beijing and who had clamored for the overthrow of most veteran cadres, including Zhou Enlai. He declared that Lin Biao was the "backstage boss" of all these activities.[132]

In the hope that he could use Mao's change of mood to redress some of the most obvious absurdities of the Cultural Revolution, Zhou spearheaded a campaign against ultraleftism as represented by Lin Biao. Throughout 1972, he made critical remarks about the practice of engaging in empty talk about politics not only by Lin Biao but also by former CCRG members, who had fallen into disgrace. He challenged the sacred tenet of "putting politics in command," which, in his view, led to negligence in economic policy. The result of this type of attitude was, in

Zhou's view, the poor quality of Chinese products. At the end of 1971, Zhou was informed that, of the forty MiG-6 fighter planes produced in Chinese factories, seven were unusable. He seized on this issue to attack problems related to the quality of a wide array of products, ranging from canned food to clothing to trucks. He also ordered the restoration of regulations and discipline in management, which had been abolished during the chaotic years, and introduced emergency measures to improve quality control in production. Most of all, he encouraged cadres to improve their professional work. On his instruction, in early 1972, a conference on national planning produced a report on the restoration of discipline in enterprises. The importation of scientific and industrial equipment from Western countries, criticized as "worshiping everything foreign," was also resumed after Zhou convinced Mao of the necessity of buying Western equipment to produce chemical fertilizer and synthetic fibers.[133]

Many problems had arisen in the agricultural sector, which were mainly due to the practice of egalitarianism among members of the people's communes. This practice made it impossible for peasants to develop sideline occupations such as raising poultry or growing vegetables, which were criticized as "capitalistic." Initiated by Zhou, a Central Committee document began to allow peasants to engage in a small measure of private activity.

Zhou's efforts at rectification extended to culture, education, and scientific research. Emphasizing that ultraleftism had brought about the degeneration of art, he derided fashionable revolutionary songs and dances, which, in his view, were characterized by high-pitched singing and rigidity of movement at the expense of sentiment and rhythm.

In May 1972, the State Council discussed the situation at schools and universities. This was the first time since the beginning of the Cultural Revolution that officials in charge of education had the opportunity to vent their anxieties about the damage left-wing policies had inflicted on the educational system. Contrary to the practice of recruiting students among workers, peasants, and soldiers, which had been hailed as one of the "newly emerging things" of the Cultural Revolution, Zhou defended the old system of selecting students among senior middle-school graduates, although it had been condemned as a bourgeois educational policy. He obtained widespread support for this in educational circles and among parents. He instructed the Chinese Academy of Sciences and Beijing University to resume basic theoretical studies that had been discarded as useless.[134]

Much of Zhou's energy was devoted to the rehabilitation of high-ranking cadres and government officials. In early 1972, 669 people, most of them officials and some well-known representatives of literature and art, remained under examination by the first and the third offices of the CCEG. Some were incarcerated at the notorious Qincheng Prison near Beijing, others were in custody in different locations in the capital, and still others were held in May Seventh Cadre Schools in the countryside. Several hundred PLA officers were either purged or still under investigation by the second office of the CCEG.[135]

In April 1972, two ministers died in custody, due to lack of medical treatment. Seizing the opportunity, Zhou issued instructions to the Ministry of Public Health to restore the medical system of high-ranking cadres and to give all of them a checkup. More than five hundred cadres were examined at Beijing's hospitals. The checkup was a turning point for many of them. Those who were in the cadre schools in the countryside were called back to Beijing for the checkup and never returned to the labor camps. Some of them obtained their rehabilitation.[136]

To promote the return to duty of more high-ranking cadres, Zhou instructed the *People's Daily* to publish an editorial condemning Lin Biao's treatment of them as a manifestation of ultraleftism. Encouraged by Zhou's efforts, Wang Ruoshui, the deputy director of *People's Daily*, devoted an entire page of the 14 October issue to the repudiation of anarchism and to the unjustifiable persecution of cadres. This was the strongest criticism of the practices of the Cultural Revolution hitherto made public.

In the course of 1973, Zhou succeeded in rehabilitating 175 PLA officers, most of whom had been purged by Lin Biao. The rehabilitation of Party and government officials proved more difficult because of the opposition of the radical members of the Politburo. Zhou had only limited leverage from Mao's bout of nostalgia, so he was able to free from custody just a few veteran cadres (including Zhu De, Chen Yun, Li Fuchun, and Nie Rongzhen). Deng Xiaoping's rehabilitation in March 1973 was particularly significant. Although only Mao had the authority to reverse the verdict on the "second most important capitalist roader in the party," it was Zhou who suggested that Deng resume his post as vice premier.[137]

Zhou's drive against ultraleftism within the framework of the campaign against Lin Biao soon met with resistance from the Jiang Qing group, which perceived it as a denunciation of the Cultural Revolution to which their political fate was linked. In retaliation, Zhang Chunqiao instructed the Shanghai paper *Wenhuibao* to publish a report on 4 November, about a workers' meeting at which, it was said, the participants had angrily denounced the *People's Daily* articles of 14 October as a "negation of the Cultural Revolution and a repudiation of the masses." Two days later, the same paper published an editorial arguing that Lin Biao's political line was one of "right opportunism." An important member of the Shanghai Party committee called the *People's Daily* from Shanghai to ask who the "backstage boss" of its October articles was. Zhang felt strong enough to confront Zhou directly on the issue, while Jiang Qing issued the statement that she considered Lin's activities ultrarightist, not ultraleftist. A number of military commanders in the Beijing Military Region also started discussing the fundamental nature of Lin's political line.[138]

Challenged by the Shanghai *Wenhuibao* and feeling increasingly confused about the issue, Wang Ruoshui felt compelled to submit the matter to Mao, who, alone, had the authority to settle it. He wrote a letter to the Chairman, drawing his attention to the controversies between *Wenhuibao* and the *People's Daily*, and between Zhou Enlai and Zhang Chunqiao, declaring himself in full agreement with the premier's views.

Zhou had initiated the campaign against ultraleftism in the belief that he acted in compliance with Mao's changed attitude after the Lin Biao affair. But Mao, once more, proved to be unpredictable. Although Zhou's appraisal of Mao's intentions was not entirely mistaken, his own instinct for restoring more sensible policies pushed him beyond the limits of Mao's tolerance. On 17 December, Mao summoned Zhang Chunqiao and Yao Wenyuan to his office, where he told them that he disagreed with Wang Ruoshui's views on ultraleftism. He emphasized that Lin Biao's politics had been ultrarightist, since he had practiced revisionism, attempted to split the Party, and betrayed the Party and the nation. And he ordered them not to "criticize ultraleft trends of thought too much."[139]

This was the final verdict on the matter. Zhou Enlai not only had to retract his campaign against ultraleftism but also was left with the embarrassing task of notifying the heads of the mass media that Lin Biao had been a rightist. On 19 December, Zhou called the chief editors of the *People's Daily* to a meeting attended by Politburo members including Jiang Qing, Zhang Chunqiao, and Yao Wenyuan. In his opening speech he once more adjusted to Mao's interpretation supporting the criticism of Lin Biao's ultrarightism. He flatly dismissed his own previous remarks about ultraleftism, declaring that they had not referred to the political line pursued by Lin Biao. Linking the campaign against ultraleftism with Lin Biao could only lead to the repudiation of the masses, he said. Zhou concluded that Wang, by publishing the three articles on Lin Biao's ultraleftism, had erred. Wang tried to defend himself but was quickly overwhelmed by sharp accusations from Jiang Qing, Zhang Chunqiao, and Yao Wenyuan. They condemned Wang for his attempt to "erect differences between Zhou and other Politburo members" on this question—differences that, in their view, did not exist. After the meeting, all criticism of ultraleftism was halted. Zhou thus suffered his first defeat since the Lin Biao affair.[140]

In August 1973, the tenth national congress of the CCP was convened to officially end the purge of Lin Biao and his supporters and to amend the Party constitution, which, in 1969 included the statement that Lin Biao was "Comrade Mao Zedong's close comrade-in-arms and his successor." The collapse of the Lin Biao group also demanded the reorganization of the Party leadership, which became the most significant outcome of the congress. The tripartite structure established by the ninth Party congress was replaced with a new structure in which power was divided between the veteran revolutionaries associated with Zhou Enlai and the radicals, or Cultural Revolution faction, which was considerably diminished. Of the fourteen members of the CCRG nominated in May 1966, only four (Kang Sheng, Jiang Qing, Zhang Chunqiao, and Yao Wenyuan) had survived the political struggles of the previous years. But even though the veterans were numerically stronger, they had not yet fully revived politically and had to face the markedly aggressive radicals, who, on national scale, wielded the greater influence through their control of the media.[141]

Both the veteran revolutionaries represented by Zhou and the radicals headed by Jiang Qing consolidated their position in the Central Committee at the expense of the military, which had been overrepresented at the previous congress. Zhou became one of the five vice chairmen of the Party and one of the nine members of the Politburo's Standing Committee. Most important was the return to leading positions of veteran revolutionaries and, most important, Deng Xiaoping—formerly called "the second top Party person in power traveling the capitalist road." Now rehabilitated after three and a half years in exile, Deng returned to Beijing in March 1973 and was reinstated as vice premier. At the end of the year, Mao ordered his nomination to the Politburo and to the Central Military Commission. Thereafter he became actively involved in political, military, and Party matters at highest level.[142]

## Breakthrough in Foreign Policy

During the Cultural Revolution, Chinese foreign relations underwent a series of major transformations. As part of restoring order in the late 1960s, Mao altered his views on China's role on the international scene. He no longer accepted the isolation to which his country was reduced while his major objective of Chinese foreign policy was based on his visions of China as the center of world revolution dominated by Mao Zedong Thought.

Such a view had never been Zhou Enlai's perspective of Chinese foreign policy. For years, he had labored to make his five principles of peaceful coexistence acceptable to the rest of the world. During the first part of the Cultural Revolution, he tried to maintain normal diplomatic relations but China's contacts with foreign countries were soon reduced to a minimum or, in many cases, completely forsaken. Its former great ally, the Soviet Union, and its followers had turned into foes, while its great enemy, the United States, continued to be perceived as the head of the "imperialist camp" and its increasingly active presence in Vietnam was considered a major threat to China's security. For this reason Vietnam had become the only significant exception in this gloomy picture of isolation. As a promoter of revolutionary struggle in the Third World, China supported the Vietnamese Communist Party. In 1965, U.S. involvement in Vietnam escalated as 3,500 U.S. Marines arrived in Da Nang. Zhou responded to their arrival by saying, "China will send the people of South Vietnam all the necessary material aid, including arms and other war matériel ... [and will] send our own men whenever the South Vietnamese want them."[143] During most of the Cultural Revolution, China sent substantial aid to Vietnam in the form of military equipment, engineering, communications, logistics as well as food, uniforms, edible oils, soap, and the like.

By the end of the 1960s, however, the Soviet Union was considered more of a threat than the United States. In addition to the virulent ideological battles between the CCP and the CPSU, the Soviet invasion of Czechoslovakia in 1968 and the announcement of the Brezhnev doctrine that declared the determination of the Soviet Union to intervene in the internal affairs of Socialist States, contributed considerably to a further deterioration in relations between the two countries. Moreover, numerous border incidents since October 1964 in Xinjiang and along the Heilongjiang (Amur) river reached a peak with armed clashes on Zhenbao Island on 2 and 15 March 1969, bringing the two countries close to the brink of war. Mao insisted that China prepare for war mentally and materially, and the Central Military Commission proposed increasing military expenses by 34 percent that year.[144] Zhou Enlai initiated a diplomatic offensive, releasing a series of protest notes against the Soviet government. Ultimately, it was the increasing threat of war with the Soviet Union that motivated the Chinese leaders to seek a rapprochement with the United States.

The sense of urgency heightened when news spread that the Soviet Union was considering a pre-emptive nuclear strike on Chinese nuclear installations. Chinese apprehension had reached the point that the leaders refused to talk with their Soviet counterparts, who insisted that the issue be discussed at highest level. Zhou was expected to lead a delegation to Hanoi on 8 September to attend Ho Chi Minh's funeral; he went to Vietnam four days earlier to pay his respects and returned to Beijing the same day, thus avoiding any contact with the Soviet delegation. But Aleksei Kosygin, Chairman of the Soviet Council of Ministers, had expected Zhou in Hanoi. He informed the Chinese ambassador in Hanoi that he wanted to meet Zhou in Beijing. With Mao's approval, Zhou agreed to a meeting but, to demonstrate Chinese displeasure at the Soviet threats of war, insisted that it take place at Beijing airport. The discussions between the two leaders, laden with mutual accusations of warmongering, nonetheless ended with an agreement to maintain the status quo along the border and to conduct border talks at the vice ministerial level.[145]

Despite the relaxation of tensions, Mao and Zhou remained skeptical about Soviet intentions. The talks will be a "smokescreen," Mao said, a cunning maneuver to divert Chinese attention from a Soviet surprise attack. He issued instructions to accelerate the third-line construction, which, was carried out on a massive scale between 1969 and 1971, absorbing large quantities of investment and human resources. A few weeks before the border talks opened, the air force was put on the highest alert. Fearing that the Soviet Union might take advantage of the National Day celebrations on 1 October to launch an attack on Beijing, Lin Biao suggested draining all of Beijing's large reservoirs, on which the capital depended for its water supply. Arguing that such drainage would cause considerable technical problems, Zhou was able to oppose this plan. But as the Sino-Soviet border talks approached, war preparations became increasingly rushed. Since Mao expected a military attack at any moment, he decided to evacuate the leaders, including those who had been purged and were under arrest. As the only major leader to remain in Beijing, Zhou moved to a secret location from which he organized the exodus and directed government affairs. Mao was relocated to Wuhan, whereas Lin Biao was sent to Suzhou. Those leaders who were under investigation were moved to different provinces: Liu Shaoqi and Xu Xiangqian were sent to Kaifeng in Henan province, Chen Yun and Deng Xiaoping to Nanchang in Jiangxi province, and Chen Yi to Shijiazhuang in Hebei province. Government staff and functions were reduced, and large parts of ministries and other institutions evacuated to diverse locations throughout China. Zhou ordered mass meetings to be held to inform people of their imminent departure. They were allowed to take only a few belongings. Any possessions requiring heavy transport had to be sold or simply abandoned. Apartments had to be returned to the government. Trains were allocated to each ministry to transport its personnel to their destinations. The efficiency with which the spectacular relocation from Beijing and other major cities was organized, and the orderly manner in which it was executed bore the brand of Zhou's impressive organizational talent.[146]

A few days before the Soviet delegation was expected to arrive in Beijing, the military alert was again reinforced. At Zhou's side, General Huang Yongsheng, the general chief of staff, ensured the army's readiness in case of a military attack.

The Sino-Soviet border talks began on 20 October, but the surprise attack for which Zhou and the military had prepared in such great detail failed to materialize. A month later, the stage of emergency was canceled. Although the threat of war was not realized, the border talks dragged on for several weeks without result. From the start of the negotiations Zhou had been pessimistic about their outcome, and he became convinced that the Soviet delegation did not respect the understanding that he had reached with Kosygin during their meeting at the airport. In December 1969, after Soviet military forces entered Afghanistan, he broke off negotiations.[147]

In the late 1960s the foreign minister and most of his deputies, and the department heads of the ministry were still under investigation while only about 30 percent of the Foreign Ministry staff was active in Beijing.

The rest had been relocated to cadre schools, where they were occupied with the campaign to purify class ranks and to discover "516 elements" among their colleagues at the Ministry. They also were engaged in farm labor and animal husbandry. But it was during this period of reduced efficiency among the foreign policy apparatus that major changes in Sino-American relations took place. The powerful and hostile neighbor on China's northern border and the growing U.S. presence in Vietnam compelled Mao to re-examine China's security alternatives. In the process, he ignored the Foreign Ministry and even bypassed Zhou, even though he was considered the foremost expert on foreign relations in China. Mao addressed himself to the four marshals, Chen Yi, Ye Jianying, Xu Xiangqian, and Nie Rongzhen. Although inactive, Chen Yi was still the foreign minister, while the other three occupied high-level military positions and had long-standing experience in foreign policy. They were asked to form a study group to examine China's security problems. The marshals produced a general appraisal about the threat of war as well as a number of operational reports. They did not entirely discount the possibility of a Soviet attack against China, but expressed doubts about Soviet military ability to wage a war. In their view, the Soviet Union had overextended itself in Czechoslovakia and along the 7,000-mile-long Sino-Soviet border. Arguing against the possibility, often invoked by official Chinese propaganda, that the Soviet Union might join with the United States in a war against China, they carefully suggested improving relations with the United States. They were aware of the subtle changes in the attitude of the United States toward China initiated by the administration of Richard Nixon since it came to office in 1968. The first foreign policy report of the Nixon administration, issued in February 1969, stated that "the Chinese are a great and vital people who should not be isolated from the international community." The report further stated that it would be to the benefit of "stability in Asia and in the world, that we take whatever steps we can towards improved practical relations with Beijing."[148] This provided the basis for a different approach to the United States.

As a first step Zhou began to closely monitor developments in U.S. policy toward China. He instructed the Foreign Ministry to keep him informed on all aspects of American attitudes toward China, including minor incidents such as the arrest, by local Guangdong security officers, of two Americans whose boat had entered Chinese territorial waters near Hong Kong. The case was referred to Zhou, who summoned officials of the Foreign Ministry and the Ministry of Public Security to a meeting on 16 July 1969. The meeting started at ten o'clock in the morning, an unusual hour for Zhou, who normally started his daily activities around midday, and an indication of the great importance that he placed on the incident. In this instance, his instructions were to avoid publicity and to refrain from open denunciation of the Americans as "agents of the CIA." After some investigation, they were found to be students, and Zhou ordered their release.[149]

The four marshals also suggested that, in view of the tense situation on the northern border, it would be useful for China to become more active on the international and diplomatic scene. One of the first steps toward greater opening to the world was the restraint imposed on official propaganda and the dissemination of Mao Zedong Thought, which until this point had been a major "diplomatic" activity. Chinese diplomats, journalists, students, and technicians, regardless of where they were stationed, vigorously distributed propaganda in the form of Mao badges and the "little red book." Left-wingers among overseas Chinese frequently supported such activities. Initially, Zhou had tried to avoid this type of propaganda in foreign affairs. In December 1967, he had warned students going abroad that "Chairman Mao's words cannot be used indiscriminately." His ideas cannot "be imposed on others, not even on the people of the Soviet Union."[150] But it took some time before Mao realized that dissemination of ideas, implying that China was at the center of world revolution and calling for rebellion against established "bourgeois authorities," did more harm than good to the international reputation of his country. He became aware that, if he wanted to lead China out of its isolation, it would be necessary to curb such propaganda activities. During 1968, Mao issued several statements confirming his new approach to Chinese propaganda in foreign countries. He forbade the presentation of Mao badges to guests at receptions organized by the Foreign Ministry; he deleted references to the doctrine of "invincible Marxism, Leninism, and Mao Zedong Thought" and to "Chairman Mao's Proletarian Revolutionary Line" from documents written by the CCRG and the Foreign Ministry, remarking that "all this is useless and will only antagonize others."[151]

It was a delicate matter to change a course that had become ingrained in the minds of Chinese citizens like a religious dogma. But Mao had opened the door toward change, even if only a crack, so Zhou used every opportunity to correct the prevailing trend. He followed through with instructions about the use of propaganda in foreign countries, issuing a document on the "reform of propaganda in foreign countries" that said Chinese diplomats "must fight against formalism and propaganda imposed on others" and "overcome self-glorification in propaganda to foreign countries." In October 1970, Zhou told delegates to a conference on foreign trade that they should change their practice of using Chairman Mao's quotations on the packaging of the goods to be exported. Mao's quotations were not to be used nor was the idea to be further cultivated that China was the center of world revolution. It was an erroneous trend in foreign affairs as well as a sign of chauvinism and of imposition upon others, he said. For Zhou it was a victory over his left-wing enemies whom he never officially acknowledged as such. But he criticized them by innuendo when he attacked the media they controlled. Referring to the *People's Daily*—controlled by Jiang Qing and her acolytes—he said that it "sometimes lacked good style" and, since the beginning of the Cultural Revolution, was using "empty words, reprimands, or plain rudeness" in their reporting about foreign countries.[152]

At a national conference on foreign affairs in May 1971, Zhou delivered a major address on the new approach to foreign policy and the errors committed in the past, which, he said, consisted mainly of using inappropriate language. "I do not agree with the term 'Soviet revisionists' or with the tendency to refer to some East European countries as belonging to the revisionist camp," he said. And he warned against the indiscriminate use of such oversimplified terms as "imperialists, revisionists, and reactionaries."[153]

In February 1971, the British mission to China moved into a new office building. The British chargé d'affaires celebrated the event with a reception, which was attended by a number of officials from the Foreign Ministry. The next day, Zhou summoned some of those who had been at the reception to ask whether any of them had explained to the British the background of the incident that had led to the burning of their mission in August 1967. Because the Foreign Ministry officials had not received any instructions about this matter, they had, of course, remained silent. But Zhou criticized them for their lack of initiative, saying, "It was a handful of hooligans who burned down the old building of the mission, and they were condemned by the CCP and the government. You should have explained this to the British representatives. You could have said this in front of the other foreign ambassadors." On 2 March 1971 he personally met with the British chargé d'affaires to explain the events.[154]

Mao made some efforts at elucidating some of the strange events that had taken place in previous years. In 1970 and 1971 he blamed them on the 516 Group. He told visitors from Romania, North Korea, and Burma as well as to Edgar Snow that there had been a good deal of trouble in the country. One day it was Zhou Enlai who should have been overthrown, another day it was Li Xiannian, and yet another day someone else. He did not understand all this, he said, adding that it was one of the great results of the Cultural Revolution that the evil 516 Group had become exposed. Since its "backstage bosses" were now known and under investigation, there would be no further obstacles to normalizing relations with other countries.[155]

Between 1966 and 1969, Chinese ambassadors were not stationed in foreign capitals. They had been summoned to Beijing to take part in the Cultural Revolution. To repair relations with foreign countries, diplomatic ties had to be re-established at ambassadorial rank. Since most senior ambassadors had been criticized by their own embassy staff, they needed political upgrading before being sent abroad. Zhou insisted that the ambassadors be invited to the ninth congress of the CCP in April 1969 and recommended that they be elected to the new Central Committee, a suggestion that Mao readily accepted. In June 1969 Zhou issued instructions to the Foreign Ministry to dispatch a group of ambassadors to Albania, Vietnam, France, and Sweden.[156] Over the next few years, Zhou dispatched ambassadors to all the countries with which China already had diplomatic relations. In the first half of the 1970s, largely because relations with the United States had become normalized, more than sixty additional countries established diplomatic relations with the People's Republic.

A certain formalism with respect to protocol concerning the exchange of ambassadorial credentials created some misgivings in the Foreign Ministry, which required Zhou's intervention. According to diplomatic convention, it is the head of state who appoints ambassadors and who signs their credentials. These credentials are in turn presented to the head of state receiving the ambassador. But Liu Shaoqi, who formally remained the head of state despite his downfall, was no longer on active duty. This formalism became a concrete problem when Pakistan appointed a new ambassador to China and Pakistan's Foreign Ministry raised the question: to whom should its new ambassador present his credentials. Zhou suggested that, for the time being, letters of credence should be addressed to the vice president without mentioning a specific name. Credentials of Chinese ambassadors to be sent abroad should be signed by Vice President Dong Biwu.[157]

## A New Start with the United States

On Chinese National Day on 1 October 1970, Edgar Snow and his wife were invited onto the rostrum above the main entrance to the Forbidden City, where Mao presided over the festivities. The next day, the front page of *People's Daily* was largely occupied by a picture of Mao and the Snows, an arrangement that Zhou had personally supervised. On 28 December, Mao gave a lengthy interview to Snow, in which he stated that he had lost interest in the talks that had been taken place for a number of years between the Chinese and the American ambassadors in Warsaw. He thought that if problems between the United States and China were to be solved it would be better if he talked to President Nixon directly. He would be willing to talk to Nixon, he said, regardless of whether anything was accomplished. Nixon might come to China either as a tourist or as a president.[158]

At the same time, the Nixon administration was making attempts to develop better communication with the Chinese authorities through its diplomatic representation in Warsaw, where the only direct contact existed between the two countries. Subjects of discussion at the Warsaw talks were limited, and the talks had reached a stalemate. In December 1969, at a reception at a Yugoslav clothing exhibition, the U.S. ambassador to Poland, Walter Stoessel—at a reception at a Yugoslav clothing exhibition—approached Chinese diplomats in attendance. But when Li Juqing, the second secretary of the Chinese embassy, and his interpreter saw the American diplomat approaching them, they avoided him. Later, the U.S. ambassador caught up with the Chinese interpreter to convey the message that he wanted to talk to the Chinese chargé d'affaires, as President Nixon wished to open negotiations with China on major issues. The Chinese embassy reported the event to the government in Beijing. Zhou had no response about talks with Nixon, but he instructed the embassy representative to invite the American diplomat for further talks.[159]

This was not the only time that Chinese diplomats tried to avoid contact with their American counterparts. At the end of 1969, the Chinese embassies in Bern and Paris also received requests from American diplomats for a meeting. They asked for instructions on how to respond.

The Foreign Ministry, drilled in Cultural Revolution tactics, drafted a carefully worded reply informing the embassies that they should not accept requests for meetings with the Chinese ambassador and the chargé d'affaires. Ordinary staff members at the embassies could consent to a meeting, but they should not venture any opinions and certainly should refrain from replying to any question. They should go to meetings with American diplomats only in pairs; they should not talk, but only listen carefully. Zhou agreed with this suggestion: "We have to listen to what the other side has to say.... We will reply when the time is ripe for us."[160]

In spite of these slight changes in the Chinese attitude, not much could be accomplished through normal diplomatic channels. Contacts were finally established through a somewhat tortuous, albeit efficient, channel that also guaranteed discretion. President Nixon, wary of inefficient diplomatic channels, asked the presidents of Romania and Pakistan, both of whom had good relations with the Chinese government, to convey his intention to develop contact with the Chinese authorities. In March 1970, the president of Pakistan, Agha Mohammed Yahya Khan, summoned the Chinese ambassador, Zhang Tong, and told him that he had a message from President Nixon to the Chinese government. It stated that the U.S. government wanted to transmit, through the Pakistan's president, any oral messages on subjects of interest to both the United States and China. Zhang Tong was stunned, for a few days earlier he had received a circular from the Chinese Foreign Ministry according to which the Nepalese ambassador to China had told Zhou that the United States hoped to establish a direct dialogue, above the ambassadorial level, with the Chinese authorities. Zhou had politely but firmly denied the request. Because Zhang had not received different instructions, his reply to President Khan was along the same lines. But when Zhou received Zhang's report, the situation had already changed. He instructed the Foreign Ministry to send a telegram to Zhang, indicating that the Chinese authorities were interested this kind of oral communications. During his next audience with Khan, Zhang received another message from the United States. President Khan told him that, if Beijing agreed, President Nixon was prepared to open direct channels from the White House to Zhongnanhai, with assurance of complete discretion. The existence of such a channel, he conveyed through Khan, would not be known to anyone outside the White House. On 21 March Zhang sent Nixon's message to Zhou, who then indicated that he was willing to open this channel of communications.

During the next few months, oral messages began to flow, in great secrecy, between the Chinese and U.S. leaders. If Zhou wanted to communicate with the Americans, he would send a message to Zhang, who then called President Khan on his private line to request a meeting. When he saw Khan, Zhang read the message to him. Khan would write it down and then read it back to the ambassador to ensure that there was no misunderstanding. Only then would it be transmitted to Washington. Pakistan's ambassador to the United States would pass messages to Khan, who then telephoned the Chinese ambassador to convey the message personally. It was through this channel that Kissinger's secret mission to China was arranged.[161]

## Ping-Pong Diplomacy

The various political campaigns had caught up with well-known athletes. If they had won international contests, they were in view of the new policy of opening up international contacts, it was decided that a Chinese team should participate in the world table tennis championship in Japan in April 1971. This was the first time since the beginning of the Cultural Revolution that a Chinese team was allowed to take part in an international sports event. When meeting with other contestants, the Chinese athletes were expected to follow a strict code of behavior. Zhou stipulated that the team should not take the initiative of talking to or exchanging greetings with the American team. If they had to play the Americans, they should shake hands and greet them, but they should not exchange banners with the other team.[162] Such a scenario allowed little scope for friendly relations between the American and the Chinese team members. Nonetheless, the contacts between the teams—later called "ping-pong policy"—were a major step in the establishment of Sino-American relations at the highest level.

Henry Kissinger and, later, John Holdridge attribute the initiative for ping-pong policy to Zhou Enlai. "It was an inspired and theatrical piece of diplomacy that had the attributes of Zhou Enlai's sophistication, wisdom and strategic planning," wrote Holdridge.[163] The Chinese interpretation, however, indicates that Zhou was much too cautious to take an initiative that would certainly have widespread consequences for his country's foreign policy. Chinese authors attribute the first step toward establishing contact to members of the U.S. team and to American journalists who were covering the event. According to this view, they approached the Chinese delegation several times to express their friendship and their desire to visit China. This was reported to Beijing, where both the State Sports Commission and the Foreign Ministry discussed the issue. A majority argued that, since Mao had already told Edgar Snow that he would welcome President Nixon, it would not be right to invite the American athletes ahead of the president. A minority defended the opposite view, believing that it would be a sign of good will to invite the American athletes at that time. Finally, the ministry and the Sports Commission issued a joint recommendation addressed to Zhou, stating that "the time is not ripe for such a visit ... and we are convinced that there will be other opportunities in the future." Zhou approved these conclusions, adding, "We should clearly tell the [American team's] representative that we Chinese people are firmly against the conspiracy of 'two Chinas.'" But this was not the final word on the matter. The recommendation was submitted to Mao. It was understood that, because the table tennis tournament was to due to end on 7 April, if Mao had not given his instruction on the matter by the afternoon of 6 April, Zhou's conclusions would be transmitted to the Chinese team in Japan. Mao apparently found it difficult to come to a decision. It was not until midnight on 6 April that he made up his mind to invite the American athletes.

After the decision was made, Zhou organized the visit with his usual courtesy. On 14 April he received the American table tennis team—as well as teams from Canada, Colombia, Great Britain, and Nigeria—in the Great Hall of the People, where he said that the visit would open "the doors for friendly exchanges between our two peoples."[164]

The evolution of contacts between Kissinger and Zhou ushered in an entirely new phase of Chinese activities in international relations. The U.S. government had decided to maintain strict secrecy about Kissinger's visit to China.[165] This decision created some suspicion among Chinese leaders. But in China, too, the new course of Chinese foreign policy at first remained a secret, confined to a restricted number of people at the highest echelons. Officials at lower levels, as well as the Chinese people, were not informed, much less prepared, for this major policy change. During the secret contacts between Kissinger and Zhou, anti-American rhetoric continued unabated in the Chinese media, and for most government officials it was unthinkable that a high-ranking U.S. official would be cordially received in China. Only in May 1971—barely two months before Kissinger's arrival in Beijing—Zhou recommended to

Mao that leading members of the ministries and the PLA be informed about the pending visit. Zhou also established a working group under the direction of Ye Jianying to prepare for the visit.

While the Chinese leaders were hesitant about informing their own inner circle about changing relations with the United States, Zhou considered it necessary to give China's closest allies advance notice of Kissinger impending arrival. He paid secret visits to North Korea and North Vietnam to tell their governments about the unprecedented event. Both governments expressed understanding of the Chinese desire to improve relations with the United States. Only Albania, also informed, reacted negatively and expressed strong disapproval of China's changed attitude toward the United States.[166]

When Kissinger arrived in Beijing on 9 July, the central government was in a deep crisis that a short two months later would end in the disappearance of Lin Biao, Mao's designated successor. Mao was so deeply preoccupied with this emergency that when Zhou appeared at his residence to report about his first discussions with Kissinger, he refused to listen. Only after he had received the latest information about the internal situation was he ready to give a fair hearing to Zhou's report.

Taiwan, Vietnam, and Indochina were the thorny issues in his discussions with Kissinger, but Zhou established a friendly atmosphere, stating that the differences between the two countries should not jeopardize their common efforts to find a basis of equality and friendship for relations between them. But Mao, after hearing Zhou's report on his first talks with the U.S. National Security Adviser, began to ruminate about "world revolution," instructing Zhou to convey to Kissinger and his aides the basics on the subject. He insisted that Zhou expound Mao's views on "great disorder under heaven," the "excellence of the situation" (in China), and that China was "prepared for the United States, the Soviet Union, and Japan to come and carve up the country." Zhou faithfully carried out these instructions during his second meeting with Kissinger, lecturing his American guests on the world situation characterized by chaos and conflicts, the upsurge of the revolutionary struggle, the readiness of the People's Republic to face collusion of the superpowers against it, to fight a protracted war against any aggressor, and similar propaganda.

Kissinger was taken somewhat by surprise by the sudden transformation of the hitherto genial and urbane Zhou and his tirade, which, according to Kissinger, was pronounced "with little rhetorical flourish." He began to refute Zhou's arguments, but Zhou, after having made his statement, seemed to have lost interest in the subject. He reminded his guests that lunch would be served. Over a succulent Peking duck, the atmosphere became relaxed once more.[167]

Differences emerged regarding the draft of the communiqué announcing President Nixon's visit to China. As was the case for the invitation to the American table tennis team, the Chinese wanted to give the impression that the United States had solicited the invitation, so the two high-ranking Foreign Ministry officials in charge of drafting the communiqué suggested that Nixon had sought out the Chinese. This was "in the best of Middle Kingdom tradition" as Kissinger wrote.[168] After consultation with Mao, Zhou overruled the wording. The final text of the communiqué reads: "Knowing of President Nixon's expressed desire to visit the People's Republic of China, Premier Zhou Enlai, on behalf of the Government of the People's Republic of China, has extended an invitation to President Nixon to visit China at an appropriate date before May 1972." By mutual consent this statement was made public simultaneously in China and in the United States.

The announcement of the impending visit of the U.S. president to China stunned the world. Its immediate impact was a UN General Assembly vote, on 25 October, to admit the People's Republic as a member. For many years, Zhou had sent regular telegrams to the United Nations, claiming what he considered China's rightful seat at the General Assembly and the Security Council and protesting Taiwan's occupation of that seat. Now that the battle was finally won, Zhou hesitated in responding to the United Nations. First, he did not want to create the impression that the Chinese government would be in great hurry to join the organization. Second, he was concerned about whether China was sufficiently prepared to participate in UN debates, because of its diplomats' long isolation. When Zhou discussed the issue with Foreign Ministry officials, some of them expressed skepticism about the United Nations, saying that it was a forum of discussion for bourgeois politicians and an instrument dominated by the two superpowers, the United States and the Soviet Union. It was a bureaucratic organization where people drank coffee, chatted, and engaged in oral argument, an organization that was unable to speak up for the rights of oppressed nations. While the discussions were going on, Wang Hairong, Mao's grand niece, appeared at the meeting hall, saying that Mao wanted to see Zhou, Ye Jianying, Ji

Pengfei, Qiao Guanhua, Xiong Xianghui, and Tang Wensheng immediately. When they arrived at Mao's residence, he said, "Hasn't the secretary-general of the United Nations sent a cable inviting us? We will send a delegation now. Let Qiao [Guanhua] be the head of the delegation."[169]

On 8 November, Mao and Zhou met with all the members of the Chinese delegation in a briefing session that lasted the entire night. The main message conveyed was that the struggle had to continue. "Only by getting into the tiger's den can you get the tiger's cub," Mao said.

Zhou wanted to avoid creating the impression that the People's Republic was anxious to participate in UN deliberations on China's membership. In his view, China's position on the issue of Taiwan's UN presence had prevailed while the United States had finally failed in their effort to keep China out of the organization. By resuming its seat at the United Nations in November 1971, Beijing was, in fact, doing the United States a favor. His approach to Nixon's visit was similar. It was presented in a way reminiscent of dynastical practice in which foreign dignitaries paid homage to the Middle Kingdom. In November 1971, Zhou told the British writer Neville Maxwell that "President Nixon himself knocked at our door, expressing his wish to come to Beijing for talks." In a speech on the international situation in December, Zhou declared that Nixon would come like a woman without morals, "dressed up elaborately to present herself at the door" (*shuzang daban, songshang menlai*). Nixon's eagerness to come to China, he said, was due to the external and domestic difficulties that he was having. Internationally he had to face problems in Vietnam and the expanding Soviet influence in Europe and the Middle East. Domestically, Zhou suggested, Nixon was "under immense pressure engendered by the American people to improve Sino-American relations."[170]

Whatever rhetoric might have surrounded Zhou's statements on Nixon's visit, he gave every detail of the organization of the event his full attention. During his preparations, he encountered a number of difficulties with Jiang Qing and her coterie, who took exception to several aspects of his arrangements. The Ministry of Culture, one of Jiang's strongholds, objected to playing the American anthem "America the Beautiful," which Zhou had chosen for a banquet in Nixon's honor. Jiang Qing resented the activities of an American broadcasting team that wanted to film Nixon's visit in China, on the grounds that it was "doing propaganda for Nixon on Chinese soil."

Zhou was eager to demonstrate to the world that China—which, for years, had emphasized Sino-American differences and even hostility— would not succumb to any American attempt to seek reconciliation at the expense of basic principles. He therefore considered unacceptable any communiqué that would paper over such differences. Zhou insisted on a text that would set forth agreements and disagreements between the two parties. The Shanghai Communiqué, signed on 28 February, reflected this particular need. It clearly stated the conflicting views between the two countries on Vietnam, Korea, Japan, and South Asia.

Relations between the two countries thereafter developed rapidly on a working level through the U.S. and Chinese embassies in Paris and Ottawa. In February 1973, Kissinger raised the issue of a more direct exchange with Zhou, proposing trade representatives, consulates, or liaison offices in Beijing and Washington. As a counteroffer, he promised the withdrawal of all remaining U.S. forces from Taiwan and the termination of official ties with Taiwan. Although this promise was not entirely kept and the United States continued to be officially present in Taiwan, China agreed to the opening of liaison offices in their respective capitals.[171]

With respect to foreign relations, 1972 belonged to Zhou. His efforts at reorienting Chinese foreign policy enhanced his international image. High-level visitors from abroad paid homage to his intellectual abilities, charm, negotiating skills, grasp of details as well as analytical powers. Mao could hardly tolerate that Zhou, and not he himself, was widely considered as the architect of the new Chinese foreign policy thus overshadowing him in international stature. In July 1973, Mao began to criticize the Foreign Ministry, whose appraisal of the world situation he did not appreciate. He complained that the Foreign Ministry was sending him "shit documents" that he refused to read. He would not read the premier's speeches either, he said. In Mao's view, the ministry failed to discuss "important matters" with him while producing reports on "minor matters." He warned that "if the situation does not improve, revisionism is bound to occur." Mao's criticism threw Zhou into a panic. He wrote a letter to Mao, declaring that he was responsible for the ministry's errors and that "the mistakes the Chairman has pointed to have to do with my political thinking and my style of work."[172]

During 1973, the Sino-American normalization process slowed down. Kissinger went to Beijing about twice a year, recalling that after November 1973 his visits "either were downright chilly or were holding actions"[173] The timing coincides with the continued campaign against Zhou, who had come under sustained criticism. Zhou's handling of Sino-American relations and the Taiwan issue were significant elements of the campaign, which accused him of "capitulation" to the United States. At several meetings of the Politburo, enlarged by officials from the Foreign Ministry, Zhou made self-criticisms and listened to the denunciations by not only his senior colleagues but also his own subordinates. [174]

## Illness and Setbacks

Deng's rehabilitation was not only a sign of Mao's changing policies after the death of Lin Biao, but also a necessity because of the deterioration in Zhou's physical condition. In May 1972, he was diagnosed with bladder cancer. His doctors did not break the news about his condition to him. At high leadership level it was customary to first inform Mao on such matters as serious illness among his senior colleagues, through Wang Dongxing, Mao's chief security officer. While Zhou continued to work tirelessly, his doctors were waiting for instructions from the Chairman to start Zhou's treatment.[175] Mao did not take the matter seriously. He rambled about doctors who are always looking for illness because they had nothing better to do. He asked Li Zhisui, his own physician, how it was possible to tell that someone had bladder cancer by looking at his urine. When Dr. Li finally convinced him that Zhou had cancer, Mao thought that further laboratory tests would not be necessary. Cancer cannot be cured, he said, and treatment only caused pain and mental anguish. "If I have cancer," he declared, "I definitely will not have it treated."[176] The doctor's hands were tied. Zhou received no treatment, so his health was left to deteriorate. In January 1973, as blood discharged with his urine, his physical condition could no longer be kept a secret from him. Shocked, Zhou listed to the explanations of his doctor, Zhang Zuoliang, without uttering a word. Dr. Zhang tried to alleviate his concerns, saying that the cancer was still at an early stage and that the best specialists in China would be consulted to determine the appropriate therapy. He and his colleagues agreed that, at that point, Zhou's cancer should be treated with cauterization instead of surgery. Again the doctors needed Mao's approval for the intervention, which took another two months to achieve. On 10 March, in a house in the scenic western hills of Beijing, Zhou had a cystoscopy and a local cauterization of the bladder. The intervention was successful in preventing future discharges of blood in his urine. With his wife, Zhou took a week's rest—the longest in many years. Then he was back in Zhongnanhai, coping with his usual workload. Dr. Zhang had prescribed two sessions a week of chemotherapy, but Zhou did not believe that he had the time to attend these sessions regularly.[177]

The physical condition of the then eighty-year-old Mao was equally tenuous. He had developed a pulmonary heart condition and suffered from a rare motor neuron disease and muscular atrophy in his arms and legs. His speech had become increasingly slurred, and his eyesight had deteriorated considerably.[178] The two ailing men were ruling a country devastated by the Cultural Revolution and a population exhausted by one political campaign after the other. Disillusionment and weariness as well as discontent and loathing of Mao's personality cult were widespread among cadres at various levels and among the population. Revolutionary aspirations existed only in the rhetoric of the mass media controlled by Jiang Qing and her sycophants. The society was characterized by sluggishness, procrastination, and depression. Living standards deteriorated. Most May Seventh Cadre Schools—with the exception of those under the Foreign Ministry, hence under Zhou's responsibility—closed and released their inmates, who returned to the cities to look for work. More than ten million young people who had been sent to the countryside returned to the cities completely disillusioned. People everywhere yearned for a normal life, stability, and improvement in their living standards. But, in an effort to resist the popular desire to return to normalcy and to recover some of the old order, Mao issued a call "to go against the tide," designed to persuade people that only through the Cultural Revolution would it be possible for China to maintain its specific form of socialism and to progress toward communism. For Mao, the defense of the Cultural Revolution was a priority. During his lifetime, Mao said, he had only two major achievements to his credit: the victory over the Guomindang and the Cultural Revolution.[179]

Mao's remarks provided Jiang Qing and her group with room for another attack on Zhou. His efforts to restore some degree of normalcy in society and particularly in the educational sector were construed as a "relapse into right deviation"—an attempt to reestablish the old order that had existed before the Cultural Revolution. To support their contentions, they cited measures such as the reintroduction of entrance examinations to universities by the State Council. According to Jiang Qing, this was a principle that would restore giving "priority to intellectual capacities." A young man in Liaoning who had handed in a blank paper at a university entrance examination was hailed as a hero who dared to "go against the tide." He was invited to join the CCP, admitted to a college, where, shortly thereafter, he joined the administrative board. The following year, he was elected to the National People's Congress.[180]

There are many other examples of similar conflicts between Zhou and the radical faction. The old educational system not only was criticized for discriminating against the working class but also was accused of killing children. An example was the much publicized Tanghe Incident of July 1973. A fifteen-year-old girl from Tanghe county in Henan province wrote an improvised verse on her English examination: "I am Chinese. Why should I learn English, Without learning the a, b, c, I can still be a successor [to Mao's revolutionary cause]." Her teacher reprimanded her, and the school authorities encouraged her schoolmates to discuss the problem. Feeling humiliated, she drowned herself in a river. Learning about the incident, Jiang Qing sent a delegation to the county to investigate, which determined that the school was an outstanding example of bourgeois restoration in education. Both the principal of the school and the girl's teacher were arrested.

In another case, a twelve-year-old pupil at a Beijing primary school became a national heroine. In a letter to *Beijing ribao* (Beijing Daily), she complained about her teacher, who, she believed, had unjustly disciplined her. Her letter was published with excerpts from the girl's diary, and with an editorial comment emphasizing that this was a typical example of the impact of the revisionist line on education and demonstrated that traditional concepts were far from eliminated. The girl, by "going against the tide," had the courage to oppose the restoration of the Confucian concept of "dignity of the teacher" (*shidao zunyan*). The newspaper appealed to students to learn from this case.[181] Criticism of right deviation in education swept the country, condemning all efforts to reform the school system and restore it to normalcy. The widespread desire to reform the education system, which had become a strong social current, was at least temporarily suppressed. But the major threat to greater stability came from Mao. In bad health and wary of living under the same roof with his wife, Jiang Qing, he became more and more inaccessible. In his isolation, he began to rely on intermediaries to communicate with Zhou and other senior colleagues. In 1973, five young women, known as the "five golden flowers," had access to Mao. All of them were employed in the Foreign Ministry, where, to the dismay of many officials with long years of experience, they quickly rose through the ranks. Wang Hairong, the director of the Protocol Department, was promoted to vice minister in 1974. Her close friend, Tang Wensheng (Nancy Tang), who was born in the United States, was an English interpreter who had risen to become deputy director of the Department of the Americas and Oceania. She was further promoted, in August 1973, to become an alternate member of the tenth Central Committee. Zhang Hanzhi, also an English interpreter, became the deputy director of the Asian Department. Qi Zonghua and Luo Xu, both French interpreters, had risen to become deputy director of the West European and the African Departments, respectively. Mao made Wang Hairong and Nancy Tang his principal liaisons with the Foreign Ministry. To reinforce their status, Mao requested that they attend Politburo meetings, beginning in November 1973. Zhou, who always adapted to Mao's quirks, showed them respect and used their services whenever he wanted to communicate with Mao. Even Mao's wife had to go through them if she wanted to communicate with the Chairman.[182]

Wang and Tang followed Mao's whims. When Mao was displeased with Zhou, they played up to him. This was the case in mid-1973, when the foreign press was celebrating Zhou as the architect of the breakthrough in Sino-American relations, while little mention was made of Mao. In Chinese politics, the rigid hierarchical system precluded having the premier, as Mao's subordinate, receive more credit for this policy than Mao. Wang and Tang drew Mao's attention to the foreign press, which he normally never read. They also brought him an article published in an internal newspaper at the Foreign Ministry, which Mao normally did not read either. The article covered the June 1973 visit of Leonid Brezhnev, the Soviet leader, to Washington, and concluded that the Soviet Union and the United States were attempting "joint domination of the world." While Zhou found the analysis remarkable and praised its author—something that rarely happened—for Mao this was once more an opportunity to strongly complain about the Foreign Ministry. Zhou's talks with Kissinger in November 1973 again provoked Mao's ire. In an amiable atmosphere, the two statesmen reviewed the world situation, expressed satisfaction about the establishment of the liaison offices in Beijing and Washington, and decided on a number of common projects for the year to come. But one of the interpreters reported to Mao that Zhou had talked about a number of subjects for which he did not have Mao's prior approval, nor did he account to Mao afterward. She also said that Zhou and Ye Jianying, who was also present at the talks, were afraid of the American atom bomb. Mao immediately concluded that Zhou and

Ye were guilty of "rightist deviation" and of having surrendered to the United States.[183]

On 17 November, Mao convened a meeting at his office in Zhongnanhai with Zhou and leading cadres of the Foreign Ministry. This was another opportunity to voice his criticism of Zhou, who, in his talks with Kissinger, had talked about two possibilities for solving the Taiwan problem: peaceful and military. Mao declared that this was wrong. "We will fight," he said. "Remember when we were in northern Shaanxi, even for a small fortified village we had to fight. It would not have surrendered if we had not fought." And he demanded criticism of Zhou by an enlarged Politburo, to which he invited Tang and Wang. The criticism meeting started the same evening and went on for several evenings. Beginning 21 November, as more participants were added, the meeting was moved to the Great Hall of the People. The Foreign Ministry was represented by vice ministers Ji Pengfei, Zhong Xidong, and Qiao Guanhua, Ambassaor Huang Zhen, and four of the "golden flowers," Wang, Tang, Zhang Hanzhi, and Luo Xu. Other participants were Geng Biao, the head of the Central Liaison Department, the leaders of eight military regions, Wang Hongwen, and Jiang Qing. All of them vociferously criticized Zhou. Were they convinced that Zhou had made mistakes or were they just following orders? It appears that Qiao Guanhua, who had worked under Zhou since the 1930s, did not believe in Zhou's guilt and later regretted what he had said at the meeting.[184] Jiang Qing, however, was particularly harsh. For her, this was an occasion to destroy Zhou. She accused the premier of being anxious to replace Mao and, more significantly, declared that his case was one of "the eleventh-line struggle." This was an extremely serious accusation. In the history of the CCP, all the major leaders that Mao had purged were involved in a "line struggle." They were a total of ten, from Chen Duxiu and Qu Qiubai to Liu Shaoqi and Lin Biao, who, after his defection, became the subject of the tenth-line struggle. By linking Zhou with the "eleventh-line struggle," Jiang Qing clearly aimed at his elimination.

In Mao's mind, however, she had gone too far. On 9 December, he talked to Wang and Tang, saying that the "the meetings of the Politburo in November were very successful. But someone said one or two wrong sentences. One was the reference to the 'eleventh-line struggle.' There is no such struggle. The other was that the premier is too anxious to replace me. But it is not the premier who is too anxious, it is Jiang Qing herself."[185]

This ended one of the most serious crises in Zhou Enlai's political life. Mao once again refused to overthrow Zhou, recognizing that he was the only leader capable of running the country. Although he clearly resented the recognition that Zhou had earned internationally, and he was eager to teach him a lesson and to put him in his place, he was also aware that he needed Zhou's talents.

But Zhou's Enlai's ordeal was not over. In 1974, the campaign against a "relapse into right deviation" evolved into a campaign to criticize Lin Biao and Confucius. In the tortuous logic of the Cultural Revolution, the rather unexpected linkage between Lin Biao and Confucius was established after a number of scrolls written in Lin's calligraphy were discovered at his former residence. They were copies of quotations from the teachings of Confucius. Confucius had been dead for two thousand years but, in Mao's view, he represented retrogression and all the vices of the old society. Shortly thereafter a third person, Zhou Gong, was added to the slogan to criticize Lin and Confucius. Zhou Gong was the name of the famous Duke of Zhou who, in the twelfth century B.C.E., served King Cheng of the Western Zhou dynasty. But it is also a respectful address for someone named Zhou. Zhou Enlai had been known as Zhou Gong among his noncommunist friends when he was active as the CCP representative in Guomindang areas in the 1940s.

In response to Mao's instruction to criticize Confucius, in the second half of 1973, Jiang Qing and her radical associates compiled material about "Lin Biao and the doctrine of Confucius and Mencius," which the Party authorities distributed throughout the country for the purpose of political studies. On 24 and 25 January 1974, she called two meetings attended by ten thousand people each to start the campaign to "criticize Lin, criticize Confucius" (*pi Lin, pi Kong*). A group of writers recruited from among professors at Beijing and Qinghua Universities, the Central Party School, and other academic institutions published a plethora of articles on the subject in the official press. This was followed by a series of publications criticizing "the present-day Confucius," an attack on Zhou by innuendo. But the insinuations became increasingly transparent. Jiang Qing declared that there was a "chief Confucius in the Party," who, according to one of her supporters, was "neither Liu Shaoqi, nor Lin Biao." In April 1974, *Red Flag* depicted Zhou in the role of Confucius as prime minister of the State of Lu, who was critically ill; and *Beijing Daily* described Confucius as a sick man whose arm, like Zhou's, was bent at the elbow. Zhou was likened to several other prime ministers in Chinese history, one of whom was alleged to have been a slave owner who "vigorously promoted a reactionary political line" and another who was described as "a very shrewd old bureaucrat ... good at handling human relations," who was "ambiguous and who, in order not to offend anybody, never revealed his true attitude," a portrait of Zhou that was not too far off the mark.[186]

When the campaign against Lin, Confucius, and the Duke of Zhou became increasingly centered on Zhou, his physical condition declined. A second cauterization in March 1974 did not yield satisfactory results. In April, his doctors suggested surgery but did not receive official approval. Zhou received regular blood transfusions for hematuria at his residence, but his condition continued to deteriorate. The tumor in his bladder grew larger and metastasized. His urethra became worse, making urination difficult and painful. Desperate about an inability to treat their patient properly, his medical team continued to report to the Center about Zhou's health and asked to be allowed to perform surgery without delay. Ye Jianying, Zhang Chunqiao, Wang Dongxing, and others received the team at the Great Hall of the People. The physicians' report was followed by a long silence. Finally, Zhang Chunqiao declared that the premier was the country's chief manager of Party, government, and military affairs. This made him indispensable and irreplaceable. In addition, Zhang said, Zhou was scheduled to meet a number of foreign visitors at the end of May. Only after that could surgery be considered.

The last foreign visitor scheduled at that time was the Malaysian prime minister, Tun Abdul Razak Bin Datuk Hussein, who visited China from 28 May to 2 June. Zhou negotiated with him over the establishment of diplomatic relations between China and Malaysia. While they talked in the Great Hall of the People, a medical team with all the necessary equipment was installed in an adjacent room, ready for any emergency. On 1 June, Zhou's surgery was finally scheduled. After an apparently successful operation, Zhou seemed to be recovering.[187]

As the campaign to criticize Lin and Confucius unfolded, reinstated veteran cadres were again attacked, leading organs in many localities and work units again became paralyzed, and armed battles among rival factions restarted. As a result, industrial production fell dramatically during the first five months of 1974. Fearing a reoccurrence of the situation of 1967, Mao ordered that the campaign against Lin and Confucius be directed by Party committees; that no mass organizations be established; and that no exchange of experiences among different professions and trades or between different localities take place.[188] Although he was concerned with maintaining a certain degree of radicalism, he did not want to be confronted with another bout of upheaval and disorder. His deteriorating health may have contributed to this attitude. He had increasing difficulty in speaking, standing up, and walking. In the spring of 1974, he developed cataracts and began to lose his eyesight.[189]

Vulnerable and exposed as he was in the campaign against "relapse into right deviation," Zhou could seek solace only in the fact that Mao had no doubts about his loyalty. The Chairman wanted him to be admonished, not eliminated. This became clear on 17 July, when Zhou left the hospital to attend a Politburo meeting that Mao had called. There, Mao warned Jiang Qing to be more careful in her relations with others, not to treat them harshly or charge them with unjustified accusations. He declared openly: "Jiang Qing does not speak for me, she speaks only for herself"; and he warned her not to "form a small group of four people" or a "Shanghai gang." This was the first time that Mao had raised the question of the Gang of Four, as the group was later called, which comprised Jiang Qing, Zhang Chunqiao, Wang Hongwen, and Yao Wenyuan. Clearly, Mao did not support Jiang Qing's activities aimed at making Zhou the prime target of the campaign against Lin, Confucius, and the Duke of Zhou. Without Mao's explicit support, the campaign could not go beyond attacking Zhou by innuendo. Nonetheless, Zhou was defenseless before the allegorical attacks against him. In addition to his normally heavy workload, he believed that he had to closely observe the progress of the campaign and to handle the problems that developed because of it.

Mao was now clearly preoccupied with stability and order. "Eight years have passed since the Great Proletarian Cultural Revolution started," said Mao. "It is preferable to have stability now. The Party and the nation should unite."[190] In early 1975, Mao decided to convene the fourth National People's Congress, which had been delayed by the Lin Biao affair. One of the main issues at the congress was the redistribution of power in the government, especially the composition of the State Council. Jiang Qing and her group, whose major stronghold was the media, wielded little influence in government affairs. Dissatisfied with these limitations, they attempted to advance their own status at the forthcoming congress.

But the focus of attention was the premiership. Zhou's illness suggested that he would not be able to hold the post for much longer even if he were renominated at the congress. The radicals attempted to promote Zhang Chunqiao as a candidate to the post, but the appointment of Deng Xiaoping, on 4 October 1973, to the position of first vice premier suggested that Deng had the better chances. This could not but anger Jiang Qing and her associates, who were offended by Deng's rehabilitation, not to mention the possibility that Deng might be nominated premier after Zhou's death. Since they did not have the means to vent their dissatisfaction on Mao, in their resentment, they focused on Deng and Zhou. In the spring of 1974, they clashed on the issue of Deng's mission to the sixth special session of the UN General Assembly. Cognizant of the complicated relations within the Politburo, the Foreign Ministry sent Wang Hairong and Nancy Tang to Mao to discuss the composition of the Chinese delegation to the special session. Would Mao agree that Deng should lead the delegation? Mao reacted positively. On 22 March, the Foreign Ministry sent a memorandum to Zhou suggesting that Deng, accompanied by Vice Foreign Minister Qiao Guanhua, should address the UN General Assembly on behalf of China. Both Mao and Zhou approved the suggestion. After learning about this, Jiang Qing angrily summoned Wang Hairong and Nancy Tang to her office. Upon their arrival, she demanded that the Foreign Ministry revoke its memorandum. Zhou Enlai, considering Jiang Qing's weight and Mao's unpredictable relationship with her, approached Mao again on that matter to seek his support. Mao, in his usual prima donna fashion, replied through one of his secretaries that it had been his idea to send Deng abroad. If, however, all the members of the Politburo were against his decision, Deng should not go, Mao said. Jiang Qing was not so easily deterred. She continued to telephone Wang Hairong and Nancy Tang, demanding the withdrawal of the Foreign Ministry memorandum.

To clear up the matter, Zhou called a meeting of the Politburo, at which all but Jiang Qing agreed that Deng should go to the United Nations. Mao finally corroborated the decision in a letter to Jiang Qing, where he made it clear that she should not oppose Deng's mission to New York.[191]

Since his reinstatement to the Politburo, Deng—less diplomatic and more daring than Zhou—had frequently butted heads with Jiang Qing. He clashed with her at a Politburo meeting on 17 October over a policy that Zhou had advocated in the early 1970s of buying ships from other countries in order to improve China's merchant fleet. In Jiang Qing's perception, this policy represented a "slavish comprador philosophy," whereas the first ocean-going cargo ship designed and built in China (called the *Fang Qing*) as a symbol of Mao's policy of self-reliance and independence. After the ship returned from its maiden voyage to Europe, Jiang Qing became aware that the political commissar assigned to the ship had made a number of critical remarks about the quality of the freighter, which had suffered a number of mechanical failures during the trip. Moreover, he was said to have made a few sarcastic remarks about Jiang Qing's model operas. This was construed as a counterrevolutionary incident, which led to the man's arrest. At the Politburo meeting, Jiang Qing attempted to coax Deng into accepting the accusations against him. Deng refused to commit himself, sharp words were exchanged, and Deng left the meeting in protest.

Jiang Qing was outraged. After discussing the issue with the other members of the Gang of Four (Wang Hongwen, Zhang Chunqiao, Yao Wenyuan), Jiang Qing decided to send Wang Hongwen to Changsha to see Mao.[192] Wang reported to him about the events at the Politburo meeting, accusing Deng of plotting to protect the Ministry of Communications, which, in Wang's view, had followed Liu Shaoqi's revisionist line, since it had preferred to rent or buy foreign ships rather than build them in China. In addition, Wang reported that the atmosphere in Beijing had become as tense as that during the 1970 Lushan conference. In Wang's opinion, this was not due in the least to Zhou, who, despite being seriously ill, was receiving many people at the hospital. Hinting that the old guard was plotting to gain power, Wang said that Deng Xiaoping, Ye Jianying, and Li Xiannian were among Zhou's most frequent visitors.

According to Zhang Yufeng, Mao's private secretary, the only other person present at Wang's meeting with the Chairman, Mao was not impressed with Wang's version of events. He told Wang to talk things over with Deng if he had any disagreement with him and advised him to develop his contacts with Zhou Enlai and Ye Jianying and to reduce his involvement with Jiang Qing.[193]

Other attempts to undermine Zhou's and Deng's positions in Mao's eyes were equally unsuccessful. Zhang Chunqiao declared that China's foreign trade deficit was a direct result of the policy of "worshipping foreign things" pursued by the State Council. Moreover, he compared the agitation at the October Politburo meeting to the "February Countercurrent" of 1967. Mao, still in Changsha, stated that Zhou "was the premier and he will remain the premier" (*yinwei zongli haishi zongli*), and he repeated that Wang Hongwen should take charge of preparations for the congress jointly with Zhou. Concerning the conflict in the Politburo over the *Feng Qing* Incident, Mao said only that he intended to announce Deng's promotion to the posts of vice chairman of the Party, first vice premier, vice chairman of the Central Military Commission and general chief of staff, which consolidated not only Deng's position but also Zhou's.

With Mao's support, Zhou began to organize the National People's Congress. From 20 October until mid-December, he consulted numerous times with Deng, Ye Jianying, Li Xiannian, and others about the composition of the National People's Congress and the State Council. Other Politburo members were called to the hospital to be briefed about Mao's instructions and to discuss various problems related to the forthcoming congress. On 6 November, he wrote to Mao to express his support for Deng's promotions. Although seriously ill, he told Mao that he would be able to attend the congress if it took place soon.[194]

Despite the nomination of Deng Xiaoping to several key positions, Jiang Qing continued to believe in her own importance to Mao's goal of preserving the Cultural Revolution. In the struggle for power, she wrote to Mao to assure the promotion of some of her own people. But Mao, who showed no interest in her suggestions, wrote the following comment on her letter: "Do not make too many appearances in public, and refrain from commenting on too many documents. Do not take it upon yourself to organize the cabinet." On 19 November, Jiang Qing wrote to Mao again, complaining that she had not been assigned any work since the ninth Party congress. But she was again rebuffed. Mao wrote back to her that her work "consists of following the internal and external situation," which, he emphasized, was "an important responsibility."[195]

Zhou was aware that the Gang of Four was fighting for control of a number of ministries. After discussing the question with Deng and other veteran leaders, he decided to compromise and to leave the Ministry of Culture, the Ministry of Public Health, and the Sports Commission to Jiang Qing's faction. The Ministry of Education, to which she also aspired, was kept under the control of the veterans. As for other ministries and commissions, the Cultural Revolution faction was assigned a number of posts as deputy ministers and as members of the ministerial Party groups.

Zhou's cancer spread to his colon, yet he considered it his duty to continue to work for the preparation of the congress. On 23 December, he left the hospital against medical advice and, with Wang Hongwen, flew to Changsha to report to Mao directly about the matter. It was particularly important to obtain Mao's approval for the lists of candidates for ministerial posts and National People's Congress positions that Zhou had established. According to Ye Jianying, only the premier would be able to win the Chairman's support for the proposed nominations, which were vital for the future of the Party and the state. He asked Dr. Zhang to organize a medical team to accompany the premier to Changsha and back.[196]

Mao met with Zhou and Wang four times between 23 and 27 December and approved without modification the list of candidates for the chairman- and vice-chairmanship of the congress presented to him by Zhou.

But Mao again expressed concern about a united leadership and apprehension about Jiang Qing's group, which should "no longer function as a Gang of Four," adding that "people at the center are not numerous, [so] they should unite." He also made some comments about different leaders. "Deng Xiaoping," he said, was a "person of rare talent" (*rencai nande*). Pointing to Wang Hongwen, his designated successor, he added that Deng was "stronger than him politically." Concerning Jiang Qing, he said that she had gained merit by fighting against Liu Shaoqi, and in criticizing Lin Biao and Confucius, but she should not engage in sectarian activities. Wang Hongwen, he said, should make a self-criticism, because, in spite of Mao's warnings, he had continued to team up with Jiang Qing, Zhang Chunqiao, and Yao Wenyuan. His disillusionment with Wang was obvious. His chosen successor had disappointed him, and he began to make it clear that Wang's status as Mao's successor was in jeopardy.

Mao's praise of Deng, his renewed trust in him and his criticism of the Gang of Four gave Zhou some consolation. After his return to the hospital in Beijing, he engaged in hectic work. On 10 January 1975, he called a Central Committee meeting to brief its members about his talks with Mao and to approve the nominations of the leading cadres of the State Council. A few days later, a Central Committee document announced the nomination of Deng to the posts of vice chairman of the Central Military Commission and as general chief of staff, and that of Zhang Chunqiao as director of the PLA General Political Department. Mao, while granting his favors to the old guard, did not ignore the supporters of Cultural Revolution policies.

The fourth National People's Congress convened from 13 to 17 January 1975. The ailing Zhou left the hospital again to deliver the keynote speech at the congress, the report on the work of the government, in which he reiterated the concept, previously introduced by the third congress, of developing the economy in two stages. "The first stage," he said, "that is, before 1980, is to build an independent and relatively comprehensive industrial and economic system; the second stage is to accomplish the modernization of agriculture, industry, national defense, and science and technology before the end of the century."[197]

The congress reinstated Zhou as premier and nominated twelve vice premiers. Six of them were veteran cadres (Deng Xiaoping, Li Xiannian, Chen Xilian, Wang Zhen, Yu Qiuli, and Gu Mu), one belonged to the Gang of Four (Zhang Chunqiao), and the other five were promoted during the Cultural Revolution, either from local leading posts (Ji Dengkui, Hua Guofeng) or from the grass roots (Chen Yonggui, Wu Guixian, and Sun Jian).[198] At a meeting of the State Council, Zhou informed the participants about Mao's comments on Deng and declared that Deng would be in charge during his absence. The struggle for power was resolved, at least temporarily, in favor of Zhou and his supporters.

## The Final Year

Zhou was exhausted from his activities surrounding the congress. He had developed a tumor in the large intestine close to the liver and, at the end of March 1975, he underwent his third operation. But he still refused to stop working. On 3 April he received the prime minister of Tunisia, Hedi Nouira in the hospital, and on 19 April, he met with the North Korean leader Kim Il Sung, who had come to see his old friend for what would turn out to be the last time. Although extremely weak, Zhou insisted on getting up and dressing for the occasion. But his feet were so swollen that he could not put on his shoes, and a special pair of cotton shoes had to be made for him.[199]

After an absence of ten months, the Chairman returned to the capital. One of his first actions was to call a meeting of the Politburo that Zhou left the hospital in order to attend. As usual, Mao did most of the talking at the meeting, albeit with considerable difficulty. He rambled on a number of subjects, including eggs being too rich in cholesterol, the interpretation of one of his poems, and a poem written by the Song dynasty poet Xin Qiji. But his principal message was the need for stability and unity. He again warned Jiang Qing not to take part in a Gang of Four. "Why are you still doing it?" he asked her. He raised the issue of criticizing empiricism (that is, the policies implemented by Zhou Enlai and other veteran revolutionaries), a campaign initiated by Zhang Chunqiao and Yao Wenyuan in March. According to Zhang and Yao, Zhou was pragmatic and ignored Marxism. In their view, empiricism was the main danger confronting the Party.

Jiang Qing came up with yet another idea to marginalize veteran cadres, namely, to accuse them of engaging in the use of a "back door," or using personal relations to obtain results—a practice already rampant among high-ranking cadres. Most people were well aware of this practice, which only a few enjoyed, and the back door issue could have turned into one of the rare popular campaigns launched by Jiang Qing. But Mao, thinking that it might divert from the rather abstract issue of Lin Biao and Confucius, interrupted the campaign and ordered that the "Gang of Four" should be criticized at the Politburo. At the same time, he deflated the issue, saying: "I do not think the matter is serious. So do not make a fuss over it."[200]

Jiang Qing and her acolytes were criticized at Politburo meetings on 27 May and 3 June. This was the first time since the beginning of the Cultural Revolution that veteran cadres had the opportunity to criticize the new appointees openly. The irony was that the meetings were presided over by Deng, who had been overthrown at the beginning of the Cultural Revolution. The tide had indeed turned in favor of the veteran cadres, but the question that remained open was, for how long?

Deng was not new to the State Council. He had been acting premier whenever Zhou was abroad. Although both men were pragmatic and matter-of-fact, their styles were quite different. Where Zhou was cautious, conciliatory, and detail-oriented, Deng was decisive, forceful, and focused on the big picture. He was like a commander in chief, who designed broad policy directions and decided on the course of the country, while Zhou had always been a thoughtful and hard-working chief executive who implemented policy decisions. Deng, encouraged by Mao's support, used all his energy to correct leftist mistakes and to promote economic readjustment and social consolidation, most notably in 1975. He not only revived Zhou's 1972 anti-leftist campaign but carried it out in a more systematic manner and on a larger scale.

Deng's policies were bound to meet with resistance from the radicals, who soon found another pretense for launching a counterattack in the form of a campaign that, this time, was directed against "capitulationism." It was symbolized by the Chinese classical novel *Shui hu zhuan* (Water Margin), on which Mao had commented, in the spring of 1975, that "the good thing about the book is its description about capitulation. It can be used as a negative example to enable people to recognize capitulationists."

Mao's comment was recorded as usual, and public discussions about *Water Margin*, in the light of Mao's latest interpretation, were promoted by the media at the end of August. Jiang Qing took the lead in applying the lessons to be drawn from the novel to Zhou's and Deng's policies. Their efforts to restore order, discipline, rules, and regulations were equated with capitulation to the capitalist class. Both were likened to Song Jiang, the main figure in the novel who, in the interpretation of the radicals, had betrayed the cause of revolting peasants led by Cao Gai and capitulated to the emperor. In mid-September, at a conference on agriculture, Jiang Qing's assaults culminated in the statement that there were people who used Chairman Mao as a figurehead, just as Song Jiang had used Cao Gai. Referring to Song Jiang's acceptance of a number of officers and officials to the uprising army, she said, "Someone has enlisted a number of local despots into the government," thus hinting that some veteran cadres had been reinstalled in different positions by Zhou and Deng.[201]

Zhou had no means of reacting to these increasingly rampant attacks. In late August his doctors found that his cancer had metastasized and was now incurable. Zhou was dying. Yet, against his doctors' advice, he received an official delegation from Romania on 7 September. He jokingly told his guests that he had received an invitation from Karl Marx (a common saying among Chinese leaders indicating that someone was going to die and meet with Karl Marx in the next world), which was impossible to refute. Throughout his life, Zhou had received numerous foreign guests. The meeting with the Romanians was his last.[202]

Although his days were numbered, he continued to observe the political situation closely. Deng's energetic efforts to solve the most critical problems in a society that had been tormented by irrational radical policies gave him great satisfaction, but he was concerned about the unexpected movement to comment on *Water Margin*. He had no doubt that Jiang Qing's attacks on capitulationism were directed at himself and at Deng as the representatives of a policy of normalization and pragmatism. Moreover, the media, on a massive scale, were again commenting on the "Wu Hao notice"— implying capitulation to the Guomindang—a Damocles sword hanging over him that had already been held against him in 1967 and again in 1972. But as a lifelong leader of the CCP, he knew how cruel and ruthless inner-party struggles could be. As the head of the CCEG, he could not have failed to notice how "evidence" was fabricated to prove that Liu Shaoqi, He Long, Bo Yibo, and many others had betrayed the Party. The very existence of the "Wu Hao notice" constituted a grave threat to him. Its authenticity was of no importance, and there was no defense.

To prolong Zhou's life, his doctors had scheduled another surgical procedure on 20 September. Deng Xiaoping, Ye Jianying, Zhang Chunqiao, Li Xiannian, Wang Dongxing, and Deng Yingchao were at the hospital awaiting the outcome. The operating team was ready to begin and was expecting Zhou to be wheeled into the operating room. Thirty minutes passed, but Zhou did not arrive. Finally Deng Yingchao went to see him. She returned, saying that he was deeply absorbed in writing. Sometime later Dr. Zhang also went to Zhou's room, finding him so deeply engrossed in writing that he dared not interrupt him. After another twenty minutes, Zhou rang his bell. When his wife entered the room, Zhou handed her a thick envelope containing a letter to Mao and other documents.[203] Deeply distressed by the accusations against him, which, he feared, his opponents might continue to spread after his death, he wanted to defend himself by making his case known to the entire nation. When he was wheeled into the operation room, he suddenly cried out: "I am loyal to the party and the people. I am not a capitulationist."[204]

Because of his deteriorating health, Mao lived in growing seclusion. At the end of September he called his nephew Mao Yuanxin, then thirty-four years old, to Beijing to act as his liaison with the Politburo. Before he joined Mao's staff, Yuanxin, the son of Mao's brother Zemin, had risen to become political commissar of the Shenyang Military Region. Yuanxin was a confirmed radical and a stout believer in the Cultural Revolution. His nomination to this key post made it possible to isolate Mao even further from such major leaders as Zhou and Deng Xiaoping. Through him Mao learned that there was a trend to denigrate the Cultural Revolution, "a gust of wind ... even stronger than the movement to criticize ultraleftism in 1972." Yuanxin also informed the Chairman that Deng Xiaoping seldom mentioned the achievements of the Cultural Revolution in his many speeches, that he failed to criticize Liu Shaoqi's revisionist line, and that he had reduced Mao's three recent instructions (to study Marxism, to achieve stability and unity, and to promote the national economy) to one: promotion of the economy.

Mao's sensitivity to anything that put the Cultural Revolution in question remained so strong that he had a dramatic change of heart regarding Deng. He remarked to his nephew that Deng's attitude reflected "dissatisfaction with the Cultural Revolution in the first place and an attempt to settle accounts with it in the second place." He gave instructions to criticize Deng at the Politburo and ordered him discharged from all functions other than those in foreign affairs. In late November, Deng was officially condemned as being "unhappy about the Cultural Revolution," "bent on settling accounts with it," and responsible for "rightist attempts to reverse correct verdicts." A campaign against him was organized accordingly.[205]

Zhou was greatly distressed by the sudden change in Mao's attitude. Although accustomed to Mao's capriciousness, this change of attitude toward Deng was undeniably an unpleasant surprise. Zhou's nurse, who read the newspaper to him every day, described him as wordlessly looking at the ceiling, shaking his head, and sighing from time to time. "There are a lot of things in my heart that I have not said," Zhou told his wife, who replied that she, too, was carrying a lot of things in her heart[206] But Zhou did not confide his true thinking to anyone, not even his lifelong companion.

Even in the final days of his life, when he was barely able to speak, Zhou, in his mind, was still deeply involved in politics. He told Ye Jianying, who was a regular visitor, to be careful in handling relations with the Gang of Four so that power would not fall into their hands. On 20 December, he called Luo Qingchang, who was in charge of Taiwan affairs, to the hospital to talk about some questions concerning Taiwan. Zhou reminded him of certain people still in Taiwan who had made significant contributions to the united front between the CCP and the Guomindang during the early period of the anti-Japanese war. As an example, he mentioned Zhang Xueliang, still in Chiang Kai-shek's custody. He asked Luo not to forget these old friends when the Taiwan problem was solved. This was the last time that he summoned one of his subordinates to his sickbed to talk about work. According to the records, from March to September 1975, Zhou held 102 discussions with people about various problems and met foreign visitors 34 times in the hospital, left the hospital 7 times to take part in meetings and 4 times to pay visits to other people, and held meetings at the hospital 3 times.[207]

During the last few months of his life, Zhou suffered physical and mental anguish from the cancer that was taking his life. His doctors left no stone unturned in their efforts to prolong his life. In all, he had thirteen operations, five of them major. He had eighty-nine blood transfusions. He had numerous tubes running from various places in his body: for blood transfusion, for glucose and other fluids, and for nourishment as well as catheters for urine elimination. His doctors repeatedly gave him injections of painkillers. Mao, in deteriorating physical condition himself, never came to visit him. It is doubtful that he would have shown compassion for his faithful premier, even if he had been in better health. The two had not met since the Politburo meeting in May 1975. Deng, Zhou's protégé and the man capable of carrying on his policies, was not able to visit him, being under fire by the mass media that—with Mao's blessing—made him a political outcast. The only frequent visitor was his old colleague Ye Jianying, who increased his visits to once a day after Zhou's condition became critical in December. Once, after a long talk with Zhou, Ye confided to two of Zhou's assistants who were taking turns keeping watch over him twenty-four hours a day, that the premier had kept a lot of grievances to himself and that, if he decided to talk, they should be ready to take down whatever he might have to say. But Zhou never took the opportunity to unburden himself of his thoughts before he died.

On New Year's day 1976, the newspapers published two poems Mao had written in 1965. Zhou, in a final demonstration of his devotion to Mao, asked his assistants to read them to him. Afterward, Zhou's condition deteriorated further. On 5 January, he fell into a coma and two days later, at 11 P.M., awoke for the last time. Opening his eyes to find his doctors watching him, he said in a weak voice that there was nothing more they could do for him—they should take care of their other patients, who needed them more. These were Zhou's last words. He died on 8 January at 9:57 A.M., at seventy-eight years old."[208]

# Epilogue

The year 1976 was one of the most eventful in the history of the People's Republic—a history shaped by powerful personalities. Three of those towering figures passed away that year. First, Zhou Enlai died on January 8, Marshal Zhu De, (an outstanding revolutionary) on 6 July, while Mao Zedong disappeared on 9 September.

Zhou's death inspired the first spontaneous popular protest movement since the spanning of the Cultural Revolution. A few days after Zhou's death, Deng Xiaoping eulogized him, in what would be his last public appearance until 1978 During the Qingming festival in early April, when the Chinese traditionally mourn their dead and sweep their graves, thousands of poems and funeral wreaths were left at Tiananmen Square; millions of people poured into the Square to pay tribute to Zhou and to vent their resentment of the Gang of Four. The demonstrations were quickly suppressed as counterrevolutionary.

The public was by this time generally demoralized and weary of the never-ending political campaigns, with mounting discontent due to poor living conditions. They focused on Zhou, whom many referred to as "our beloved Premier Zhou," as a symbol of reason and rectitude. Indirectly, by praising his qualities, they found a way to express that discontent.

At the same time, the Chinese Communist Party had lost popularity and much of the prestige that had been attached to it before outbreak of the Cultural Revolution. Mao Zedong's charisma had faded, and his responsibility for many disastrous policy decisions was increasingly revealed to the public. After his return to power in 1978, Deng was confronted with a dilemma. Although he thought that Mao should bear the blame for the disastrous policies of the previous two decades, he did not want the prestige of the Party to be entirely destroyed in the process, since the Party was the foundation of his own political power. Given Mao's myriad arbitrary misdeeds, at the hands of which many leaders and a majority of the population had suffered, it was not difficult to separate Mao from the Party. Besides the entire leadership was accomplice to Mao's rise to the pinnacle of power. In this difficult moment of transition, a different standard bearer was therefore needed to serve as the symbolic focus for all that was positive and worthwhile in the Party's past: someone who had the stature and the popularity. Zhou Enlai was the obvious choice. He was projected as a pillar of righteousness, humanity, managerial efficiency, and devotion to his work.

By 1998, the centenary of Zhou's birth, tributes to him had reached the level of a personality cult. At meetings in his honor held by the Central Committee, the State Council, and the Ministry of Foreign Affairs, Party dignitaries of the highest level eulogized him, offering their highest respects. Memorial halls were erected in his honor at Tianjin University, where hundreds of scholars gathered to recount Zhou Enlai's great achievements. No critical or negative comments were tolerated (as this author personally witnessed). A replica of his office at Zhongnanhai, in the center of a vast park, was built at his ancestral home in Shaoxing. Visitors were allowed to file past and to glimpse through the windows, but not to enter. All over the country, in places where Zhou had been active, special exhibitions were organized to which busloads of schoolchildren, soldiers, and others were transported so that they could learn about Zhou Enlai's peerless service to the nation. The entire mass media was systematically utilized to highlight his great deeds and his benign image. A documentary and a feature film were produced about him. Since the 1980s, no fewer than five hundred books and more than five thousand articles have been published about him. Everywhere he was hailed as a great revolutionary and political leader, who had devoted himself to the cause of making his country prosperous and strong. He was placed on a pedestal as someone who was extremely hard-working and plain-living, modest and prudent, selfless and endowed with all virtues. In sum, a man without flaw.

But the real Zhou was not a paragon. Above all, he was a survivor. In China, it required toughness and ruthlessness to outlast, for more than half a century, the incessant infighting that was endemic in the Chinese Communist Party. To hold the post of prime minister for twenty-six years, working under the command of one of the most powerful, capricious, and distrustful emperors in Chinese history, called for adroitness, adaptability, and the capacity for shaping his positions according to the political winds, notwithstanding his own convictions.

To dissociate Zhou Enlai from Mao Zedong, as official propaganda has attempted to do, contradicts reality, for there was clearly a strong link between Mao's policy decisions and Zhou's faithful implementation of them. In an interview with the Italian journalist Oriana Fallaci in August 1980, Deng Xiaoping declared that, in the last years of his life, Zhou did not always say what he wanted to or act as he would have liked to. This may be so. Nonetheless strong collusion between the Chairman and his prime minister had existed ever since 1956, when Zhou had endangered his career by criticizing "rash advance" in economic policy. Zhou played an active role in the early purges of major leaders during the Cultural Revolution. Following Mao's instructions, he guided the unprecedented "power seizures" and the formation of the revolutionary committees throughout the country; he cooperated with the radicals of the Cultural Revolution Group in the campaign to "purify class ranks"; he headed the redoubtable Special Case Group responsible for the examination of all high-ranking cadres above the level of vice minister or vice provincial governor who had been accused of being "renegades, special agents, capitalist roaders, antiparty and antisocialist elements or counter-revolutionary revisionists."

Political survival clearly required Zhou to faithfully execute Mao's arbitrary instructions. For this he had not much choice, any defiance by him would have unavoidably resulted in his downfall, since an array of radicals was closely watching him and waiting for him to take a false step to oust him from power. But he did do great things, too, for which history will remember him. As an outstanding administrator, with remarkable ability of coherent governance, he ran the country ably, even in the midst of tremulousness; Zhou had equally shown an uncanny ability of going around all over China maintaining roots with the people—roots for which they loved him. Also within the suffocating atmosphere of terror and arbitrariness, he did try to avoid, wherever possible, the excesses of violence and made myriad efforts to soften the impact of mass movements that were reeling out of control. For all this he will be remembered, despite the fact that he served one of the most brutal tyrants of the century—comparable to Hitler and Stalin.

# Landmarks in the Life of Zhou Enlai

*March 1898*
Born in Huai'an

*March 1924*
Appointed Political Director of the Whampoa Military Academy

*March 1925*
Appointed Director of the Political Department of the Northern Expedition Army with the rank of Major General

*August 1925*
Marries Deng Yingchao

*March 1927*
Organises worker's uprising in Shanghai

*April–May 1927*
Elected member of the Central Committee and the Politburo of the Communist Party

*July 1927*
Elected member of the Standing Committee of the new Provincial Center

*November 1927*
Re-elected as a member of the Standing Committee at the enlarged Politburo meeting of the Provisional Center

*January 1928*
Appointed by the Politburo as Director in charge of propaganda, military affairs, investigation, secret service, communications and publications

*June 1928*
Elected as member of the Politburo and Standing Committee

*July 1928*
Appointed as General Secretary of the Standing Committee

*July–September 1928*
Elected alternate member of the Executive Committee of the Comintern (Communist International)

*August 1929*
Appointed Director of the department of militay affairs of the central Committee

*January 1931*
Though criticised by the Comintern, he continues to retain his membership of the Standing Committee

*September 1931*
Leaves Shanghai for Jiangxi province to become Secretary of the Central Committee's bureau in Soviet areas, and to become in charge of the Red Army

*December 1931*
Arrives in Ruijin to take over the Central Committee Bureau

*August 1932*
Appointed Chairman of the newly established Supreme Military Committee (Mao is member of the Committee)

*October 1932*
Takes over as the Political Comissar of the first front army after Mao is deprived of his post in the Red Army at the Ningdu Conference

*February–March 1932*
Appointed General Political Comissar for the Red Army and the First Front Army as the provincial center moves from Shanghai to Jiangxi province

*December 1933*
Appointed Vice-Chairman of the newly established Central Revolutionary Committee (Zhu De is the Chairman)

*January 1934*
In the new reshuffle, elected as member of the Standing Committee of the Central Committee

*July 1934*
Appointed member of the three men group to lead the Long March

*January 1935*
Entrusted at Zunyi Conference with the responsibility of making final decisions in military affairs (Mao is appointed his assistant)

*November 1935*
Establishment in northern Shaanxi by the Politburo of a Central Organisation Department under his direction

*October 1936*
Appointed Vice-Chairman of the enlarged Central Military Commission after integration of the three main armies

*August 1937*
Appointed by the Politburo as one of the two Deputy Secretaries of the new Revolutionary Military Commission

*December 1937*
Nominated by the Politburo as member of the Central Committee's Yangzi Bureau charged with the Party's work in the southern provinces

*February 1938*
Appointed Deputy Director of the political department of the Military
Commission of the Nationalist Government

*December 1938*
Arrives in Chongqing for negotiations with Guomindang

*January 1939*
Appointed Secretary of the South China Bureau

*March 1943*
While still in Chongqing retains his place in the Politburo

*June 1945*
Elected to the thirteen member Politburo and the five member Secretariat
(Mao is the chairman)

*November 1946*
On his return from Chongqing to Yan'an appointed as Vice-Chairman of
the Military Commission and acting chief of staff

*October 1949*
Appointed Premier and Foreign Minister of the People's Republic of
China and Vice-Chairman of the Military Commission

*July 1954*
Leads China's Delegation to the Geneva Conference

*April 1955*
Participates in the Bandung Conference

*April 1969*
Ranks third, after Mao and Lin Biao in the Standing Committee at the
Ninth Party Congress

*January 1976*
Dies in Beijing

# Notes

**Introduction**

1.  Chae-Jin Lee, *Zhou Enlai: The Early Years* (Stanford: Stanford University Press, 1994), 170.
2.  *Asahi shimbun*, 23 January 1976.
3.  Henry Kissinger, *The White House Years* (Boston: Little, Brown, 1979), 745.
4.  Dick Wilson, "Zhou Enlai: The Man and His Work", *World Affairs,* no. 2 (1998), 29.

**Chapter 1**

1.  Before 1914 Huai'an was called Shanyang.
2.  Chen Duo, "Zhou Enlai Shaoxing jiashi ji zuju kao" (A Study of Zhou Enlai's Shaoxing Family and Ancestral Home), in *Zhou Enlai qingnian shidai* (Zhou Enlai's Youthful Period) (Tianjin: Zhou Enlai jinianguan, 1980–1986), no. 7 (1986), 58–62.
3.  Lee, *Zhou Enlai: The Early Years*, 9.
4.  "Zhou Enlai tong Li Boman tan geren jingli" (Zhou Enlai Discusses His Personal History with Lieberman), *Liaowang,* 8 January 1984, 26–29.
5.  Edgar Snow, *Red Star Over China* (Harmondsworth: Penguin Books, 1978), 46.
6.  Quoted in Jin Chongji et al., *Zhou Enlai zhuan, 1889–1949* (Biography of Zhou Enlai, 1889–1949) (Beijing: Zhongyang wenxuan chubanshe, 1989), 3.
7.  Kai-yu Hsu, *Chou En-lai: China's Grey Eminence* (Garden City, NY: Doubleday, 1968), p. 25.
8.  "Zhou Enlai tong Li Boman."
9.  Ibid.
10. Lee, *Zhou Enlai: The Early Years*, 13.
11. *Zhou Enlai nianpu, 1898–1949* (A Chronology of Zhou Enlai's Life, 1898–1949) (Beijing: Zhongyang wenxian chubanshe, 1989), 3.

12. Lin Yutang, *The Wisdom of China* (Bombay: Jaico, 1955), 213–218, 329–352.

13. Jin et al., *Zhou Enlai zhuan, 1889–1949*, 4; see also Hu Hua, *The Early Life of Zhou Enlai* (Beijing: Foreign Languages Press, 1980), 3–4.

14. Mukden was later called Fengtian and is now called Shenyang.

15. *Zhou zongli yu guxiang* (Premier Zhou and His Hometown) (Nanjing: Jiangsu renmin chubanshe, 1979), 104–106.

16. Lee, *Zhou Enlai: The Early Years*, 25.

17. Jin et al., *Zhou Enlai zhuan, 1898–1949*, 19.

18. Lee, *Zhou Enlai: The Early Years*, 41–43.

19. Ibid., 37–41, 47–49.

20. Jin et al., *Zhou Enlai zhuan, 1898–1949*, 19.

21. *Zhou Enlai nianpu, 1898–1949*, 14–16.

22. Lee, *Zhou Enlai: The Early Years*, 64.

23. *Zhou Enlai nianpu, 1898–1949*, 17–19.

24. Percy Jucheng Fang and Lucy Guinong Fang, *Zhou Enlai: A Profile* (Beijing: Foreign Languages Press, 1986), 15–16.

25. *Zhou Enlai nianpu, 1898–1949*, 22.

26. Ibid.

27. See, for example, his warnings against a potential Japanese threat expressed in a composition written in 1915 and in a speech delivered on the occasion of a speech contest in October 1916 in *Tianjin wenshi ziliao xuanji* (Selected Material of Tianjin History) (Tianjin: Tianjin renmin chubanshe, 1981), no. 15, 11–12; *Xiaofeng*, 8 November 1916; ibid., 37–41.

28. Jin et al., *Zhou Enlai zhuan 1898–1949*, 24.

29. *Zhou Enlai nianpu, 1898–1949*, 27.

30. Lee, *Zhou Enlai: The Early Years*, 91.

31. Liu Yan and Mi Zhenbo, *Zhou Enlai yanjiu wenxuan* (Selected Articles on Zhou Enlai) (Tianjin: Nankai daxue chubanshe, 1987), 85; Jin et al., *Zhou Enlai zhuan, 1898–1949*, 33.

32. Lee, *Zhou Enlai: The Early Years*, 102–104.

33. In 1915, the journal was called *Qingnian zazhi* (Youth Magazine). It was renamed *Xin qingnian* (New Youth) in 1916.

34. Quoted in Su Kaiming, *Modern China: A Topical History, 1840–1983* (Beijing: New World Press, 1985), 99.

35. Jin et al., *Zhou Enlai zhuan, 1989-1949*, 28–29; Jonathan Spence, *The Gate of Heavenly Peace: The Chinese and Their Revolution, 1895–1980* (Harmondsworth: Penguin Books, 1982), 155.

36. Lee, *Zhou Enlai: The Early Years*, 127.

37. Ibid., 134.
38. Liu and Mi, *Zhou Enlai yanjiu wenxuan*, 9.
39. Lee, *Zhou Enlai: The Early Years*, 136–138, 141.
40. *Yishebao,* 30 January 1920, quoted in ibid., 204.
41. Ibid., 141–148.
42. *Zhou Enlai nianpu*, 45.
43. Jin et al., *Zhou Enlai zhuan, 1898–1949*, 55.
44. Liu and Mi, *Zhou Enlai yanjiu wenxuan*, 102.
45. Quoted in Lee, *Zhou Enlai: The Early Years*, 161.
46. This question gave rise to controversies in China. It was an important issue for both the CCP and the Guomindang, where seniority of membership played a significant role. Zhou's admission to the CCP had been thought to have taken place in 1922. However, in May 1985, the Organization Department of the CCP Central Committee declared that, according to its findings, he had joined in 1921. See Liu and Mi, *Zhou Enlai yanjiu wenxuan*, 121.
47. Lee, *Zhou Enlai: The Early Years,* 158. Zhang Shenfu and Liu Qingyang left the CCP to join the China Democratic League. Liu rejoined the CCP in 1961. She held a number of positions in the PRC: vice chairwoman of the All-China Democratic Women's Federation, vice president of the China Red Cross, member of the National People's Congress. Cai Hesen and his wife, Xiang Jingyu, were executed in 1931 and 1928, respectively. Cai's sister, Cai Chang, became a member of the CCP Central Committee in 1945 and Chairwoman of the All-China Democratic Women's Federation. Li Fuchun was Vice premier and Minister of Heavy Industries. Li Lisan was Minister of Labor. Li Weihan was Director of the CCP United Front Department; Chen Yi was Marshal of the PLA, Mayor of Shanghai, Vice premier, Minister of Foreign Affairs; Nie Rongzhen was Marshal of the PLA; Zhao Shiyan was executed in Shanghai in 1927. Deng Xiaoping was paramount leader of the PRC from the late 1970s to his death in 1997.
48. Jin et al., *Zhou Enlai zhuan, 1898–1949*, 62–64
49. Lee, *Zhou Enlai: The Early Years*, 157; see also Nie Rongzhen, *Inside the Red Star: The Memoirs of Marshal Nie Rongzhen* (Beijing: New World Press, 1988), 17.
50. Richard Evans, *Deng Xiaoping and the Making of Modern China* (London: Penguin Books, 1997), 19.
51. Jin et al., *Zhou Enlai zhuan, 1898–1949*, 79.

**Chapter 2**

1. On the origin of the collaboration between the Guomindang and the CCP,

see Tony Saich, "Henk Sneevliet and the Origins of the First United Front", *Issues and Studies*, August 1986, 117–151. The literature on Soviet advisers in China is abundant. For example, see especially Dan N. Jacobs, *Borodin, Stalin's Man in China* (Cambridge, MA: Harvard University Press, 1981); Martin C. Wilbur and Julie Lien-ying How, *Missionaries of Revolution: Soviet Advisors and Nationalist China, 1920–1927* (Cambridge, MA: Harvard University Press, 1989).

2.   Martin C. Wilbur, *The National Revolution in China* (Cambridge: Cambridge University Press, 1983), 2–8.

3.   Liu and Mi, *Zhou Enlai yanjiu wenxian,* 188; see also Dieter Heinzig, *Sowjetische Militärberater bei der Kuomintang, 1923–1927* (Baden-Baden: Nomos Verlagsgesellschaft, 1978), 159–160.

4.   Hu Sheng, *A Concise History of the Communist Party of China* (Beijing: Foreign Languages Press, 1994), 43.

5.   Claude Cadart and Cheng Yinxiang, *Mémoires de Peng Shuzhi, L'envol du communism en Chine* (Paris: Gallimard, 1983), 461–463; Zhang Wenhe, *Shenhuo zhong de Zhou Enlai* (Beijing: Jiefangjun chubanshe, 1999), 50–51.

6.   Ibid., 40–41.

7.   Hu, *A Concise History*, 71.

8.   Nie, *Inside the Red Star,* 40–41.

9.   Sterling Seagrave, *The Soong Dynasty* (London: Sidgwick and Jackson, 1985), 215–217; Denis Twitchett and John K. Fairbank, vol. eds., *The Cambridge History of China*, vol. 12, part 1 (Cambridge: Cambridge University Press, 1983), 620–621.

10.   *Zhou Enlai nianpu, 1898–1949*, 98.

11.   Jin et al., *Zhou Enlai zhuan, 1898–1949*, 131.

12.   *Zhongguo gongchandang lishi, 1919–1949* (History of the Chinese Communist Party, 1919–1949) (Beijing: Renmin chubanshe, 1991), vol. 1, 216.

13.   Jin et al., *Zhou Enlai zhuan, 1898–1949*, 142–143.

14.   Nie, *Inside the Red Star*, 51.

15.   Roy Hofheinz, "The Autumn Harvest Insurrection," *The China Quarterly*, no. 32 (October 1967), 37–87; *Zhongguo gongchandang liushinian dashi jianji* (A Brief Account of Major Events of the Sixty-Year History of the CCP) (Beijing: Guofeng daxue chubanshe, 1986), 105–106.

16.   Party History Research Center of the Central Committee of the Chinese Communist Party, comp., *History of the Chinese Communist Party: A Chronology of Events (1919–1990)* (hereafter cited as *History of the CCP*) (Beijing: Foreign Langauges Press, 1991), 53.

17.   Benjamin I. Schwartz, *Chinese Communism and the Rise of Mao*

(Cambridge, MA: Harvard University Press, 1951), 95.

18. *Zhou Enlai nianpu, 1898–1949*, 127, 134.

19. Ibid., 170–173.

20. Lu Xingdou, ed., *Zhou Enlai he ta de shiye* (Zhou Enlai and His Cause) (Beijing: Zhonggong dangshi chubanshe, 1990), 35.

21. Jin et al., *Zhou Enlai zhuan, 1898–1949*, 208.

22. In a speech to the Politburo, on 17 February 1930; see Gao Wenqian, "Zhou Enlai yu Zhonggong sanci 'zuo'qing cuowu" (Zhou Enlai and the Three "Left" Deviations of the CCP), *Xinhua wenzhai*, no. 12 (1988).

23. The resolution was adopted by the CCP Politburo on 11 June 1930; summary in Hsiao Tso-liang, *Power Relations within the Chinese Communist Movement, 1930–1934* (Seattle: University of Washington Press, 1961), 19–20.

24. Jin et al., *Zhou Enlai zhuan, 1898–1949*, 230–231.

25. Jin Chongji, "Tong Deng dajie de jici tanhua" (An Interview with Elder Sister Deng Yingchao), *Dangde wenxian*, no. 6 (1992), 16.

26. Lin Nong, "Zhou Enlai yu zhongyang teke" (Zhou Enlai and the Central Special Department), *Junshi*, no. 33 (1991); see also Yu Maochun, *OSS in China* (New Haven: Yale University Press, 1996), 33–35.

27. Mu Xin, *Chen Geng tongzhi zai Shanghai—zai zhongyang teke de douzheng jingli* (Comrade Chen Geng in Shanghai: His Fighting Experience within the Special Service Section of the Central Committee) (Beijing: Wenshi ziliao chubanshe, 1980), 34–35.

28. Fang Ke and Dan Mu, *Zhonggong qingbao shounao Li Kenong* (CCP Intelligence Chief Li Kenong) (Beijing: Zhongguo shehui kexue chubanshe, 1996), 37–43.

29. Ibid.

30. Mu Xin, *Chen Geng tongzhi zai Shanghai*, 82–83.

31. Frederic Wakeman, *Policing Shanghai, 1927–1937* (Berkeley: University of California Press, 1996), 141–155, 158–159; see also Patricia Stranahan, *Underground: The Shanghai Communist Party and the Politics of Survival, 1927–1937* (Lanham, MD: Rowman and Littlefield, 1998), 119.

32. Yin Qi, *Pan Hannian de qingbao shengya* (Pan Hannian's Intelligence Career) (Beijing: Renmin chubanshe, 1996), 16; Jin Feng, *Deng Yingchao zhuan* (Biography of Deng Yingchao) (Beijing: Renmin chubanshe, 1993), 173.

33. Yin, *Pan Hannian de qingbao shengya*, 52.

34. *Zhongguo gongchandang lishi*, 300.

35. Ibid., 137, 301, 312, 315; see also Zhen Fulin, ed., *Zhonggong dangshi*

*zhishi shouce* (Handbook of CCP History) (Beijing: Beijing chubanshe, 1985), 807.

36. Liu Bingrong, *Suqu [sufan] da jishi* (Facts About [the Elimination of Counterrevolutionaries] in the Soviet Areas) (Shijiazhuang: Huashan wenyi chubanshe, 1993), vol. 1, 199.

37. Quoted in Philip Short, *Mao: A Life* (New York: Henry Holt, 1999), 199, 274.

38. Hu Shiyan et al., *Chen Yi zhuan* (Biography of Chen Yi) (Beijing: Dangdai Zhongguo chubanshe, 1991), 126.

39. *History of the CCP*, 73.

40. Dai Xiangqing, "Lun AB tuan he Futian shijian" (On the AB Group and the Futian Incident), *Zhonggong dangshi yanjiu*, no. 2 (1989), 22; Chiang Baiying, "Minxi suqu de suqing minzhudang yuan'an" (The Wrong Case of Elimination of Social Democrats in West Fujian), *Zhonggong dangshi yanjui*, no. 4 (1989), 33; Liu, *Suqu [sufan] da jishi*, vol. 2, 615; Cao Ying, "Xiang Ying de huihuang yu shilue" (Xiang Ying's Ups and Downs), *Yuanhuang chunqiu,* no. 4 (1998), 46.

41. Jin et al., *Zhou Enlai zhuan, 1898–1949*, 245–246.

42. Huang Shaoqun, "Zhongyang suqu shiqidi Zhou Enlai yu Mao Zedong" (Zhou Enlai and Mao Zedong in the Central Soviet Area), *Danxiao luntan*, no. 1 (1989), 31.

43. Jin et al., *Zhou Enlai zhuan, 1898–1949*, 241.

44. *Selected Works of Mao Zedong*, vol. 1 (Beijing: Foreign Language Press, 1975), 121.

45. Schwartz, *Chinese Communism,* 189–190.

46. Jin et al., *Zhou Enlai zhuan, 1898–1949*, 193.

47. *Selected Works of Mao Zedong*, vol. 3 (Beijing: Foreign Languages Press, 1960), 197–198.

48. *Zhongguo gongchandang lishi*, vol. 1, 344.

49. Huang Yunsheng, "Ningdu huiyi shimo" (Ningdu Conference, from Beginning to End), *Dangde wenxian*, no. 2 (1990), 42–44.

50. See Edward L. Dreyer, *China at War, 1901–1949* (London: Longman, 1995), 187.

51. Stuart Schram, *Mao Zedong Unrehearsed* (Harmondsworth: Penguin, 1974), 269.

52. *Zhou Enlai nianpu, 1898–1949*, 246; *Zhongguo gongshandang lishi*, 267, 272.

53. According to Dreyer, blockhouse tactics were inspired by a strategy used by Zeng Guofan to suppress the Nian rebellion in the nineteenth century; see

Dreyer, *China at War*, 191.

54. *History of the CCP*, 89.

55. The twelve-member Politburo included Bo Gu, Zhang Wentian, Zhou Enlai, Wang Ming, Xiang Ying, Wang Jiaxiang, and Mao Zedong; see *History of the CCP*, 89.

56. Dreyer, *China at War*, 192

57. Huang Shaoqun, "Zhou Enlai zai changzheng zhong de teshu gongxian" (Zhou Enlai's Special Contribution During the Long March), *Dangde wenxian,* no. 5 (1996), 11.

58. Jin et al., *Zhou Enlai zhuan, 1898–1949*, 278.

59. Harrison E. Salisbury, *The Long March: The Untold Story* (New York: McGraw-Hill, 1987), 111–113.

60. Jin et al., *Zhou Enlai zhuan, 1898–1949*, 278.

61. Ibid., 282.

62. *Zhou Enlai nianpu, 1898–1949*, 271.

63. The meeting was attended by six members of the Politburo (Zhou Enlai, Mao Zedong, Zhu De, Chen Yun, Luo Fu, Bo Gu); alternate members Wang Jiaxiang, Deng Fa (the security chief), Liu Shaoqi; and He Kequan (Kai Feng), leader of the Communist Youth League. See Salisbury, *The Long March*, 121. Military commanders of the Red Army headquarters and various army groups also attended: Liu Bocheng, Li Fuchun, Lin Biao, Nie Rongzhen, Peng Dehuai, Yang Shangkun, and Li Zhuoran, as well as Deng Xiaoping as secretary-general of the Central Committee, and Otto Braun and his interpreter, Wu Xiuquan, as observers (*History of the CCP*, 95).

64. Lu Xingdou, *Zhou Enlai he tade shiye*, 79.

65. Zeng Jingzhong, "Mao zai Zhongguo gongchandang lingdao diwei queli he gonggu" (The Establishment and Consolidation of Mao Zedong's Leading Position in the Chinese Communist Party), *Zhonggong dangshi yanjiu,* no. 4 (1998), 59. Zeng Jingzhong, a scholar at the Institute of Modern History at the Chinese Academy of Social Sciences, quotes Mao's statement confirming this decision. "Later [after the Zunyi conference] we set up a group of three; the head was Zhou Enlai. I myself and Wang Jaixiang were members" (ibid.). See also *History of the CCP*, 95. Thomas Kampen reached a similar conclusion in "The Zunyi Conference and Further Steps in Mao's Rise to Power," *The China Quarterly*, no. 117 (March 1989), 118–134.

66. Dick Wilson, *The Long March, 1935* (Harmondsworth: Penguin Books, 1971), 175–184; Hu, *A Concise History*, 185.

67. Chang Kuo-t'ao (Zhang Guotao), *The Rise of the Chinese Communist Party:*

*The Autobiography of Chang Kuo-t'ao* (Lawrence: University Press of Kansas, 1971–1972), vol. 1, 420–428; see also Hu, *A Concise History*, 186.

68. Jin et al., *Zhou Enlai zhuan, 1898–1949*, 322.

69. See John W. Garver, "The Origins of the Second United Front: The Comintern and the Chinese Communist Party," *The China Quarterly*, no. 113 (March 1988), 29–59; and Otto Braun, *Comintern Agent in China, 1932–1939* (London: Hurst, 1982), 170.

70. Xiang Qing, "Bayi xuanyan xingcheng lishi guocheng" (The Historical Process of the Appearance of the August 1 Manifesto), in *Dangshi ziliao congkan* (Compendium of Material on Party History) no. 3 (1982), 101; Garver, "The Origins of the Second United Front," 34–35; "Report on an Investigation of the Peasant Movement in Hunan" (March 1927), in *Selected Works of Mao Zedong*, vol. 1 (1951), 23–62.

71. Quoted in Shum Kui-Kwong, *The Chinese Communists' Road to Power: The Anti-Japanese National United Front, 1935–1945* (Hong Kong: Oxford University Press, 1988), 51–52, 56–57.

72. Ibid., 56–57.

73. Jin et al., *Zhou Enlai zhuan, 1898–1949*, 306.

74. Ibid., 308; Shum, *Chinese Communists' Road to Power*, 60.

75. Snow, *Red Star over China*, 82.

76. Zhang Kuitang, "Zhou Enlai yu Zhang Xueliang," in Yang Shengqun, ed., *Zhonggong dangshi zhongda shijian shushi* (Factual Accounts of Major Events in CCP History) (Beijing: Renmin chubanshe, 1993), 144.

77. Zhang Peisen et al., "Zhang Wentian yu Xian shibian," in Liu Wusheng (ed.), *Zhonggong dangshi fengyun lu* (Record of the Stormy Years in Party History) (Beijing: Renmin chubanshe), 179; Li Haiwen, "Zhou Enlai yu Xian shibian" (Zhou Enlai and the Xian Incident) in Liu Wusheng, *Zhonggong dangshi fengyun lu*, 34–35.

78. Lin et al., *Zhou Enlai zhuan, 1898–1949*, 338.

79. Ibid., 147–148; *Lianhe bao*, 21 May 1991.

80. Shum, *The Chinese Communists' Road to Power*, 106–197.

81. Ibid., 108.

82. Zhen, *Zhonggong dangshi zhishi shouce*, 105.

83. *Selected Works of Mao Zedong*, vol. 2 (Beijing: Foreign Languages Press, 1965), 61–70.

84. Shum, *The Chinese Communists' Road to Power*, 114–117.

85. Tong Xiaopeng, *Fengyun sishinian* (Forty Stormy Years) (Beijing: Zhongyang wenxian chubanshe, 1996), vol. 1, 129.

86. *Zhou Enlai nianpu, 1898–1949*, 402; Bai Shouyi, ed., *An Outline History of*

*China (1919–1949)* (Beijing: Foreign Languages Press, 1993), 402.

87. Shum, *The Chinese Communists' Road to Power*, 122.
88. Tong, *Fenyun sishinian*, vol. 1, 143.
89. Ibid., 160–165; Chang, *The Rise of the Communist Party*, 580.
90. Lu Rongbin, *Zhou Enlai zai guotongqu* (Zhou Enlai in Guomindamg Areas) (Beijing: Zhonggong zhongyang dangxiao chubanshe, 1996), 44–45, 51.
91. Theodore H. White, *In Search of History: A Personal Adventure* (New York: Harper & Row, 1978), 66–70.
92. Tong, *Fengyun sishinian*, vol. 1, 193.
93. Ibid., 158–159.
94. Jin et al., *Zhou Enlai zhuan, 1898–1949*, 436.
95. A special committee (*tewei*) was established to handle recruitment and organization of party affairs at an intermediary stage before a party committee as such could be established either at county or at provincial level.
96. *Selected Works of Mao Zedong*, vol. 2, 435.
97. Lu, *Zhou Enlai zai guotongqu*, 84.
98. Liu Xiao, "Zhou Enlai yao wo jingshang" (Zhou Enlai Wanted Me to Do Business), *Yanhuang chunqiu*, no. 6 (1966).
99. Li Maosheng, *Kong Xiangxi zhuan* (Biography of H.H. Kung) (Beijing: Zhongguo guangbo dianshi chubanshe, 1992); Yu, *OSS in China*, 45; Fang and Dan, *Zhonggong qingbao shounao Li Kenong*, 90.
100. Fang and Dan, *Zhonggong qingbao shounao Li Kenong*, 100–102.
101. Shum, *The Chinese Communists' Road to Power*, 184–185.
102. Lu, *Zhou Enlai zai guotongqu*, 117, 121; Tong, *Fengyun sishinian*, vol. 1, 221, 233.
103. Tong, *Fengyun sishinian*, vol. 1, 245.
104. *Selected Works of Zhou Enlai* (Beijing: Foreign Languages Press, 1981), vol. 1, 128.
105. Jin et al., *Zhou Enlai zhuan, 1898–1949*, 511–513.
106. *Selected Works of Mao Zedong*, vol. 3, 27.
107. Yin, *Pan Hannian de qingbao shengya*, 134.
108. Xiong Xianghui, *Dixia Shiernian yu Zhou Enlai* (Twelve Years of Underground Work and Zhou Enlai) (Beijing: Zhonggong zhonyang dangxiao chubanshe, 1991), 96.
109. Fang and Dan, *Zhonggong qingbao shounao Li Kenong*, 252–253.
110. Xiong, *Dixia shiernian yu Zhou Enlai*, 21–25.
111. Ibid., 119, 122.
112. Xue Yu, "Zhou Enlai yu dang de yingbi zhanxian" (Zhou Enlai and the

Secret Party Front), *Zhongong dangshi yanjiu,* no. 1 (1998), 69.

113. Yin, *Pan Hannian de qingbao shenya,* 244; Jin et al., *Zhou Enlai zhuan, 1898–1949,* 412.

114. Fang and Dan, *Zhonggong qingbao shounao Li Kenong,* 37–43.

115. Liu and Mi, *Zhou Enlai yanjiu wenxuan,* 407.

116. Meng Zhen, "Guanyu songdai de dongxi" (Something about the Soong Dynasty), *Jiushiniandai,* no. 9 (1985), 76–77.

117. White, *In Search of History,* 118.

118. Ibid., 407.

119. Liu and Mi, *Zhou Enlai yanjiu wenxuan,* 399–403.

120. Dogmatism: well versed in Marxism but not in Chinese realities; subjectivism: having the ability to engage in discourse about Marxism but inexperienced in Chinese revolutionary realities; sectarianism: the belief that one represents real Marxism and Chinese revolutionaries are "indigenous," that is, ignorant of Marxism.

121. Yang, *Zhonggong dangshi yu Yan'an zhengfeng,* vol. 2, 279, 289; "A Brief Review of Study Organizations in Yen'an," quoted in Warren Kuo, *Analytical History of the Chinese Communist Party,* vol. 4 (Taipei: Institute of International Relations, 1971), 557–594.

122. *History of the CCP,* 151; see also Roderick MacFarquhar and John K. Fairbank, vol. eds., *The Cambridge History of China,* vol. 14 (Cambridge: Cambridge University Press, 1987), 60.

123. "Hu Qiaomu huiyi Yan'an zhengfeng" (Hu Qiaomu Remembers the Yan'an Rectification Campaign), *Dangde wenxian,* no. 2 (1994), 59.

124. *Liu Shaoqi xuanji* (Selected Works of Liu Shaoqi) (Beijing: Renmin chubanshe, 1981), vol. 1, 291.

125. *Selected Works of Zhou Enlai,* vol. 1, 156–157.

126. Hu, "Hu Qiaomu huiyi Yan'an zhengfeng", 66–68.

127. Jin et al., *Zhou Enlai zhuan, 1898–1949,* 561–563.

128. *Selected Works of Mao Zedong,* vol. 3, 211.

129. Hu, "Hu Qiaomu huiyi Yan'an zhengfeng", 69.

130. Jin et al., *Zhou Enlai zhuan, 1898–1949,* 555–556.

131. Ivo Babac, ed., *The Diary of George Dimitrov, 1933–1949* (New Haven: Yale University Press, 2003), 290.

132. *Liu Shaoqi xuanji,* vol. 1, 314.

133. Hu, *Concise History,* 249–252; Carollee J. Carter, *Mission to Yenan, American Liaison with the Chinese Communists, 1944–1947* (Lexington: University Press of Kentucky, 1997), 16–17, 20–22.

134. Recalling rebel territory during the American Civil War, the members of the

American team in China had given the name "Dixie" to the communist-controlled areas in China (ibid., 25).

135. *Zhou Enlai nianpu, 1898–1949*, 578, 585, 681; see also *Hu Qiaomu huiyi Mao Zedong* (Hu Qiaomu Recalls Mao Zedong) (Beijing: Renmin chubanse, 1994), 338, 341, 361.

136. John K. Fairbank and Albert Feuerwerker, vol. eds., *The Cambridge History of China*, vol. 13, part 2 (Cambridge: Cambridge University Press, 1986), 714.

137. *Selected Works of Zhou Enlai*, vol. 1, 229.

138. Shao Kuo-kang, *Zhou Enlai and the Foundations of Chinese Foreign Policy* (Houndmills and London: Macmillan, 1996), 110–114.

139. *Selected Works of Zhou Enlai*, vol. 1, 230.

140. *Selected Works of Mao Zedong*, vol. 3, 331, 335.

141. Ibid.

142. Ibid., 252.

143. *Hu Qiaomu huiyi Mao Zedong*, 403.

144. Jin et al., *Zhou Enlai zhuan, 1898–1949*, 603.

145. *The Cambridge History of China*, vol. 12, part 2, 724; *History of the CCP*, 170.

146. *Hu Qiaomun huiyi Mao Zedong*, 404, 410.

147. Wu Xiuquan, *Wangshi changsang* (Memoirs of the Past) (Shanghai: Shanghai wenyi chubanshe, 1986), 158. Wu Xiuquan was Mao's and Zhou's Russian translator. At the time of the civil war, he was a leading officer on Lin Biao's staff. See also *Zhongguo gongchandang lishi*, vol. 1, 680.

148. *The Cambridge History of China*, vol. 13, part 2, 726; see also Tang Tsou, *America's Failure in China* (Chicago: University of Chicago Press, 1963), 305, 727.

149. Wu Xiuquan, *Wangshi changsang*, 682.

150. *The Cambridge History of China*, vol. 13, part 2, 727.

151. Michael H. Hunt, *The Genesis of Chinese Communist Foreign Policy* (New York: Columbia University Press, 1996), 166; Liu, *Zhonggong dangshi fenyunlu*, 43.

152. *Zhou Enlai nianpu, 1898–1949*, 632; Hunt, *The Genesis of Chinese Communist Foreign Policy*, 166.

153. *The Cambridge History of China*, vol. 13, part 2, 636–637, 729–730; *History of the CCP*, 174.

154. Hunt, *The Genesis of Chinese Communist Foreign Policy*, 167.

155. Ibid., *Hu Qiaomu huiyi Mao Zedong*, 438.

156. Liu, *Zhonggong dangshi fengyun lu*, 48.
157. *Selected Works of Zhou Enlai*, vol. 1, 286.
158. For a more detailed account of the military situation, see Dreyer, *China at War*, 320–324.
159. Wu, *Wangshi changsang*, 669.
160. Zhang Wenjin, *Zhou Enlai yu Maxi'er shihua* (Zhou Enlai and Marshall in China), in Liu Wusheng, *Zhonggong dangshi fengyun lu*, 53–54; Dreyer, *China at War*, 319–320.
161. *The Cambridge History of China*, vol. 13, part 2, 763; Bai Shouyi, ed., *An Outline History of China, 1919-1949* (Beijing: Foreign Languages Press, 1993), 243–244.
162. Xiong, *Dixia shiernian yu Zhou Enlai*, 12, 65–66.
163. Tong, *Fengyun sishinian*, vol. 1, 494–497; Dreyer, *China at War*, 343.
164. Jin et al., *Zhou Enlai zhuan, 1898–1949*, 682.
165. *Hu Qiaomu huiyi Mao Zedong*, 482, 695; *Zhou Enlai nianpu, 1898–1949*, 729.
166. *Selected Works of Mao Zedong*, vol. 4, 133–134.
167. *History of the CCP*, 192.
168. *Zhou Enlai nianpu, 1898–1949*, 492, 732.
169. Jin et al., *Zhou Enlai zhuan, 1898–1949*, 694; Tong, *Fengyun sishinian*, vol. 1, 537–539.
170. *Zhou Enlai nianpu, 1898–1949*, 756.
171. For an examination of the competition between the CCP and the GMD at universities between 1937 and 1945, see Hu Kuo-tai, "The Struggle between the Kuomintang and the Chinese Communist Party on Campus during the War of Resistance, 1937–45," *The China Quarterly*, no. 118 (June 1989), 300–323.
172. Tong, *Fengyun sishinian*, vol. 1, 537–539.
173. Ibid., 734; *Selected Works of Mao Zedong*, vol. 4, 261.
174. *The Cambridge History of China*, vol. 13, part 2, 764.
175. Ibid., 775–777.
176. *Selected Works of Mao Zedong*, vol. 4, 261, 281, 289.
177. Ibid., 309.
178. Cold War International History Project (hereafter cited as CWIPH), "Rivals and Allies: Stalin, Mao, and the Chinese Civil War, January 1949," *Cold War International History Project Bulletin* (hereafter cited as *CWIHP Bulletin*), issue 6–7 (Winter 1995/96), p. 29.
179. Pei Jianzhang, *Xin Zhongguo waijiao fengyun* (Major Events in New China's Foreign Relations) (Beijing: Shijie zhishi chubanshe, 1990), vol. 1, 16. The

announcement of his appointment was made at the second session of the seventh Central Committee, held from 5 to 13 March, 1949 (ibid., 745); Jin et al., *Zhou Enlai zhuan, 1898–1949*, 743.
180. Ibid., 753, 755, 757.

**Chapter 3**
1. Tong, *Fengyu sishinian,* vol. 2, 18.
2. Jin, *Deng Yingchao zhuan,* 462.
3. Cheng Hua, ed., *Zhou Enlai he ta de mishumen* (Zhou Enlai and His Secretaries) (Beijing: Zhongguo guangbo dianshi chubanshe, 1992), 283–284.
4. Ibid.
5. *Zhou Enlai nianpu, 1898–1949,* 284; Quan Yanchi, *Zouxia shentan de Zhou Enlai* (Zhou Enlai Descends from His Shrine) (Beijing: Zhonggong zhongyang dangxiao chubanshe, 1993), 109.
6. Li Hong et al., *Zhou Enlai he Deng Yingchao* (Zhou Enlai and Deng Yingchao) (Beijing: Zhonggong zhongyang dangxiao chubanshe, 1994), 94.
7. In the early 1950s the Chinese government implemented a wage scale of twenty-eight grades. Zhou was in grade 2, where he earned a monthly salary that, in time, increased from RMB400 to 500. His wife, who was grade 6, earned between RMB300 and 400. His brother's salary was a small fraction of that amount.
8. Li et al., *Zhou Enlai he Deng Yingchao,* 54–55; Yang Hong, "Yanhe zhizi" (The Sons of the Yan River), *Dadi,* no. 1 (1992).
9. Author's interview with Qian Jiadong, Beijing, April 1998.
10. Ibid.
11. Quan, *Zouxia shentan de Zhou Enlai,* 174.
12. *Selected Works of Mao Zedong,* vol. 4, 415, 419.
13. Tong, *Fengyun sishinian,* vol. 2, 24; Israel Epstein, *Women in World History: Soong Ching Ling (Mme. Sun Yatsen),* 2nd ed. (Beijing: New World Press, 1995), 479.
14. Hu Sheng, *Zhongguo gongchandang de qishinian* (Seventy Years of the Chinese Communist Party) (Beijing: Zhonggong dangshi chubanshe, 1991), 38.
15. *Zhou Enlai nianpu, 1898–1949,* 832; *History of the CCP,* 210–214; Tong, *Fengyun sishinian,* vol. 2, 51.
16. Lin Yunhui et al., *Kaige xingjinde shiqi* (Period of Marching in Triumph) (Zhengzhou: Henan renmin chubanshe, 1989), 38.
17. An Jianshe, *Zhou Enlai de zuihou suiyue, 1966–1976* (Zhou Enlai's Final

Years, 1966–1976) (Beijing: Zhongyang wenxian chubanshe, 1995), 207; Pei, *Xin Zhongguo waijiao fengyun*, 92.

18. Xu Jingli, *Lingqi luzao* (Making a Fresh Start) (Beijing: Shijie zhishi chubanshe, 1998), 194.

19. Li Xiannian et al., *Bujin de sinian* (Endless Memories) (Beijing: Zhongyang wenxian chubanshe, 1987), 426; *Zhou Enlai waijiao wenxuan* (Selected Works of Zhou Enlai on Foreign Affairs) (Beijing: Zhongyang wenxian chubanshe, 1987), 426

20. Xu, *Lingqi luzao*, 190.

21. Jin Chongji et al., *Zhou Enlai zhuan, 1949–76* (Beijing: Zhongyang wenxian chubanshe, 1998), vol. 1, 32, 43.

22. Pei, *Xin Zhongguo waijiao fengyun*, vol. 1, 25, 30.

23. *Selected Works of Mao Zedong*, vol. 4, 317

24. Xu, *Lingqi luzao*, 273, 290–308; Han Nianlong et al., eds., *Dangdai Zhongguo waijiao* (Contemporary Chinese Diplomacy) (Beijing: Zhonguo shehui kexue chubanshe, 1992), 18.

25. *CWIHP*, Bulletin 6–7 (Winter 1995/96).

26. Short, *Mao, A life*, 424.

27. Wu, *Wangsi changsang*, 182.

28. Quoted in Sergei N. Goncharov, John W. Lewis, and Xue Litai, *Uncertain Partners: Stalin, Mao and the Korean War* (Stanford: Stanford University Press, 1993), 101, 114, 120–121.

29. Li Ping, *Kaiguo zongli Zhou Enlai* (Zhou Enlai, The First Premier of the Nation) (Beijing: Zhonggong zhongyang dangxiao chubanshe, 1994), 246.

30. Hao Yufan and Zhai Zhihai, "China's Decision to Enter the Korean War: History Revisited," *The China Quarterly*, no. 121 (March 1990), 100; Goncharov et al., *Uncertain Partners*, 153; Zhonggong zhongyang wenxian yanjiushi, ed., *Zhou Enlai nianpu, 1949–1976* (Beijing: Zhongyang wenxian chubanshe, 1997), vol. 1, 51.

31. Qin Shi, "1950 jiefang Taiwan jihua geqian de muhou" (The Postponement of the 1950 Liberation of Taiwan: Events Behind the Scenes), *Bainianchao*, no. 1 (1997), 42–44; Yao Xu, *Cong Yalu dao Banmendian* (From the Yalu to Panmunjom) (Beijing: Renmin chubanshe, 1985), 22; quoted in Hao and Zhai, "China's Decision to Enter the Korean War," 100.

32. *Zhou Enlai nianpu, 1949–1976*, vol. 1, 51.

33. Lei Yingfu, "Kang Mei yuan Chao jige zhongda juece de huiyi" (Some Important Decisions Concerning the Korean War), *Dangde wenxian*, no. 61 (1993), 78; Qing, "1950 jiefang Taiwan jihua geqian de muhou," 38–40.

34. Goncharov et al., *Uncertain Partners*, 171–172; Hao and Zhai, "China's

Decision to Enter the Korean War", 101; Lei, "Kang Mei yuan Chao jige zhongda juece de huiyi," 79–80.

35. Lei Yingfu, "Kang Mei yuan Chao zhanzheng jige zhongda juece de huiyi" (Reminiscence of Major Decisions Made on the Korean War), *Dangde wenxian*, no. 1 (1994), 25.

36. Chai Chengwen and Zhao Yongtian, *Banmendian tanpan* (The Panmunjom Negotiations) (Beijing: Jiefangjun chubanshe, 1992), 58.

37. Bo Yibo, *Ruogan zhongda juece yu shijian de huigu* (Recollections on Some Important Decisions and Events) (Beijing: Zhonggong dangxiao chubanshe, 1991), vol. 1, 43.

38. Nie, *Inside the Red Star*, 634–635.

39. Alexandre Y. Mansourov, trans. and with an article, "Stalin, Mao, Kim, and China's Decision to Enter the Korean War, September 16–October 15, 1950: New Evidence from the Russian Archives," *CWIHP Bulletin*, issues 6–7 (Winter 1995/96).

40. Ibid.

41. *Zhou Enlai junshi wenxuan* (Selected Articles by Zhou Enlai on Military Affairs) (Beijing: Renmin chubanshe, 1997), vol. 4, 64.

42. Quoted in Mansourov, "Stalin, Mao, Kim, and China's Decision to Enter the Korean War," 114.

43. Li Qi, ed., *Zai Zhou Enlai shenbian de rizi* (My Days Working for Zhou Enlai) (Beijing: Zhongyang wenxian chubanshe, 1998), 394; Han et al., *Dangdai zhongguo waijiao* (Contemporary Chinese Diplomacy) (Beijing: Zhongguo shehui kexue chubanshe, 1992), 37.

44. Quoted in Goncharov et al., *Uncertain Partners*, 180.

45. Qing, "1950 jiefang Taiwan jihua geqian de muhou."

46. Ibid.

47. Jin et al., *Zhou Enlai zhuan, 1949–1976*, vol. 1 62; Xiong, "Zhou Enlai mimi fangsu" (Zhou Enlai's Secret Mission to the Soviet Union), *Dangde wenxian*, no. 3 (1994).

48. *Zhou Enlai junshi wenxuan*, vol. 4, 100.

49. Wang Yan et al., *Peng Dehuai zhuan* (Biography of Peng Dehuai) (Beijing: Dangdai Zhongguo chubanshe, 1993), 454–455.

50. Hong Xuezhi, *Kang Mei yuan Chao zhanzheng huiyi* (Recollections of the War to Resist U.S. Aggression and Aid Korea) (Beijing: Jiefangjun wenyi chubanshe, 1990), 174; Chai and Zhao, *Banmendian tanpan*, 119.

51. Wu Lengxi, *Yi Mao Zhuxi* (In Memory of Chairman Mao) (Beijing: Xinhua chubanshe, 1995), 6; Goncharov et al., *Uncertain Partners*, 159.

52. Shao, *Zhou Enlai and the Foundations of Chinese Foreign Policy*, 211–215.

53.   Zhai Qiang, "China and the Geneva Conference of 1954," *The China Quarterly*, no. 129 (March 1992), 103–122; Pei, *Xin Zhongguo waijiao fengyun*, vol. 1, p. 130; Qian Jiadong, Zhou's secretary for foreign affairs, also said that no one could remember that the premier had attempted to shake hands with Dulles. See Cheng, *Zhou Enlai he ta de mishumen*, 240, and Zhai, "China and the Geneva Conference of 1954," 110.

54.   Wang Bingnan, "Zhongmei huitan jiunian" (Recollection of the Nine-year Sino-American Talks), *Shijie zhishi*, no. 8 (1985).

55.   Anthony Eden, *Full Circle* (Boston: Houghton Mifflin, 1960), 138.

56.   Humphrey Trevelyan, *Living with the Communists* (Boston: Gambit, 1971), 82–83.

57.   Pei Jianzhang, ed., *Yanjiu Zhou Enlai: Waijiao sixiang yu shijian* (Studies on Zhou Enlai: Thought and Practice in Foreign Affairs) (Beijing: Shijie zhishi chubanshe, 1989), 254–255, 257.

58.   Keith C. Ronald, *The Diplomacy of Zhou Enlai* (New York: St. Martin's Press, 1989), 79; Zhai, "China and the Geneva Conference of 1954," 111.

59.   Shao, *Zhou Enlai and the Foundation of Chinese Foreign Policy*, 189.

60.   Steve Tsang, "Target Zhou Enlai: The 'Kashmir Princess' Incident in 1955," *The China Quarterly*, no. 139 (September 1994), 766–782.

61.   Tong, *Fengyun sishinian*, vol. 2, 91–92.

62.   *Zhou Enlai waijiao wenxuan*, 121.

63.   Zhou Enlai, *China and the Asian-African Conference* (Beijing: Foreign Languages Press, 1955), 47.

64.   Jin et al., *Zhou Enlai zhuan, 1949–1976*, vol. 1, 74.

65.   Harish Kapur, *The Awakening Giant: China's Ascension to World Politics* (Alpen aan den Rijn: Sijthoff and Noordhoff, 1981), 235.

66.   Pei, *Yanjiu Zhou Enlai*, 65; *History of the CCP*, 235.

67.   Shi Zhe, *Zai lishi juren shenbian* (Working Beside a Historical Giant) (Beijing: Zhongyang wenxian chubanshe, 1991), 520–521.

68.   CWIHP, "Talks Between Stalin and Zhou Enlai on 3 September 1952," *CWIHP Bulletin*, issues 6–7 (Winter 1995/96); *Zhou Enlai nianpu, 1949–1976*, vol. 1, 260; Bo, *Ruogan zhongda juece yu shijian de huigu*, vol. 1, 297–300.

69.   Ibid., 309–310.

70.   Ibid., 197.

71.   In 1959 Zhu De confessed in a self-criticism that he had supported Gao Gang; see Cong Jin, *Quzhe fazhan de suiyue* (Years of Advance in Zig-Zags) (Zhengzhou: Henan renmin chubanshe, 1989), 306. Peng Dehuai was condemned by Mao for having acted in unison with Gao in 1953; see Li Rui,

*Lushan huiyi shilu* (A Factual Record of the Lushan Conference) (Hunan: Chuqiu chubanshe, 1988); Lin Biao's support was publicized after his death; see Lin Qingshan, *Lin Biao zhuan* (Biography of Lin Biao) (Beijing: Zhishi chubanshe, 1988), 86–91.

72. *Selected Works of Deng Xiaoping* (Beijing: Foreign Languages Press, 1994), vol. 2, 292.

73. *Selected Works of Mao Zedong*, vol. 2, 224.

74. Ibid., vol. 5, 162.

75. *History of the CCP*, 244; Lin, *Kaige xingjin de shiqi*, 333.

76. *Zhou Enlai jingji wenxian* (Selected Works of Zhou Enlai on the Economy) (Beijing: Zhongyang wenxian chubanshe, 1993), 131.

77. Lin, *Kaige xingjin de shiqi*, 576.

78. Qing, "1950 jiefang Taiwan jihua geqian de muhou," 48.

79. Bo, *Ruogan zhongda juece yu shijian de huigu*, vol. 1, 521, 531, 541; *Selected Works of Zhou Enlai*, vol. 2, 195–196.

80. Bo, *Ruogan zhongda juece yu shijian de huigu*, vol. 1, 538. The editorial was published in the *People's Daily* on 20 June 1956.

81. Li Rui, *Dayuejin qinli* (My Personal Experiences in the Great Leap Forward) (Shanghai: Shanghai yandong chubanshe, 1996), 48.

82. Cong, *Quzhe fazhan de suiyue*, 112.

83. Frederic C. Teiwes with Warren Sun, *China's Road to Disaster* (Armonk, NY: M.E. Sharpe, 1999), 70–74.

84. Xiong Huayuan and Liao Xinwen, *Zhou Enlai zhongli shengya* (Premier Zhou Enlai's Life) (Beijing: Renmin chunbanshe, 1997), 240–241, 244.

85. Fan Ruoyu, "Zai Zhou Enlai shengbian rizili," *Wenzhai xunkan* (1986), 186; Nan Xingzhou, *Zhou Enlai yisheng* (The Life of Zhou Enlai) (Beijing: Zhongguo qingnian chubanshe, 1987), 478–479.

86. Cong, *Quzhe fazhan de suiyue*, 123–127.

87. Xiong and Liao, *Zhou Enlai zhongli shengya*, 249.

88. Lin et al., *Kaige xingjin de shiqi*, 212.

89. *Selected Works of Zhou Enlai*, vol. 2, 71–79; Barbara Barnouin and Yu Changgen, *Ten Years of Turbulence: The Chinese Cultural Revolution* (London: Keagan Paul International, 1993), 261.

90. Barnouin and Yu, *Ten Years of Turbulence*, 261.

91. *Selected Works of Mao Zedong*, vol. 5, 121–122, 225.

92. *Selected Works of Zhou Enlai*, vol. 2, 170.

93. Ibid., 174–178.

94. Hu, *Zhongguo gongchandang de qishinian*, 363.

95. These were the targets of the second five-year plan (1957–1962), drawn up

under Zhou's direction. See *Zhou Enlai jingji wenxian*, 291, 304.

96.  Bo, *Ruogan zhongda juece yu shijian de huigu*, vol. 2, 690–691.

97.  Cheng, *Zhou Enlai he tade mishumen*, 19.

98.  Bo, *Ruogan zhongda juece yu shijian de huigu*, vol. 2, 690.

99.  Wu, *Yi Mao zhuxi*, 133–135.

100. Li, *Lushan huiyi shilu*, 19, 88.

101. *Zhou Enlai nianpu, 1949–1976*, vol. 2, 241–242.

102. Peng, *Memoirs of a Chinese Marshal*, 517.

103. Namely the "general line" (of socialism), the Great Leap Forward, and the People's Communes.

104. Li, *Lushan huiyi shilu*, 153, 164–176, 243–249, 284.

105. Cong, *Quzhe fazhan de suiyue*, 302; Peng Dehuai died in 1974. He was officially rehabilitated in 1978.

106. Bo, *Ruogan zhongda juece yu shijian de huigu*, vol. 2, 884–886.

107. Li, *Kaiguo zongli Zhou Enlai*, 374.

108. "Communist wind" refers to exaggerated and hasty eagerness to change the ownership system based on the commune to collective ownership by the state.

109. Cao Yingwang, ed., *Zhou Enlai de zhihui* (Zhou Enlai's Intelligence) (Beijing: Zhonggong zhongyang dangxiao chubanshe, 1994), 17.

110. Ibid., 287–288.

111. *Zhou Enlai nianpu, 1949–1976*, vol. 2, 366.

112. Gu Baozi, "Dayuejin hou de Zhou Enlai" (Zhou Enlai after the Great Leap Forward), *Zhonghua ernu*, no. 3 (1993).

113. *Zhou Enlai nianpu, 1949-1976*, vol. 2, 369.

114. Cong, *Quzhe fazhan de suiyue*, 370–371; Li, *Bujin de sinian*, 231–233.

115. Li, *Bujin de sinian*, 232–233.

116. *Cambridge History of China*, vol. 14, part 1, 73.

117. Zhen Xiaoying, ed., *Zhou Enlai dangxing de kaimo* (Zhou Enlai, a Model Party Member) (Beijing: Zhonggong zhongyang dangxiao chubanshe, 1989), 86.

118. *History of the CCP*, 228.

119. Bo, *Ruogan zhongda juece yu shijian de huigu*, vol. 2, 897; Dong Bian, *Mao Zedong he ta de mishu Tian Jiaying* (Mao Zedong and His Secretary Tian Jiaying) (Beijing: Zhongyang wenxian chubanshe, 1990), 59.

120. *Liu Shaoqi xuanji*, vol. 2, 1985, 256–257, 351–354.

121. Roderick MacFarquhar, *The Origins of the Cultural Revolution* (London: Oxford University Press, 1997), vol. 3, 152–153.

122. Schram, *Mao Tse-tung Unrehearsed*, 165, 167, 175.

123. Ibid., 410–411; MacFarquhar, *Origins of the Cultural Revolution*, vol. 3, 166–167.

124. *Selected Works of Zhou Enlai*, vol. 2, 361; Cong, *Quzhe fazhan de suiyue*, 407–408; MacFarquhar, *Origins of the Cultural Revolution*, vol. 3, 175–177.

125. MacFarquhar, *Origins of the Cultural Revolution*, vol. 3, 175–177.

126. *Selected Works of Zhou Enlai*, vol. 2, 366–382; Merle Goldman, *China's Intellectuals, Advice and Dissent* (Cambridge, MA: Harvard University Press, 1981), 20–21; Hu et al., *Chen Yi zhuan*, 531.

127. Hu et al., *Chen Yi zhuan*, 531.

128. *Zhou Enlai tongyi zhanxian wenxuan* (Selected Works of Zhou Enlai on the United Front) (Beijing: Renmin chubanshe, 1988), 426.

129. Hu Sheng, "Hu Qiaomu he dangshi gongzuo" (Hu Qiaomu and Party History Work), *Zhonggong dangshi yanjiu*, no. 1 (1994), 75; MacFarquhar, *Origins of the Cultural Revolution*, vol. 3, 247–248.

130. Bo, *Ruogan zhongda juece yu shijian de huigu*, vol. 2, 1006–1007; Tong, *Fengyun sishinian*, vol. 2, 264–266.

131. In 1958: 2.1 billion yuan; in 1959: 6.5 billion yuan; in 1960: 8.189 billion yuan; in 1961: 1.09 billion yuan. The money supply for 1961 was estimated at 12.5 billion yuan and was expected to increase to more than 15 billion yuan in 1962. See Cong, *Quzhe fazhan de suiyue*, 414.

132. Bo, *Ruogan zhongda juece yu shijian de huigu*, vol. 2, 173, 298.

133. Lin, *Kaige xingjin de shiqi*, 576; Jin et al., *Zhou Enlai zhuan, 1949–1976*, 675–676.

134. *Selected Works of Zhou Enlai*, vol. 2, 383–385, 392–393.

135. *History of the CCP*, 300; Jin et al., *Zhou Enlai zhuan, 1949–1976*, vol. 2, 683; Cong, *Quzhe fazhan de suiyue*, 421, 425.

136. People's communes were composed of production brigades, which, in turn, were made up of production teams grouping individual farmers.

137. MacFarquhar, *Origins of the Cultural Revolution*, vol. 3, 211.

138. Dong, *Mao Zedong he ta de mishu Tian Jiaying*, 50.

139. *Selected Works of Deng Xiaoping*, vol. 1, 318.

140. Dong, *Mao Zedong he ta de mishu Tian Jiaying*, 69.

141. Bo, *Ruogan zhongda juece yu shijian de huigu*, vol. 2, 1086.

142. Jin et al., *Zhou Enlai zhuan, 1949–1946*, vol. 2, 690–691.

143. *Ziliao xuanbian* (Selected Reference Material) (Beijing, 1967), 269–271.

144. Short, *Mao, A Life*, 446.

145. *Zhou Enlai nianpu, 1949–1976*, vol. 2, 494; Jin et al., *Zhou Enlai zhuan, 1949–1976*, vol. 2, 692.

146. Schram, *Mao Tse-tung Unrehearsed*, 189.

147. *Zhou Enlai nianpu, 1949–1976*, vol. 2, 498; Jin et al., *Zhou Enlai zhuan, 1949–1976*, vol. 2, 692; Wu, *Yi Mao Zhuxi*, 3–5.

148. Wu Lengxi participated in these meetings in his capacity as the head of the Xinhua News Agency and editor-in-chief of *Renmin ribao* (People's Daily), Wu, *Yi Mao Zhuxi*, 10.

149. *Zhou Enlai nianpu, 1949–1976*, vol. 1, 563.

150. Wu, *Yi Mao Zhuxi*, 12–13.

151. Ibid., 14.

152. *Zhou Enlai nianpu, 1949–1976*, vol. 1, 633.

153. Ronald C. Keith, *The Diplomacy of Zhou Enlai* (London: MacMillan, 1990), 93; Cong, *Quzhe fazhan de suiyue*, 316.

154. Shao, *Zhou Enlai and the Foundations of Chinese Foreign Policy*, 163; *Zhou Enlai nianpu, 1949–1976*, vol. 2, 4–7.

155. Keith, *The Diplomacy of Zhou Enlai*, 96; *Zhou Enlai nianpu, 1949–1976*, vol. 2, 5.

156. Pei, *Xin Zhongguo waijiao fengyun*, vol. 2, 26.

157. *Zhou Enlai nianpu, 1949–1976*, vol. 2, 6.

158. Ibid., 12; Pei, *Xin Zhongguo waijiao fengyun*, vol. 2, 28; Keith, *The Diplomacy of Zhou Enlai*, 98–99.

159. *Zhou Enlai nianpu, 1949–1976*, vol. 2, 15.

160. *The Polemics on the General Line of the International Communist Movement* (Beijing: Foreign Languages Press, 1965), 544–545.

161. Pei, *Yanjiu Zhou Enlai*, 163; Pei, *Xin Zhongguo waijiao fengyun*, vol. 1, 94.

162. The group comprised Chen Boda, alternate member of the Politburo, editor in chief of *Red Flag* and Mao's chief aide on ideological questions; Yao Zhen, vice minister of the Central Propaganda Department; Wu Lengxi; Wang Li, deputy head of the Central Liaison Department; Deng Liqun, Hu Sheng, and Fan Ruoyu, all deputy chief editors of *Hongqi* (Red Flag); see also MacFarquhar, *Origins of the Cultural Revolution*, vol. 3, 360.

163. *Zhou Enlai nianpu, 1949–1976*, vol. 2, 441, 686; *History of the CCP*, 313.

164. Pei, *Yanjiu Zhou Enlai*, 167.

165. Harish Kapur, *The Awakening Giant*, 246–255.

166. Xiong Huayuan, *Zhou Enlai zongli shenya* (Premier Zhou Enlai's Life) (Beijing: Renmin chubanshe, 1987), 432.

167. Other members were He Long, Li Fuchun, Li Xiannian, Nie Rongzhen, Bo Yibo, Lu Dingyi, Luo Ruiqing, and seven ministers; see Xiong and Liao, *Zhou Enlai zongli shengya*, 433.

168. CWIHP, "Zhou Enlai's Speech at the War-Planning Meeting of the Central Military Commission, 21 May 1965," *CWIHP Bulletin*.

169. Sun Dongsheng, "Wo guo jingji jianshe zhanlue buju de dazhuanbian" (The Major Transformation of Our National Economic Startegy), *Dangde wenxuan,* no. 5 (1995), 44; Niu Jun, "Lun liushi niandai Zhongguo dui Mei zhangfu zhuanbian de lishi zhijing" (On the Historical Background of the Change of China's U.S. Policy in the 1960s), *Dangdai Zhongguoshi yanjiu,* no. 1 (2000).

170. Jin et al., *Zhou Enlai zhuan, 1949–1976,* vol. 2, 817; *History of the CCP,* 317; Li, *Lushan huiyi shilu,* 153.

171. Paul Kennedy, *The Rise and Fall of the Great Powers* (New York: Random House, 1987), 405.

172. Zhu Zhongli, "Suowei 'san he yi shao' wenti zhenxiang" (The Truth about the So-Called "Three Peacefuls and One Less"), *Dangde wenxian,* no. 5 (1993).

173. *Zhou Enlai nianpu, 1949–1976,* vol. 2, 496.

174. Tong, *Fengyun sishinian,* vol. 2, 219–220.

175. *Zhou Enlai nianpu, 1949–1976,* vol. 2, 655, 663, 707.

176. *Zhou Enlai waijiao wenxuan,* vol. 4, 461, 528.

177. *Zhou Enlai nianpu, 1949–1976,* vol. 2, 724; *History of the CCP,* 316.

178. Tong, *Fengyun sishinian,* 222.

## Chapter 4

1. The song runs: "The east is red, the sun rises, China brought forth a Mao Zedong, He works for the people's well being, He is the people's great savior."

2. Xiong, *Zhou Enlai zongli shenya,* 448–451; Chen Huangmei, ed., *Zhou Enlai yu yishujiamen* (Zhou Enlai and the Artists) (Beijing: Zhongyang wenxian chubanshe, 1992), 292.

3. Edgar Snow, *The Long Revolution* (New York: Random House, 1971), 58–69.

4. For a more detailed analysis of the evolution of Mao's thinking, see Barnouin and Yu, *Ten Years of Turbulence,* 10; Mao's original statement to that effect was published in *Peking Review,* no. 34 (1967).

5. Jin et al., *Zhou Enlai zhuan, 1949–1976,* vol. 2, 883.

6. Shuai Dongbing, *Peng Zhen zai wenhua dageming qianxi* (Peng Zhen on the Eve of the Cultural Revolution) (Beijing: Zhonggong zhongyang dangxiao chubanshe, 1993), 58; Jin Chunming, *Wenhua dageming shigao* (A Preliminary History of the Cultural Revolution) (Chengdu: Sichuan renmin chubanshe, 1995), 140.

7. Li Ping, *Wenhua dageming zhong de Zhou Enlai* (Zhou Enlai in the Cultural Revolution) (Beijing: Zhonggong zhongyang dangxiao chubanshe, 1991), 3; Peng Cheng, *Zhongguo zhengju beiwanglu* (A Memorandum on the Chinese

Political Situation) (Beijing: Jiefangjun chubanshe, 1989), 72.

8.  Shuai, *Peng Zhen zai wenhua dageming qianxi*, 74.

9.  Zhi Ling and Zhi Zhen, "Wu Han he 'Hai Rui baguan'" (Wu Han and "Hai Rui Dismissed from Office"), in Zhou Ming, *Lishi zai zheli chensi* (Pondering History) (Beijing: Huaxia chubanshe, 1986), vol. 2, 13–14.

10. Shuai, *Peng Zhen zai wenhua dageming qianxi*, 239–243.

11. Zhang Yaoci, *Huiyi Mao Zedong* (Remembering Mao Zedong) (Beijing: Zhonggong zhongyang dangxiao chubanshe, 1996), 30.

12. Dian Dian, *Feifan de niandai* (Extraordinary Years) (Shanghai: Wenyi chubanshe, 1992), 203.

13. Dian Dian, "Dian Dian jiyi" (Dian Dian's Recollections), *Dangdai,* no. 5 (1998), 30.

14. The other two were Lu Dingyi (head of the CCP Propaganda Department) and Yang Shangkun (chief of the CCP General Office). All four were condemned as the "Peng-Luo-Lu-Yang Anti-Party Clique." See Barnouin and Yu, *Ten Years of Turbulence*, 63–71.

15. "Zhongguo gongchandang weiyuanhui tongzhi, 5.16" (Circular of the CCP Central Committee, May 16, 1966), *Renmin ribao*, 17 May 1967.

16. *Zhou Enlai nianpu, 1949–1976*, vol. 3, 32–33.

17. Jin et al., *Zhou Enlai zhuan, 1949–1976*, vol. 2, 884.

18. The appointment of work teams was a typical Chinese method to implement policies at the grass-roots level. Work teams were usually made up of cadres of all grades up to ministerial rank and assigned to certain areas or institutions to verify and to impose proper application of rules; Wang Nianyi, *Dadongluan de niandai* (Years of Turmoil) (Zhengzhou: Henan renmin chubanshe, 1988), 33, 34.

19. *History of the CCP*, 327, 328.

20. *Renmin ribao*, 5 August 1967.

21. Gao Wenqiàn, "Ji wenhua dageming zhong de Zhou Enlai" (Zhou Enlai in the Cultural Revolution), in Zhou, *Lishi zai zheli chensi*, vol. 1, 58.

22. Li, *Wenhua dageming zhong de Zhou Enlai*, 5.

23. Lin Qing, *Zhou Enlai zaixiang shengya* (Zhou Enlai's Premiership) (Beijing: Changcheng wenhua chuban gongsi, 1991), 75; Jin Chunming, *Wenhua dageming shigao* (A preliminary History of the Cultural Revolution) (Chengdu: Sichuan renmin chubanshe, 1995) 184.

24. *Renmin ribao,* 27 March 1967.

25. Gu Mu et al., *Women de Zhou Zongli* (Our Premier Zhou) (Beijing: Zhongyang wenxian chubanshe, 1991), 483; Jin et al., *Zhou Enlai zhuan, 1949–1976,* vol. 4, 1876–1884.

26. Wang, *Dadongluan de niandai*, 77.
27. Barnouin and Yu, *Ten years of Turbulence*, 99; *Women de Zhou zongli*, 43; Jin Chunming et al., *Wenge shiqi guaishi guaiyu* (The Absurdities of the Cultural Revolution) (Beijing: Qiushi chubanshe, 1989), 288.
28. *Hongqi*, 2 October 1966; Li, *Wenhua dageming zhong de Zhou Enlai*, 104.
29. Wang, *Dadongluan de niandai*, 80.
30. Zhang Yunsheng, *Maojiawan jishi* (A Factual Account of Maojiawan) (Beijing: Chunqiu chubanshe, 1988), 60.
31. An Jianshe, *Zhou Enlai de zuihou suiyue, 1966–1976* (Zhou Enlai's Final Years, 1966–1976) (Beijing: Zhongyang wenxuan chubanshe, 1995), 14.
32. Zhou, *Lishi zai zheli chensi*, vol. 5, 75.
33. Li, *Wenhua dageming zhongde Zhou Enlai*, 7.
34. "Circular on how Industrial and Transport Enterprises and Capital Construction Units Should Carry out the Cultural Revolution," in *History of the CCP*, 327. The circular stated: "In view of the fact that these enterprises and units (including units of construction and design) have to fulfill state quotas, the Cultural Revolution should be combined there with the four cleans movement and be carried out in conformity with the provisions in the Twenty-three-point Directive and the plans formulated by the local authorities, and by stages and groups, under sound leadership."
35. Su Caiqing, "Wenge chuqi jinji zhanxiande yanzhong douzheng" (Sharp Conflicts on the Economic Front at the Beginning of the Cultural Revolution), in Tan Zhongji et al., eds., *Shinian hou de pingshou* (Critical Comments after Ten Years) (Beijing: Dangshi cailiao chubanshe, 1987), 42.
36. Gu Mu, "Huiyu qin'ai de Zhou Zongli" (In Memory of Our Beloved Premier Zhou), in Gu Mu et al., *Women de Zhou zongli*, 18, 20, 24.
37. *Peking Review*, no. 39 (1966).
38. "Regulations Concerning the Cultural Revolution in Rural Areas Below the County Level" of 14 September 1966 specified that students and Red Guards "shall not go" to these areas; the "Circular on Grasping Revolution and Practicing Production" required that measures be taken in industrial, agricultural, transport, financial, and trade departments to ensure the normal processes of production and that Red Guards should stay away from these sectors. See *History of the CCP*, 330; Li, *Wenhua dageming zhong de Zhou Enlai*, 6.
39. Li, *Wenhua dageming zhong de Zhou Enlai*, 26.
40. Yu Gong, *Lin Biao shijian zhenxiang* (The True Story of the Lin Biao Affair) (Beijing: Zhongguo guangbo dianshe chubanshe, 1988), 397, 398; *History of the CCP*, 332.

41. *History of the CCP*, 332.
42. Su Caiqing, "Hongweibing yundong jiqi lishi jiaoxun" (The Red Guard Movement and Its Lessons), *Dangxiao ziliao*, 1987, 54–55.
43. Ibid., 55.
44. Li, *Wenhua dageming zhong de Zhou Enlai*, 21.
45. *History of the CCP*, 334.
46. Zhou Enlai's speech of 10 January 1967, in Editorial Department of the *Zhonggong yanjiu* Press, comp., *Zhonggong wenhua dageming zhongyao wenjian huibian* (A Collection of Important Documents on the Cultural Revolution) (Taipei: Zhonggong yanjiu zazhishe, 1973), 223.
47. *Zhou Enlai nianpu, 1949–1976*, vol. 3, 113.
48. Li, *Wenhua dageming zhong de Zhou Enlai*, 17.
49. Jin, *Wenhua dageming jianshi*, 10.
50. *History of the CCP*, 336.
51. Lin, *Zhou Enlai zaixiang shengya*, 126.
52. Wang Nianyi, "Guanyu eryue niliu de yixie zilian" (Some Facts about the February Adverse Current), *Dangshi yanjiu ziliao*, no. 1 (1990).
53. Ibid.
54. *Zhou Enlai nianpu, 1949–1976*, vol. 3, 127–130.
55. Gu et al., *Women de Zhou Zongli*, 45.
56. Barnouin and Yu, *Ten years of Turbulence*, 121; Thomas Robinson, *The Cultural Revolution in China* (Berkeley: University of California Press, 1971), 222.
57. Xiao Di, "Lishi burong wangji" (History Should Never Be Forgotten), *Landun*, no. 7 (1985).
58. Editorial Department of the *Zhonggong yanjiu* Press, *Zhonggong wenhua dageming zhongyao wenjian huibian*, 254.
59. Quan Yanchi, *Hongqiang neiwai* (Inside and Outside the Red Wall) (Beijing: Kunlun chubanshe, 1989), 107, 127; Quan Yanchi, *Zouxia shentan de Mao Zedong* (Mao Zedong Descends from His Shrine) (Beijing: Zhongwai wenhua chuban gongsi, 1989), 131.
60. Lin Qingshan, *Jiang Qing chenfu lu* (The Rise and Fall of Jiang Qing) (Beijing: Zhongguo xinwen chubanshe, 1988), 122.
61. Dong Baocun, *Yang Yu Fu shijian zhenxiang* (The Truth about the Yang-Yu-Fu Incident) (Beijing: Jiefangjun chubanshe, 1987), 83.
62. Li Tien-min, *Chou En-lai* (Taipei: Institute of International Relations, 1974), 343–344.
63. Barnouin and Yu, *Ten Years of Turbulence*, 43, 44.
64. Editorial Department of the *Zhonggong yanjiu* Press, *Zhonggong wenhua*

*dageming zhongyao wenjian huibian*, 237–240.

65. Text of Zhou's speech before the ninth Party congress, 1969, held at the library of Fairbank Center for East Asian Research, Harvard University.

66. Lin Biao's speech before the ninth Party congress, 1969 held at library of the Fairbank Center for East Asian Research, Harvard University.

67. Zhang, *Maijiawan jishi*, 99.

68. "Decision Instructing the PLA to Give Firm Support to the Revolutionary Left," in *History of the CCP*, 335.

69. Wang Li, *Xianchang lishi: Wenhua dageming jishi* (On the Scene of History: Chronicle of the Cultural Revolution) (Hong Kong: Oxford University Press, 1993), 39.

70. Chen Zaidao, "Wuhan qierling shijianxiang" (The Truth about the Wuhan Incident of 20 July), in Peng, *Zhongguo zhenju beiwanglu*, 25.

71. Wu Qingyong, *Zhou Enlai zai wenhua dageming zhong* (Zhou Enlai in the Cultural Revolution) (Beijing: Zhongtong dangshi chubanshi, 1998), 32.

72. Zhang Songshan, "Yi ge zhongyang zhuan'an zuzhang de chanhui" (Repentance of a Central Case Group Leader), *Yanhuang chunqiu*, no. 4 (1994), 23.

73. Song Renqiong, *Song Renqiong huiyilu* (The Memoirs of Song Renqiong) (Beijing: Jiefangjun chubanshe, 1996).

74. Li Ke and Hao Shengzhang, *Wenhua dageming zhong de renmin jiefangjun* (The People's Liberation Army in the Cultural Revolution) (Beijing: Zhongyang danshi ziliao chubanshe, 1989), 248.

75. Michael Schoenhals, "The Central Case Examination Group, 1966–1979," *The China Quarterly*, no. 145 (March 1996), 87–111.

76. Ye Yonglie, *Jiang Qing zhuan* (Biography of Jiang Qing) (Beijing: Zuojia chubanshe, 1993), 422.

77. Yang, *Zhonggong dangshi zhongda shijian shushi*, 265–267.

78. "Zhongyang shouzhang zhongyao jianghua" (Important Speeches by Central Leaders), 27 March 1968, *Waijiaobu dalianchou*, 1968, 5.

79. Liu Zhende, *Wo wei Shaoqi dang mishu* (I Worked as Shaoqi's Secretary) (Beijing: Zhongyang wenxian chubanshe, 1994), 285.

80. Editorial Department of the *Zhonggong yanjiu* Press, *Zhonggong wenhua dageming zhongyao wenjian huibian*, 237–240; Xu Xuan and Jin Chunming, *Wenhua dageming jianshi* (A Brief History of the Cultural Revolution) (Beijing: Zhonggong dangshi chubanshe, 1996), 196.

81. Quan Yanchi, *He Long yu Xue Ming* (He Long and Xue Ming) (Guangzhou: Guangdong luyou chubanshe, 1997), 369, 375.

82. Zhou, *Lishi zai zheli chensi*, vol. 1, 157, 160.

83.  An, *Zhou Enlai de zuihou suiyue*, 209.

84.  At that time, thirty-seven ministries and commissions, as well as some thirty special offices functioned under the State Council. They were divided into administrative systems, each of which was headed by a vice premier. Chen Yi was in charge of the foreign affairs system, which incorporated all ministries, special offices, and agencies dealing with political and trade relations with foreign countries and with overseas Chinese.

85.  An, *Zhou Enlai de zuihou suiyue*, 210–211.

86.  *Waishi fenglei* (Events in Foreign Relations), a Red Guard tabloid (Beijing: 12 August 1967).

87.  Tie Zhuwei, *Chen Yi yuanshuai zai wenhua dagemingzhong* (Marshal Chen Yi in the Cultural Revolution) (Beijing: Jiefangjun wenyi chubanshe, 1986), 171.

88.  Luo Yincai, "Chen Yi zai suowei eryue niliu zhong jiejian guiguo liuxuesheng daibiao" (Chen Yi Met with Representatives of Students Returned from Abroad), *Zhongyang wenxian*, no. 4 (1990), 65.

89.  In Cultural Revolution language, the degree of condemnation was expressed by different slogans. "Criticize and repudiate" (*pipan*) or "bombard" (*paohong*) implied that a person could be submitted to struggle sessions but that, if he confessed his mistakes, he would be reinstated in his position. "Down with" and "smash" (*daodong*) implied that a person would be removed from office. It was the latter fate that Zhou wanted to avoid for Chen Yi; see An, *Zhou Enlai de zuihou suiyue*, 222.

90.  Barnouin and Yu, *Ten Years of Turbulence*.

91.  *Waishi fenglei.*

92.  Author's interview with Zhang Dianqing, a former rebel leader at the Foreign Ministry, Beijing, March 1998.

93.  Ibid.,

94.  Barnouin and Yu, *Ten Years of Turbulence*, 143–150, 217–221; see also Tie, *Chen Yi yuanshuai zai wenhua dagemingzhong*, 257.

95.  Tie, *Chen Yi yuanshuai zai wenhua dagemingzhong*, 326.

96.  An article in the *People's Daily* stated that the Cultural Revolution "fundamentally defeated the global counterrevolutionary strategy of U.S. imperialism," which had always aimed at promoting "peaceful evolution" in China, and "prevented a big reverse and retrogression of world history; it has reopened that channel leading to communism that was blocked by modern revisionism, and advanced the international communist movement and world revolution to an entirely new stage." The article concluded that the Cultural Revolution "is a gigantic struggle of strategic importance between world revolutionary forces and counterrevolutionary forces." The article was

reprinted in *Peking Review*, no. 14 (1967).

97. Barbara Barnouin and Yu Changgen, *Chinese Foreign Policy During the Cultural Revolution* (London: Keagan Paul International 1997), 61.

98. Lu Dan, "Guoji tekui lieche zai bianchui xiaozhen beijie" (International Express Intercepted at a Small Border Town), *Yanhuang chunqiu*, no. 9 (1993).

99. Yang Zanxian, "Zhongguo liuxuesheng Mosike hongchang liuxueji" (The Bloodshed of Chinese Students at the Red Square in Moscow), *Bainiancao*, no. 3 (1998).

100. Barnouin and Yu, *Ten Years of Turbulence*, 69.

101. Yu Changgen, "Zhou Enlai yaokung fanying kangbao neimu" (The Inside Story of Hong Kong's Fight against the British Violent Suppression in 1967), *Jiushi niandai*, May, June, 1996.

102. Clare Hollingworth, *Mao* (London: Triad Paladin Grafton Books, 1987), 169; Barnouin and Yu, *Chinese Foreign Policy during the Cultural Revolution*, 71; Han et al., *Dangdai Zhongguo waijiao*, 211. The British chargé d'affaires, Donald Hopson, described the events in a letter to his wife, published in Hollingworth, *Mao*, 169

103. There is a discrepancy between Chinese and British records about the involvement of British diplomats in the incident. According to the *Times* of London, Donald Hopson was severely injured by the Red Guards. For his bravery, he was given an award by the Queen (see clippings of the *Times*). But at the meeting on the night of the twenty-second, neither the Beijing Garrison nor the Foreign Ministry reported to Zhou that British diplomats had been mistreated. According to them, the building was empty when the Red Guards broke into it. The British diplomats had apparently left through the garden (author interview with Zhang Jingnan, a team leader of the Red Flag Rebels Corps of the Red Guards of the Beijing Foreign Language Institute, who had himself stormed the building and confirmed that they found no one on the premises).

104. Liu Pingping et al., "Huainian women de baba Liu Shaoqi" (In Memory of Our Father Liu Shaoqi), in Zhou, *Lishi zai zheli chensi*, vol. 1, 31.

105. Quan Yanchi, *Yang Chengwu zai 1967* (Yang Chengwu in 1967) (Guangzhou: Guangdong luyou chubanshe, 1997), 179; *Zhou Enlai nianpu, 1949–1976*, vol. 3, 182.

106. *Zhou Enlai nianpu, 1949–1976*, vol. 3, 183; Wang, *Xianchang lishi*, 57.

107. "Zhongyang shouzhang zai Beijingshi geming weiyuanhui changwei kuoda huiyishang zhongyao jianghua" (Important Speeches of Central Leaders at the Enlarged Meeting of the Standing Committee of the Beijing

Revolutionary Committee on 1 September 1967), *Wenge xiaobao*, 1 September 1967.

108. *Renmin ribao*, 5 September 1967.

109. *Xinhua News Agency*, 9 September 1968.

110. The difficulty of reaching agreements within revolutionary committees is demonstrated in detail by the example of Hubei province and its provincial capital, Wuhan, in Wang Shaoguang, *Failure of Charisma* (Hong Kong: Oxford University Press, 1995), 193–195.

111. This was referred as the movement of "one smashing and three anti's" (*yida sanfan*) with the emphasis on the "destructive activities of counterrevolutionaries" (Hao and Duan, *Zhongguo gongchandang liushinian*, 609).

112. *Zhou Enlai nianpu, 1949–1976*, vol. 3, 347.

113. Wang, *Dadongluan de niandai*, 337.

114. Transcript of Zhou Enlai's speech at a meeting of the Political Department of a revolutionary committee in Jiangsu, 1967. (personal collection of a member of the Committee)

115. Among them were Xiao Hua, head of the General Political Department of the PLA; Yang Chengwu, acting general chief of staff; Yu Lijin, political commissar of the air force; Fu Chongbi, commander of the Beijing Garrison; and Wang Li, Guan Feng, and Qi Benyu, members of the CCRG.

116. Hao and Duan, *Zhongguo gongchandang liushinian*, 609.

117. Author's interview with several former Foreign Ministry rebels, Beijing, November 1998.

118. "Zongli guanyu jiushiyiren dazebaode zhongyao zhishi" (The Premier's Important Instructions to the Ninety-One Persons Who Wrote the Poster), Beijing, Foreign Ministry tabloid, February 1968.

119. *Zhou Enlai nianpu, 1949–1976*, vol. 3, 50.

120. Transcript of Ma Wenbo's speech of 20 March, 1870 at the Foreign Ministry. (private collection)

121. Author's interview with former rebel leaders, Beijing, March 1998.

122. *Zhou Enlai nianpu, 1949–1976*, vol. 3, 402, 406, 413, 433.

123. Author's interview with Yao Dengshan and others who belonged to the twenty "516 counterrevolutionaries" designated by Zhou Enlai, Beijing, March 1997 and 1998.

124. After the ninth Party congress, the remaining members of the CCRG were elected to the Politburo, where they represented what is here called the "Cultural Revolution faction." The CCRG thus became superfluous and dissolved.

125. Shao Yihai, *Lianhe jiandui de fumie* (The Collapse of the Joint Fleet) (Zhengzhou: Chunqiu chubanshe, 1988), 257–266, 290.

126. Guo Simin, *Wo yanzhong de Mao Zedong* (Mao as I Saw Him) (Shijiazhuang: Hebei renmin chubanshe, 1990), 255.

127. Xu Wenyi, "Lin Biao jihui renwang xiangchang ji" (On-the-Spot Investigation of Lin Biao's Air Crash), in Yu Gong, *Lin Biao shijian zhenxiang*, 157, 160, 164, 173.

128. Fu Hao, "Jiu yao san shijian bubai" (More about the 13 September Incident), in Pei, *Xin Zhongguo waijiao fengyun*, vol. 1, 181, 183; Shao, *Lianhe jiandui de fumie*, 293.

129. Li and Hao, *Wenhua dageming zhong de renmin jiefangjun*, 136–137.

130. Zhang Yufeng, "Mao Zedong Zhou Enlai wannian er san shi" (A few Remarks about Mao Zedong's and Zhou Enlai's Last Years), *Yanhuang zisun*, no. 1 (1989).

131. Jin, *Wenhua dageming shigao*, 348.

132. Li and Hao, *Wenhua dageming zhong de renmin jiefangjun*, 140.

133. An Jianshe, "Zhou Enlai lingdao 1972 nian qianhou pipan jizuo sichaode douzheng" (Zhou Enlai Led the Criticism of Ultraleftism in 1972), *Dangde wenxian*, no. 1 (1993), 24–25; Tong, *Fengyun sishinian*, vol. 2, 475.

134. Li, *Wenhua dageming zhong de Zhou Enlai*, 26, 29.

135. Song, *Song Renqiong huiyilu*; An, *Zhou Enlai de zuihou suiyue*, 307.

136. Tong, *Fengyun sishinian*, vol. 2, 472.

137. Li, *Kaiguo zongli Zhou Enlai*, 480–482; Jin, *Wenhua dageming shigao*, 350.

138. Wang Ruoshui, "Cong pizuo daoxiang fanyou" (From Criticizing "Left" to Opposing Right), *Mingbao yuekan*, no. 3 (1989), 5; An, "Zhou Enlai lingdao 1972 nian qianhou pipan jizuo sichao de douzheng," 27.

139. Peng, *Zhongguo zhengju beiwanglu*, 36; Jin, *Wenhua dageming shigao*, 354.

140. Wang, "Cong pizuo daoxiang fanyou," 8–10.

141. The Politburo of the tenth Central Committee comprised Mao Zedong and the veteran revolutionaries: Zhou Enlai, Wei Guoqing, Ye Jianying, Liu Bocheng, Zhu De, Xu Shiyou, Chen Xilian, Li Xiannian, Li Desheng, and Dong Biwu; the radicals: Kang Sheng, Jiang Qing, Wang Hongwen, Zhang Chunqiao, and Yao Wenyuan; those in the "gray zone" were Hua Guofeng, Ji Dengkui, Wu De, Wang Dongxing, and Chen Yonggui. See Barnouin and Yu, *Ten Years of Turbulence*, 251.

142. Hao and Duan, *Zhongguo gongchandang liushinian*, 632.

143. *Peking Review*, no. 15 (1965).

144. Barnouin and Yu, *Chinese Foreign Policy during the Cultural Revolution*, 86–90.

145. Ibid.
146. Chen Dengde, *Mao Zedong + Nikesen zai 1972* (Mao Zedong and Nixon in 1972) (Beijing: Kunlun chubanshe, 1988), 33.
147. Barnouin and Yu, *Foreign Policy during the Cultural Revolution*, 94–95.
148. Ibid., 63–64, 100.
149. Chen, *Mao Zedong + Nikesen zai 1972*, 16.
150. Ibid., 64.
151. *Zhou Enlai nianpu, 1949–1976*, vol. 2, 207; Wang, *Da dongluan de niandai*, 458–560.
152. Ibid., 250, 398, 456–457.
153. *Zhou Enlai nianpu, 1949–1976*, 450.
154. Ibid., 438–440.
155. Xu Dashen, ed., *Zhonghua renmin gongheguo shilu* (Changchun: Jilin renmin chubanshe, 1994), 603–604, 637, 662, 732.
156. Geng Biao, *Huiyi lu (1949–1992)*(Geng Biao's Reminiscnece) (Nanjing: Jiangsu renmin chubanshe, 1998), 241–242.
157. *Zhou Enlai nianpu, 1949–1976*, 265.
158. Snow, *The Long Revolution*, 171–173.
159. Barnouin and Yu, *Foreign Policy during the Cultural Revolution*, 101.
160. *Zhou Enlai nianpu, 1949–1976*, 341.
161. Ibid., 356; Qian Jiang, "Dui dakai zhong-mei guanxi qi zhongyao zuoyang de Bajisitan qudao" (The Important Role of the Pakistani Channel in the Breakthrough of the Sino-American Relations), *Zhongheng*, no. 6 (1998).
162. *Diaoyutai dang'an*, vol. 1, 361–363.
163. John H. Holdridge, *Crossing the Divide: An Insider's Account of the Normalization of U.S.-China Relations* (Lanham, MD: Rowman & Littlefield, 1997), 48.
164. *Diaoyutai dang'an*, vol. 1, 362; Qian Jiang, *Pingpang waijiao shimo* (The Story of Ping-Pong Diplomacy) (Beijing: Dongfang chubanshe, 1987), 120–158.
165. Kissinger, *The White House Years*, 725.
166. Barnouin and Yu, *Chinese Foreign Policy*, 104–105.
167. Wei Shiyan, "Kissinger mimi fang hua neimu" (With Kissinger on His Secret Visit to China), in Liu, *Zhonggong dangshi fengyunlu*, 113–114; Kissinger, *The White House Years*, 750.
168. Kissinger, *The White House Years*, 752.
169. Xiong Xianghui, "Mao Zedong meiyou xiangdaode shengli" (A Victory Mao Did Not Expect), *Bainianchao*, no. 1 (1997); Weng Ming, *Waijiaoguan zai liangheguo* (The Foreign Minister's First Visit to the

United Nations) (Beijing: Zhongguo huaqiao chubanshe, 1995), 7–9.

170. Barnouin and Yu, *Chinese Foreign Policy During the Cultural Revolution*, 108–109.

171. Ibid., 110–111.

172. *Zhou Enlai nianpu, 1949–1976*, vol. 3, 603–604.

173. Henry Kissinger, *Years of Upheaval* (New York: Little, Brown and Co., 1982), 182, 698.

174. Barnouin and Yu, *Foreign Policy during the Cultural Revolution*, 111.

175. Zhang Zuoliang, "Zhou Enlai de zuihou 1,323 tian" (Zhou Enlai's Last 1,323 Days), *Zhongguo zuojia*, no. 1 (1997).

176. Li Zhisui, *The Private Life of Chairman Mao* (New York: Random House, 1994), 572–573.

177. Zhang, "Zhou Enlai de 1,323 tian."

178. Li, *Private Life of Chairman Mao*, 580–581.

179. Barnouin and Yu, *Ten Years of Turbulence*, 2.

180. Gao Gao and Yan Jianqi, *Wenhua dageming shinian shi* (A History of the Ten-Year Cultural Revolution) (Tianjin: Tianjin renmin chubanshe, 1986), 480.

181. Wang, *Dadongluan de niandai*, 484, 488.

182. Ma Jisen, *The Cultural Revolution in the Foreign Ministry of China* (Hong Kong: The Chinese University Press, 2004), 353, 360.

183. Ibid., 362.

184. Author's Interview with Zhang Hanzhi, Qiao Guanhua's widow, Beijing, March 1998.

185. Peng, *Zhongguo zhengju beiwanglu*, 38–39; *History of the CCP*, 362–364.

186. Wang, *Dadongluan de niandai*, 438, 469.

187. Zhang, "Zhou Enlai de 1,323 tian."

188. Barnouin and Yu, *Ten Years of Turbulence*, 268–269.

189. Li, *Private Life of Chairman Mao*, 592.

190. *History of the CCP*, 364–365.

191. Su Caiqing, "Sirenbang dui Deng Xiaoping chuxi lianda zhi jienan" (The Attempts of the Gang of Four to Prevent Deng Xiaoping from Going to New York), *Zhonggong dangshi cailiao*, no. 58 (1996); Peng, *Zhongguo zhengju beiwanglu*, 41.

192. Tong, *Fengyun sishinian*, 536.

193. Ye Yongli, *Wang Hongwen xingshuailai* (The Vicissitudes of Wang Hongwen) (Changchun: Shidai wenyi chubanshe, 1989), 409.

194. Tong, *Fengyun sishinian*, 537; An, *Zhou Enlai de zuihou suiyue*, 332.

195. Peng, *Zhongguo zhengju beiwanglu*, 45–46; Gao and Yan, *Wenhua dageming*

*shinian shi*, 75.

196. Zhang, "Zhou Enlai de 1,323 tian."

197. Peng, *Zhongguo zhengju beiwanglu*, 46–47; *History of the CCP*, 366.

198. Peng, *Zhongguo zhengju beiwanglu*, 48.

199. Zhou, *Lishi zai zheli chensi*, vol. 1, 77; Peng, *Zhongguo zhengju beiwanglu*, 50.

200. Ibid., 49–51.

201. Jia Sinan, ed., *Mao Zedong renji jiaowang shilu* (Mao's Relations with Other People) (Nanjing: Jiangsu wenyi chubanshe, 1989), 353–355.

202. Fang and Fang, *Zhou Enlai: A Profile*, 189–190.

203. Zhang, "Zhou Enlai de 1,323 tian."

204. Zhou, *Lishi zai zheli chensi*, vol. 1, 79.

205. Barnouin and Yu, *Ten Years of Turbulence*, 287.

206. Quan, *Zouxia shentan de Zhou Enlai*, 399.

207. Tong, *Fengyun sishinian*, vol. 2, 566; Zhou, *Lishi zai zheli chensi*, vol. 1, 77.

208. Quan Ye, "Zhou Enlai shishi quangguocheng jishi" (A Full Account of Zhou Enlai's Death), *Yanhuang zisun* (September 1989).

# Selected Bibliography

**Books**

An Jianshe. *Zhou Enlai de zuihou suiyue, 1966–1976* (Zhou Enlai's Final Years, 1966–1976). Beijing: Zhongyang wenxian chubanshe, 1995.

Bai Shouyi (ed.). *An Outline History of China, 1919–1949*. Beijing: Foreign Languages Press, 1993.

Banac, Ivo (ed.). *The Diary of Georgi Dimitrov, 1933–1949*. New Haven and London: Yale University Press, 2003.

Barnouin, Barbara, and Yu Changgen. *Ten Years of Turbulence: The Chinese Cultural Revolution*. London: Keagan Paul International, 1993.

———. *Chinese Foreign Policy during the Cultural Revolution*. London: Keagan Paul International, 1997.

Bo Yibo. *Ruogan zhongda juece yu shijian de huigu* (Recollections on Some Important Decisions and Events). 2 vols. Beijing: Zhonggong dangxiao chubanshe, vol. 1, 1991; vol. 2, 1993.

Braun, Otto. *Comintern Agent in China, 1932–1939*. London: Hurst, 1982.

Cadart, Claude, and Cheng Yingxiang. *Mémoires de Peng Shuzhi: envol du communism en Chine*. Paris: Gallimard, 1983.

Cai Kaisong et al. (eds.). *Zhou Enlai de gushi* (Stories about Zhou Enlai). Beijing: Zhonggong dangshi chubanshe, 1993.

Cao Hua et al. *Da kang zheng* (Big Confrontation). Beijing: Tuanjie chubanshe, 1993.

Cao Yingwang (ed.). *Zhou Enlai de zhihui* (Zhou Enlai's Intelligence). Beijing: Zhonggong zhongyang dangxiao chubanshe, 1994.

Chai Chengwen, and Zhao Yongtian. *Banmendian tanpan* (Panmunjom Negotiations). Beijing: Jiefangjun chubanshe, 1992.

Chang Kuo-t'ao. *The Rise of the Chinese Communist Party, 1921–1927*. Lawrence: University Press of Kansas, 1971.

Chen Dengdee. *Mao Zedong + Nixon zai 1972* (Mao Zedong and Nixon in 1972). Beijing: Kunlun chubanshe, 1988.

Chen Huangmei (ed.). *Zhou Enlai yu yishujiamen* (Zhou Enlai and Artists). Beijing: Zhongyang wenxian chubanshe, 1992.

Chen Shiyu et al. *Zhonggong dangshi zhongda shijian shushi* (Major Events in the History of the Chinese Communist Party). Beijing: Renmin chubanshe, 1993.

Cheng Hua (ed.). *Zhou Enlai he ta de mishumen* (Zhou Enlai and His Secretaries). Beijing: Zhongguo guangbo dianshi chubanshe, 1992.

*China's Foreign Relations: A Chronology of Events: 1949–1988*. Beijing: Foreign Languages Press, 1989.

Chow Tse-tsung. *The May Fourth Movement: Intellectual Revolutionaries in Modern China*. Cambridge, MA: Harvard University Press, 1960.

Cold War International History Project. "Rivals and Allies: Stalin, Mao, and the Chinese Civil War, January 1949." *Cold War International History Project Bulletin*, issue 6–7 (Winter 1995/96).

Cong Jin. *Quzhe fazhan de suiyue* (Years of Politics with Changing Directions). Zhengzhou: Henan renmin chubanshe, 1989.

Cui Qi (ed.). *Zhou Enlai zhenglun xuan* (Selected Articles of Zhou Enlai on Politics). Beijing: Zhongyang wenxian chubanshe, 1993.

Deng Xiaoping. *Selected Works of Deng Xiaoping*. 3 vols. Beijing: Foreign Languages Press, vol. 1, 1992; vol. 2, 1994; vol. 3, 1995.

Dian Dian. *Feifan de niandai* (Extraordinary Years). Shanghai: Shanghai wenyi chubanshe, 1992.

Dong Baocun. *Yang Yu Fu shijian zhenxiang* (The Truth about the Yang-Yu-Fu Incident). Beijing: Jiefangjun chubanshe, 1987.

———. *Zai lishi de xuanwozhong* (In the Whirlpools of History). Beijing: Zhongwai wenhua chubanshe, 1990.

———. *Tan Zhenlin waizhuan* (An Unofficial Biography of Tan Zhenlin). Beijing: Zuojia chubanshe, 1991.

Dong Bian. *Mao Zedong he ta de mishu Tian Jiaying* (Mao Zedong and His Secretary Tian Jiaying). Beijing: Zhongyang wenxian chubanshe, 1990.

Dreyer, Edward L. *China at War, 1901–1949*. London: Longman, 1995.

Editorial Department of the *Zhonggong yanjiu* Press (comp.). *Zhonggong wenhua dageming zhongyao wenjian huibian* (A Collection of Important Documents on the Cultural Revolution). Taipei: Zhonggong yanjiu zazhishe, 1973.

Faligot, Roger, and Remi Kauffer. *Kang Sheng et les services secrets chinois, 1927–1987*. Paris: Robert Laffont, 1987.

Fan Shuo. *Ye Jianying zai 1976* (Ye Jianying in 1976). Beijing: Zhonggong zhongyang dangxiao chubanshe, 1990.

Fan Xiao (ed.). *Zhonggong dangshi bianyilu* (Controversial Issues in CCP History). Taiyuan: Shanxi jiaoyu chubanshe, 1992.

Fang Ke, and Dan Mu. *Zhonggong qingbao shounao Li Kenong* (CCP Intelligence Chief Li Kenong). Beijing: Zhongguo shehui kexue chubanshe, 1996.

Fang, Percy Jucheng, and Lucy Guinong Fang. *Zhou Enlai: A Profile*. Beijing: Foreign Languages Press, 1986.

Gao Gao, and Yan Jiaqi. *Wenhua dageming shinian shi* (A History of the Ten-Year Cultural Revolution). Tianjin: Tianjin renmin chubanshe, 1986.

Gao Wenqian. *Wannian Zhou Enlai* (Zhou Enlai in His Later Years). New York: Mingjing chubanshe, 2003.

Gao Xin, and He Pin. *Gaogan dang'an* (Biographies of High-Ranking Cadres). Taipei: Xinwen wenhua gongsi, 1993.

Goldman, Merle. *China's Intellectuals: Advise and Dissent*. Cambridge, MA: Harvard University Press, 1981.

Goncharov, Sergei N., John W. Lewis, and Xue Litai. *Uncertain Partners: Stalin, Mao and the Korean War*. Stanford: Stanford University Press, 1993.

*Gongheguo zouguo de lu—jianguo yilai zhongyao wenxian xuanbian* (The Road of the Republic—Important Documents Since the Founding of the PRC). Beijing: Zhongyang wenxian chubanshe, 1991.

Gu Baozi. *Hongqiang li de shunjian* (A Flash Inside the Red Walls). Beijing: Jiefangjun wenyi chubanshe, 1992.

Gu Mu et al. *Women de Zhou Zongli* (Our Premier Zhou). Beijing: Zhongyang wenxian chubanshe, 1991.

Guan Weixun. *Wo suo zhidao de Ye Qun* (Ye Qun as I Knew Her). Beijing: Zhongguo wenxue chubanshe, 1993.

*Guanyu jianguo yilai dang de ruogan lishi wenti de jueyi* (Resolution on Certain Questions in CCP History Since the Founding of the PRC). Beijing: Renmin chubanshe, 1985.

Guo Simin (ed.). *Wo yanzhong de Mao Zedong* (Mao Zedong as I Saw Him). Shijiazhuang: Hebei renmin chubanshe, 1990.

———. *Wo yanzhong de Zhou Enlai* (Zhou Enlai as I Saw Him). Shijiazhuang: Hebei renmin chubanshe, 1993.

Han Nianlong et al. (ed.). *Dangdai Zhongguo waijiao* (Contemporary Chinese Diplomacy). Beijing: Zhonguo shehui kexue chubanshe, 1992.

Han Suyin. *Eldest Son: Zhou Enlai and the Making of Modern China, 1898–1976*. London: Pimlico, 1994.

Hao Mengbi, and Duan Haoran (eds.). *Zhongguo gongchandang liushinian* (Sixty Years of the CCP). Beijing: Jiefangjun chubanshe, 1984.

Hei Yannan. *Shinian dongluan* (A Decade of Turbulence). Xi'an: Guoji wenhua chuban gongsi, 1988.

Heinzig, Dieter. *Sowietische Militarberater bei der Kuomintang 1923–1927*. Baden-Baden: Nomos Verlagsgesellschaft, 1978.

Hong Xuezhi. *Kang Mei yuan Chao zhanzheng huiyi* (Recollections of the War to Resist U.S. Aggression and Aid Korea). Beijing: Jiefangjun wenyi chubanshe, 1991.

Hu Qiaomu. *Hu Qiaomu huiyi Mao Zedong* (Hu Qiaomu Recalls Mao Zedong). Beijing: Renmin chubanshe, 1994.

Hu Hua. *The Early Life of Zhou Enlai*. Beijing: Foreign Languages Press, 1980.

Hu Sheng. *A Concise History of the Communist Party of China*. Beijing: Foreign Languages Press, 1994.

———. *Diguozhuyi yu Zhongguo zhengzhi* (Imperialism and Chinese Politics). Beijing: Renmin chubanshe, 1978.

Hu Shiyan et al. *Chen Yi zhuan* (Biography of Chen Yi). Beijing: Dangdai Zhongguo chubanshe, 1991.

Huang Zheng (ed.). *Liu Shaoqi de zuihou suiyue, 1966–1969* (Liu Shaoqi's Final Years, 1966–1969). Beijing: Zhongyang wenxian chubanshe, 1996.

Hunt, Michael H. *The Genesis of Chinese Communist Foreign Policy*. New York: Columbia University Press, 1996.

Hsiao Tso-liang. *Power Relations within the Chinese Communist Movement, 1930–1934*. Seattle: University of Washington Press, 1961.

Hsu, Kai-yu. *Chou Enlai: China's Grey Eminence*. Garden City, NY: Doubleday, 1968.

Jacobs, Dan N. *Borodin, Stalin's Man in China*. Cambridge, MA: Harvard University Press, 1981.

Ji Ming et al. *Zhou Enlai de waijiao yishu* (Zhou Enlai's Diplomacy). Jinan: Shandong daxue chubanshe, 1992.

Jia Sinan. *Mao Zedong renji jiaowang shilu* (Mao's Relations with Other

People). Nanjing: Jiangsu wenyi chubanshe, 1989.

Jin Chongji et al. (eds.). *Zhou Enlai zhuan, 1898–1949* (Biography of Zhou Enlai, 1898–1949). Beijing: Zhongyang wenxian chubanshe, 1989.

———. *Zhou Enlai zhuan, 1949–1976* (Biography of Zhou Enlai, 1949–1976), 2 vols. Beijing: Zhongyang wenxian chubanshe, 1998.

Jin Chunming. *Wenhua dageming shigao* (A Preliminary History of the Cultural Revolution). Chengdu: Sichuan renmin chubanshe, 1995.

——— et al. *Wenge shiqi guaishi guaiyu* (The Absurdities of the Cultural Revolution). Beijing: Qiushi chubanshe, 1989.

Jin Feng. *Deng Yingchao zhuan* (Biography of Deng Yinchao). Beijing: Renmin chubanshe, 1993.

Kapur, Harish. *The Awakening Giant: China's Ascension in World Politics*. Alpen Aan Den Rijn: Sifthoff and Noordhoff, 1981

Keith, Ronald C. *The Diplomacy of Zhou Enlai*. London: MacMillan, 1990.

Kissinger, Henry. *The White House Years*. Boston: Little, Brown, 1979.

———. *Years of Upheaval*. New York: Little, Brown and Co., 1982.

Kolakowski, Leszek. *Main Currents of Marxism: Its Origins, Growth and Dissolution*. 3 vols. Oxford: Oxford University Press, 1987.

Kuo, Warren. *Analytical History of the Chinese Communist Party*, book 4. Taipei: Institute of International Relations, 1971.

Lee, Chae-Jin. *Zhou Enlai: The Early Years*. Stanford: Stanford University Press, 1994.

Li Hong et al. (ed.). *Zhou Enlai he Deng Yingchao* (Zhou Enlai and Deng Yingchao). Beijing: Zhonggong zhongyang dangxiao chubanshe, 1994.

Li Jian. *Zhongnanhai yongtanlu* (Zhongnanhai Aria). Beijing: Beijing shifan daxue chubanshe, 1992.

Li Ke, and Hao Shengzhang. *Wenhua dageming zhong de renmin jiefangjun* (The People's Liberation Army in the Cultural Revolution). Beijing: Zhonggong dangshi ziliao chubanshe, 1989.

Li Maosheng. *Kong Xiangxi zhuan* (Biography of H.H. Kung). Beijing: Zhongguo guangbo dianshi chubanshe, 1992.

Li Ping. *Kaiguo zongli Zhou Enlai* (Zhou Enlai, The First Premier of the Nation). Beijing: Zhonggong zhongyang dangxiao chubanshe, 1994.

———. *Wenhua dageming zhong de Zhou Enlai* (Zhou Enlai in the Cultural Revolution). Beijing: Zhonggong zhongyang dangxiao chubanshe, 1991.

Li Qi (ed.). *Zai Zhou Enlai shenbian de rizi* (My Days Working for Zhou Enlai). Beijing: Zhongyang wenxian chubanshe, 1998.

Li Rui. *Dayuejin qinli* (My Personal Experiences in the Great Leap Forward). Shanghai: Shanghai yandong chubanshe, 1996.

———. *Lushan huiyi shilu* (A Factual Record of the Lushan Conference). Hunan: Chunqiu chubanshe, 1988.

Li Tien-min. *Chou En-lai*. Taipei: Institute of International Relations, 1974.

Li Weihan. *Huiyi yu yanjiu* (Recollections and Studies). Beijing: Zhonggong dangshi ziliao chubanshe, 1986.

Li Xiannian et al. *Bujin de sinian* (Endless Memories). Beijing: Zhongyang wenxian chubanshe, 1987.

Li Yinqiao. *Zai Mao Zedong shenbian shiwunian* (Fifteen Years with Mao Zedong). Shijiazhuang: Hebei renmin chubanshe, 1991.

Li Zhisui. *The Private Life of Chairman Mao*. New York: Random House, 1994.

Liao Xinwen (ed.). *Qingyi yu shiye zai Zhou Enlai xinzhong* (Zhou Enlai: Friendship and Cause). Beijing: Zhongyang wenxian chubanshe, 1991.

*Lin fuzhuxi zai jiuda jianghua* (Vice Chairman Lin's Speech at the Ninth Party Congress). Kunming junqu zhengzhibu yin, 1969.

Lin Qing. *Zhou Enlai zaixiang shengya* (Zhou Enlai's Premiership). Beijing: Changcheng wenhua chuban gongsi, 1991.

Lin Qingshan. *Fengyun shinian yu Deng Xiaoping* (Ten Years of Turmoil and Deng Xiaoping). Beijing: Jiefangjun chubanshe, 1989.

———. *Jiang Qing chenfu lu* (The Rise and Fall of Jiang Qing). Beijing: Zhongguo xinwen chubanshe, 1988.

———. *Lin Biao zhuan* (Biography of Lin Biao). Beijing: Zhishi chubanshe, 1988.

Lin Yunhui et al. *Kaige xingjin de shiqi* (Times of Marching in Triumph). Zhengzhou: Henan renmin chubanshe, 1989.

Liu Bingrong. *Suqu sufan da jishi* (Facts about the Elimination of Counterrevolutionaries in the Soviet Areas). 2 vols. Shijiazhuang: Huashan wenyi chubanshe, 1993.

Liu Jingshan et al. *Zhou Enlai de guanli yishu* (Zhou Enlai's Talent for Administration). Jinan: Shandong daxue chubanshe, 1992.

———. *Zhou Enlai de siwei yishu* (Zhou Enlai's Way of Thinking). Jinan: Shandong daxue chubanshe, 1992.

Liu Jintian, and Shen Xueming (ed.). *Lijie zhonggong zhongyang weiyuan renmin cidian, 1921–1987* (Biographies of CCP Central

Committee Members, 1921–1987). Beijing: Zhonggong dangshi chubanshe, 1992.

Liu Shaoqi. *Liu Shaoqi xuanji* (Selected Works of Liu Shaoqi). Beijing: Renmin chubanshe, 1985.

Liu Suinian, and Wu Qungan. *China's Socialist Economy: An Outline History 1949–1984.* Beijing: Beijing Review, 1986.

Liu Wusheng (ed.). *Zhonggong dangshi fengyunlu* (Major Events in CCP History). Beijing: Renmin chubanshe, 1990.

Liu Yan, and Mi Zhenbo. *Zhou Enlai yanjiu wenxuan* (Selected Articles on Zhou Enlai). Tianjin: Nankai daxue chubanshe, 1987.

Liu Yan et al. *Zhongwai xuezhe lun Zhou Enlai* (Chinese and Foreign Scholars on Zhou Enlai). Tianjin: Nankai daxue chubanshe, 1990.

Liu Zhende. *Wo wei Shaoqi dang mishu* (I Worked as [Liu] Shaoqi's Secretary). Beijing: Zhongyang wenxian chubanshe, 1994.

Lu Rongbin. *Zhou Enlai zai guotongqu* (Zhou Enlai in Guomindang Areas). Beijing: Zhonggong zhongyang dangxiao chubanshe, 1996.

Lu Xingdou (ed.). *Zhou Enlai he ta de shiye* (Zhou Enlai and His Cause). Beijing: Zhonggong dangshi chubanshe, 1990.

MacFarquhar, Roderick. *The Origins of the Cultural Revolution.* 3 vols. London: Oxford University Press; New York: Columbia University Press, vols. 1 and 2, 1983; vol. 3, 1997.

———, and John K. Fairbank (vol. eds.). *The Cambridge History of China*, vols. 14. Cambridge: Cambridge University Press, 1987.

*Mao Zedong Biography: Assessment, Reminiscences.* Beijing: Foreign Languages Press, 1986.

Mao Zedong. *Jianguo yilai Mao Zedong wengao* (Mao Zedong's Writings since the Founding of the PRC). 13 vols. Beijing: Zhongyang wenxian chubanshe, 1987–1996.

———. *Mao zhuxi shici* (Chairman Mao's Poems). Beijing: Renmin wenxue chubanshe, 1974.

———. *Selected Works of Mao Zedong.* 5 vols. Beijing: Foreign Languages Press, vols. 1–4, 1965; vol. 5, 1977.

Maxwell, Neville. *India's China War.* London: Jonathan Cape, 1970.

McNamara, Robert. *In Retrospect: The Tragedy and Lessons of Vietnam.* New York: Vintage Books, 1996.

Nan Xingzhou. *Zhou Enlai yisheng* (The Life of Zhou Enlai). Beijing: Zhongguo qingnian chubanshe, 1987.

Nathan, Andrew J. The Great Wall and the Empty Fortress. New York: W.W. Norton, 1997.

Nie Rongzhen. *Inside the Red Star: The Memoirs of Marshal Nie Rongzhen*. Beijing: New World Press, 1988.

Party History Research Center of the Central Conmmittee of the Chinese Communist Party, comp. *History of the Chinese Communist Party: A Chronology of Events, 1919–1990*. Beijing: Foreign Languages Press, 1991.

Pei Jianzhang (ed.). *Yanjiu Zhou Enlai: Waijiao sixiang yu shijian* (Studies on Zhou Enlai: Thought and Practice in Foreign Affairs). Beijing: Shijie zhishi chubanshe, 1989.

———. *Xin Zhongguo waijiao fengyun* (Major Events in New China's Foreign Relations). 3 vols. Beijing: Shijie zhishi chubanshe, vol. 1, 1990; vol. 2, 1991; vol. 3, 1994.

Peng Cheng. *Zhongguo zhengju beiwanglu* (A Memorandum on the Chinese Political Situation). Beijing: Jiefangjun chubanshe, 1989.

Peng Dehuai. *Memoirs of a Chinese Marshal*. Beijing: Foreign Languages Press, 1984.

*The Polemics on the General Line of the International Communist Movement*. Beijing: Foreign Languages Press, 1965.

Qian Jiang. *Pingpang waijiao shimo* (The Story of Ping-Pong Diplomacy). Beijing: Dongfang chubanshe, 1987.

Qin Xiaoying et al. *Buxu chuan junzhuang de jiangjun* (A General Deprived of His Uniform). Beijing: Huaxia chubanshe, 1988.

Quan Yanchi. *He Long yu Xue Ming* (He Long and Xue Ming). Guangzhou: Guangdong luyou chubanshe, 1997.

———. *Hongqiang neiwai* (Inside and Outside the Red Walls). Beijing: Kunlun chubanshe, 1989.

———. *Tao Zhu zai wenhua dageming zhong* (Tao Zhu in the Cultural Revolution). Beijing: Zhonggong zhongyang dangxiao chubanshe, 1991.

———. *Yang Chengwu zai 1967* (Yang Chengwu in 1967). Guangzhou: Guangdong luyou chubanshe, 1997.

———. *Zouxia shentan de Mao Zedong* (Mao Zedong Descends from His Shrine). Beijing: Zhongwai wenhua chuban gongsi, 1989.

———. *Zouxia shentan de Zhou Enlai* (Zhou Enlai Descends from His Shrine). Beijing: Zhonggong zhongyang dangxiao chubanshe, 1993.

*Quotations from Chairman Mao Tse-tung*. Beijing: Foreign Languages Press, 1968.

*Resolution on CCP History, 1949–81*. Beijing: Foreign Languages Press, 1981.

Robinson, Thomas. *The Cultural Revolution in China.* Berkeley: University of California Press, 1971.

Salisbury, Harrison. *The Long March: The Untold Story.* New York: McGraw-Hill, 1987.

Schram, Stuart. *Mao Tse-tung Unrehearsed.* Harmondsworth, UK: Penguin, 1974.

Schwartz, Benjamin I. *Chinese Communism and the Rise of Mao.* Cambridge, MA: Harvard University Press, 1951.

Seagrave, Sterling. *The Soong Dynasty.* London: Sidgwick and Jackson, 1985.

*Selected Articles: Criticizing Lin Biao and Confucius.* 2 vols. Beijing: Foreign Languages Press, vol. 1, 1974; vol. 2, 1975.

Shan Shaojie. *Mao Zedong zhizheng chunqiu, 1949–1976* (Mao in Power, 1949–1976). Hong Kong: Mingjing chubanshe, 2001.

Shao, Kuo-kang. *Zhou Enlai and the Foundations of Chinese Foreign Policy.* Houndmills and London, UK: Macmillan, 1996.

Shao Yihai. *Lianhe jiandui de fumie* (The Collapse of the Joint Fleet). Zhengzhou: Chunqiu chubanshe, 1988.

Sheng Yue. *Mosike zhongshan daxue he Zhongguo geming* (Sun Yat-sen University in Moscow and the Chinese Revolution). Beijing: Dangdai lishi ziliao chubanshe, 1980.

Shi Shanyu et al. *Dangshi zhishi jicheng, 1921–1991* (A Collection of Major Events in CCP History, 1921–1991). Beijing: Changzheng chubanshe, 1991.

Shi Zhe. *Zai lishi juren shenbian* (Working Beside a Historical Giant). Beijing: Zhongyang wenxian chubanshe, 1991.

Short, Philip. *Mao: A Life.* New York: Henry Holt, 1999.

Shuai Dongbing. *Peng Zhen zai wenhua dageming qianxi* (Peng Zhen on the Eve of the Cultural Revolution). Beijing: Zhonggong zhongyang dangxiao chubanshe, 1993.

Shum, Kui-Kwong. *The Chinese Communists' Road to Power: The Anti-Japanese National United Front, 1935–1945.* Hong Kong: Oxford University Press, 1988.

Si Ren et al. *Wenhua dageming fengyun renwu fangtanlu* (Interviews with Men of the Cultural Revolution). Beijing: Zhongyang minzu xueyuan chubanshe, 1993.

Snow, Edgar. *The Long Revolution.* New York: Random House, 1971.

———. *Red Star over China.* Harmondsworth, UK: Penguin Books, 1978.

Song Renqiong. *Song Renqiong huiyilu* (The Memoirs of Song Renqiong). Beijing: Jiefangjun chubanshe, 1996.

Spence, Jonathan. *The Gate of Heavenly Peace: The Chinese and Their Revolution 1895–1980*. Harmondsworth, UK: Penguin Books, 1982.

Stranahan, Patricia. *Underground: The Shanghai Communist Party and the Politics of Survival*. Lanham, MD: Rowman and Littlefield, 1998.

Su Kaiming. *Modern China: A Topical History, 1840–1983*. Beijing: New World Press, 1985.

Tan Zongji et al. *Shinian hou de pingshuo* (Critical Comments after Ten Years). Beijing: Dangshi ziliao chubanshe, 1987.

*The Tenth National Congress of the CCP: Documents*. Beijing: Foreign Languages Press, 1973.

Tie Zhuwei. *Chen Yi yuanshuai zai wenhua dageming zhong* (Marshal Chen Yi in the Cultural Revolution). Beijing: Jiefangjun wenyi chubanshe, 1986.

Tong Xiaopeng. *Fengyun sishinian* (Forty Stormy Years). Beijing: Zhongyang wenxian chubanshe, 1996.

Tu Men, and Kong Di. *Gongheguo zuida yuan'an* (The Cases of the Largest Injustice in the Republic). Beijing: Falue chubanshe, 1993.

Tuchman, Barbara W. *Stilwell and the American Experience in China, 1911–45*. Toronto: Bantam Books, 1972.

Twitchett, Denis, and John K. Fairbank (vol. eds.). *The Cambridge History of China*, vol. 12, part 1. Cambridge: Cambridge University Press, 1983.

U.S. Department of State. *United States Relations with China, with Special Reference to the Period 1944–1949*. Washington, DC: GPO, 1949. [Reissued by Lyman Van Slyke as *China White Paper*, 2 vols. Stanford: Stanford University Press, 1967.]

Wakeman, Frederic. *Policing Shanghai, 1927–1937*. Berkeley: University of California Press, 1996.

Wang Dongxing. *Mao Zedong yu Lin Biao fangeming jituan de douzheng* (Mao Zedong's Struggle with Lin Biao's Counterrevolutionary Group). Beijing: Zhongyang wenxian chubanshe, 1997.

Wang Li. *Xianchang lishi: Wenhua dageming jishi* (On the Scene of History: Chronicle of the Cultural Revolution). Hong Kong: Oxford University Press, 1993.

Wang Nianyi. *Dadongluan de niandai* (Years of Turmoil). Zhengzhou: Henan renmin chubanshe, 1988.

Wang Yan et al. *Peng Dehuai zhuan* (Biography of Peng Dehuai). Beijing:

Dangdai Zhongguo chubanshe, 1993.

Wang Yongsheng et al. *Zhou Enlai de yuyan yishu* (Zhou Enlai, A Master of Languages). Jinan: Shandong daxue chubanshe, 1992.

Wen Lequn et al. *Wenge zhong de mingren zhisheng* (Rising Stars during the Cultural Revolution). Beijing: Zhongyang minzu xueyuan chubanshe, 1993.

Wei, William. *Counterrevolution in China: The Nationalists in Jiangxi during the Soviet Period*. Ann Arbor: University of Michigan Press, 1985.

*Wenxian he yanjiu* (Documents and Studies). Beijing: Zhongyang wenxian chubanshe, 1987.

White, Theodore H. *In Search of History: A Personal Adventure*. New York: Harper & Row, 1978.

Whitson, William W. *The Chinese High Command: A History of Chinese Communist Military Politics, 1927–71*. New York: Praeger, 1973.

Wilbur, C. Martin. *The Nationalist Revolution in China, 1923–1928*. Cambridge: Cambridge University Press, 1983.

———, and How Julie Lien-ying. *Documents on Communism, Nationalism, and Soviet Advisers in China, 1918–1927: Papers Seized in the 1927 Peking Raid*. New York: Columbia University Press, 1956.

———. *Missionaries of Revolution: Soviet Advisers and Nationalist China, 1920–1927*. Cambridge, MA: Harvard University Press, 1989.

Wilson, Dick. *The Long March, 1935*. Harmondsworth, UK: Penguin Books, 1971.

———. *China's Revolutionary War*. London: Weidenfeld and Nicholson, 1991.

———. *Zhou Enlai, A Biography*. New York, Viking, 1984

Witke, Roxane. *Comrade Chiang Ch'ing*. Boston: Little, Brown, 1977.

*Wuchan jieji wenhua dageming shengli wansui* (Long Live the Great Proletarian Cultural Revolution). Beijing: Xinhua yinshuachang, 1969.

Wu Lengxi. *Yi Mao Zhuxi* (In Memory of Chairman Mao). Beijing: Xinhua chubanshe, 1995.

———. *Shenian lunzheng, 1956–1966; Zhong Su guanxi huiyilu* (Ten Years of Polemics, 1956–1966; Record of Sino-Soviet Relations). 2 vols. Beijing: Zhongyang wenxian chubanshe, 1999.

Wu Qingtong. *Zhou Enlai zai wenhua dageming zhong* (Zhou Enlai in the Cultural Revolution). Beijing: Zhonggong dangshi chubanshe, 1998.

Wu Xiuquan. *Wangshi changsang* (Memories of the Past). Shanghai:

Shanghai wenyi chubanshe, 1986.

Xi Xuan, and Jin Chunming. *Wenhua dageming jianshi* (A Short History of the Cultural Revolution). Beijing: Zhonggong dangshi chubanshe, 1996.

Xia Honggen (ed.). *Dangshi zhishi zhenwenlu* (Episodes in CCP History). Beijing: Jiefangjun chubanshe, 1988.

Xia Zhongcheng. *Yafei xiongfeng* (Strong Winds in Asia and Africa). Beijing: Shijie zhishi chubanshe, 1993.

Xiao Di et al. (eds.). *Wenge zhimi* (The Enigmatic Cultural Revolution). Beijing: Zhaohua chubanshe, 1993.

Xiao Sike. *Chaoji shenpan* (Super Trial). Jinan: Jinan chubanshe, 1992.

Xiao Yanzhong (ed.). *Wannian Mao Zedong* (Mao in His Later Years). Beijing: Chunqiu chubanshe, 1989.

Xiong Huayuan, and Liao Xinwen. *Zhou Enlai zongli shengya* (Premier Zhou Enlai's Life). Beijing: Renmin chubanshe, 1997.

Xiong Xianghui. *Dixia shiernian yu Zhou Enlai* (Twelve Years Underground and Zhou Enlai). Beijing: Zhonggong zhongyang dangxiao chubanshe, 1991.

Xu Dashen (ed.). *Zhonghua renmin gongheguo shilu* (Chronicle of the People's Republic of China). Changchun: Jilin renmin chubanshe, 1994.

Xu Jingli. *Lingqi luzao* (Making a Fresh Start). Beijing: Shijie zhishi chubanshi, 1998.

Xu Xuan, and Jin Chunming. *Wenhua dageming shigao* (A Preliminary History of the Cultural Revolution). Chengdu: Sichuan renmin chubanshe, 1995.

Yan Changlin. *Jingwei Mao Zedong jishi* (Memories of Mao's Guard). Changchun: Jilin renmin chubanshe, 1992.

Yang Mingwei, and Chen Yangyong. *Zhou Enlai waijiao fengyun* (Zhou Enlai's Diplomatic Career). Beijing: Jiefangjun wenyi chubanshe, 1995.

Yang Shengqun (ed.). *Zhonggong dangshi zhongda shijian shushi* (Factual Accounts of Major Events in CCP History). Beijing: Renmin chubanshe, 1993.

Yang Zhongmei. *Zunyi huiyi yu Yanan zhengfeng* (The Zunyi Conference and the Yanan Rectification Campaign). Hong Kong: Benma chubanshe, 1988.

Yao Wenyuan. *On the Social Basis of the Lin Biao Anti-Party Clique*. Beijing: Foreign Languages Press, 1975.

*Ye Jianying zhuanlue* (A Brief Biography of Ye Jianying). Beijing: Junshi kexue chubanshe, 1987.

Ye Yonglie. *Jiang Qing zhuan* (Biography of Jiang Qing). Beijing: Zuojia chubanshe, 1993.

——. *Wang Hongwen xingshuailu* (The Vicissitudes of Wang Hongwen). Changchun: Shidai wenyi chubanshe, 1989.

——. *Yaoshi fuzi* (The Yaos: Father and Son). Dalian: Dalian chubanshe, 1989.

——. *Zhang Chunqiao fuchenshi* (The Rise and Fall of Zhang Chunqiao). Changchun: Shidai wenyi chubanshe, 1988.

——. *Zhang Chunqiao zhuan* (The Biography of Zhang Chunqiao). Beijing: Zuojia chubanshe, 1993.

Yin Qi. *Pan Hannian de qingbao shengya* (Pan Hannian's Intelligence Career). Beijing: Renmin chubanshe, 1996.

Yu Gong. *Lin Biao shijian zhenxiang* (The True Story of the Lin Biao Affair). Beijing: Zhongguo guangbo dianshi chubanshe, 1988.

Yu Maochun. *OSS in China*. New Haven: Yale University Press, 1996.

Zhang Chunqiao. *On Exercising All-Round Dictatorship over the Bourgeoisie*. Beijing: Foreign Languages Press, 1975.

Zhang Hanzhi. *Wo yu Qiao Guanhua* (Qiao Guanhua and I). Beijing: Zhongguo qingnian chubanshe, 1994.

Zhang Quanzhen (ed.). *Zhou Enlai de ganqing shijie* (Zhou Enlai's Feelings). Jinan: Shandong daxue chubanshe, 1992.

Zhang Wenhe. *Shenghuo zhong de Zhou Enlai* (Zhou Enlai's Life). Beijing: Jiefangjun chubanshe, 1999.

Zhang Yaoci. *Huiyi Mao Zedong* (Reminiscences of Mao Zedong). Beijing: Zhonggong zhongyang dangxiao chubanshe, 1996.

Zhang Yunsheng. *Maojiawan jishi* (A Factual Account of Maojiawan). Beijing: Chunqiu chubanshe, 1988.

Zhang Zuoliang. *Zhou Enlai de zuihou shinian* (Zhou Enlai's Last Ten Years). Shanghai: Shanghai renmin chubanshe, 1997.

Zhen Fulin (ed.). *Zhonggong dangshi zhishi shouce* (Handbook of CCP History). Beijing: Beijing chubanshe, 1985.

Zhen Xiaoying. *Zhou Enlai dangxing de kaimo* (Zhou Enlai, a Model Party Member). Beijing: Zhonggong zhongyang dangxiao chubanshe, 1998.

Zheng Derong (ed.). *Xin Zhongguo jishi, 1949–1984* (A Chronology of New China). Changchun: Dongbei shifan daxue chubanshe, 1986.

*Zhonggong zhongyang erzhong quanhui ziliao* (Materials from the

Second Plenum of the Central Committee of the CCP). Shanghai:
1929.

*Zhongguo gongchandang lishi, 1919–1949* (The History of the Chinese
Communist Party, 1919–1949), vol. 1. Beijing: Renmin chubanshe,
1991.

*Zhongguo gongchandang dijiuci quanguo daibiao dahui wenjian huibian*
(Documents of the CCP's Ninth National Congress). Kunming:
Kunming junqu zhengzhibu, 1969.

*Zhongguo gongchandang liushinian dashi jianjie* (A Brief Account of
Major Events in the Sixty-Year History of the CCP). Beijing:
Guofang daxue chubanshe, 1986.

*Zhongguo renmin jiefangjun jiangshuai minglu* (Who's Who of PLA
Marshals and Generals). Beijing: Jiefangjun chubanshe, 1986.

Zhou Enlai. *Report to the Tenth National Congress of the CCP*. Beijing:
Foreign Languages Press, 1973.

———. *Report on the Work of Government*. Beijing: Foreign Languages
Press, 1975.

———. *Selected Works of Zhou Enlai*. 2 vols. Beijing: Foreign
Languages Press, vol. 1, 1981; vol. 2, 1989.

*Zhou Enlai jingji wenxian* (Selected Works of Zhou Enlai on the
Economy). Beijing: Zhongyang wenxian chubanshe, 1993.

*Zhou Enlai junshi wenxuan* (Selected Articles by Zhou Enlai on Military
Affairs). 4 vols. Beijing: Renmin chubanshe, 1997.

*Zhou Enlai lun wenyi* (Zhou Enlai on Literature and Art). Beijing:
Renmin wenxue chubanshe, 1979.

*Zhou Enlai nianpu, 1898–1949* (A Chronology of Zhou Enlai's Life,
1898–1949). Beijing: Zhongyang wenxian chubanshe, 1989.

*Zhou Enlai nianpu, 1949–1976* (A Chronology of Zhou Enlai's Life,
1949–1976). 3 vols. Beijing: Zhongyang wenxian chubanshe, 1997.

*Zhou Enlai shuxin xuanji* (Selected Letters of Zhou Enlai). Beijing:
Zhongyang wenxian chubanshe, 1988.

*Zhou Enlai tongyi zhanxian wenxuan* (Selected Works of Zhou Enlai on
the United Front). Beijing: Renmin chubanshe, 1984.

*Zhou Enlai waijiao wenxuan* (Selected Works of Zhou Enlai on Foreign
Affairs). Beijing: Zhongyang wenxian chubanshe, 1990.

*Zhou Enlai yanjiu wenxuan* (Selected Works of Zhou Enlai). Tianjin:
Nankai daxue chubanshe, 1987.

*Zhou Enlai zai wenhua dageming zhong* (Zhou Enlai in the Cultural
Revolution). Beijing: Zhonggong dangxiao chubanshe, 1990.

Zhou Ming (ed.). *Lishi zai zheli chensi* (Pondering History). 6 vols. Vols. 1–3, Beijing: Huaxia chubanshe, 1986; vols. 4–6, Taiyuan: Beiyue wenyi chubanshe, 1989.

Zhou Xin (trans.). *The Vladimirov Diaries*. Taipei: United Daily Press, 1976.

Zhu Lin. *Dashi furen huiyilu* (Reminiscences of an Ambassador's Wife). Beijing: Shijie zhishi chubanshe, 1991.

### Contributions (Books) and Articles

An Jianshe. "Zhou Enlai lingdao de 1972 nian qianhou pipan jizuo sichao de douzheng" (Zhou Enlai Led the Criticism of Ultraleftism in 1972). *Dangde wenxian*, no. 1 (1993).

———. "Zhou Enlai tichu pipan jizuo" (Criticism of Ultra-leftism Initiated by Zhou Enlai). *Dangde wenxian*, no. 2 (1990).

Barnouin, Barbara. "The Man and His Work: Zhou Enlai during the Cultural Revolution." *World Affairs*, April– June 1998.

———. "Le processus de décision en polititique étrangère dans la Chine de Mao Zedong." *Relations Internationales*, no. 85 (1996).

Cao Ying. "Xiang Ying de huihuang yu shiluo" (Xiang Ying's Glories and Regrets). *Yuanhuang chunqiu*, no. 4 (1998).

Chai Chengwen. "Zhou Enlai lingdao women jinxing zhongsu bianjie tanpan" (Working under Zhou's Guidance in Sino-Soviet Border Talks). *Dangde wenxian*, no. 3 (1991).

"Chen Boda tan Zhou Enlai" (Chen Boda's Statement on Zhou Enlai). In *Selected Works of Zhou Enlai*. Hong Kong: Yishan Book Co., 1967.

Chen Zaidao. "Wuhan 7–20 shijian" (The Wuhan July 20 Event). In Qin Xiaoying et al., *Buxu chuan junzhuang de jiangjun* (A General Deprived of His Uniform).

Chen Shuliang. "Xin zhongguo waijiao de weida kaituozhe" (Great Path-Breaker of New China's Foreign Relations). In Li Xiannian et al. *Bujin de sinian* (Endless Memories).

Chen Xuewei. "Wenhua dageming shinian de jingji jianshe" (Economic Construction in the 10 Year Cultural Revolution). In Tan Zongji et al., *Shinian hou de pingshuo* (Critical Comments after Ten Years).

Chiang Baiying. "Minxi suqu de suqing shihui minzhudang yuan'an" (The Unjust Case of Elimination of Social Democrats in West Fujian). *Zhonggong dangshi yanjiu*, no. 4 (1989).

Dai Xiangqing. "Lun AB tuan he Futian shibian" (On the AB Group and the Futian Incident). *Zhonggong dangshi yanjiu*, no. 2 (1989).

Dian Dian. "Dian Dian jiyi" (Dian Dian's Recollections). *Dangdai*, no. 5 (1998).

Du Weidong. "Zhenbaodao zhanzheng milu" (Behind the Fighting of Zhenbao Island). *Gongming*, no. 6 (1992).

Fan Ruoyu. "Zai Zhou Enlai shenbian de rizi li" (The Days with Zhou Enlai). *Wenzhai xunkan*, no. 186 (1986).

Fan Zhenshui. "Zhongguo yiliaozu yu Ho Chi Minh" (Chinese Medical Teams and Ho Chi Minh). In Pei Jianzhang (ed.), *Xin Zhongguo waijiao fengyun* (Major Events in New China's Foreign Relations), vol. 2.

"Fangwen Jiang Zuoshou" (Interview with Jiang Zuoshou—Brigade Leader of 8341 Troops). *Zhonghua ernu*, no. 3, 1994.

Fu Bei. "Mao Zedong ping *Shuihu* zhenxiang" (Mao's Comment on Water Margin). *Zhuiqiu*, no. 5 (1988).

Fu Hao. "Jiu yao san shijian bubai" (More on the September 13 Event). In Pei Jianzhang (ed.), *Xin Zhongguo waijiao fengyun*, vol. 1.

Gao Wenqian. "Ji wenhua dageming zhong de Zhou Enlai" (Zhou Enlai in the Cultural Revolution). In Zhou Ming (ed.), *Lishi zai zheli chensi* (Pondering History), vol. 1.

———. "Zhou Enlai yu zhonggong sanci 'zuo' qing cuowu" (Zhou Enlai and the Three 'Left' Mistakes of the CCP). *Xinhua wenzhai*, no. 12 (1988).

Garver, John W. "The Origins of the Second United Front: the Comintern and the Chinese Communist Party." *The China Quarterly*, no. 113 (March 1988).

Gong Yuzhi. "[Eryue tigang] he donghu zhixing" (The February Outline Report and the Voyage to the East Lake). *Bainianchao*, no. 3 (1998).

Gu Baozi. "Dayuejin hou de Zhou Enlai" (Zhou Enlai after the Great Leap Forward). *Zhonghua ernu*, no. 3 (1993).

Hao Yufan, and Zhai Zhihai. "China's Decision to Enter the Korean War: History Revisited." *The China Quarterly*, no. 121 (March 1990).

He Ding. "Peng Dehuai zuihou haizai zhandou" (Peng Dehuai's Persistent Struggle during His Last Days). *Yan Huang chunqiu*, no. 12 (1998).

He Shaoqi. "Zhou Enlai zai Zunyi huiyi qianhou" (Zhou Enlai Before and After the Zunyi Conference). *Dangde wenxian*, no. 2 (1989).

Hu Kuo-tai. "The Struggle between the Kuomintang and the Chinese Communist Party on Campus During the War of Resistance, 1937–45." *The China Quarterly*, no. 118 (June 1989).

"Hu Qiaomu huiyi Yanan zhengfeng" (Hu Qiaomu Remembers the Yanan Rectification Campaign). *Dangde wenxian*, no. 2 (1994).

Hu Sheng. "Hu Qiaomu he dangshi gongzuo" (Hu Qiaomu and Party History Work). *Zhonggong dangshi yanjiu*, no. 1 (1994).

Huang Hua. "Nanjing jiefang chuqi wo tong Situleiding de jici jiechu" (My Contacts with Leighton Stuart in Nanjing at the Beginning of the Liberation). In Pei Jianzhang (ed.), *Xin Zhongguo waijiao fengyun*, vol. 1.

Huang Shaoqun. "Lun zhongyang suqu shiqi Zhou Enlai yu Mao Zedong de guanxi" (Relationship between Zhou Enlai and Mao Zedong during the Period of Central Soviet Areas). *Xinhua wenzhai* , December 1989.

———. "Zhou Enlai zai changzheng zhongde teshu gongxian" (Zhou Enlai's Special Contribution during the Long March). *Dangde wenxian*, no. 5 (1996).

Huang Yunsheng. "Ningdu huiyi shimo" (Ningdu Conference, from Beginning to End). *Dangde wenxian*, no. 2 (1990).

Huang Zheng. "Liu Shaoqi yu wenge chuqi gongzuozu" (Liu Shaoqi and the Work Team Policy). *Dangde wenxian*, no. 6 (1992).

———. "Liu Shaoqi yu wenhua dageming" (Liu Shaoqi and the Cultural Revolution). *Dangde wenxian*, no. 5 (1988).

Interviews with former Foreign Ministry officials in Beijing, March 1993.

Interviews with members of "Bu zheng chun bingtuan" (The Spring Heralding Corps) in Beijing, November 1996.

Interview with Yao Dengshan in Beijing, March 1993.

Interviews with Zhang Kesi, former leader of "Da lian chou" (The Preparatory Committee of Great Alliance of the Foreign Ministry) in Beijing, March 1993.

Ji Pengfei. "Zhou zongli yu zhongri jianjiao" (Premier Zhou and the Sino-Japanese Diplomatic Relations). *Renmin ribao*, 26 September 1993.

"Ji Pengfei liuyue liuri de baogao" (Ji Pengfei's Report on June 6 in the Foreign Ministry). *Waijiaobu*, 1966.

"Ji Pengfei liuyue ershisiri de baogao" (Ji Pengfei's Report on June 24 in the Foreign Ministry). *Waijiaobu*, 1966.

Jin Chongji. "Tong Deng dajie de jici tanhua" (Talks with Elder Sister Deng). *Dangde wenxian*, no. 6 (1992).

Jue Shi. "Zhou Enlai yu kangzhan chuqi de Changjiang ju" (Zhou Enlai and the Changjiang Bureau of the Party at the Early Stage of Anti-

Japanese War). *Zhonggong dangshi yanjiu*, no. 2 (1988).

Kong Jianmin. "Zhongguo dasanxian jianshe de jiannan licheng" (The Difficult Path of China's Third Line Construction). *Zhuiqiu*, no. 1 (1989).

Kong Jiesheng. "Zhou Enlai yu shenhua de zhongjie" (Zhou Enlai and the End of a Myth). *Zhengming*, March 1994.

Lei Yingfu. "Kang Mei yuan Chao jige zhongda juece de huiyi" (Some Important Decisions Concerning the Korean War). *Dangde wenxian*, no. 6 (1993).

Li Chengrui. "Dayuejin yinqide renkou biandong" (Demographic Changes Caused by the Great Leap Forward). *Zhonggong dangshi yanjiu*, no. 2 (1997).

Li Desheng. "Cong Lushan huiyi dao jiuyaosan shijian" (From the Lushan Conference to the September 13 Incident). *Yanhuang chunqiu*, no. 11 (1993).

Li Desheng. "Zhou Enlai danchen juishi zhounian jinianri" (In Memory of Zhou Enlai's Ninetieth Birthday). *Renmin ribao*, 7 March 1988.

Li Dihua. "Jianguoqian waishi gongzuo de pianduan huiyi" (Some Recollections of Diplomatic Work before the Founding of the PRC). In Pei Jianzhang (ed.), *Xin Zhongguo waijiao fengyun*, vol. 2.

Li Haiwen. "Zhonggong zhongyang jiujing heshi jueding zhiyuanjun chuguo zuozhan" (The Decision to Send Volunteers to Fight in Korea). *Dangde wenxian*, no. 5 (1993).

Li Haiwen. "Zhou Enlai yu Xian shibian" (Zhou Enlai and the Xian Incident). In Liu Wusheng (ed.), *Zhonggong dangshi fengyunlu* (Major Events in CCP History).

Li Ping. "Zhou Enlai guanyu jingji jianshede jige zhongyao sixiang" (Some Important Views of Zhou Enlai on Economic Construction). *Renmin ribao*, 4 March 1991.

Li Ping. "Zhou Enlai zai 1930 nian" (Zhou Enlai in 1930). In Liu Wusheng (ed.), *Zhonggong danngshi fengyunlu*.

Li Xiannian. "Dangqian caizheng, xindai he shichang fangmian cunzaide wenti he ying caiqude cuoshi" (Problems in the Current Finance and Credit Market and Measures to Be Taken to Deal with Them). *Dangde wenxian*, no. 2 (1989).

Li Xuefeng. "Huiyi wengge chuqi de 'luxian cuowu'" (Recollections of the "Mistakes of Line" at the Beginning of the Cultural Revolution). *Zhonggong dangshi yanjiu*, no. 4 (1998).

Li Yueran. "Wo zai Zhou zongli shenbian gongzuo de pianduan huiyi" (A

Few Recollections about Working for Zhou Enlai). In Pei Jianzhang (ed.), *Xin Zhongguo waijiao fengyun*, vol. 1.

Liao Xinwen. "Mao Zedong juece paoji jinmen de lishi kaocha" (A Review of Mao's Decision of Shelling Quemoy). *Dangde wenxian*, no. 1 (1994).

Lin Nong. "Zhou Enlai yu zhongyang teke" (Zhou Enlai and the Special Department). *Junshi*, no. 33 (1991).

Liu Hongwei. "Sai zhenzhu de Zhongguo xin" (Pearl Buck's Love for China). *Huang chunqiu*, no. 12 (1993).

Liu pingping et al. "Huainian women de baba Liu Shaoqi" (In Memory of Our Father Liu Shaoqi). In Zhou Ming (ed.). *Lishi zai zheli chensi*, vol. 1.

Lu Dan. "Guoji tekuai lieche zai bianchui xiaozhan beijie" (International Express Intercepted at a Small Border Town). *Yanhuang chunqiu*, no. 9 (1993).

Lu Jia. "Mao Zedong meiyou tichu 'pi Zhou gong'" (Mao Didn't Suggest Criticisim of Duke Zhou). *Dangde wenxian*, no. 5 (1990).

Ma Zhisun. "Zhou Enlai de wushi jingshen yu fanmaojin fanzuoqing" (Zhou Enlai and Opposition to Rash Advance, Opposition to "Left" Orientation). *Dangde wenxian*, no. 5 (1992).

Mansourov, Alexandre Y. Trans. and with an article. "Stalin, Mao, Kim, and China's Decision to Enter the Korean War, September 16–October 15, 1950: New Evidence from the Russian Archives." *CWIHP Bulletin*, issues 6–7 (Winter 1995/96).

"Mao zhuxi, Lin fuzhuxi he zhongyang shouzhang tan wu yao liu fangeming jituan" (Chairman Mao, Vice Chairman Lin and Other Leaders on the May 16 Counterrevolutionary Clique). *Waijiaobu dalianchou* (Preparatory Committee of Great Alliance of the Foreign Ministry). Private collection, 1967.

Meng Zhen. "Something about the Soong Dynasty." *Jiushi niandai*, no. 9 (1985).

Niu Jun. "Lun liushi niandai Zhongguo dui meizhangfu zhuanbian de lishi zhijing" (On the Historical Background of the Change of China's U.S. Policy in the 1960s). *Dangdai zhongguoshi yanjiu*, no. 1 (2000).

Qiao Yi. "Liandong shijian" (The Liandong Affair). *Zhuiqiu*, no. 5 (1988).

Qing Shi. "Sidalin buxu geming" (Stalin against Revolution). *Bainianchao*, no. 3 (1998).

Quan Ye. "Zhou Enlai shishi quanguocheng jishi" (A Full Account of Zhou Enlai's Death). *Yanhuang zisun*, September 1989.

"Ri–Zhong bangjiao zhengchanghua tanpan" (Negotiations on Sino-Japanese Normalization). *Wenzhai xunkan*, no. 9 (1988).

Saich, Tony. "Henk Sneevliet and the Origins of the First United Front." *Issues and Studies* (August 1986).

Schoenhals, Michael. "The Central Case Examination Group, 1966–1979." *The China Quarterly*, no. 145 (March 1996).

Shen Zhihua. "Chaoxian zhanzheng yanjiu zongshu" (A Summary of Research on the Korean War). *Zhonggong dangshi yanjiu*, no. 6 (1996).

Shi Wei. "Maojin, fanmaojin, fanfanmaojin" (Rush Advance, Opposition to Rush Advance, Opposing the Opposition to Rush Advance). *Dangde wenxian*, no. 2 (1990).

Si Ren. "Wenhua dageming zhong de waijiaobu duoquan dongluan" (Seizing Power in the Foreign Ministry in the Cultural Revolution). *Yanhuang chunqiu*, no. 2 (1993).

Song Yan. "Shixuejia Wu Han de lishi beiju" (The Tragedy of the Hisorian Wu Han). *Yanhuang chunqiu*, no. 10 (1993).

Su Caiqing. "Hongweibing yundong jiqi lishi jiaoxun" (The Red Guard Movement and Its Lessons). *Dangxiao ziliao*, no. 8 (1987).

——. Wenge chuqi jingji zhanxian de yanzhong douzheng (Serious Conflicts in the Field of Economy in the Early Stage of the Cultural Revolution). In Tan Zongji, *Shinian hou de pingshuo*.

——. "Wenhua dageming lishi bianwu sanze" (Three Errors about the History of the Cultural Revolution). *Zhonggong dangshi yanjiu*, no. 5 (1989).

"Summary of the Forum on the Work of Literature and Art in the Armed Forces with which Comrade Lin Biao Entrusted Comrade Jiang Qing." *Peking Review*, no. 23 (1967).

"Waijiaobu wenhua dageming yundong dashiji" (Chronicle of Events of the Cultural Revolution of the Foreign Ministry, May 11, 1966–June 6, 1967). *Wailian*, 1967.

Wang Bingnan. "Zhong-Mei huitan jiunian huigu" (Reflections on the Nine-Year Sino-American Talks). *Shijie zhishi*, no. 19 (1984)–no. 8 (1985).

Wang Dongxing. "Yi Lushan jiujie erzhong quanhui" (Second Plenum of the Ninth Congress at Lushan). *Dangdai Zhongguo yanjiu,* no. 3 (1994).

"Wang Li tongzhi jiejian Yao Dengshan, waijianbu geming zaofan lianluozhan daibiao de zhongyao jianghua" (Important Speech of

Comrade Wang Li to Yao Dengshan and Representatives of the FM Revolutionary Rebels Liaison Station). *Wailian*, 1967.

Wang Lingshu. "Ji Dengkui xiaye yihou" (Ji Dengkui Retires). *Yanhuang chunqiu*, no. 4 (1993).

Wang Nianyi. "Guanyu eryue niliu de yixie ziliao" (Some Facts about the February Adverse Current). *Dangshi ziliao yanjiu*, no. 1 (1990).

Wang Ruoshui. "Cong pizuo daoxiang fanyou" (From Criticizing "Left" to Opposing Right). *Mingbao yuekan*, no. 3 (1989).

"Weiduizhang jiyi zhong de jiu yaosan qianye" (On the Eve of the Night of September 13). *Zhonghua ernu*, no. 5 (1994).

Wei Shiyan. "Geluomike yu Mao Zedong tanhua de huiyi yu shishi bufu" (Rebuttal of Gromyko's Recollection of His Talk with Mao). In Pei Jianzhang (ed.), *Xin Zhongguo waijiao fengyun*, vol. 1.

Wei Shiyan. "Jixinge dierci fanghua" (Kissinger's Second Visit to China). *Dangde wenxian*, no. 5 (1992).

Wei Shiyan. "Jixinge mimi fang Hua neimu (Insider view of Kissinger's Secret Visit to China ). In Pei Jianzhang (ed.), *Xin zhongguo waijiao fengyun*, vol. 2.

*Wenge fengyun: Pidou Chen Yi dahui zhuanji* (The Storm of the CR: Criticism and Struggle Against Chen Yi), *Beiwai Zaofantuan* (Red Guard Rebels Corps of The Beijing Foreign Languages Institute) and *Pi Chen Lianluozhan* (Criticising Chen Yi Liaison Station), 1967. Red Guard Material.

Wu De. "Lushan huiyi he Lin Biao shijian" (Lushan Conference and Lin Biao Affair). *Dangdai Zhongguo yanjiu*, no. 2 (1995).

Wu Tien-wei. "Chiang Kai-shek's March Twentieth Coup d'état of 1926." *Journal of Asian Studies*, no. 27 (May 1968).

Wu Xuewen. "Tianzhong zuge xinwen fabiao de qianqian houhou" (The Publication of the News about Tanaka Government). *Renmin ribao*, 2 October 1992.

Xia Daosheng. "Yi Zhou Enlai 1957 nian fangwen Xiongyali" (Zhou Enlai's Visit to Hungary in 1957). In Pei Jianzhang (ed.), *Xin Zhongguo waijiao fengyun*, vol. 2.

Xiao Qiming. "Jiuyaosan shijian qingliji" (Personal Experiences in the September 13 Incident). *Zhongguo laonian*, no. 6 (1992).

Xiao Xiao. "Lin Biao nuer pilu fuqing chuzou xiangqing" (Lin Biao's Daughter Discloses the Truth of Her Father's Defection). *Jingbao yuekan*, no. 6 (1988).

"Xie Fuzhi yu hongweibing tanhua" (Xie Fuzhi's Talk with the Red

Guards [on September 10, 1967]). *Zuojia wenzhai*, no. 85 (1994).

Xie Li. "Zhongfa jianjiao tanpan jishi (Negotiations for Sino-French Normalization). In Pei Jianzhang (ed.), *Xin Zhongguo waijiao fengyun*, vol. 1.

Xiong Huayuan. "Zhou Enlai mimi fang Su" (Zhou Enlai's Secret Mission to the Soviet Union). *Dangde wenxian*, no. 3 (1994).

Xiong Lei. "Mao Zedong tong Xiong Xianghui tan Lushan huiyi wenti" (Mao Talks with Xiong about Lushan Conference). *Xinguancha*, no. 18 (1986).

Xiong Xianghui. "Dakai Zhong-Mei guanxi de qianzou" (Prelude of Sino-U.S. Breakthrough). *Liaowang*, August 1992.

Xiong Xianghui. "Mao Zedong zhuxi dui Menggemali tan 'jichengren'" (Mao Talks with Montgomery about His Successor). In Pei Jianzhang (ed.), *Xin Zhongguo waijiao fengyun*, vol. 1.

Xu Hong. "Zhou Enlai de jiashi" (Zhou Enlai's Family Affairs). *Zhonghua ernu*, no. 1 (1993).

Xu Wenyi. "Lishi fuyu wode yixiang teshu shiming" (An Unusual Task Given to Me by History). In Pei Jianzhang (ed.), *Xin Zhongguo waijiao fengyun*, vol. 1.

Yan Rengeng. "Zhou Enlai yu Yan Xiu" (Zhou Enlai and Yan Xiu). *Dangde wenxian*, no. 4 (1990).

Yang Kuisong. "Dui 'Zhou Enlai Zhuan' ruogan shishi de bianzheng" (Some Facts in *Biography of Zhou Enlai* Rectified). *Dangde wenxian*, no. 4 (1990).

Yang Qinghua. "Haixia liang'an mouhe zuji shilu" (Contacts for Peace between the Two Sides of the Straits). *Yanhuang chunqiu*, no. 8 (1997).

Yang Quan. "Yanhe zhi zi" (The Son of the Yan River). *Dadi*, no. 1 (1992).

Yang Zanxian. "Zhongguo liuxuesheng Mosike hongchang liuxueji" (The Bloodshed of Chinese Students on the Red Square in Moscow). *Bainianchao*, no. 3 (1998).

Ye Fei. "Mao zhuxi zhihui paoji jinmen" (Chairman Mao in Command of the Bombardment of Quemoy). *Renmin ribao*, 24 December 1993.

Yu Changgeng. "Zhou Enlai yaokong fanying kangbao neimu" (The Inside Story of Hong Kong's Fight against the British Violent Suppression in 1967). *Jiushi niandai*, May and June 1996.

Yu Nan. "Jiujie erzhong quanhui shangde yichang fengbo" (Storm at the Second Plenum of the Ninth Central Committee). *Dangde wenxian*, no. 3 (1992).

————. Lin Biao jituan xingwang chutan (A Preliminary Study on the Rise and Fall of Lin Biao Group). In Tan Zongji et al., *Shinian hou de pingshuo*.

Yu Qiuli. "Zhongliu dizhu li wan kuanglan" (A Pillar Rock in Midstream). In Gu Mu et al., *Women de Zhou Zongli*.

Yu Zhan. "Zhou Enlai zuihou yici fang Su" (Zhou Enlai's Last Visit to the Soviet Union). *Dangde wenxian*, no. 2 (1992).

Zeng Jingzhong. "Guanyu Zunyi huiyi de jidian tantao" (A Study on the Zunyi Conference). *Zhonggong dangshi yanjiu*, no. 6 (1988).

————. "Zunyi hui yihou zhongyang sanren lingdao jigou yanjiu" (A Study on the Three Men Leading Organ after the Zunyi Conference). *Zhonggong dangshi yanjiu*, no. 4 (1989).

Zhang Hua. "Lun zhishi qingnian shangshan xiaxiang yundong" (On the Movement of Educated Youth Going to the Countryside). In Tan Zongji et al., *Shinian hou de pingshuo*.

Zhang Kuitang. "Zhou Enlai yu Zhang Xueliang de jiaowang he youyi" (Zhou Enlai's Relations and Friendship with Zhang Xueliang). *Dangde wenxian*, no. 3 (1991).

Zhang Ning. "Niuqu de hong" (A Rainbow Deformed). In Zhou Ming (ed.), *Lishi zai zheli chensi*, vol. 5.

Zhang Songshan. "Yi ge zhongyang zhuan'an zuzhang de chanhui" (Repentance of a Central Case Group Leader). *Yanhuang chunqiu*, no. 4, 1994.

Zhang Tong. "Dui yin ziwei fanjizhan qianhoude huiyi" (Recollections of Sino-Indian Border War). In Pei Jianzhang (ed.), *Xin Zhongguo waijiao fengyun*, vol. 1.

Zhang Wenjin. "Zhou Enlai yu Maxi'er shihua" (Zhou Enlai and Marshall in China). In Liu Wusheng (ed.), *Zhonggong dangshi fengyunlu*.

Zhang Yufeng. "Mao Zedong Zhou Enlai wannian ersan shi" (A Few Things about Mao Zedong and Zhou Enlai in Their Later Years). *Yanhuang zisun*, no. 1 (1989).

Zhang Zhicai et al. "Zhou Enlai he Xie Hegeng fufu" (Zhou Enlai and the Xies). *Yanhuang chunqiu*, no. 9 (July 1992).

Zhang Zuoliang. "Zhou Enlai de zuihou 1,323 tian" (Zhou Enlai's Last 1,323 Days). *Zhongguo zuojia*, no. 1 (1997).

Zhao Chunsheng. "Zhou Enlai yu heping gongchu wuxiang yuanze" (Zhou Enlai and the Five Principles of Peaceful Coexistence). *Dangde wenxian*, no. 1 (1992).

Zhou Enlai. "Chou En-lai's Internal Report to the Party on International Situation in December 1971." *Chinese Law and Government*, no. 1 (Spring 1977).

Zhou Enlai. "Chou En-lai's Report to the Party on the Problems of the Current International Situation in March 1973." *Chinese Law and Government*, 10, no. 1 (Spring 1977).

"Zhou Enlai de jianghua" (Zhou Enlai's Speeches: Sept. 20, Oct. 19, 1967; Mar. 27, Sept. 7, 1968). In *Selected Works of Zhou Enlai*, vol. 3. Hong Kong: Yishang Book Co., 1976.

"Zhou Enlai pipan Liang Shuming" (Zhou Enlai Criticizes Liang Shuming). *Wenzhai xunkan*, no. 50 (1989).

"Zhou Enlai zai jiuda jianghua" (Zhou Enlai's Speech at the Ninth Party Congress), 1969.

"Zhou Zongli de sidian zhishi" (Premier Zhou's Four-Point Instructions). *Waijiaobu*, 26 December 1966.

"Zongli guanyu jiushiyi ren dazibao de zhongyao zhishi" (The Premier's Important Instructions on the Ninety-One-Person Poster). *Waijiaobu*, 1968.

Zhu Jiamu. "Shiyijie sanzhong quanhui zhuyao wenjian xingchengde ruogan qingkuang" (The Third Plenum of the Eleventh Central Committee and the Preparation of Some Major Documents). *Dangde wenxian*, no. 1 (1999).

Zhu Zhongli. "Suowei 'san he yi shao' wenti zhenxiang" (The Truth about the So-Called 'Three Peaceful's and One Less). *Dangde wenxian*, no. 5 (1993).

Zuo Shuangwen. "Jianchi 'yige Zhongguo' lichang de guomindang yuanlao Chen Cheng" (Chen Cheng, a Guomindang Veteran Persisting in the Principle of "One China"). *Yanhuang chunqiu*, no. 4 (1996).

# Index